Deep Learning with Python

Deep Learning with Python

FRANÇOIS CHOLLET

MANNING

SHELTER ISLAND

For online information and ordering of this and other Manning books, please visit
www.manning.com. The publisher offers discounts on this book when ordered in quantity.
For more information, please contact

> Special Sales Department
> Manning Publications Co.
> 20 Baldwin Road
> PO Box 761
> Shelter Island, NY 11964
> Email: orders@manning.com

 Manning Publications Co.
20 Baldwin Road
PO Box 761
Shelter Island, NY 11964

Development editor:	Toni Arritola
Technical development editor:	Jerry Gaines
Review editor:	Aleksandar Dragosavljević
Project editor:	Tiffany Taylor
Copyeditor:	Tiffany Taylor
Proofreader:	Katie Tennant
Technical proofreaders:	Alex Ott and Richard Tobias
Typesetter:	Dottie Marsico
Cover designer:	Marija Tudor

ISBN 9781617294433
Printed in the United States of America
2 3 4 5 6 7 8 9 10 – EBM – 22 21 20 19 18 17

brief contents

contents

preface

If you've picked up this book, you're probably aware of the extraordinary progress that deep learning has represented for the field of artificial intelligence in the recent past. In a mere five years, we've gone from near-unusable image recognition and speech transcription, to superhuman performance on these tasks.

The consequences of this sudden progress extend to almost every industry. But in order to begin deploying deep-learning technology to every problem that it could solve, we need to make it accessible to as many people as possible, including non-experts—people who aren't researchers or graduate students. For deep learning to reach its full potential, we need to radically democratize it.

When I released the first version of the Keras deep-learning framework in March 2015, the democratization of AI wasn't what I had in mind. I had been doing research in machine learning for several years, and had built Keras to help me with my own experiments. But throughout 2015 and 2016, tens of thousands of new people entered the field of deep learning; many of them picked up Keras because it was—and still is—the easiest framework to get started with. As I watched scores of newcomers use Keras in unexpected, powerful ways, I came to care deeply about the accessibility and democratization of AI. I realized that the further we spread these technologies, the more useful and valuable they become. Accessibility quickly became an explicit goal in the development of Keras, and over a few short years, the Keras developer community has made fantastic achievements on this front. We've put deep learning into the hands of tens of thousands of people, who in turn are using it to solve important problems we didn't even know existed until recently.

The book you're holding is another step on the way to making deep learning available to as many people as possible. Keras had always needed a companion course to simultaneously cover fundamentals of deep learning, Keras usage patterns, and deep-learning best practices. This book is my best effort to produce such a course. I wrote it with a focus on making the concepts behind deep learning, and their implementation, as approachable as possible. Doing so didn't require me to dumb down anything—I strongly believe that there are no difficult ideas in deep learning. I hope you'll find this book valuable and that it will enable you to begin building intelligent applications and solve the problems that matter to you.

acknowledgments

I'd like to thank the Keras community for making this book possible. Keras has grown to have hundreds of open source contributors and more than 200,000 users. Your contributions and feedback have turned Keras into what it is today.

I'd also like to thank Google for backing the Keras project. It has been fantastic to see Keras adopted as TensorFlow's high-level API. A smooth integration between Keras and TensorFlow greatly benefits both TensorFlow users and Keras users and makes deep learning accessible to most.

I want to thank the people at Manning who made this book possible: publisher Marjan Bace and everyone on the editorial and production teams, including Christina Taylor, Janet Vail, Tiffany Taylor, Katie Tennant, Dottie Marsico, and many others who worked behind the scenes.

Many thanks go to the technical peer reviewers led by Aleksandar Dragosavljević — Diego Acuña Rozas, Geoff Barto, David Blumenthal-Barby, Abel Brown, Clark Dorman, Clark Gaylord, Thomas Heiman, Wilson Mar, Sumit Pal, Vladimir Pasman, Gustavo Patino, Peter Rabinovitch, Alvin Raj, Claudio Rodriguez, Srdjan Santic, Richard Tobias, Martin Verzilli, William E. Wheeler, and Daniel Williams—and the forum contributors. Their contributions included catching technical mistakes, errors in terminology, and typos, and making topic suggestions. Each pass through the review process and each piece of feedback implemented through the forum topics shaped and molded the manuscript.

On the technical side, special thanks go to Jerry Gaines, who served as the book's technical editor; and Alex Ott and Richard Tobias, who served as the book's technical proofreaders. They're the best technical editors I could have hoped for.

Finally, I'd like to express my gratitude to my wife Maria for being extremely supportive throughout the development of Keras and the writing of this book.

about this book

This book was written for anyone who wishes to explore deep learning from scratch or broaden their understanding of deep learning. Whether you're a practicing machine-learning engineer, a software developer, or a college student, you'll find value in these pages.

This book offers a practical, hands-on exploration of deep learning. It avoids mathematical notation, preferring instead to explain quantitative concepts via code snippets and to build practical intuition about the core ideas of machine learning and deep learning.

You'll learn from more than 30 code examples that include detailed commentary, practical recommendations, and simple high-level explanations of everything you need to know to start using deep learning to solve concrete problems.

The code examples use the Python deep-learning framework Keras, with Tensor-Flow as a backend engine. Keras, one of the most popular and fastest-growing deep-learning frameworks, is widely recommended as the best tool to get started with deep learning.

After reading this book, you'll have a solid understand of what deep learning is, when it's applicable, and what its limitations are. You'll be familiar with the standard workflow for approaching and solving machine-learning problems, and you'll know how to address commonly encountered issues. You'll be able to use Keras to tackle real-world problems ranging from computer vision to natural-language processing: image classification, timeseries forecasting, sentiment analysis, image and text generation, and more.

Who should read this book

This book is written for people with Python programming experience who want to get started with machine learning and deep learning. But this book can also be valuable to many different types of readers:

- If you're a data scientist familiar with machine learning, this book will provide you with a solid, practical introduction to deep learning, the fastest-growing and most significant subfield of machine learning.
- If you're a deep-learning expert looking to get started with the Keras framework, you'll find this book to be the best Keras crash course available.
- If you're a graduate student studying deep learning in a formal setting, you'll find this book to be a practical complement to your education, helping you build intuition around the behavior of deep neural networks and familiarizing you with key best practices.

Even technically minded people who don't code regularly will find this book useful as an introduction to both basic and advanced deep-learning concepts.

In order to use Keras, you'll need reasonable Python proficiency. Additionally, familiarity with the Numpy library will be helpful, although it isn't required. You don't need previous experience with machine learning or deep learning: this book covers from scratch all the necessary basics. You don't need an advanced mathematics background, either—high school–level mathematics should suffice in order to follow along.

Roadmap

This book is structured in two parts. If you have no prior experience with machine learning, I strongly recommend that you complete part 1 before approaching part 2. We'll start with simple examples, and as the book goes on, we'll get increasingly close to state-of-the-art techniques.

Part 1 is a high-level introduction to deep learning, providing context and definitions, and explaining all the notions required to get started with machine learning and neural networks:

- Chapter 1 presents essential context and background knowledge around AI, machine learning, and deep learning.
- Chapter 2 introduces fundamental concepts necessary in order to approach deep learning: tensors, tensor operations, gradient descent, and backpropagation. This chapter also features the book's first example of a working neural network.
- Chapter 3 includes everything you need to get started with neural networks: an introduction to Keras, our deep-learning framework of choice; a guide for setting up your workstation; and three foundational code examples with detailed explanations. By the end of this chapter, you'll be able to train simple neural

networks to handle classification and regression tasks, and you'll have a solid idea of what's happening in the background as you train them.

- Chapter 4 explores the canonical machine-learning workflow. You'll also learn about common pitfalls and their solutions.

Part 2 takes an in-depth dive into practical applications of deep learning in computer vision and natural-language processing. Many of the examples introduced in this part can be used as templates to solve problems you'll encounter in the real-world practice of deep learning:

- Chapter 5 examines a range of practical computer-vision examples, with a focus on image classification.
- Chapter 6 gives you practice with techniques for processing sequence data, such as text and timeseries.
- Chapter 7 introduces advanced techniques for building state-of-the-art deep-learning models.
- Chapter 8 explains generative models: deep-learning models capable of creating images and text, with sometimes surprisingly artistic results.
- Chapter 9 is dedicated to consolidating what you've learned throughout the book, as well as opening perspectives on the limitations of deep learning and exploring its probable future.

Software/hardware requirements

All of this book's code examples use the Keras deep-learning framework (https://keras.io), which is open source and free to download. You'll need access to a UNIX machine; it's possible to use Windows, too, but I don't recommend it. Appendix A walks you through the complete setup.

I also recommend that you have a recent NVIDIA GPU on your machine, such as a TITAN X. This isn't required, but it will make your experience better by allowing you to run the code examples several times faster. See section 3.3 for more information about setting up a deep-learning workstation.

If you don't have access to a local workstation with a recent NVIDIA GPU, you can use a cloud environment, instead. In particular, you can use Google Cloud instances (such as an n1-standard-8 instance with an NVIDIA Tesla K80 add-on) or Amazon Web Services (AWS) GPU instances (such as a p2.xlarge instance). Appendix B presents in detail one possible cloud workflow that runs an AWS instance via Jupyter notebooks, accessible in your browser.

Source code

All code examples in this book are available for download as Jupyter notebooks from the book's website, www.manning.com/books/deep-learning-with-python, and on GitHub at https://github.com/fchollet/deep-learning-with-python-notebooks.

Book forum

Purchase of *Deep Learning with Python* includes free access to a private web forum run by Manning Publications where you can make comments about the book, ask technical questions, and receive help from the author and from other users. To access the forum, go to https://forums.manning.com/forums/deep-learning-with-python. You can also learn more about Manning's forums and the rules of conduct at https://forums .manning.com/forums/about.

Manning's commitment to our readers is to provide a venue where a meaningful dialogue between individual readers and between readers and the author can take place. It isn't a commitment to any specific amount of participation on the part of the author, whose contribution to the forum remains voluntary (and unpaid). We suggest you try asking him some challenging questions lest his interest stray! The forum and the archives of previous discussions will be accessible from the publisher's website as long as the book is in print.

about the author

François Chollet works on deep learning at Google in Mountain View, CA. He is the creator of the Keras deep-learning library, as well as a contributor to the TensorFlow machine-learning framework. He also does deep-learning research, with a focus on computer vision and the application of machine learning to formal reasoning. His papers have been published at major conferences in the field, including the Conference on Computer Vision and Pattern Recognition (CVPR), the Conference and Workshop on Neural Information Processing Systems (NIPS), the International Conference on Learning Representations (ICLR), and others.

about the cover

The figure on the cover of *Deep Learning with Python* is captioned "Habit of a Persian Lady in 1568." The illustration is taken from Thomas Jefferys' *A Collection of the Dresses of Different Nations, Ancient and Modern* (four volumes), London, published between 1757 and 1772. The title page states that these are hand-colored copperplate engravings, heightened with gum arabic.

Thomas Jefferys (1719–1771) was called "Geographer to King George III." He was an English cartographer who was the leading map supplier of his day. He engraved and printed maps for government and other official bodies and produced a wide range of commercial maps and atlases, especially of North America. His work as a map maker sparked an interest in local dress customs of the lands he surveyed and mapped, which are brilliantly displayed in this collection. Fascination with faraway lands and travel for pleasure were relatively new phenomena in the late eighteenth century, and collections such as this one were popular, introducing both the tourist as well as the armchair traveler to the inhabitants of other countries.

The diversity of the drawings in Jefferys' volumes speaks vividly of the uniqueness and individuality of the world's nations some 200 years ago. Dress codes have changed since then, and the diversity by region and country, so rich at the time, has faded away. It's now often hard to tell the inhabitants of one continent from another. Perhaps, trying to view it optimistically, we've traded a cultural and visual diversity for a more varied personal life—or a more varied and interesting intellectual and technical life.

At a time when it's difficult to tell one computer book from another, Manning celebrates the inventiveness and initiative of the computer business with book covers based on the rich diversity of regional life of two centuries ago, brought back to life by Jefferys' pictures.

Part 1

Fundamentals of deep learning

Chapters 1–4 of this book will give you a foundational understanding of what deep learning is, what it can achieve, and how it works. It will also make you familiar with the canonical workflow for solving data problems using deep learning. If you aren't already highly knowledgeable about deep learning, you should definitely begin by reading part 1 in full before moving on to the practical applications in part 2.

What is deep learning?

This chapter covers

- High-level definitions of fundamental concepts
- Timeline of the development of machine learning
- Key factors behind deep learning's rising popularity and future potential

In the past few years, artificial intelligence (AI) has been a subject of intense media hype. Machine learning, deep learning, and AI come up in countless articles, often outside of technology-minded publications. We're promised a future of intelligent chatbots, self-driving cars, and virtual assistants—a future sometimes painted in a grim light and other times as utopian, where human jobs will be scarce and most economic activity will be handled by robots or AI agents. For a future or current practitioner of machine learning, it's important to be able to recognize the signal in the noise so that you can tell world-changing developments from overhyped press releases. Our future is at stake, and it's a future in which you have an active role to play: after reading this book, you'll be one of those who develop the AI agents. So let's tackle these questions: What has deep learning achieved so far? How significant is it? Where are we headed next? Should you believe the hype?

This chapter provides essential context around artificial intelligence, machine learning, and deep learning.

1.1   Artificial intelligence, machine learning, and deep learning

First, we need to define clearly what we're talking about when we mention AI. What are artificial intelligence, machine learning, and deep learning (see figure 1.1)? How do they relate to each other?

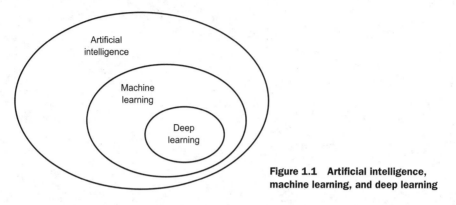

Figure 1.1   Artificial intelligence, machine learning, and deep learning

1.1.1   Artificial intelligence

Artificial intelligence was born in the 1950s, when a handful of pioneers from the nascent field of computer science started asking whether computers could be made to "think"—a question whose ramifications we're still exploring today. A concise definition of the field would be as follows: *the effort to automate intellectual tasks normally performed by humans.* As such, AI is a general field that encompasses machine learning and deep learning, but that also includes many more approaches that don't involve any learning. Early chess programs, for instance, only involved hardcoded rules crafted by programmers, and didn't qualify as machine learning. For a fairly long time, many experts believed that human-level artificial intelligence could be achieved by having programmers handcraft a sufficiently large set of explicit rules for manipulating knowledge. This approach is known as *symbolic AI*, and it was the dominant paradigm in AI from the 1950s to the late 1980s. It reached its peak popularity during the *expert systems* boom of the 1980s.

Although symbolic AI proved suitable to solve well-defined, logical problems, such as playing chess, it turned out to be intractable to figure out explicit rules for solving more complex, fuzzy problems, such as image classification, speech recognition, and language translation. A new approach arose to take symbolic AI's place: *machine learning*.

1.1.2   Machine learning

In Victorian England, Lady Ada Lovelace was a friend and collaborator of Charles Babbage, the inventor of the *Analytical Engine*: the first-known general-purpose, mechanical computer. Although visionary and far ahead of its time, the Analytical

Engine wasn't meant as a general-purpose computer when it was designed in the 1830s and 1840s, because the concept of general-purpose computation was yet to be invented. It was merely meant as a way to use mechanical operations to automate certain computations from the field of mathematical analysis—hence, the name Analytical Engine. In 1843, Ada Lovelace remarked on the invention, "The Analytical Engine has no pretensions whatever to originate anything. It can do whatever we know how to order it to perform.... Its province is to assist us in making available what we're already acquainted with."

This remark was later quoted by AI pioneer Alan Turing as "Lady Lovelace's objection" in his landmark 1950 paper "Computing Machinery and Intelligence,"[1] which introduced the *Turing test* as well as key concepts that would come to shape AI. Turing was quoting Ada Lovelace while pondering whether general-purpose computers could be capable of learning and originality, and he came to the conclusion that they could.

Machine learning arises from this question: could a computer go beyond "what we know how to order it to perform" and learn on its own how to perform a specified task? Could a computer surprise us? Rather than programmers crafting data-processing rules by hand, could a computer automatically learn these rules by looking at data?

This question opens the door to a new programming paradigm. In classical programming, the paradigm of symbolic AI, humans input rules (a program) and data to be processed according to these rules, and out come answers (see figure 1.2). With machine learning, humans input data as well as the answers expected from the data, and out come the rules. These rules can then be applied to new data to produce original answers.

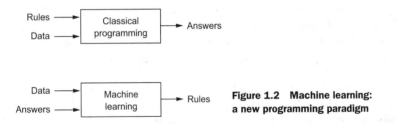

Figure 1.2 **Machine learning: a new programming paradigm**

A machine-learning system is *trained* rather than explicitly programmed. It's presented with many examples relevant to a task, and it finds statistical structure in these examples that eventually allows the system to come up with rules for automating the task. For instance, if you wished to automate the task of tagging your vacation pictures, you could present a machine-learning system with many examples of pictures already tagged by humans, and the system would learn statistical rules for associating specific pictures to specific tags.

---

[1] A. M. Turing, "Computing Machinery and Intelligence," *Mind* 59, no. 236 (1950): 433-460.

Although machine learning only started to flourish in the 1990s, it has quickly become the most popular and most successful subfield of AI, a trend driven by the availability of faster hardware and larger datasets. Machine learning is tightly related to mathematical statistics, but it differs from statistics in several important ways. Unlike statistics, machine learning tends to deal with large, complex datasets (such as a dataset of millions of images, each consisting of tens of thousands of pixels) for which classical statistical analysis such as Bayesian analysis would be impractical. As a result, machine learning, and especially deep learning, exhibits comparatively little mathematical theory—maybe too little—and is engineering oriented. It's a hands-on discipline in which ideas are proven empirically more often than theoretically.

1.1.3   Learning representations from data

To define *deep learning* and understand the difference between deep learning and other machine-learning approaches, first we need some idea of what machine-learning algorithms *do*. I just stated that machine learning discovers rules to execute a data-processing task, given examples of what's expected. So, to do machine learning, we need three things:

- *Input data points*—For instance, if the task is speech recognition, these data points could be sound files of people speaking. If the task is image tagging, they could be pictures.
- *Examples of the expected output*—In a speech-recognition task, these could be human-generated transcripts of sound files. In an image task, expected outputs could be tags such as "dog," "cat," and so on.
- *A way to measure whether the algorithm is doing a good job*—This is necessary in order to determine the distance between the algorithm's current output and its expected output. The measurement is used as a feedback signal to adjust the way the algorithm works. This adjustment step is what we call *learning*.

A machine-learning model transforms its input data into meaningful outputs, a process that is "learned" from exposure to known examples of inputs and outputs. Therefore, the central problem in machine learning and deep learning is to *meaningfully transform data*: in other words, to learn useful *representations* of the input data at hand—representations that get us closer to the expected output. Before we go any further: what's a representation? At its core, it's a different way to look at data—to *represent* or *encode* data. For instance, a color image can be encoded in the RGB format (red-green-blue) or in the HSV format (hue-saturation-value): these are two different representations of the same data. Some tasks that may be difficult with one representation can become easy with another. For example, the task "select all red pixels in the image" is simpler in the RG format, whereas "make the image less saturated" is simpler in the HSV format. Machine-learning models are all about finding appropriate representations for their input data—transformations of the data that make it more amenable to the task at hand, such as a classification task.

Let's make this concrete. Consider an x-axis, a y-axis, and some points represented by their coordinates in the (x, y) system, as shown in figure 1.3.

As you can see, we have a few white points and a few black points. Let's say we want to develop an algorithm that can take the coordinates (x, y) of a point and output whether that point is likely to be black or to be white. In this case,

- The inputs are the coordinates of our points.
- The expected outputs are the colors of our points.
- A way to measure whether our algorithm is doing a good job could be, for instance, the percentage of points that are being correctly classified.

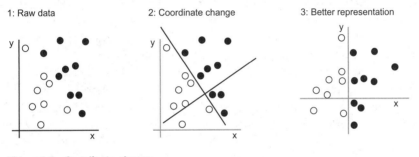

Figure 1.3
Some sample data

What we need here is a new representation of our data that cleanly separates the white points from the black points. One transformation we could use, among many other possibilities, would be a coordinate change, illustrated in figure 1.4.

Figure 1.4   Coordinate change

In this new coordinate system, the coordinates of our points can be said to be a new representation of our data. And it's a good one! With this representation, the black/white classification problem can be expressed as a simple rule: "Black points are such that $x > 0$," or "White points are such that $x < 0$." This new representation basically solves the classification problem.

In this case, we defined the coordinate change by hand. But if instead we tried systematically searching for different possible coordinate changes, and used as feedback the percentage of points being correctly classified, then we would be doing machine learning. *Learning*, in the context of machine learning, describes an automatic search process for better representations.

All machine-learning algorithms consist of automatically finding such transformations that turn data into more-useful representations for a given task. These operations can be coordinate changes, as you just saw, or linear projections (which may destroy information), translations, nonlinear operations (such as "select all points such that $x > 0$"), and so on. Machine-learning algorithms aren't usually creative in finding these transformations; they're merely searching through a predefined set of operations, called a *hypothesis space*.

So that's what machine learning is, technically: searching for useful representations of some input data, within a predefined space of possibilities, using guidance from a feedback signal. This simple idea allows for solving a remarkably broad range of intellectual tasks, from speech recognition to autonomous car driving.

Now that you understand what we mean by *learning*, let's take a look at what makes *deep learning* special.

1.1.4   The "deep" in deep learning

Deep learning is a specific subfield of machine learning: a new take on learning representations from data that puts an emphasis on learning successive *layers* of increasingly meaningful representations. The *deep* in *deep learning* isn't a reference to any kind of deeper understanding achieved by the approach; rather, it stands for this idea of successive layers of representations. How many layers contribute to a model of the data is called the *depth* of the model. Other appropriate names for the field could have been *layered representations learning* and *hierarchical representations learning*. Modern deep learning often involves tens or even hundreds of successive layers of representations—and they're all learned automatically from exposure to training data. Meanwhile, other approaches to machine learning tend to focus on learning only one or two layers of representations of the data; hence, they're sometimes called *shallow learning*.

In deep learning, these layered representations are (almost always) learned via models called *neural networks*, structured in literal layers stacked on top of each other. The term *neural network* is a reference to neurobiology, but although some of the central concepts in deep learning were developed in part by drawing inspiration from our understanding of the brain, deep-learning models are *not* models of the brain. There's no evidence that the brain implements anything like the learning mechanisms used in modern deep-learning models. You may come across pop-science articles proclaiming that deep learning works like the brain or was modeled after the brain, but that isn't the case. It would be confusing and counterproductive for newcomers to the field to think of deep learning as being in any way related to neurobiology; you don't need that shroud of "just like our minds" mystique and mystery, and you may as well forget anything you may have read about hypothetical links between deep learning and biology. For our purposes, deep learning is a mathematical framework for learning representations from data.

What do the representations learned by a deep-learning algorithm look like? Let's examine how a network several layers deep (see figure 1.5) transforms an image of a digit in order to recognize what digit it is.

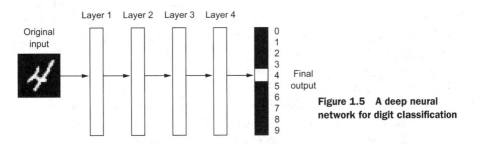

Figure 1.5 A deep neural network for digit classification

As you can see in figure 1.6, the network transforms the digit image into representations that are increasingly different from the original image and increasingly informative about the final result. You can think of a deep network as a multistage information-distillation operation, where information goes through successive filters and comes out increasingly *purified* (that is, useful with regard to some task).

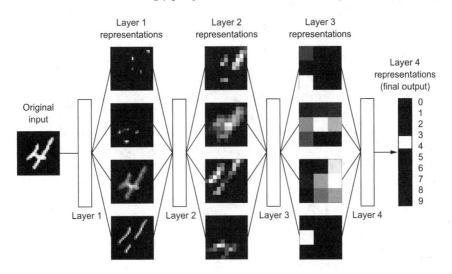

Figure 1.6 Deep representations learned by a digit-classification model

So that's what deep learning is, technically: a multistage way to learn data representations. It's a simple idea—but, as it turns out, very simple mechanisms, sufficiently scaled, can end up looking like magic.

1.1.5 Understanding how deep learning works, in three figures

At this point, you know that machine learning is about mapping inputs (such as images) to targets (such as the label "cat"), which is done by observing many examples of input and targets. You also know that deep neural networks do this input-to-target mapping via a deep sequence of simple data transformations (layers) and that these data transformations are learned by exposure to examples. Now let's look at how this learning happens, concretely.

The specification of what a layer does to its input data is stored in the layer's *weights*, which in essence are a bunch of numbers. In technical terms, we'd say that the transformation implemented by a layer is *parameterized* by its weights (see figure 1.7). (Weights are also sometimes called the *parameters* of a layer.) In this context, *learning* means finding a set of values for the weights of all layers in a network, such that the network will correctly map example inputs to their associated targets. But here's the thing: a deep neural network can contain tens of millions of parameters. Finding the correct value for all of them may seem like a daunting task, especially given that modifying the value of one parameter will affect the behavior of all the others!

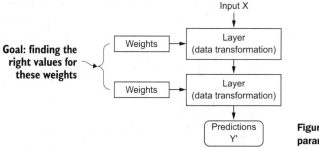

Figure 1.7   A neural network is parameterized by its weights.

To control something, first you need to be able to observe it. To control the output of a neural network, you need to be able to measure how far this output is from what you expected. This is the job of the *loss function* of the network, also called the *objective function*. The loss function takes the predictions of the network and the true target (what you wanted the network to output) and computes a distance score, capturing how well the network has done on this specific example (see figure 1.8).

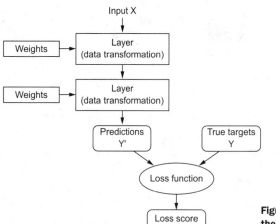

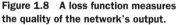

Figure 1.8   A loss function measures the quality of the network's output.

The fundamental trick in deep learning is to use this score as a feedback signal to adjust the value of the weights a little, in a direction that will lower the loss score for the current example (see figure 1.9). This adjustment is the job of the *optimizer*, which implements what's called the *Backpropagation* algorithm: the central algorithm in deep learning. The next chapter explains in more detail how backpropagation works.

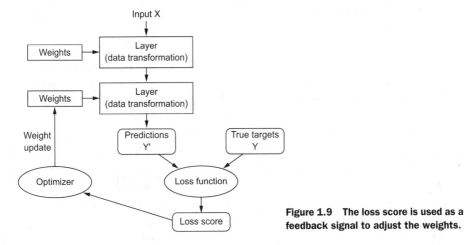

Figure 1.9   The loss score is used as a feedback signal to adjust the weights.

Initially, the weights of the network are assigned random values, so the network merely implements a series of random transformations. Naturally, its output is far from what it should ideally be, and the loss score is accordingly very high. But with every example the network processes, the weights are adjusted a little in the correct direction, and the loss score decreases. This is the *training loop*, which, repeated a sufficient number of times (typically tens of iterations over thousands of examples), yields weight values that minimize the loss function. A network with a minimal loss is one for which the outputs are as close as they can be to the targets: a trained network. Once again, it's a simple mechanism that, once scaled, ends up looking like magic.

1.1.6   *What deep learning has achieved so far*

Although deep learning is a fairly old subfield of machine learning, it only rose to prominence in the early 2010s. In the few years since, it has achieved nothing short of a revolution in the field, with remarkable results on perceptual problems such as seeing and hearing—problems involving skills that seem natural and intuitive to humans but have long been elusive for machines.

In particular, deep learning has achieved the following breakthroughs, all in historically difficult areas of machine learning:

- Near-human-level image classification
- Near-human-level speech recognition
- Near-human-level handwriting transcription
- Improved machine translation

- Improved text-to-speech conversion
- Digital assistants such as Google Now and Amazon Alexa
- Near-human-level autonomous driving
- Improved ad targeting, as used by Google, Baidu, and Bing
- Improved search results on the web
- Ability to answer natural-language questions
- Superhuman Go playing

We're still exploring the full extent of what deep learning can do. We've started applying it to a wide variety of problems outside of machine perception and natural-language understanding, such as formal reasoning. If successful, this may herald an age where deep learning assists humans in science, software development, and more.

1.1.7   *Don't believe the short-term hype*

Although deep learning has led to remarkable achievements in recent years, expectations for what the field will be able to achieve in the next decade tend to run much higher than what will likely be possible. Although some world-changing applications like autonomous cars are already within reach, many more are likely to remain elusive for a long time, such as believable dialogue systems, human-level machine translation across arbitrary languages, and human-level natural-language understanding. In particular, talk of *human-level general intelligence* shouldn't be taken too seriously. The risk with high expectations for the short term is that, as technology fails to deliver, research investment will dry up, slowing progress for a long time.

This has happened before. Twice in the past, AI went through a cycle of intense optimism followed by disappointment and skepticism, with a dearth of funding as a result. It started with symbolic AI in the 1960s. In those early days, projections about AI were flying high. One of the best-known pioneers and proponents of the symbolic AI approach was Marvin Minsky, who claimed in 1967, "Within a generation … the problem of creating 'artificial intelligence' will substantially be solved." Three years later, in 1970, he made a more precisely quantified prediction: "In from three to eight years we will have a machine with the general intelligence of an average human being." In 2016, such an achievement still appears to be far in the future—so far that we have no way to predict how long it will take—but in the 1960s and early 1970s, several experts believed it to be right around the corner (as do many people today). A few years later, as these high expectations failed to materialize, researchers and government funds turned away from the field, marking the start of the first *AI winter* (a reference to a nuclear winter, because this was shortly after the height of the Cold War).

It wouldn't be the last one. In the 1980s, a new take on symbolic AI, *expert systems*, started gathering steam among large companies. A few initial success stories triggered a wave of investment, with corporations around the world starting their own in-house AI departments to develop expert systems. Around 1985, companies were spending over $1 billion each year on the technology; but by the early 1990s, these systems had proven expensive to maintain, difficult to scale, and limited in scope, and interest died down. Thus began the second AI winter.

We may be currently witnessing the third cycle of AI hype and disappointment—and we're still in the phase of intense optimism. It's best to moderate our expectations for the short term and make sure people less familiar with the technical side of the field have a clear idea of what deep learning can and can't deliver.

1.1.8   *The promise of AI*

Although we may have unrealistic short-term expectations for AI, the long-term picture is looking bright. We're only getting started in applying deep learning to many important problems for which it could prove transformative, from medical diagnoses to digital assistants. AI research has been moving forward amazingly quickly in the past five years, in large part due to a level of funding never before seen in the short history of AI, but so far relatively little of this progress has made its way into the products and processes that form our world. Most of the research findings of deep learning aren't yet applied, or at least not applied to the full range of problems they can solve across all industries. Your doctor doesn't yet use AI, and neither does your accountant. You probably don't use AI technologies in your day-to-day life. Of course, you can ask your smartphone simple questions and get reasonable answers, you can get fairly useful product recommendations on Amazon.com, and you can search for "birthday" on Google Photos and instantly find those pictures of your daughter's birthday party from last month. That's a far cry from where such technologies used to stand. But such tools are still only accessories to our daily lives. AI has yet to transition to being central to the way we work, think, and live.

Right now, it may seem hard to believe that AI could have a large impact on our world, because it isn't yet widely deployed—much as, back in 1995, it would have been difficult to believe in the future impact of the internet. Back then, most people didn't see how the internet was relevant to them and how it was going to change their lives. The same is true for deep learning and AI today. But make no mistake: AI is coming. In a not-so-distant future, AI will be your assistant, even your friend; it will answer your questions, help educate your kids, and watch over your health. It will deliver your groceries to your door and drive you from point A to point B. It will be your interface to an increasingly complex and information-intensive world. And, even more important, AI will help humanity as a whole move forward, by assisting human scientists in new breakthrough discoveries across all scientific fields, from genomics to mathematics.

On the way, we may face a few setbacks and maybe a new AI winter—in much the same way the internet industry was overhyped in 1998–1999 and suffered from a crash that dried up investment throughout the early 2000s. But we'll get there eventually. AI will end up being applied to nearly every process that makes up our society and our daily lives, much like the internet is today.

Don't believe the short-term hype, but do believe in the long-term vision. It may take a while for AI to be deployed to its true potential—a potential the full extent of which no one has yet dared to dream—but AI is coming, and it will transform our world in a fantastic way.

1.2 Before deep learning: a brief history of machine learning

Deep learning has reached a level of public attention and industry investment never before seen in the history of AI, but it isn't the first successful form of machine learning. It's safe to say that most of the machine-learning algorithms used in the industry today aren't deep-learning algorithms. Deep learning isn't always the right tool for the job—sometimes there isn't enough data for deep learning to be applicable, and sometimes the problem is better solved by a different algorithm. If deep learning is your first contact with machine learning, then you may find yourself in a situation where all you have is the deep-learning hammer, and every machine-learning problem starts to look like a nail. The only way not to fall into this trap is to be familiar with other approaches and practice them when appropriate.

A detailed discussion of classical machine-learning approaches is outside of the scope of this book, but we'll briefly go over them and describe the historical context in which they were developed. This will allow us to place deep learning in the broader context of machine learning and better understand where deep learning comes from and why it matters.

1.2.1 Probabilistic modeling

Probabilistic modeling is the application of the principles of statistics to data analysis. It was one of the earliest forms of machine learning, and it's still widely used to this day. One of the best-known algorithms in this category is the Naive Bayes algorithm.

Naive Bayes is a type of machine-learning classifier based on applying Bayes' theorem while assuming that the features in the input data are all independent (a strong, or "naive" assumption, which is where the name comes from). This form of data analysis predates computers and was applied by hand decades before its first computer implementation (most likely dating back to the 1950s). Bayes' theorem and the foundations of statistics date back to the eighteenth century, and these are all you need to start using Naive Bayes classifiers.

A closely related model is the *logistic regression* (logreg for short), which is sometimes considered to be the "hello world" of modern machine learning. Don't be misled by its name—logreg is a classification algorithm rather than a regression algorithm. Much like Naive Bayes, logreg predates computing by a long time, yet it's still useful to this day, thanks to its simple and versatile nature. It's often the first thing a data scientist will try on a dataset to get a feel for the classification task at hand.

1.2.2 Early neural networks

Early iterations of neural networks have been completely supplanted by the modern variants covered in these pages, but it's helpful to be aware of how deep learning originated. Although the core ideas of neural networks were investigated in toy forms as early as the 1950s, the approach took decades to get started. For a long time, the missing piece was an efficient way to train large neural networks. This changed in the mid-1980s,

when multiple people independently rediscovered the Backpropagation algorithm—
a way to train chains of parametric operations using gradient-descent optimization
(later in the book, we'll precisely define these concepts)—and started applying it to
neural networks.

The first successful practical application of neural nets came in 1989 from Bell
Labs, when Yann LeCun combined the earlier ideas of convolutional neural networks
and backpropagation, and applied them to the problem of classifying handwritten
digits. The resulting network, dubbed *LeNet*, was used by the United States Postal Ser-
vice in the 1990s to automate the reading of ZIP codes on mail envelopes.

1.2.3   Kernel methods

As neural networks started to gain some respect among researchers in the 1990s,
thanks to this first success, a new approach to machine learning rose to fame and
quickly sent neural nets back to oblivion: kernel methods. *Kernel methods* are a group of
classification algorithms, the best known of which is the *support vector machine* (SVM).
The modern formulation of an SVM was developed by Vladimir
Vapnik and Corinna Cortes in the early 1990s at Bell Labs and
published in 1995,[2] although an older linear formulation was
published by Vapnik and Alexey Chervonenkis as early as 1963.[3]

SVMs aim at solving classification problems by finding good
decision boundaries (see figure 1.10) between two sets of points
belonging to two different categories. A decision boundary can
be thought of as a line or surface separating your training data
into two spaces corresponding to two categories. To classify new
data points, you just need to check which side of the decision
boundary they fall on.

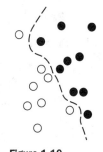

Figure 1.10
A decision boundary

SVMs proceed to find these boundaries in two steps:

1   The data is mapped to a new high-dimensional representation where the
    decision boundary can be expressed as a hyperplane (if the data was two-
    dimensional, as in figure 1.10, a hyperplane would be a straight line).
2   A good decision boundary (a separation hyperplane) is computed by trying to
    maximize the distance between the hyperplane and the closest data points from
    each class, a step called *maximizing the margin*. This allows the boundary to gen-
    eralize well to new samples outside of the training dataset.

The technique of mapping data to a high-dimensional representation where a classification problem becomes simpler may look good on paper, but in practice it's
often computationally intractable. That's where the *kernel trick* comes in (the key idea
that kernel methods are named after). Here's the gist of it: to find good decision

[2] Vladimir Vapnik and Corinna Cortes, "Support-Vector Networks," *Machine Learning* 20, no. 3 (1995): 273–297.
[3] Vladimir Vapnik and Alexey Chervonenkis, "A Note on One Class of Perceptrons," *Automation and Remote Con-
    trol* 25 (1964).

hyperplanes in the new representation space, you don't have to explicitly compute the coordinates of your points in the new space; you just need to compute the distance between pairs of points in that space, which can be done efficiently using a *kernel function*. A kernel function is a computationally tractable operation that maps any two points in your initial space to the distance between these points in your target representation space, completely bypassing the explicit computation of the new representation. Kernel functions are typically crafted by hand rather than learned from data—in the case of an SVM, only the separation hyperplane is learned.

At the time they were developed, SVMs exhibited state-of-the-art performance on simple classification problems and were one of the few machine-learning methods backed by extensive theory and amenable to serious mathematical analysis, making them well understood and easily interpretable. Because of these useful properties, SVMs became extremely popular in the field for a long time.

But SVMs proved hard to scale to large datasets and didn't provide good results for perceptual problems such as image classification. Because an SVM is a shallow method, applying an SVM to perceptual problems requires first extracting useful representations manually (a step called *feature engineering*), which is difficult and brittle.

1.2.4   *Decision trees, random forests, and gradient boosting machines*

Decision trees are flowchart-like structures that let you classify input data points or predict output values given inputs (see figure 1.11). They're easy to visualize and interpret. Decisions trees learned from data began to receive significant research interest in the 2000s, and by 2010 they were often preferred to kernel methods.

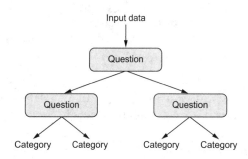

Figure 1.11   **A decision tree: the parameters that are learned are the questions about the data. A question could be, for instance, "Is coefficient 2 in the data greater than 3.5?"**

In particular, the *Random Forest* algorithm introduced a robust, practical take on decision-tree learning that involves building a large number of specialized decision trees and then ensembling their outputs. Random forests are applicable to a wide range of problems—you could say that they're almost always the second-best algorithm for any shallow machine-learning task. When the popular machine-learning competition website Kaggle (http://kaggle.com) got started in 2010, random forests quickly became a favorite on the platform—until 2014, when *gradient boosting machines* took over. A gradient boosting machine, much like a random forest, is a machine-learning technique based on ensembling weak prediction models, generally decision trees. It uses *gradient boosting*, a way to improve any machine-learning model by iteratively training new models that specialize in addressing the weak points of the previous models. Applied to decision trees, the use of the gradient boosting technique results in models that strictly outperform random forests most of the time, while having similar properties. It may be one of the best, if not *the* best, algorithm for dealing with nonperceptual data today. Alongside deep learning, it's one of the most commonly used techniques in Kaggle competitions.

1.2.5   Back to neural networks

Around 2010, although neural networks were almost completely shunned by the scientific community at large, a number of people still working on neural networks started to make important breakthroughs: the groups of Geoffrey Hinton at the University of Toronto, Yoshua Bengio at the University of Montreal, Yann LeCun at New York University, and IDSIA in Switzerland.

In 2011, Dan Ciresan from IDSIA began to win academic image-classification competitions with GPU-trained deep neural networks—the first practical success of modern deep learning. But the watershed moment came in 2012, with the entry of Hinton's group in the yearly large-scale image-classification challenge ImageNet. The ImageNet challenge was notoriously difficult at the time, consisting of classifying high-resolution color images into 1,000 different categories after training on 1.4 million images. In 2011, the top-five accuracy of the winning model, based on classical approaches to computer vision, was only 74.3%. Then, in 2012, a team led by Alex Krizhevsky and advised by Geoffrey Hinton was able to achieve a top-five accuracy of 83.6%—a significant breakthrough. The competition has been dominated by deep convolutional neural networks every year since. By 2015, the winner reached an accuracy of 96.4%, and the classification task on ImageNet was considered to be a completely solved problem.

Since 2012, deep convolutional neural networks (*convnets*) have become the go-to algorithm for all computer vision tasks; more generally, they work on all perceptual tasks. At major computer vision conferences in 2015 and 2016, it was nearly impossible to find presentations that didn't involve convnets in some form. At the same time, deep learning has also found applications in many other types of problems, such as natural-language processing. It has completely replaced SVMs and decision trees in a wide range of applications. For instance, for several years, the European Organization for Nuclear Research, CERN, used decision tree–based methods for analysis of particle data from the ATLAS detector at the Large Hadron Collider (LHC); but CERN eventually switched to Keras-based deep neural networks due to their higher performance and ease of training on large datasets.

1.2.6   What makes deep learning different

The primary reason deep learning took off so quickly is that it offered better performance on many problems. But that's not the only reason. Deep learning also makes problem-solving much easier, because it completely automates what used to be the most crucial step in a machine-learning workflow: feature engineering.

Previous machine-learning techniques—shallow learning—only involved transforming the input data into one or two successive representation spaces, usually via simple transformations such as high-dimensional non-linear projections (SVMs) or decision trees. But the refined representations required by complex problems generally can't be attained by such techniques. As such, humans had to go to great lengths to make the initial input data more amenable to processing by these methods: they had to manually engineer good layers of representations for their data. This is called *feature engineering*. Deep learning, on the other hand, completely automates this step: with deep learning, you learn all features in one pass rather than having to engineer them yourself. This has greatly simplified machine-learning workflows, often replacing sophisticated multistage pipelines with a single, simple, end-to-end deep-learning model.

You may ask, if the crux of the issue is to have multiple successive layers of representations, could shallow methods be applied repeatedly to emulate the effects of deep learning? In practice, there are fast-diminishing returns to successive applications of shallow-learning methods, because *the optimal first representation layer in a three-layer model isn't the optimal first layer in a one-layer or two-layer model*. What is transformative about deep learning is that it allows a model to learn all layers of representation *jointly*, at the same time, rather than in succession (*greedily*, as it's called). With joint feature learning, whenever the model adjusts one of its internal features, all other features that depend on it automatically adapt to the change, without requiring human intervention. Everything is supervised by a single feedback signal: every change in the model serves the end goal. This is much more powerful than greedily stacking shallow models, because it allows for complex, abstract representations to be learned by breaking them down into long series of intermediate spaces (layers); each space is only a simple transformation away from the previous one.

These are the two essential characteristics of how deep learning learns from data: the *incremental, layer-by-layer way in which increasingly complex representations are developed*, and the fact that *these intermediate incremental representations are learned jointly*, each layer being updated to follow both the representational needs of the layer above and the needs of the layer below. Together, these two properties have made deep learning vastly more successful than previous approaches to machine learning.

1.2.7 *The modern machine-learning landscape*

A great way to get a sense of the current landscape of machine-learning algorithms and tools is to look at machine-learning competitions on Kaggle. Due to its highly competitive environment (some contests have thousands of entrants and million-dollar prizes) and to the wide variety of machine-learning problems covered, Kaggle offers a realistic way to assess what works and what doesn't. So, what kind of algorithm is reliably winning competitions? What tools do top entrants use?

In 2016 and 2017, Kaggle was dominated by two approaches: gradient boosting machines and deep learning. Specifically, gradient boosting is used for problems where structured data is available, whereas deep learning is used for perceptual problems such as image classification. Practitioners of the former almost always use the excellent XGBoost library, which offers support for the two most popular languages of data science: Python and R. Meanwhile, most of the Kaggle entrants using deep learning use the Keras library, due to its ease of use, flexibility, and support of Python.

These are the two techniques you should be the most familiar with in order to be successful in applied machine learning today: gradient boosting machines, for shallow-learning problems; and deep learning, for perceptual problems. In technical terms, this means you'll need to be familiar with XGBoost and Keras—the two libraries that currently dominate Kaggle competitions. With this book in hand, you're already one big step closer.

1.3   Why deep learning? Why now?

The two key ideas of deep learning for computer vision—convolutional neural networks and backpropagation—were already well understood in 1989. The Long Short-Term Memory (LSTM) algorithm, which is fundamental to deep learning for timeseries, was developed in 1997 and has barely changed since. So why did deep learning only take off after 2012? What changed in these two decades?

In general, three technical forces are driving advances in machine learning:

- Hardware
- Datasets and benchmarks
- Algorithmic advances

Because the field is guided by experimental findings rather than by theory, algorithmic advances only become possible when appropriate data and hardware are available to try new ideas (or scale up old ideas, as is often the case). Machine learning isn't mathematics or physics, where major advances can be done with a pen and a piece of paper. It's an engineering science.

The real bottlenecks throughout the 1990s and 2000s were data and hardware. But here's what happened during that time: the internet took off, and high-performance graphics chips were developed for the needs of the gaming market.

1.3.1   Hardware

Between 1990 and 2010, off-the-shelf CPUs became faster by a factor of approximately 5,000. As a result, nowadays it's possible to run small deep-learning models on your laptop, whereas this would have been intractable 25 years ago.

But typical deep-learning models used in computer vision or speech recognition require orders of magnitude more computational power than what your laptop can deliver. Throughout the 2000s, companies like NVIDIA and AMD have been investing billions of dollars in developing fast, massively parallel chips (graphical processing units [GPUs]) to power the graphics of increasingly photorealistic video games—cheap, single-purpose supercomputers designed to render complex 3D scenes on your screen in real time. This investment came to benefit the scientific community when, in 2007, NVIDIA launched CUDA (https://developer.nvidia.com/about-cuda), a programming interface for its line of GPUs. A small number of GPUs started replacing massive clusters of CPUs in various highly parallelizable applications, beginning with physics modeling. Deep neural networks, consisting mostly of many small matrix multiplications, are also highly parallelizable; and around 2011, some researchers began to write CUDA implementations of neural nets—Dan Ciresan[4] and Alex Krizhevsky[5] were among the first.

---

[4] See "Flexible, High Performance Convolutional Neural Networks for Image Classification," *Proceedings of the 22nd International Joint Conference on Artificial Intelligence* (2011), www.ijcai.org/Proceedings/11/Papers/210.pdf.

[5] See "ImageNet Classification with Deep Convolutional Neural Networks," *Advances in Neural Information Processing Systems* 25 (2012), http://mng.bz/2286.

What happened is that the gaming market subsidized supercomputing for the next generation of artificial intelligence applications. Sometimes, big things begin as games. Today, the NVIDIA TITAN X, a gaming GPU that cost $1,000 at the end of 2015, can deliver a peak of 6.6 TFLOPS in single precision: 6.6 trillion `float32` operations per second. That's about 350 times more than what you can get out of a modern laptop. On a TITAN X, it takes only a couple of days to train an ImageNet model of the sort that would have won the ILSVRC competition a few years ago. Meanwhile, large companies train deep-learning models on clusters of hundreds of GPUs of a type developed specifically for the needs of deep learning, such as the NVIDIA Tesla K80. The sheer computational power of such clusters is something that would never have been possible without modern GPUs.

What's more, the deep-learning industry is starting to go beyond GPUs and is investing in increasingly specialized, efficient chips for deep learning. In 2016, at its annual I/O convention, Google revealed its tensor processing unit (TPU) project: a new chip design developed from the ground up to run deep neural networks, which is reportedly 10 times faster and far more energy efficient than top-of-the-line GPUs.

1.3.2 Data

AI is sometimes heralded as the new industrial revolution. If deep learning is the steam engine of this revolution, then data is its coal: the raw material that powers our intelligent machines, without which nothing would be possible. When it comes to data, in addition to the exponential progress in storage hardware over the past 20 years (following Moore's law), the game changer has been the rise of the internet, making it feasible to collect and distribute very large datasets for machine learning. Today, large companies work with image datasets, video datasets, and natural-language datasets that couldn't have been collected without the internet. User-generated image tags on Flickr, for instance, have been a treasure trove of data for computer vision. So are YouTube videos. And Wikipedia is a key dataset for natural-language processing.

If there's one dataset that has been a catalyst for the rise of deep learning, it's the ImageNet dataset, consisting of 1.4 million images that have been hand annotated with 1,000 image categories (1 category per image). But what makes ImageNet special isn't just its large size, but also the yearly competition associated with it.[6]

As Kaggle has been demonstrating since 2010, public competitions are an excellent way to motivate researchers and engineers to push the envelope. Having common benchmarks that researchers compete to beat has greatly helped the recent rise of deep learning.

1.3.3 Algorithms

In addition to hardware and data, until the late 2000s, we were missing a reliable way to train very deep neural networks. As a result, neural networks were still fairly shallow,

---

[6] The ImageNet Large Scale Visual Recognition Challenge (ILSVRC), www.image-net.org/challenges/LSVRC.

using only one or two layers of representations; thus, they weren't able to shine against more-refined shallow methods such as SVMs and random forests. The key issue was that of *gradient propagation* through deep stacks of layers. The feedback signal used to train neural networks would fade away as the number of layers increased.

This changed around 2009–2010 with the advent of several simple but important algorithmic improvements that allowed for better gradient propagation:

- Better *activation functions* for neural layers
- Better *weight-initialization schemes*, starting with layer-wise pretraining, which was quickly abandoned
- Better *optimization schemes*, such as RMSProp and Adam

Only when these improvements began to allow for training models with 10 or more layers did deep learning start to shine.

Finally, in 2014, 2015, and 2016, even more advanced ways to help gradient propagation were discovered, such as batch normalization, residual connections, and depthwise separable convolutions. Today we can train from scratch models that are thousands of layers deep.

1.3.4   *A new wave of investment*

As deep learning became the new state of the art for computer vision in 2012–2013, and eventually for all perceptual tasks, industry leaders took note. What followed was a gradual wave of industry investment far beyond anything previously seen in the history of AI.

In 2011, right before deep learning took the spotlight, the total venture capital investment in AI was around $19 million, which went almost entirely to practical applications of shallow machine-learning approaches. By 2014, it had risen to a staggering $394 million. Dozens of startups launched in these three years, trying to capitalize on the deep-learning hype. Meanwhile, large tech companies such as Google, Facebook, Baidu, and Microsoft have invested in internal research departments in amounts that would most likely dwarf the flow of venture-capital money. Only a few numbers have surfaced: In 2013, Google acquired the deep-learning startup DeepMind for a reported $500 million—the largest acquisition of an AI company in history. In 2014, Baidu started a deep-learning research center in Silicon Valley, investing $300 million in the project. The deep-learning hardware startup Nervana Systems was acquired by Intel in 2016 for over $400 million.

Machine learning—in particular, deep learning—has become central to the product strategy of these tech giants. In late 2015, Google CEO Sundar Pichai stated, "Machine learning is a core, transformative way by which we're rethinking how we're doing everything. We're thoughtfully applying it across all our products, be it search, ads, YouTube, or Play. And we're in early days, but you'll see us—in a systematic way— apply machine learning in all these areas."[7]

---

[7] Sundar Pichai, Alphabet earnings call, Oct. 22, 2015.

As a result of this wave of investment, the number of people working on deep learning went in just five years from a few hundred to tens of thousands, and research progress has reached a frenetic pace. There are currently no signs that this trend will slow any time soon.

1.3.5 *The democratization of deep learning*

One of the key factors driving this inflow of new faces in deep learning has been the democratization of the toolsets used in the field. In the early days, doing deep learning required significant C++ and CUDA expertise, which few people possessed. Nowadays, basic Python scripting skills suffice to do advanced deep-learning research. This has been driven most notably by the development of Theano and then TensorFlow—two symbolic tensor-manipulation frameworks for Python that support autodifferentiation, greatly simplifying the implementation of new models—and by the rise of user-friendly libraries such as Keras, which makes deep learning as easy as manipulating LEGO bricks. After its release in early 2015, Keras quickly became the go-to deep-learning solution for large numbers of new startups, graduate students, and researchers pivoting into the field.

1.3.6 *Will it last?*

Is there anything special about deep neural networks that makes them the "right" approach for companies to be investing in and for researchers to flock to? Or is deep learning just a fad that may not last? Will we still be using deep neural networks in 20 years?

Deep learning has several properties that justify its status as an AI revolution, and it's here to stay. We may not be using neural networks two decades from now, but whatever we use will directly inherit from modern deep learning and its core concepts. These important properties can be broadly sorted into three categories:

- *Simplicity*—Deep learning removes the need for feature engineering, replacing complex, brittle, engineering-heavy pipelines with simple, end-to-end trainable models that are typically built using only five or six different tensor operations.
- *Scalability*—Deep learning is highly amenable to parallelization on GPUs or TPUs, so it can take full advantage of Moore's law. In addition, deep-learning models are trained by iterating over small batches of data, allowing them to be trained on datasets of arbitrary size. (The only bottleneck is the amount of parallel computational power available, which, thanks to Moore's law, is a fast-moving barrier.)
- *Versatility and reusability*—Unlike many prior machine-learning approaches, deep-learning models can be trained on additional data without restarting from scratch, making them viable for continuous online learning—an important property for very large production models. Furthermore, trained deep-learning models are repurposable and thus reusable: for instance, it's possible to take a deep-learning model trained for image classification and drop it into a video-processing pipeline. This allows us to reinvest previous work into increasingly

complex and powerful models. This also makes deep learning applicable to fairly small datasets.

Deep learning has only been in the spotlight for a few years, and we haven't yet established the full scope of what it can do. With every passing month, we learn about new use cases and engineering improvements that lift previous limitations. Following a scientific revolution, progress generally follows a sigmoid curve: it starts with a period of fast progress, which gradually stabilizes as researchers hit hard limitations, and then further improvements become incremental. Deep learning in 2017 seems to be in the first half of that sigmoid, with much more progress to come in the next few years.

Before we begin: the mathematical building blocks of neural networks

This chapter covers

- A first example of a neural network
- Tensors and tensor operations
- How neural networks learn via backpropagation and gradient descent

Understanding deep learning requires familiarity with many simple mathematical concepts: tensors, tensor operations, differentiation, gradient descent, and so on. Our goal in this chapter will be to build your intuition about these notions without getting overly technical. In particular, we'll steer away from mathematical notation, which can be off-putting for those without any mathematics background and isn't strictly necessary to explain things well.

To add some context for tensors and gradient descent, we'll begin the chapter with a practical example of a neural network. Then we'll go over every new concept that's been introduced, point by point. Keep in mind that these concepts will be essential for you to understand the practical examples that will come in the following chapters!

After reading this chapter, you'll have an intuitive understanding of how neural networks work, and you'll be able to move on to practical applications—which will start with chapter 3.

2.1 A first look at a neural network

Let's look at a concrete example of a neural network that uses the Python library Keras to learn to classify handwritten digits. Unless you already have experience with Keras or similar libraries, you won't understand everything about this first example right away. You probably haven't even installed Keras yet; that's fine. In the next chapter, we'll review each element in the example and explain them in detail. So don't worry if some steps seem arbitrary or look like magic to you! We've got to start somewhere.

The problem we're trying to solve here is to classify grayscale images of handwritten digits (28 × 28 pixels) into their 10 categories (0 through 9). We'll use the MNIST dataset, a classic in the machine-learning community, which has been around almost as long as the field itself and has been intensively studied. It's a set of 60,000 training images, plus 10,000 test images, assembled by the National Institute of Standards and Technology (the NIST in MNIST) in the 1980s. You can think of "solving" MNIST as the "Hello World" of deep learning—it's what you do to verify that your algorithms are working as expected. As you become a machine-learning practitioner, you'll see MNIST come up over and over again, in scientific papers, blog posts, and so on. You can see some MNIST samples in figure 2.1.

> **Note on classes and labels**
>
> In machine learning, a *category* in a classification problem is called a *class*. Data points are called *samples*. The class associated with a specific sample is called a *label*.

 **Figure 2.1 MNIST sample digits**

You don't need to try to reproduce this example on your machine just now. If you wish to, you'll first need to set up Keras, which is covered in section 3.3.

The MNIST dataset comes preloaded in Keras, in the form of a set of four Numpy arrays.

Listing 2.1 Loading the MNIST dataset in Keras

```
from keras.datasets import mnist

(train_images, train_labels), (test_images, test_labels) = mnist.load_data()
```

train_images and train_labels form the *training set*, the data that the model will learn from. The model will then be tested on the *test set*, test_images and test_labels.

The images are encoded as Numpy arrays, and the labels are an array of digits, ranging from 0 to 9. The images and labels have a one-to-one correspondence.

Let's look at the training data:

```
>>> train_images.shape
(60000, 28, 28)
>>> len(train_labels)
60000
>>> train_labels
array([5, 0, 4, ..., 5, 6, 8], dtype=uint8)
```

And here's the test data:

```
>>> test_images.shape
(10000, 28, 28)
>>> len(test_labels)
10000
>>> test_labels
array([7, 2, 1, ..., 4, 5, 6], dtype=uint8)
```

The workflow will be as follows: First, we'll feed the neural network the training data, `train_images` and `train_labels`. The network will then learn to associate images and labels. Finally, we'll ask the network to produce predictions for `test_images`, and we'll verify whether these predictions match the labels from `test_labels`.

Let's build the network—again, remember that you aren't expected to understand everything about this example yet.

Listing 2.2   The network architecture

```
from keras import models
from keras import layers

network = models.Sequential()
network.add(layers.Dense(512, activation='relu', input_shape=(28 * 28,)))
network.add(layers.Dense(10, activation='softmax'))
```

The core building block of neural networks is the *layer*, a data-processing module that you can think of as a filter for data. Some data goes in, and it comes out in a more useful form. Specifically, layers extract *representations* out of the data fed into them—hopefully, representations that are more meaningful for the problem at hand. Most of deep learning consists of chaining together simple layers that will implement a form of progressive *data distillation*. A deep-learning model is like a sieve for data processing, made of a succession of increasingly refined data filters—the layers.

Here, our network consists of a sequence of two `Dense` layers, which are densely connected (also called *fully connected*) neural layers. The second (and last) layer is a 10-way *softmax* layer, which means it will return an array of 10 probability scores (summing to 1). Each score will be the probability that the current digit image belongs to one of our 10 digit classes.

To make the network ready for training, we need to pick three more things, as part of the *compilation* step:

- *A loss function*—How the network will be able to measure its performance on the training data, and thus how it will be able to steer itself in the right direction.
- *An optimizer*—The mechanism through which the network will update itself based on the data it sees and its loss function.
- *Metrics to monitor during training and testing*—Here, we'll only care about accuracy (the fraction of the images that were correctly classified).

The exact purpose of the loss function and the optimizer will be made clear throughout the next two chapters.

Listing 2.3   The compilation step

```
network.compile(optimizer='rmsprop',
                loss='categorical_crossentropy',
                metrics=['accuracy'])
```

Before training, we'll preprocess the data by reshaping it into the shape the network expects and scaling it so that all values are in the [0, 1] interval. Previously, our training images, for instance, were stored in an array of shape (60000, 28, 28) of type uint8 with values in the [0, 255] interval. We transform it into a float32 array of shape (60000, 28 * 28) with values between 0 and 1.

Listing 2.4   Preparing the image data

```
train_images = train_images.reshape((60000, 28 * 28))
train_images = train_images.astype('float32') / 255

test_images = test_images.reshape((10000, 28 * 28))
test_images = test_images.astype('float32') / 255
```

We also need to categorically encode the labels, a step that's explained in chapter 3.

Listing 2.5   Preparing the labels

```
from keras.utils import to_categorical

train_labels = to_categorical(train_labels)
test_labels = to_categorical(test_labels)
```

We're now ready to train the network, which in Keras is done via a call to the network's fit method—we *fit* the model to its training data:

```
>>> network.fit(train_images, train_labels, epochs=5, batch_size=128)
Epoch 1/5
60000/60000 [==============================] - 9s - loss: 0.2524 - acc: 0.9273
Epoch 2/5
51328/60000 [=========================>.....] - ETA: 1s - loss: 0.1035 - acc: 0.9692
```

Two quantities are displayed during training: the loss of the network over the training data, and the accuracy of the network over the training data.

We quickly reach an accuracy of 0.989 (98.9%) on the training data. Now let's check that the model performs well on the test set, too:

```
>>> test_loss, test_acc = network.evaluate(test_images, test_labels)
>>> print('test_acc:', test_acc)
test_acc: 0.9785
```

The test-set accuracy turns out to be 97.8%—that's quite a bit lower than the training set accuracy. This gap between training accuracy and test accuracy is an example of *overfitting*: the fact that machine-learning models tend to perform worse on new data than on their training data. Overfitting is a central topic in chapter 3.

This concludes our first example—you just saw how you can build and train a neural network to classify handwritten digits in less than 20 lines of Python code. In the next chapter, I'll go into detail about every moving piece we just previewed and clarify what's going on behind the scenes. You'll learn about tensors, the data-storing objects going into the network; tensor operations, which layers are made of; and gradient descent, which allows your network to learn from its training examples.

2.2 Data representations for neural networks

In the previous example, we started from data stored in multidimensional Numpy arrays, also called *tensors*. In general, all current machine-learning systems use tensors as their basic data structure. Tensors are fundamental to the field—so fundamental that Google's TensorFlow was named after them. So what's a tensor?

At its core, a tensor is a container for data—almost always numerical data. So, it's a container for numbers. You may be already familiar with matrices, which are 2D tensors: tensors are a generalization of matrices to an arbitrary number of dimensions (note that in the context of tensors, a *dimension* is often called an *axis*).

2.2.1 Scalars (0D tensors)

A tensor that contains only one number is called a *scalar* (or scalar tensor, or 0-dimensional tensor, or 0D tensor). In Numpy, a `float32` or `float64` number is a scalar tensor (or scalar array). You can display the number of axes of a Numpy tensor via the `ndim` attribute; a scalar tensor has 0 axes (`ndim == 0`). The number of axes of a tensor is also called its *rank*. Here's a Numpy scalar:

```
>>> import numpy as np
>>> x = np.array(12)
>>> x
array(12)
>>> x.ndim
0
```

2.2.2 Vectors (1D tensors)

An array of numbers is called a *vector*, or 1D tensor. A 1D tensor is said to have exactly one axis. Following is a Numpy vector:

```
>>> x = np.array([12, 3, 6, 14])
>>> x
array([12, 3, 6, 14])
>>> x.ndim
1
```

This vector has five entries and so is called a *5-dimensional vector*. Don't confuse a 5D vector with a 5D tensor! A 5D vector has only one axis and has five dimensions along its axis, whereas a 5D tensor has five axes (and may have any number of dimensions along each axis). *Dimensionality* can denote either the number of entries along a specific axis (as in the case of our 5D vector) or the number of axes in a tensor (such as a 5D tensor), which can be confusing at times. In the latter case, it's technically more correct to talk about *a tensor of rank 5* (the rank of a tensor being the number of axes), but the ambiguous notation *5D tensor* is common regardless.

2.2.3 Matrices (2D tensors)

An array of vectors is a *matrix*, or 2D tensor. A matrix has two axes (often referred to *rows* and *columns*). You can visually interpret a matrix as a rectangular grid of numbers. This is a Numpy matrix:

```
>>> x = np.array([[5, 78, 2, 34, 0],
                  [6, 79, 3, 35, 1],
                  [7, 80, 4, 36, 2]])
>>> x.ndim
2
```

The entries from the first axis are called the *rows*, and the entries from the second axis are called the *columns*. In the previous example, [5, 78, 2, 34, 0] is the first row of x, and [5, 6, 7] is the first column.

2.2.4   *3D tensors and higher-dimensional tensors*

If you pack such matrices in a new array, you obtain a 3D tensor, which you can visually interpret as a cube of numbers. Following is a Numpy 3D tensor:

```
>>> x = np.array([[[5, 78, 2, 34, 0],
                   [6, 79, 3, 35, 1],
                   [7, 80, 4, 36, 2]],
                  [[5, 78, 2, 34, 0],
                   [6, 79, 3, 35, 1],
                   [7, 80, 4, 36, 2]],
                  [[5, 78, 2, 34, 0],
                   [6, 79, 3, 35, 1],
                   [7, 80, 4, 36, 2]]])
>>> x.ndim
3
```

By packing 3D tensors in an array, you can create a 4D tensor, and so on. In deep learning, you'll generally manipulate tensors that are 0D to 4D, although you may go up to 5D if you process video data.

2.2.5   *Key attributes*

A tensor is defined by three key attributes:

- *Number of axes (rank)*—For instance, a 3D tensor has three axes, and a matrix has two axes. This is also called the tensor's ndim in Python libraries such as Numpy.
- *Shape*—This is a tuple of integers that describes how many dimensions the tensor has along each axis. For instance, the previous matrix example has shape (3, 5), and the 3D tensor example has shape (3, 3, 5). A vector has a shape with a single element, such as (5,), whereas a scalar has an empty shape, ().
- *Data type* (usually called dtype in Python libraries)—This is the type of the data contained in the tensor; for instance, a tensor's type could be float32, uint8, float64, and so on. On rare occasions, you may see a char tensor. Note that string tensors don't exist in Numpy (or in most other libraries), because tensors live in preallocated, contiguous memory segments: and strings, being variable length, would preclude the use of this implementation.

To make this more concrete, let's look back at the data we processed in the MNIST example. First, we load the MNIST dataset:

```
from keras.datasets import mnist
(train_images, train_labels), (test_images, test_labels) = mnist.load_data()
```

Next, we display the number of axes of the tensor `train_images`, the `ndim` attribute:

```
>>> print(train_images.ndim)
3
```

Here's its shape:

```
>>> print(train_images.shape)
(60000, 28, 28)
```

And this is its data type, the `dtype` attribute:

```
>>> print(train_images.dtype)
uint8
```

So what we have here is a 3D tensor of 8-bit integers. More precisely, it's an array of 60,000 matrices of 28 × 8 integers. Each such matrix is a grayscale image, with coefficients between 0 and 255.

Let's display the fourth digit in this 3D tensor, using the library Matplotlib (part of the standard scientific Python suite); see figure 2.2.

Listing 2.6 Displaying the fourth digit

```
digit = train_images[4]

import matplotlib.pyplot as plt
plt.imshow(digit, cmap=plt.cm.binary)
plt.show()
```

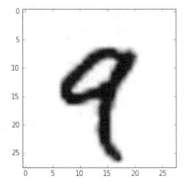

Figure 2.2 The fourth sample in our dataset

2.2.6 *Manipulating tensors in Numpy*

In the previous example, we *selected* a specific digit alongside the first axis using the syntax train_images[i]. Selecting specific elements in a tensor is called *tensor slicing*. Let's look at the tensor-slicing operations you can do on Numpy arrays.

The following example selects digits #10 to #100 (#100 isn't included) and puts them in an array of shape (90, 28, 28):

```
>>> my_slice = train_images[10:100]
>>> print(my_slice.shape)
(90, 28, 28)
```

It's equivalent to this more detailed notation, which specifies a start index and stop index for the slice along each tensor axis. Note that : is equivalent to selecting the entire axis:

```
>>> my_slice = train_images[10:100, :, :]     ◁──┐ Equivalent to the
>>> my_slice.shape                                 previous example
(90, 28, 28)
>>> my_slice = train_images[10:100, 0:28, 0:28]  ◁──┐ Also equivalent to the
>>> my_slice.shape                                     previous example
(90, 28, 28)
```

In general, you may select between any two indices along each tensor axis. For instance, in order to select 14×14 pixels in the bottom-right corner of all images, you do this:

```
my_slice = train_images[:, 14:, 14:]
```

It's also possible to use negative indices. Much like negative indices in Python lists, they indicate a position relative to the end of the current axis. In order to crop the images to patches of 14×14 pixels centered in the middle, you do this:

```
my_slice = train_images[:, 7:-7, 7:-7]
```

2.2.7 *The notion of data batches*

In general, the first axis (axis 0, because indexing starts at 0) in all data tensors you'll come across in deep learning will be the *samples axis* (sometimes called the *samples dimension*). In the MNIST example, samples are images of digits.

In addition, deep-learning models don't process an entire dataset at once; rather, they break the data into small batches. Concretely, here's one batch of our MNIST digits, with batch size of 128:

```
batch = train_images[:128]
```

And here's the next batch:

```
batch = train_images[128:256]
```

And the nth batch:

```
batch = train_images[128 * n:128 * (n + 1)]
```

When considering such a batch tensor, the first axis (axis 0) is called the *batch axis* or *batch dimension*. This is a term you'll frequently encounter when using Keras and other deep-learning libraries.

2.2.8 Real-world examples of data tensors

Let's make data tensors more concrete with a few examples similar to what you'll encounter later. The data you'll manipulate will almost always fall into one of the following categories:

- *Vector data*—2D tensors of shape (samples, features)
- *Timeseries data or sequence data*—3D tensors of shape (samples, timesteps, features)
- *Images*—4D tensors of shape (samples, height, width, channels) or (samples, channels, height, width)
- *Video*—5D tensors of shape (samples, frames, height, width, channels) or (samples, frames, channels, height, width)

2.2.9 Vector data

This is the most common case. In such a dataset, each single data point can be encoded as a vector, and thus a batch of data will be encoded as a 2D tensor (that is, an array of vectors), where the first axis is the *samples axis* and the second axis is the *features axis*.

Let's take a look at two examples:

- An actuarial dataset of people, where we consider each person's age, ZIP code, and income. Each person can be characterized as a vector of 3 values, and thus an entire dataset of 100,000 people can be stored in a 2D tensor of shape (100000, 3).
- A dataset of text documents, where we represent each document by the counts of how many times each word appears in it (out of a dictionary of 20,000 common words). Each document can be encoded as a vector of 20,000 values (one count per word in the dictionary), and thus an entire dataset of 500 documents can be stored in a tensor of shape (500, 20000).

2.2.10 Timeseries data or sequence data

Whenever time matters in your data (or the notion of sequence order), it makes sense to store it in a 3D tensor with an explicit time axis. Each sample can be encoded as a sequence of vectors (a 2D tensor), and thus a batch of data will be encoded as a 3D tensor (see figure 2.3).

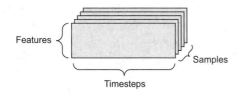

Features

Samples

Timesteps

Figure 2.3 A 3D timeseries data tensor

The time axis is always the second axis (axis of index 1), by convention. Let's look at a few examples:

- A dataset of stock prices. Every minute, we store the current price of the stock, the highest price in the past minute, and the lowest price in the past minute. Thus every minute is encoded as a 3D vector, an entire day of trading is encoded as a 2D tensor of shape (390, 3) (there are 390 minutes in a trading day), and 250 days' worth of data can be stored in a 3D tensor of shape (250, 390, 3). Here, each sample would be one day's worth of data.

- A dataset of tweets, where we encode each tweet as a sequence of 280 characters out of an alphabet of 128 unique characters. In this setting, each character can be encoded as a binary vector of size 128 (an all-zeros vector except for a 1 entry at the index corresponding to the character). Then each tweet can be encoded as a 2D tensor of shape (280, 128), and a dataset of 1 million tweets can be stored in a tensor of shape (1000000, 280, 128).

2.2.11 *Image data*

Images typically have three dimensions: height, width, and color depth. Although grayscale images (like our MNIST digits) have only a single color channel and could thus be stored in 2D tensors, by convention image tensors are always 3D, with a one-dimensional color channel for grayscale images. A batch of 128 grayscale images of size 256 × 256 could thus be stored in a tensor of shape (128, 256, 256, 1), and a batch of 128 color images could be stored in a tensor of shape (128, 256, 256, 3) (see figure 2.4).

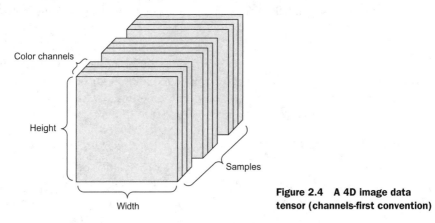

Color channels

Height

Width

Samples

Figure 2.4 A 4D image data tensor (channels-first convention)

There are two conventions for shapes of images tensors: the *channels-last* convention (used by TensorFlow) and the *channels-first* convention (used by Theano). The TensorFlow machine-learning framework, from Google, places the color-depth axis at the end: (samples, height, width, color_depth). Meanwhile, Theano places the color depth axis right after the batch axis: (samples, color_depth, height, width). With the Theano convention, the previous examples would become (128, 1, 256, 256) and (128, 3, 256, 256). The Keras framework provides support for both formats.

2.2.12 Video data

Video data is one of the few types of real-world data for which you'll need 5D tensors. A video can be understood as a sequence of frames, each frame being a color image. Because each frame can be stored in a 3D tensor (height, width, color_depth), a sequence of frames can be stored in a 4D tensor (frames, height, width, color_depth), and thus a batch of different videos can be stored in a 5D tensor of shape (samples, frames, height, width, color_depth).

For instance, a 60-second, 144 × 256 YouTube video clip sampled at 4 frames per second would have 240 frames. A batch of four such video clips would be stored in a tensor of shape (4, 240, 144, 256, 3). That's a total of 106,168,320 values! If the dtype of the tensor was float32, then each value would be stored in 32 bits, so the tensor would represent 405 MB. Heavy! Videos you encounter in real life are much lighter, because they aren't stored in float32, and they're typically compressed by a large factor (such as in the MPEG format).

2.3   *The gears of neural networks: tensor operations*

Much as any computer program can be ultimately reduced to a small set of binary operations on binary inputs (AND, OR, NOR, and so on), all transformations learned by deep neural networks can be reduced to a handful of *tensor operations* applied to tensors of numeric data. For instance, it's possible to add tensors, multiply tensors, and so on.

In our initial example, we were building our network by stacking Dense layers on top of each other. A Keras layer instance looks like this:

```
keras.layers.Dense(512, activation='relu')
```

This layer can be interpreted as a function, which takes as input a 2D tensor and returns another 2D tensor—a new representation for the input tensor. Specifically, the function is as follows (where W is a 2D tensor and b is a vector, both attributes of the layer):

```
output = relu(dot(W, input) + b)
```

Let's unpack this. We have three tensor operations here: a dot product (dot) between the input tensor and a tensor named W; an addition (+) between the resulting 2D tensor and a vector b; and, finally, a relu operation. relu(x) is max(x, 0).

> **NOTE**   Although this section deals entirely with linear algebra expressions, you won't find any mathematical notation here. I've found that mathematical concepts can be more readily mastered by programmers with no mathematical background if they're expressed as short Python snippets instead of mathematical equations. So we'll use Numpy code throughout.

2.3.1   *Element-wise operations*

The relu operation and addition are *element-wise* operations: operations that are applied independently to each entry in the tensors being considered. This means these operations are highly amenable to massively parallel implementations (*vectorized* implementations, a term that comes from the *vector processor* supercomputer architecture from the 1970–1990 period). If you want to write a naive Python implementation of an element-wise operation, you use a for loop, as in this naive implementation of an element-wise relu operation:

```
def naive_relu(x):
    assert len(x.shape) == 2      ◁——— x is a 2D Numpy tensor.

    x = x.copy()                  ◁——— Avoid overwriting the input tensor.
    for i in range(x.shape[0]):
        for j in range(x.shape[1]):
            x[i, j] = max(x[i, j], 0)
    return x
```

You do the same for addition:

```
def naive_add(x, y):
    assert len(x.shape) == 2
    assert x.shape == y.shape

    x = x.copy()
    for i in range(x.shape[0]):
        for j in range(x.shape[1]):
            x[i, j] += y[i, j]
    return x
```

x and y are 2D Numpy tensors.

Avoid overwriting the input tensor.

On the same principle, you can do element-wise multiplication, subtraction, and so on.

In practice, when dealing with Numpy arrays, these operations are available as well-optimized built-in Numpy functions, which themselves delegate the heavy lifting to a Basic Linear Algebra Subprograms (BLAS) implementation if you have one installed (which you should). BLAS are low-level, highly parallel, efficient tensor-manipulation routines that are typically implemented in Fortran or C.

So, in Numpy, you can do the following element-wise operation, and it will be blazing fast:

```
import numpy as np

z = x + y

z = np.maximum(z, 0.)
```

←—— **Element-wise addition**

←—— **Element-wise relu**

2.3.2 *Broadcasting*

Our earlier naive implementation of `naive_add` only supports the addition of 2D tensors with identical shapes. But in the `Dense` layer introduced earlier, we added a 2D tensor with a vector. What happens with addition when the shapes of the two tensors being added differ?

When possible, and if there's no ambiguity, the smaller tensor will be *broadcasted* to match the shape of the larger tensor. Broadcasting consists of two steps:

1. Axes (called *broadcast axes*) are added to the smaller tensor to match the `ndim` of the larger tensor.
2. The smaller tensor is repeated alongside these new axes to match the full shape of the larger tensor.

Let's look at a concrete example. Consider X with shape `(32, 10)` and y with shape `(10,)`. First, we add an empty first axis to y, whose shape becomes `(1, 10)`. Then, we repeat y 32 times alongside this new axis, so that we end up with a tensor Y with shape `(32, 10)`, where `Y[i, :] == y` for i in `range(0, 32)`. At this point, we can proceed to add X and Y, because they have the same shape.

In terms of implementation, no new 2D tensor is created, because that would be terribly inefficient. The repetition operation is entirely virtual: it happens at the algorithmic level rather than at the memory level. But thinking of the vector being repeated 10 times alongside a new axis is a helpful mental model. Here's what a naive implementation would look like:

```
def naive_add_matrix_and_vector(x, y):          x is a 2D Numpy tensor.
    assert len(x.shape) == 2
    assert len(y.shape) == 1                     y is a Numpy vector.
    assert x.shape[1] == y.shape[0]

    x = x.copy()                                 Avoid overwriting
    for i in range(x.shape[0]):                  the input tensor.
        for j in range(x.shape[1]):
            x[i, j] += y[j]
    return x
```

With broadcasting, you can generally apply two-tensor element-wise operations if one tensor has shape (a, b, … n, n + 1, … m) and the other has shape (n, n + 1, … m). The broadcasting will then automatically happen for axes a through n – 1.

The following example applies the element-wise `maximum` operation to two tensors of different shapes via broadcasting:

```
import numpy as np
                                            x is a random tensor with
x = np.random.random((64, 3, 32, 10))      shape (64, 3, 32, 10).
y = np.random.random((32, 10))
                                           y is a random tensor
z = np.maximum(x, y)                       with shape (32, 10).

                                     The output z has shape
                                     (64, 3, 32, 10) like x.
```

2.3.3 *Tensor dot*

The dot operation, also called a *tensor product* (not to be confused with an element-wise product) is the most common, most useful tensor operation. Contrary to element-wise operations, it combines entries in the input tensors.

An element-wise product is done with the * operator in Numpy, Keras, Theano, and TensorFlow. dot uses a different syntax in TensorFlow, but in both Numpy and Keras it's done using the standard dot operator:

```
import numpy as np

z = np.dot(x, y)
```

In mathematical notation, you'd note the operation with a dot (.):

```
z = x . y
```

Mathematically, what does the dot operation do? Let's start with the dot product of two vectors x and y. It's computed as follows:

```
def naive_vector_dot(x, y):
    assert len(x.shape) == 1           x and y are Numpy vectors.
    assert len(y.shape) == 1
    assert x.shape[0] == y.shape[0]
```

```
    z = 0.
    for i in range(x.shape[0]):
        z += x[i] * y[i]
    return z
```

You'll have noticed that the dot product between two vectors is a scalar and that only vectors with the same number of elements are compatible for a dot product.

You can also take the dot product between a matrix x and a vector y, which returns a vector where the coefficients are the dot products between y and the rows of x. You implement it as follows:

```
import numpy as np

def naive_matrix_vector_dot(x, y):
    assert len(x.shape) == 2
    assert len(y.shape) == 1
    assert x.shape[1] == y.shape[0]

    z = np.zeros(x.shape[0])
    for i in range(x.shape[0]):
        for j in range(x.shape[1]):
            z[i] += x[i, j] * y[j]
    return z
```

> x is a Numpy matrix.

> y is a Numpy vector.

> The first dimension of x must be the same as the 0th dimension of y!

> This operation returns a vector of 0s with the same shape as y.

You could also reuse the code we wrote previously, which highlights the relationship between a matrix-vector product and a vector product:

```
def naive_matrix_vector_dot(x, y):
    z = np.zeros(x.shape[0])
    for i in range(x.shape[0]):
        z[i] = naive_vector_dot(x[i, :], y)
    return z
```

Note that as soon as one of the two tensors has an `ndim` greater than 1, `dot` is no longer symmetric, which is to say that `dot(x, y)` isn't the same as `dot(y, x)`.

Of course, a dot product generalizes to tensors with an arbitrary number of axes. The most common applications may be the dot product between two matrices. You can take the dot product of two matrices x and y (`dot(x, y)`) if and only if `x.shape[1] == y.shape[0]`. The result is a matrix with shape (`x.shape[0]`, `y.shape[1]`), where the coefficients are the vector products between the rows of x and the columns of y. Here's the naive implementation:

```
def naive_matrix_dot(x, y):
    assert len(x.shape) == 2
    assert len(y.shape) == 2
    assert x.shape[1] == y.shape[0]

    z = np.zeros((x.shape[0], y.shape[1]))
    for i in range(x.shape[0]):
        for j in range(y.shape[1]):
            row_x = x[i, :]
            column_y = y[:, j]
            z[i, j] = naive_vector_dot(row_x, column_y)
    return z
```

> x and y are Numpy matrices.

> The first dimension of x must be the same as the 0th dimension of y!

> This operation returns a matrix of 0s with a specific shape.

> Iterates over the rows of x ...

> ... and over the columns of y.

To understand dot-product shape compatibility, it helps to visualize the input and output tensors by aligning them as shown in figure 2.5.

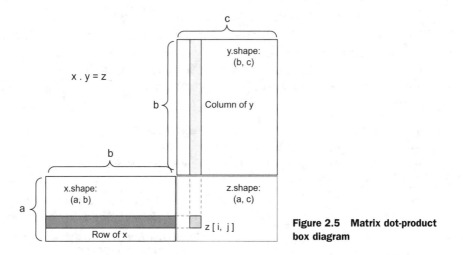

Figure 2.5   **Matrix dot-product box diagram**

x, y, and z are pictured as rectangles (literal boxes of coefficients). Because the rows and x and the columns of y must have the same size, it follows that the width of x must match the height of y. If you go on to develop new machine-learning algorithms, you'll likely be drawing such diagrams often.

More generally, you can take the dot product between higher-dimensional tensors, following the same rules for shape compatibility as outlined earlier for the 2D case:

```
(a, b, c, d) . (d,) -> (a, b, c)
(a, b, c, d) . (d, e) -> (a, b, c, e)
```

And so on.

2.3.4   *Tensor reshaping*

A third type of tensor operation that's essential to understand is *tensor reshaping*. Although it wasn't used in the Dense layers in our first neural network example, we used it when we preprocessed the digits data before feeding it into our network:

```
train_images = train_images.reshape((60000, 28 * 28))
```

Reshaping a tensor means rearranging its rows and columns to match a target shape. Naturally, the reshaped tensor has the same total number of coefficients as the initial tensor. Reshaping is best understood via simple examples:

```
>>> x = np.array([[0., 1.],
                  [2., 3.],
                  [4., 5.]])
>>> print(x.shape)
(3, 2)
```

```
>>> x = x.reshape((6, 1))
>>> x
array([[ 0.],
       [ 1.],
       [ 2.],
       [ 3.],
       [ 4.],
       [ 5.]])
>>> x = x.reshape((2, 3))
>>> x
array([[ 0.,   1.,   2.],
       [ 3.,   4.,   5.]])
```

A special case of reshaping that's commonly encountered is *transposition*. *Transposing* a matrix means exchanging its rows and its columns, so that x[i, :] becomes x[:, i]:

```
>>> x = np.zeros((300, 20))        ◁─┐  Creates an all-zeros matrix
>>> x = np.transpose(x)               │  of shape (300, 20)
>>> print(x.shape)
(20, 300)
```

2.3.5 Geometric interpretation of tensor operations

Because the contents of the tensors manipulated by tensor operations can be interpreted as coordinates of points in some geometric space, all tensor operations have a geometric interpretation. For instance, let's consider addition. We'll start with the following vector:

```
A = [0.5, 1]
```

It's a point in a 2D space (see figure 2.6). It's common to picture a vector as an arrow linking the origin to the point, as shown in figure 2.7.

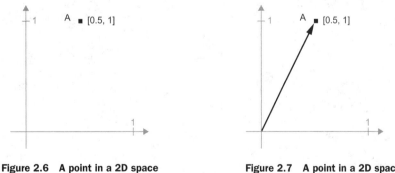

Figure 2.6 A point in a 2D space

Figure 2.7 A point in a 2D space pictured as an arrow

Let's consider a new point, B = [1, 0.25], which we'll add to the previous one. This is done geometrically by chaining together the vector arrows, with the resulting location being the vector representing the sum of the previous two vectors (see figure 2.8).

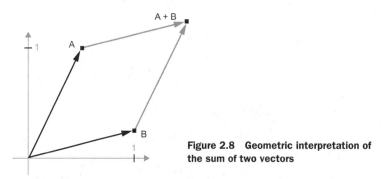

Figure 2.8 Geometric interpretation of the sum of two vectors

In general, elementary geometric operations such as affine transformations, rotations, scaling, and so on can be expressed as tensor operations. For instance, a rotation of a 2D vector by an angle theta can be achieved via a dot product with a 2 × 2 matrix R = [u, v], where u and v are both vectors of the plane: u = [cos(theta), sin(theta)] and v = [-sin(theta), cos(theta)].

2.3.6   *A geometric interpretation of deep learning*

You just learned that neural networks consist entirely of chains of tensor operations and that all of these tensor operations are just geometric transformations of the input data. It follows that you can interpret a neural network as a very complex geometric transformation in a high-dimensional space, implemented via a long series of simple steps.

In 3D, the following mental image may prove useful. Imagine two sheets of colored paper: one red and one blue. Put one on top of the other. Now crumple them together into a small ball. That crumpled paper ball is your input data, and each sheet of paper is a class of data in a classification problem. What a neural network (or any other machine-learning model) is meant to do is figure out a transformation of the paper ball that would uncrumple it, so as to make the two classes cleanly separable again. With deep learning, this would be implemented as a series of simple transformations of the 3D space, such as those you could apply on the paper ball with your fingers, one movement at a time.

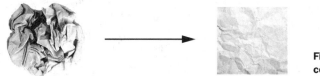

Figure 2.9   Uncrumpling a complicated manifold of data

Uncrumpling paper balls is what machine learning is about: finding neat representations for complex, highly folded data manifolds. At this point, you should have a pretty good intuition as to why deep learning excels at this: it takes the approach of incrementally decomposing a complicated geometric transformation into a long chain of elementary ones, which is pretty much the strategy a human would follow to uncrumple a paper ball. Each layer in a deep network applies a transformation that disentangles the data a little—and a deep stack of layers makes tractable an extremely complicated disentanglement process.

2.4   *The engine of neural networks: gradient-based optimization*

As you saw in the previous section, each neural layer from our first network example transforms its input data as follows:

```
output = relu(dot(W, input) + b)
```

In this expression, W and b are tensors that are attributes of the layer. They're called the *weights* or *trainable parameters* of the layer (the kernel and bias attributes, respectively). These weights contain the information learned by the network from exposure to training data.

Initially, these weight matrices are filled with small random values (a step called *random initialization*). Of course, there's no reason to expect that relu(dot(W, input) + b), when W and b are random, will yield any useful representations. The resulting representations are meaningless—but they're a starting point. What comes next is to gradually adjust these weights, based on a feedback signal. This gradual adjustment, also called *training*, is basically the learning that machine learning is all about.

This happens within what's called a *training loop*, which works as follows. Repeat these steps in a loop, as long as necessary:

1 Draw a batch of training samples x and corresponding targets y.
2 Run the network on x (a step called the *forward pass*) to obtain predictions y_pred.
3 Compute the loss of the network on the batch, a measure of the mismatch between y_pred and y.
4 Update all weights of the network in a way that slightly reduces the loss on this batch.

You'll eventually end up with a network that has a very low loss on its training data: a low mismatch between predictions y_pred and expected targets y. The network has "learned" to map its inputs to correct targets. From afar, it may look like magic, but when you reduce it to elementary steps, it turns out to be simple.

Step 1 sounds easy enough—just I/O code. Steps 2 and 3 are merely the application of a handful of tensor operations, so you could implement these steps purely from what you learned in the previous section. The difficult part is step 4: updating the network's weights. Given an individual weight coefficient in the network, how can you compute whether the coefficient should be increased or decreased, and by how much?

One naive solution would be to freeze all weights in the network except the one scalar coefficient being considered, and try different values for this coefficient. Let's say the initial value of the coefficient is 0.3. After the forward pass on a batch of data, the loss of the network on the batch is 0.5. If you change the coefficient's value to 0.35 and rerun the forward pass, the loss increases to 0.6. But if you lower the coefficient to 0.25, the loss falls to 0.4. In this case, it seems that updating the coefficient by -0.05

would contribute to minimizing the loss. This would have to be repeated for all coefficients in the network.

But such an approach would be horribly inefficient, because you'd need to compute two forward passes (which are expensive) for every individual coefficient (of which there are many, usually thousands and sometimes up to millions). A much better approach is to take advantage of the fact that all operations used in the network are *differentiable*, and compute the *gradient* of the loss with regard to the network's coefficients. You can then move the coefficients in the opposite direction from the gradient, thus decreasing the loss.

If you already know what *differentiable* means and what a *gradient* is, you can skip to section 2.4.3. Otherwise, the following two sections will help you understand these concepts.

2.4.1   What's a derivative?

Consider a continuous, smooth function `f(x) = y`, mapping a real number x to a new real number y. Because the function is *continuous*, a small change in x can only result in a small change in y—that's the intuition behind continuity. Let's say you increase x by a small factor `epsilon_x`: this results in a small `epsilon_y` change to y:

```
f(x + epsilon_x) = y + epsilon_y
```

In addition, because the function is *smooth* (its curve doesn't have any abrupt angles), when `epsilon_x` is small enough, around a certain point p, it's possible to approximate f as a linear function of slope a, so that `epsilon_y` becomes a * epsilon_x:

```
f(x + epsilon_x) = y + a * epsilon_x
```

Obviously, this linear approximation is valid only when x is close enough to p.

The slope a is called the *derivative* of f in p. If a is negative, it means a small change of x around p will result in a decrease of `f(x)` (as shown in figure 2.10); and if a is positive, a small change in x will result in an increase of `f(x)`. Further, the absolute value of a (the *magnitude* of the derivative) tells you how quickly this increase or decrease will happen.

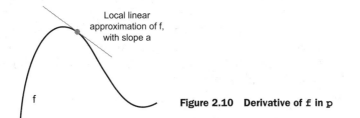

Figure 2.10   Derivative of `f` in p

For every differentiable function `f(x)` (*differentiable* means "can be derived": for example, smooth, continuous functions can be derived), there exists a derivative function `f'(x)` that maps values of x to the slope of the local linear approximation of f in those points. For instance, the derivative of `cos(x)` is `-sin(x)`, the derivative of `f(x) = a * x` is `f'(x) = a`, and so on.

If you're trying to update x by a factor `epsilon_x` in order to minimize `f(x)`, and you know the derivative of `f`, then your job is done: the derivative completely describes how `f(x)` evolves as you change x. If you want to reduce the value of `f(x)`, you just need to move x a little in the opposite direction from the derivative.

2.4.2   *Derivative of a tensor operation: the gradient*

A *gradient* is the derivative of a tensor operation. It's the generalization of the concept of derivatives to functions of multidimensional inputs: that is, to functions that take tensors as inputs.

Consider an input vector x, a matrix `W`, a target y, and a loss function `loss`. You can use `W` to compute a target candidate `y_pred`, and compute the loss, or mismatch, between the target candidate `y_pred` and the target y:

```
y_pred = dot(W, x)
loss_value = loss(y_pred, y)
```

If the data inputs x and y are frozen, then this can be interpreted as a function mapping values of `W` to loss values:

```
loss_value = f(W)
```

Let's say the current value of `W` is `W0`. Then the derivative of `f` in the point `W0` is a tensor `gradient(f)(W0)` with the same shape as `W`, where each coefficient `gradient(f)(W0)[i, j]` indicates the direction and magnitude of the change in `loss_value` you observe when modifying `W0[i, j]`. That tensor `gradient(f)(W0)` is the gradient of the function `f(W) = loss_value` in `W0`.

You saw earlier that the derivative of a function `f(x)` of a single coefficient can be interpreted as the slope of the curve of `f`. Likewise, `gradient(f)(W0)` can be interpreted as the tensor describing the *curvature* of `f(W)` around `W0`.

For this reason, in much the same way that, for a function `f(x)`, you can reduce the value of `f(x)` by moving x a little in the opposite direction from the derivative, with a function `f(W)` of a tensor, you can reduce `f(W)` by moving `W` in the opposite direction from the gradient: for example, `W1 = W0 - step * gradient(f)(W0)` (where `step` is a small scaling factor). That means going against the curvature, which intuitively should put you lower on the curve. Note that the scaling factor `step` is needed because `gradient(f)(W0)` only approximates the curvature when you're close to `W0`, so you don't want to get too far from `W0`.

2.4.3   *Stochastic gradient descent*

Given a differentiable function, it's theoretically possible to find its minimum analytically: it's known that a function's minimum is a point where the derivative is 0, so all you have to do is find all the points where the derivative goes to 0 and check for which of these points the function has the lowest value.

Applied to a neural network, that means finding analytically the combination of weight values that yields the smallest possible loss function. This can be done by solving the equation `gradient(f)(W) = 0` for `W`. This is a polynomial equation of N variables, where N is the number of coefficients in the network. Although it would be possible to solve such an equation for $N = 2$ or $N = 3$, doing so is intractable for real neural networks, where the number of parameters is never less than a few thousand and can often be several tens of millions.

Instead, you can use the four-step algorithm outlined at the beginning of this section: modify the parameters little by little based on the current loss value on a random batch of data. Because you're dealing with a differentiable function, you can compute its gradient, which gives you an efficient way to implement step 4. If you update the weights in the opposite direction from the gradient, the loss will be a little less every time:

1 Draw a batch of training samples x and corresponding targets y.
2 Run the network on x to obtain predictions y_pred.
3 Compute the loss of the network on the batch, a measure of the mismatch between y_pred and y.
4 Compute the gradient of the loss with regard to the network's parameters (a *backward pass*).
5 Move the parameters a little in the opposite direction from the gradient—for example W -= step * gradient—thus reducing the loss on the batch a bit.

Easy enough! What I just described is called *mini-batch stochastic gradient descent* (mini-batch SGD). The term *stochastic* refers to the fact that each batch of data is drawn at random (*stochastic* is a scientific synonym of *random*). Figure 2.11 illustrates what happens in 1D, when the network has only one parameter and you have only one training sample.

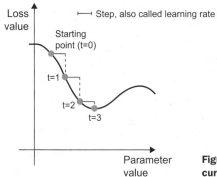

Figure 2.11 **SGD down a 1D loss curve (one learnable parameter)**

As you can see, intuitively it's important to pick a reasonable value for the `step` factor. If it's too small, the descent down the curve will take many iterations, and it could get stuck in a local minimum. If `step` is too large, your updates may end up taking you to completely random locations on the curve.

Note that a variant of the mini-batch SGD algorithm would be to draw a single sample and target at each iteration, rather than drawing a batch of data. This would be *true* SGD (as opposed to *mini-batch* SGD). Alternatively, going to the opposite extreme, you could run every step on *all* data available, which is called *batch SGD*. Each update would then be more accurate, but far more expensive. The efficient compromise between these two extremes is to use mini-batches of reasonable size.

Although figure 2.11 illustrates gradient descent in a 1D parameter space, in practice you'll use gradient descent in highly dimensional spaces: every weight coefficient in a neural network is a free dimension in the space, and there may be tens of thousands or even millions of them. To help you build intuition about loss surfaces, you can also visualize gradient descent along a 2D loss surface, as shown in figure 2.12. But you can't possibly visualize what the actual process of training a neural network looks like—you can't represent a 1,000,000-dimensional space in a way that makes sense to humans. As such, it's good to keep in mind that the intuitions you develop through these low-dimensional representations may not always be accurate in practice. This has historically been a source of issues in the world of deep-learning research.

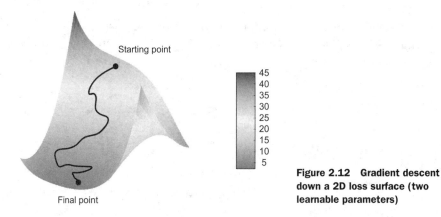

Figure 2.12   Gradient descent down a 2D loss surface (two learnable parameters)

Additionally, there exist multiple variants of SGD that differ by taking into account previous weight updates when computing the next weight update, rather than just looking at the current value of the gradients. There is, for instance, SGD with momentum, as well as Adagrad, RMSProp, and several others. Such variants are known as *optimization methods* or *optimizers*. In particular, the concept of *momentum*, which is used in many of these variants, deserves your attention. Momentum addresses two issues with SGD: convergence speed and local minima. Consider figure 2.13, which shows the curve of a loss as a function of a network parameter.

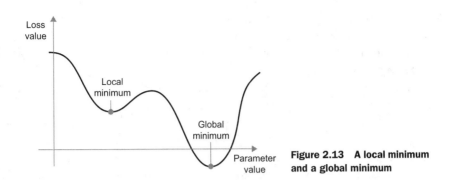

Figure 2.13 A local minimum and a global minimum

As you can see, around a certain parameter value, there is a *local minimum*: around that point, moving left would result in the loss increasing, but so would moving right. If the parameter under consideration were being optimized via SGD with a small learning rate, then the optimization process would get stuck at the local minimum instead of making its way to the global minimum.

You can avoid such issues by using momentum, which draws inspiration from physics. A useful mental image here is to think of the optimization process as a small ball rolling down the loss curve. If it has enough momentum, the ball won't get stuck in a ravine and will end up at the global minimum. Momentum is implemented by moving the ball at each step based not only on the current slope value (current acceleration) but also on the current velocity (resulting from past acceleration). In practice, this means updating the parameter w based not only on the current gradient value but also on the previous parameter update, such as in this naive implementation:

```
past_velocity = 0.
momentum = 0.1                    Constant momentum factor
while loss > 0.01:                Optimization loop
    w, loss, gradient = get_current_parameters()
    velocity = past_velocity * momentum + learning_rate * gradient
    w = w + momentum * velocity - learning_rate * gradient
    past_velocity = velocity
    update_parameter(w)
```

2.4.4 Chaining derivatives: the Backpropagation algorithm

In the previous algorithm, we casually assumed that because a function is differentiable, we can explicitly compute its derivative. In practice, a neural network function consists of many tensor operations chained together, each of which has a simple, known derivative. For instance, this is a network f composed of three tensor operations, a, b, and c, with weight matrices W1, W2, and W3:

```
f(W1, W2, W3) = a(W1, b(W2, c(W3)))
```

Calculus tells us that such a chain of functions can be derived using the following identity, called the *chain rule*: `f(g(x)) = f'(g(x)) * g'(x)`. Applying the chain rule to the computation of the gradient values of a neural network gives rise to an algorithm called *Backpropagation* (also sometimes called *reverse-mode differentiation*). Backpropagation starts with the final loss value and works backward from the top layers to the bottom layers, applying the chain rule to compute the contribution that each parameter had in the loss value.

Nowadays, and for years to come, people will implement networks in modern frameworks that are capable of *symbolic differentiation*, such as TensorFlow. This means that, given a chain of operations with a known derivative, they can compute a gradient *function* for the chain (by applying the chain rule) that maps network parameter values to gradient values. When you have access to such a function, the backward pass is reduced to a call to this gradient function. Thanks to symbolic differentiation, you'll never have to implement the Backpropagation algorithm by hand. For this reason, we won't waste your time and your focus on deriving the exact formulation of the Backpropagation algorithm in these pages. All you need is a good understanding of how gradient-based optimization works.

2.5   *Looking back at our first example*

You've reached the end of this chapter, and you should now have a general understanding of what's going on behind the scenes in a neural network. Let's go back to
the first example and review each piece of it in the light of what you've learned in the
previous three sections.

This was the input data:

```
(train_images, train_labels), (test_images, test_labels) = mnist.load_data()

train_images = train_images.reshape((60000, 28 * 28))
train_images = train_images.astype('float32') / 255

test_images = test_images.reshape((10000, 28 * 28))
test_images = test_images.astype('float32') / 255
```

Now you understand that the input images are stored in Numpy tensors, which are
here formatted as `float32` tensors of shape `(60000, 784)` (training data) and `(10000,
784)` (test data), respectively.

This was our network:

```
network = models.Sequential()
network.add(layers.Dense(512, activation='relu', input_shape=(28 * 28,)))
network.add(layers.Dense(10, activation='softmax'))
```

Now you understand that this network consists of a chain of two `Dense` layers, that
each layer applies a few simple tensor operations to the input data, and that these
operations involve weight tensors. Weight tensors, which are attributes of the layers,
are where the *knowledge* of the network persists.

This was the network-compilation step:

```
network.compile(optimizer='rmsprop',
                loss='categorical_crossentropy',
                metrics=['accuracy'])
```

Now you understand that `categorical_crossentropy` is the loss function that's used
as a feedback signal for learning the weight tensors, and which the training phase will
attempt to minimize. You also know that this reduction of the loss happens via mini-
batch stochastic gradient descent. The exact rules governing a specific use of gradient
descent are defined by the `rmsprop` optimizer passed as the first argument.

Finally, this was the training loop:

```
network.fit(train_images, train_labels, epochs=5, batch_size=128)
```

Now you understand what happens when you call `fit`: the network will start to iterate
on the training data in mini-batches of 128 samples, 5 times over (each iteration over
all the training data is called an *epoch*). At each iteration, the network will compute the
gradients of the weights with regard to the loss on the batch, and update the weights

accordingly. After these 5 epochs, the network will have performed 2,345 gradient updates (469 per epoch), and the loss of the network will be sufficiently low that the network will be capable of classifying handwritten digits with high accuracy.

At this point, you already know most of what there is to know about neural networks.

Chapter summary

- *Learning* means finding a combination of model parameters that minimizes a loss function for a given set of training data samples and their corresponding targets.

- Learning happens by drawing random batches of data samples and their targets, and computing the gradient of the network parameters with respect to the loss on the batch. The network parameters are then moved a bit (the magnitude of the move is defined by the learning rate) in the opposite direction from the gradient.

- The entire learning process is made possible by the fact that neural networks are chains of differentiable tensor operations, and thus it's possible to apply the chain rule of derivation to find the gradient function mapping the current parameters and current batch of data to a gradient value.

- Two key concepts you'll see frequently in future chapters are *loss* and *optimizers*. These are the two things you need to define before you begin feeding data into a network.

- The *loss* is the quantity you'll attempt to minimize during training, so it should represent a measure of success for the task you're trying to solve.

- The *optimizer* specifies the exact way in which the gradient of the loss will be used to update parameters: for instance, it could be the RMSProp optimizer, SGD with momentum, and so on.

Getting started
with neural networks

This chapter is designed to get you started with using neural networks to solve real problems. You'll consolidate the knowledge you gained from our first practical example in chapter 2, and you'll apply what you've learned to three new problems covering the three most common use cases of neural networks: binary classification, multiclass classification, and scalar regression.

In this chapter, we'll take a closer look at the core components of neural networks that we introduced in chapter 2: layers, networks, objective functions, and optimizers. We'll give you a quick introduction to Keras, the Python deep-learning library that we'll use throughout the book. You'll set up a deep-learning workstation, with

TensorFlow, Keras, and GPU support. We'll dive into three introductory examples of how to use neural networks to address real problems:

- Classifying movie reviews as positive or negative (binary classification)
- Classifying news wires by topic (multiclass classification)
- Estimating the price of a house, given real-estate data (regression)

By the end of this chapter, you'll be able to use neural networks to solve simple machine problems such as classification and regression over vector data. You'll then be ready to start building a more principled, theory-driven understanding of machine learning in chapter 4.

3.1   *Anatomy of a neural network*

As you saw in the previous chapters, training a neural network revolves around the following objects:

- *Layers*, which are combined into a *network* (or *model*)
- The *input data* and corresponding *targets*
- The *loss function*, which defines the feedback signal used for learning
- The *optimizer*, which determines how learning proceeds

You can visualize their interaction as illustrated in figure 3.1: the network, composed of layers that are chained together, maps the input data to predictions. The loss function then compares these predictions to the targets, producing a loss value: a measure of how well the network's predictions match what was expected. The optimizer uses this loss value to update the network's weights.

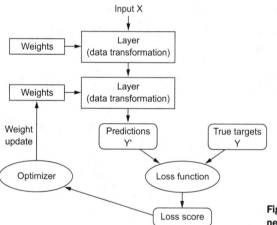

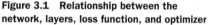

Figure 3.1   Relationship between the network, layers, loss function, and optimizer

Let's take a closer look at layers, networks, loss functions, and optimizers.

3.1.1   *Layers: the building blocks of deep learning*

The fundamental data structure in neural networks is the *layer*, to which you were introduced in chapter 2. A layer is a data-processing module that takes as input one or more tensors and that outputs one or more tensors. Some layers are stateless, but more frequently layers have a state: the layer's *weights*, one or several tensors learned with stochastic gradient descent, which together contain the network's *knowledge*.

Different layers are appropriate for different tensor formats and different types of data processing. For instance, simple vector data, stored in 2D tensors of shape (samples, features), is often processed by *densely connected* layers, also called *fully connected* or *dense* layers (the Dense class in Keras). Sequence data, stored in 3D tensors of shape (samples, timesteps, features), is typically processed by *recurrent* layers such as an LSTM layer. Image data, stored in 4D tensors, is usually processed by 2D convolution layers (Conv2D).

You can think of layers as the LEGO bricks of deep learning, a metaphor that is made explicit by frameworks like Keras. Building deep-learning models in Keras is done by clipping together compatible layers to form useful data-transformation pipe-lines. The notion of *layer compatibility* here refers specifically to the fact that every layer will only accept input tensors of a certain shape and will return output tensors of a certain shape. Consider the following example:

```
from keras import layers

layer = layers.Dense(32, input_shape=(784,))
```

A dense layer with 32 output units

We're creating a layer that will only accept as input 2D tensors where the first dimension is 784 (axis 0, the batch dimension, is unspecified, and thus any value would be accepted). This layer will return a tensor where the first dimension has been transformed to be 32.

Thus this layer can only be connected to a downstream layer that expects 32-dimensional vectors as its input. When using Keras, you don't have to worry about compatibility, because the layers you add to your models are dynamically built to match the shape of the incoming layer. For instance, suppose you write the following:

```
from keras import models
from keras import layers

model = models.Sequential()
model.add(layers.Dense(32, input_shape=(784,)))
model.add(layers.Dense(32))
```

The second layer didn't receive an input shape argument—instead, it automatically inferred its input shape as being the output shape of the layer that came before.

3.1.2 Models: networks of layers

A deep-learning model is a directed, acyclic graph of layers. The most common instance is a linear stack of layers, mapping a single input to a single output.

But as you move forward, you'll be exposed to a much broader variety of network topologies. Some common ones include the following:

- Two-branch networks
- Multihead networks
- Inception blocks

The topology of a network defines a *hypothesis space*. You may remember that in chapter 1, we defined machine learning as "searching for useful representations of some input data, within a predefined space of possibilities, using guidance from a feedback signal." By choosing a network topology, you constrain your *space of possibilities* (hypothesis space) to a specific series of tensor operations, mapping input data to output data. What you'll then be searching for is a good set of values for the weight tensors involved in these tensor operations.

Picking the right network architecture is more an art than a science; and although there are some best practices and principles you can rely on, only practice can help you become a proper neural-network architect. The next few chapters will both teach you explicit principles for building neural networks and help you develop intuition as to what works or doesn't work for specific problems.

3.1.3 Loss functions and optimizers: keys to configuring the learning process

Once the network architecture is defined, you still have to choose two more things:

- *Loss function (objective function)*—The quantity that will be minimized during training. It represents a measure of success for the task at hand.
- *Optimizer*—Determines how the network will be updated based on the loss function. It implements a specific variant of stochastic gradient descent (SGD).

A neural network that has multiple outputs may have multiple loss functions (one per output). But the gradient-descent process must be based on a *single* scalar loss value; so, for multiloss networks, all losses are combined (via averaging) into a single scalar quantity.

Choosing the right objective function for the right problem is extremely important: your network will take any shortcut it can, to minimize the loss; so if the objective doesn't fully correlate with success for the task at hand, your network will end up doing things you may not have wanted. Imagine a stupid, omnipotent AI trained via SGD, with this poorly chosen objective function: "maximizing the average well-being of all humans alive." To make its job easier, this AI might choose to kill all humans except a few and focus on the well-being of the remaining ones—because average well-being isn't affected by how many humans are left. That might not be what you intended! Just remember that all neural networks you build will be just as ruthless in lowering their loss function—so choose the objective wisely, or you'll have to face unintended side effects.

Fortunately, when it comes to common problems such as classification, regression, and sequence prediction, there are simple guidelines you can follow to choose the correct loss. For instance, you'll use binary crossentropy for a two-class classification problem, categorical crossentropy for a many-class classification problem, mean-squared error for a regression problem, connectionist temporal classification (CTC) for a sequence-learning problem, and so on. Only when you're working on truly new research problems will you have to develop your own objective functions. In the next few chapters, we'll detail explicitly which loss functions to choose for a wide range of common tasks.

3.2 Introduction to Keras

Throughout this book, the code examples use Keras (https://keras.io). Keras is a deep-learning framework for Python that provides a convenient way to define and train almost any kind of deep-learning model. Keras was initially developed for researchers, with the aim of enabling fast experimentation.

Keras has the following key features:

- It allows the same code to run seamlessly on CPU or GPU.
- It has a user-friendly API that makes it easy to quickly prototype deep-learning models.
- It has built-in support for convolutional networks (for computer vision), recurrent networks (for sequence processing), and any combination of both.
- It supports arbitrary network architectures: multi-input or multi-output models, layer sharing, model sharing, and so on. This means Keras is appropriate for building essentially any deep-learning model, from a generative adversarial network to a neural Turing machine.

Keras is distributed under the permissive MIT license, which means it can be freely used in commercial projects. It's compatible with any version of Python from 2.7 to 3.6 (as of mid-2017).

Keras has well over 200,000 users, ranging from academic researchers and engineers at both startups and large companies to graduate students and hobbyists. Keras is used at Google, Netflix, Uber, CERN, Yelp, Square, and hundreds of startups working on a wide range of problems. Keras is also a popular framework on Kaggle, the machine-learning competition website, where almost every recent deep-learning competition has been won using Keras models.

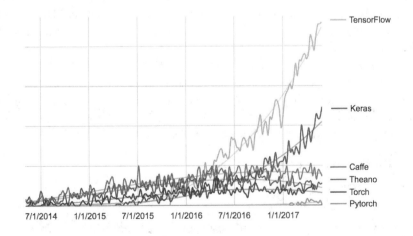

Figure 3.2 Google web search interest for different deep-learning frameworks over time

3.2.1   *Keras, TensorFlow, Theano, and CNTK*

Keras is a model-level library, providing high-level building blocks for developing deep-learning models. It doesn't handle low-level operations such as tensor manipulation and differentiation. Instead, it relies on a specialized, well-optimized tensor library to do so, serving as the *backend engine* of Keras. Rather than choosing a single tensor library and tying the implementation of Keras to that library, Keras handles the problem in a modular way (see figure 3.3); thus several different backend engines can be plugged seamlessly into Keras. Currently, the three existing backend implementations are the TensorFlow backend, the Theano backend, and the Microsoft Cognitive Toolkit (CNTK) backend. In the future, it's likely that Keras will be extended to work with even more deep-learning execution engines.

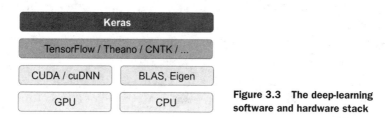

Figure 3.3   **The deep-learning software and hardware stack**

TensorFlow, CNTK, and Theano are some of the primary platforms for deep learning today. Theano (http://deeplearning.net/software/theano) is developed by the MILA lab at *Université de Montréal*, TensorFlow (www.tensorflow.org) is developed by Google, and CNTK (https://github.com/Microsoft/CNTK) is developed by Microsoft. Any piece of code that you write with Keras can be run with any of these backends without having to change anything in the code: you can seamlessly switch between the two during development, which often proves useful—for instance, if one of these backends proves to be faster for a specific task. We recommend using the TensorFlow backend as the default for most of your deep-learning needs, because it's the most widely adopted, scalable, and production ready.

Via TensorFlow (or Theano, or CNTK), Keras is able to run seamlessly on both CPUs and GPUs. When running on CPU, TensorFlow is itself wrapping a low-level library for tensor operations called Eigen (http://eigen.tuxfamily.org). On GPU, TensorFlow wraps a library of well-optimized deep-learning operations called the NVIDIA CUDA Deep Neural Network library (cuDNN).

3.2.2   *Developing with Keras: a quick overview*

You've already seen one example of a Keras model: the MNIST example. The typical Keras workflow looks just like that example:

1   Define your training data: input tensors and target tensors.
2   Define a network of layers (or *model*) that maps your inputs to your targets.

3 Configure the learning process by choosing a loss function, an optimizer, and some metrics to monitor.

4 Iterate on your training data by calling the `fit()` method of your model.

There are two ways to define a model: using the `Sequential` class (only for linear stacks of layers, which is the most common network architecture by far) or the *functional API* (for directed acyclic graphs of layers, which lets you build completely arbitrary architectures).

As a refresher, here's a two-layer model defined using the `Sequential` class (note that we're passing the expected shape of the input data to the first layer):

```
from keras import models
from keras import layers

model = models.Sequential()
model.add(layers.Dense(32, activation='relu', input_shape=(784,)))
model.add(layers.Dense(10, activation='softmax'))
```

And here's the same model defined using the functional API:

```
input_tensor = layers.Input(shape=(784,))
x = layers.Dense(32, activation='relu')(input_tensor)
output_tensor = layers.Dense(10, activation='softmax')(x)

model = models.Model(inputs=input_tensor, outputs=output_tensor)
```

With the functional API, you're manipulating the data tensors that the model processes and applying layers to this tensor as if they were functions.

> **NOTE** A detailed guide to what you can do with the functional API can be found in chapter 7. Until chapter 7, we'll only be using the `Sequential` class in our code examples.

Once your model architecture is defined, it doesn't matter whether you used a `Sequential` model or the functional API. All of the following steps are the same.

The learning process is configured in the compilation step, where you specify the optimizer and loss function(s) that the model should use, as well as the metrics you want to monitor during training. Here's an example with a single loss function, which is by far the most common case:

```
from keras import optimizers

model.compile(optimizer=optimizers.RMSprop(lr=0.001),
              loss='mse',
              metrics=['accuracy'])
```

Finally, the learning process consists of passing Numpy arrays of input data (and the corresponding target data) to the model via the `fit()` method, similar to what you would do in Scikit-Learn and several other machine-learning libraries:

```
model.fit(input_tensor, target_tensor, batch_size=128, epochs=10)
```

Over the next few chapters, you'll build a solid intuition about what type of network architectures work for different kinds of problems, how to pick the right learning configuration, and how to tweak a model until it gives the results you want to see. We'll look at three basic examples in sections 3.4, 3.5, and 3.6: a two-class classification example, a many-class classification example, and a regression example.

3.3   *Setting up a deep-learning workstation*

Before you can get started developing deep-learning applications, you need to set up your workstation. It's highly recommended, although not strictly necessary, that you run deep-learning code on a modern NVIDIA GPU. Some applications—in particular, image processing with convolutional networks and sequence processing with recurrent neural networks—will be excruciatingly slow on CPU, even a fast multicore CPU. And even for applications that can realistically be run on CPU, you'll generally see speed increase by a factor or 5 or 10 by using a modern GPU. If you don't want to install a GPU on your machine, you can alternatively consider running your experiments on an AWS EC2 GPU instance or on Google Cloud Platform. But note that cloud GPU instances can become expensive over time.

Whether you're running locally or in the cloud, it's better to be using a Unix workstation. Although it's technically possible to use Keras on Windows (all three Keras backends support Windows), We don't recommend it. In the installation instructions in appendix A, we'll consider an Ubuntu machine. If you're a Windows user, the simplest solution to get everything running is to set up an Ubuntu dual boot on your machine. It may seem like a hassle, but using Ubuntu will save you a lot of time and trouble in the long run.

Note that in order to use Keras, you need to install TensorFlow *or* CNTK *or* Theano (or all of them, if you want to be able to switch back and forth among the three backends). In this book, we'll focus on TensorFlow, with some light instructions relative to Theano. We won't cover CNTK.

3.3.1   *Jupyter notebooks: the preferred way to run deep-learning experiments*

Jupyter notebooks are a great way to run deep-learning experiments—in particular, the many code examples in this book. They're widely used in the data-science and machine-learning communities. A *notebook* is a file generated by the Jupyter Notebook app (https://jupyter.org), which you can edit in your browser. It mixes the ability to execute Python code with rich text-editing capabilities for annotating what you're doing. A notebook also allows you to break up long experiments into smaller pieces that can be executed independently, which makes development interactive and means you don't have to rerun all of your previous code if something goes wrong late in an experiment.

We recommend using Jupyter notebooks to get started with Keras, although that isn't a requirement: you can also run standalone Python scripts or run code from within an IDE such as PyCharm. All the code examples in this book are available as open source notebooks; you can download them from the book's website at www.manning .com/books/deep-learning-with-python.

3.3.2   *Getting Keras running: two options*

To get started in practice, we recommend one of the following two options:

- Use the official EC2 Deep Learning AMI (https://aws.amazon.com/amazon-ai/amis), and run Keras experiments as Jupyter notebooks on EC2. Do this if you don't already have a GPU on your local machine. Appendix B provides a step-by-step guide.
- Install everything from scratch on a local Unix workstation. You can then run either local Jupyter notebooks or a regular Python codebase. Do this if you already have a high-end NVIDIA GPU. Appendix A provides an Ubuntu-specific, step-by-step guide.

Let's take a closer look at some of the compromises involved in picking one option over the other.

3.3.3   *Running deep-learning jobs in the cloud: pros and cons*

If you don't already have a GPU that you can use for deep learning (a recent, high-end NVIDIA GPU), then running deep-learning experiments in the cloud is a simple, low-cost way for you to get started without having to buy any additional hardware. If you're using Jupyter notebooks, the experience of running in the cloud is no different from running locally. As of mid-2017, the cloud offering that makes it easiest to get started with deep learning is definitely AWS EC2. Appendix B provides a step-by-step guide to running Jupyter notebooks on a EC2 GPU instance.

But if you're a heavy user of deep learning, this setup isn't sustainable in the long term—or even for more than a few weeks. EC2 instances are expensive: the instance type recommended in appendix B (the p2.xlarge instance, which won't provide you with much power) costs $0.90 per hour as of mid-2017. Meanwhile, a solid consumer-class GPU will cost you somewhere between $1,000 and $1,500—a price that has been fairly stable over time, even as the specs of these GPUs keep improving. If you're serious about deep learning, you should set up a local workstation with one or more GPUs.

In short, EC2 is a great way to get started. You could follow the code examples in this book entirely on an EC2 GPU instance. But if you're going to be a power user of deep learning, get your own GPUs.

3.3.4   *What is the best GPU for deep learning?*

If you're going to buy a GPU, which one should you choose? The first thing to note is that it must be an NVIDIA GPU. NVIDIA is the only graphics computing company that has invested heavily in deep learning so far, and modern deep-learning frameworks can only run on NVIDIA cards.

As of mid-2017, we recommend the NVIDIA TITAN Xp as the best card on the market for deep learning. For lower budgets, you may want to consider the GTX 1060. If you're reading these pages in 2018 or later, take the time to look online for fresher recommendations, because new models come out every year.

From this section onward, we'll assume that you have access to a machine with Keras and its dependencies installed—preferably with GPU support. Make sure you finish this step before you proceed. Go through the step-by-step guides in the appendixes, and look online if you need further help. There is no shortage of tutorials on how to install Keras and common deep-learning dependencies.

We can now dive into practical Keras examples.

3.4   *Classifying movie reviews: a binary classification example*

Two-class classification, or binary classification, may be the most widely applied kind of machine-learning problem. In this example, you'll learn to classify movie reviews as positive or negative, based on the text content of the reviews.

3.4.1   *The IMDB dataset*

You'll work with the IMDB dataset: a set of 50,000 highly polarized reviews from the Internet Movie Database. They're split into 25,000 reviews for training and 25,000 reviews for testing, each set consisting of 50% negative and 50% positive reviews.

Why use separate training and test sets? Because you should never test a machine-learning model on the same data that you used to train it! Just because a model performs well on its training data doesn't mean it will perform well on data it has never seen; and what you care about is your model's performance on new data (because you already know the labels of your training data—obviously you don't need your model to predict those). For instance, it's possible that your model could end up merely *memorizing* a mapping between your training samples and their targets, which would be useless for the task of predicting targets for data the model has never seen before. We'll go over this point in much more detail in the next chapter.

Just like the MNIST dataset, the IMDB dataset comes packaged with Keras. It has already been preprocessed: the reviews (sequences of words) have been turned into sequences of integers, where each integer stands for a specific word in a dictionary.

The following code will load the dataset (when you run it the first time, about 80 MB of data will be downloaded to your machine).

Listing 3.1   Loading the IMDB dataset

```
from keras.datasets import imdb

(train_data, train_labels), (test_data, test_labels) = imdb.load_data(
    num_words=10000)
```

The argument num_words=10000 means you'll only keep the top 10,000 most frequently occurring words in the training data. Rare words will be discarded. This allows you to work with vector data of manageable size.

The variables train_data and test_data are lists of reviews; each review is a list of word indices (encoding a sequence of words). train_labels and test_labels are lists of 0s and 1s, where 0 stands for *negative* and 1 stands for *positive*:

```
>>> train_data[0]
[1, 14, 22, 16, ... 178, 32]
>>> train_labels[0]
1
```

Because you're restricting yourself to the top 10,000 most frequent words, no word index will exceed 10,000:

```
>>> max([max(sequence) for sequence in train_data])
9999
```

For kicks, here's how you can quickly decode one of these reviews back to English words:

```
word_index = imdb.get_word_index()          ◁──┐ word_index is a dictionary mapping
reverse_word_index = dict(                        words to an integer index.
    [(value, key) for (key, value) in word_index.items()])
decoded_review = ' '.join(
    [reverse_word_index.get(i - 3, '?') for i in train_data[0]])   ◁──┐
```

**Reverses it, mapping
integer indices to words**

**Decodes the review. Note that the indices
are offset by 3 because 0, 1, and 2 are
reserved indices for "padding," "start of
sequence," and "unknown."**

3.4.2   Preparing the data

You can't feed lists of integers into a neural network. You have to turn your lists into tensors. There are two ways to do that:

- Pad your lists so that they all have the same length, turn them into an integer tensor of shape (samples, word_indices), and then use as the first layer in your network a layer capable of handling such integer tensors (the Embedding layer, which we'll cover in detail later in the book).

- One-hot encode your lists to turn them into vectors of 0s and 1s. This would mean, for instance, turning the sequence [3, 5] into a 10,000-dimensional vector that would be all 0s except for indices 3 and 5, which would be 1s. Then you could use as the first layer in your network a Dense layer, capable of handling floating-point vector data.

Let's go with the latter solution to vectorize the data, which you'll do manually for maximum clarity.

Listing 3.2   Encoding the integer sequences into a binary matrix

```
import numpy as np

def vectorize_sequences(sequences, dimension=10000):        Creates an all-zero matrix
    results = np.zeros((len(sequences), dimension))    ◁──┘ of shape (len(sequences),
    for i, sequence in enumerate(sequences):                dimension)
        results[i, sequence] = 1.          ◁───┐
    return results                               Sets specific indices
                                                 of results[i] to 1s
x_train = vectorize_sequences(train_data)    ◁─── Vectorized training data
x_test = vectorize_sequences(test_data)      ◁─── Vectorized test data
```

Here's what the samples look like now:

```
>>> x_train[0]
array([ 0.,  1.,  1., ...,  0.,  0.,  0.])
```

You should also vectorize your labels, which is straightforward:

```
y_train = np.asarray(train_labels).astype('float32')
y_test = np.asarray(test_labels).astype('float32')
```

Now the data is ready to be fed into a neural network.

3.4.3 *Building your network*

The input data is vectors, and the labels are scalars (1s and 0s): this is the easiest setup you'll ever encounter. A type of network that performs well on such a problem is a simple stack of fully connected (Dense) layers with relu activations: Dense(16, activation='relu').

The argument being passed to each Dense layer (16) is the number of hidden units of the layer. A *hidden unit* is a dimension in the representation space of the layer. You may remember from chapter 2 that each such Dense layer with a relu activation implements the following chain of tensor operations:

```
output = relu(dot(W, input) + b)
```

Having 16 hidden units means the weight matrix W will have shape (input_dimension, 16): the dot product with W will project the input data onto a 16-dimensional representation space (and then you'll add the bias vector b and apply the relu operation). You can intuitively understand the dimensionality of your representation space as "how much freedom you're allowing the network to have when learning internal representations." Having more hidden units (a higher-dimensional representation space) allows your network to learn more-complex representations, but it makes the network more computationally expensive and may lead to learning unwanted patterns (patterns that will improve performance on the training data but not on the test data).

There are two key architecture decisions to be made about such a stack of Dense layers:

- How many layers to use
- How many hidden units to choose for each layer

In chapter 4, you'll learn formal principles to guide you in making these choices. For the time being, you'll have to trust me with the following architecture choice:

- Two intermediate layers with 16 hidden units each
- A third layer that will output the scalar prediction regarding the sentiment of the current review

The intermediate layers will use relu as their activation function, and the final layer will use a sigmoid activation so as to output a probability (a score between 0 and 1, indicating how likely the sample is to have the target "1": how likely the review is to be positive). A relu (rectified linear unit) is a function meant to zero out negative values (see figure 3.4), whereas a sigmoid "squashes" arbitrary values into the [0, 1] interval (see figure 3.5), outputting something that can be interpreted as a probability.

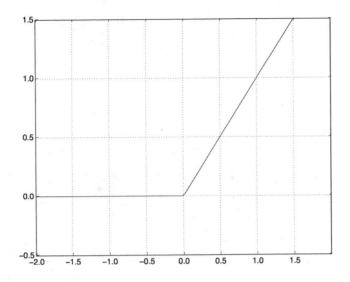

Figure 3.4　The rectified linear unit function

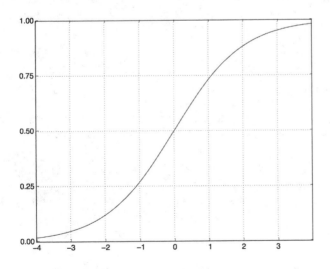

Figure 3.5　The sigmoid function

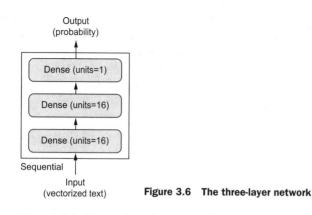

Figure 3.6   The three-layer network

Figure 3.6 shows what the network looks like. And here's the Keras implementation, similar to the MNIST example you saw previously.

Listing 3.3   The model definition

```
from keras import models
from keras import layers

model = models.Sequential()
model.add(layers.Dense(16, activation='relu', input_shape=(10000,)))
model.add(layers.Dense(16, activation='relu'))
model.add(layers.Dense(1, activation='sigmoid'))
```

What are activation functions, and why are they necessary?

Without an activation function like `relu` (also called a *non-linearity*), the `Dense` layer would consist of two linear operations—a dot product and an addition:

```
output = dot(W, input) + b
```

So the layer could only learn *linear transformations* (affine transformations) of the input data: the *hypothesis space* of the layer would be the set of all possible linear transformations of the input data into a 16-dimensional space. Such a hypothesis space is too restricted and wouldn't benefit from multiple layers of representations, because a deep stack of linear layers would still implement a linear operation: adding more layers wouldn't extend the hypothesis space.

In order to get access to a much richer hypothesis space that would benefit from deep representations, you need a non-linearity, or activation function. `relu` is the most popular activation function in deep learning, but there are many other candidates, which all come with similarly strange names: `prelu`, `elu`, and so on.

Finally, you need to choose a loss function and an optimizer. Because you're facing a binary classification problem and the output of your network is a probability (you end your network with a single-unit layer with a sigmoid activation), it's best to use the binary_crossentropy loss. It isn't the only viable choice: you could use, for instance, mean_squared_error. But crossentropy is usually the best choice when you're dealing with models that output probabilities. *Crossentropy* is a quantity from the field of Information Theory that measures the distance between probability distributions or, in this case, between the ground-truth distribution and your predictions.

Here's the step where you configure the model with the rmsprop optimizer and the binary_crossentropy loss function. Note that you'll also monitor accuracy during training.

Listing 3.4 Compiling the model

```
model.compile(optimizer='rmsprop',
              loss='binary_crossentropy',
              metrics=['accuracy'])
```

You're passing your optimizer, loss function, and metrics as strings, which is possible because rmsprop, binary_crossentropy, and accuracy are packaged as part of Keras. Sometimes you may want to configure the parameters of your optimizer or pass a custom loss function or metric function. The former can be done by passing an optimizer class instance as the optimizer argument, as shown in listing 3.5; the latter can be done by passing function objects as the loss and/or metrics arguments, as shown in listing 3.6.

Listing 3.5 Configuring the optimizer

```
from keras import optimizers

model.compile(optimizer=optimizers.RMSprop(lr=0.001),
              loss='binary_crossentropy',
              metrics=['accuracy'])
```

Listing 3.6 Using custom losses and metrics

```
from keras import losses
from keras import metrics

model.compile(optimizer=optimizers.RMSprop(lr=0.001),
              loss=losses.binary_crossentropy,
              metrics=[metrics.binary_accuracy])
```

3.4.4 Validating your approach

In order to monitor during training the accuracy of the model on data it has never seen before, you'll create a validation set by setting apart 10,000 samples from the original training data.

Listing 3.7 Setting aside a validation set

```
x_val = x_train[:10000]
partial_x_train = x_train[10000:]
```

```
y_val = y_train[:10000]
partial_y_train = y_train[10000:]
```

You'll now train the model for 20 epochs (20 iterations over all samples in the x_train and y_train tensors), in mini-batches of 512 samples. At the same time, you'll monitor loss and accuracy on the 10,000 samples that you set apart. You do so by passing the validation data as the validation_data argument.

Listing 3.8   Training your model

```
model.compile(optimizer='rmsprop',
              loss='binary_crossentropy',
              metrics=['acc'])

history = model.fit(partial_x_train,
                    partial_y_train,
                    epochs=20,
                    batch_size=512,
                    validation_data=(x_val, y_val))
```

On CPU, this will take less than 2 seconds per epoch—training is over in 20 seconds. At the end of every epoch, there is a slight pause as the model computes its loss and accuracy on the 10,000 samples of the validation data.

Note that the call to model.fit() returns a History object. This object has a member history, which is a dictionary containing data about everything that happened during training. Let's look at it:

```
>>> history_dict = history.history
>>> history_dict.keys()
[u'acc', u'loss', u'val_acc', u'val_loss']
```

The dictionary contains four entries: one per metric that was being monitored during training and during validation. In the following two listing, let's use Matplotlib to plot the training and validation loss side by side (see figure 3.7), as well as the training and validation accuracy (see figure 3.8). Note that your own results may vary slightly due to a different random initialization of your network.

Listing 3.9   Plotting the training and validation loss

```
import matplotlib.pyplot as plt

history_dict = history.history
loss_values = history_dict['loss']
val_loss_values = history_dict['val_loss']

epochs = range(1, len(acc) + 1)

plt.plot(epochs, loss_values, 'bo', label='Training loss')        ⟵  "bo" is for "blue dot."
plt.plot(epochs, val_loss_values, 'b', label='Validation loss')   ⟵
plt.title('Training and validation loss')
plt.xlabel('Epochs')                                              "b" is for "solid
plt.ylabel('Loss')                                                 blue line."
plt.legend()

plt.show()
```

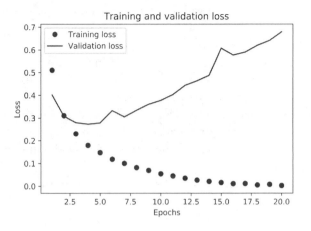

Figure 3.7 Training and validation loss

```
plt.clf()                    ⟵——— Clears the figure
acc_values = history_dict['acc']
val_acc_values = history_dict['val_acc']

plt.plot(epochs, acc, 'bo', label='Training acc')
plt.plot(epochs, val_acc, 'b', label='Validation acc')
plt.title('Training and validation accuracy')
plt.xlabel('Epochs')
plt.ylabel('Loss')
plt.legend()

plt.show()
```

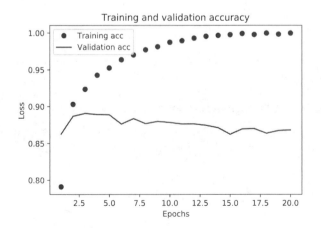

Figure 3.8 Training and validation accuracy

As you can see, the training loss decreases with every epoch, and the training accuracy increases with every epoch. That's what you would expect when running gradient-descent optimization—the quantity you're trying to minimize should be less with every iteration. But that isn't the case for the validation loss and accuracy: they seem to peak at the fourth epoch. This is an example of what we warned against earlier: a model that performs better on the training data isn't necessarily a model that will do better on data it has never seen before. In precise terms, what you're seeing is *overfitting*: after the second epoch, you're overoptimizing on the training data, and you end up learning representations that are specific to the training data and don't generalize to data outside of the training set.

In this case, to prevent overfitting, you could stop training after three epochs. In general, you can use a range of techniques to mitigate overfitting, which we'll cover in chapter 4.

Let's train a new network from scratch for four epochs and then evaluate it on the test data.

> **Listing 3.11   Retraining a model from scratch**

```
model = models.Sequential()
model.add(layers.Dense(16, activation='relu', input_shape=(10000,)))
model.add(layers.Dense(16, activation='relu'))
model.add(layers.Dense(1, activation='sigmoid'))

model.compile(optimizer='rmsprop',
              loss='binary_crossentropy',
              metrics=['accuracy'])

model.fit(x_train, y_train, epochs=4, batch_size=512)
results = model.evaluate(x_test, y_test)
```

The final results are as follows:

```
>>> results
[0.2929924130630493, 0.88327999999999995]
```

This fairly naive approach achieves an accuracy of 88%. With state-of-the-art approaches, you should be able to get close to 95%.

3.4.5   *Using a trained network to generate predictions on new data*

After having trained a network, you'll want to use it in a practical setting. You can generate the likelihood of reviews being positive by using the predict method:

```
>>> model.predict(x_test)
array([[ 0.98006207]
       [ 0.99758697]
       [ 0.99975556]
       ...,
       [ 0.82167041]
       [ 0.02885115]
       [ 0.65371346]], dtype=float32)
```

As you can see, the network is confident for some samples (0.99 or more, or 0.01 or less) but less confident for others (0.6, 0.4).

3.4.6 *Further experiments*

The following experiments will help convince you that the architecture choices you've made are all fairly reasonable, although there's still room for improvement:

- You used two hidden layers. Try using one or three hidden layers, and see how doing so affects validation and test accuracy.
- Try using layers with more hidden units or fewer hidden units: 32 units, 64 units, and so on.
- Try using the mse loss function instead of binary_crossentropy.
- Try using the tanh activation (an activation that was popular in the early days of neural networks) instead of relu.

3.4.7 *Wrapping up*

Here's what you should take away from this example:

- You usually need to do quite a bit of preprocessing on your raw data in order to be able to feed it—as tensors—into a neural network. Sequences of words can be encoded as binary vectors, but there are other encoding options, too.
- Stacks of Dense layers with relu activations can solve a wide range of problems (including sentiment classification), and you'll likely use them frequently.
- In a binary classification problem (two output classes), your network should end with a Dense layer with one unit and a sigmoid activation: the output of your network should be a scalar between 0 and 1, encoding a probability.
- With such a scalar sigmoid output on a binary classification problem, the loss function you should use is binary_crossentropy.
- The rmsprop optimizer is generally a good enough choice, whatever your problem. That's one less thing for you to worry about.
- As they get better on their training data, neural networks eventually start overfitting and end up obtaining increasingly worse results on data they've never seen before. Be sure to always monitor performance on data that is outside of the training set.

3.5   *Classifying newswires: a multiclass classification example*

In the previous section, you saw how to classify vector inputs into two mutually exclusive classes using a densely connected neural network. But what happens when you have more than two classes?

In this section, you'll build a network to classify Reuters newswires into 46 mutually exclusive topics. Because you have many classes, this problem is an instance of *multiclass classification*; and because each data point should be classified into only one category, the problem is more specifically an instance of *single-label, multiclass classification*. If each data point could belong to multiple categories (in this case, topics), you'd be facing a *multilabel, multiclass classification* problem.

3.5.1   *The Reuters dataset*

You'll work with the *Reuters dataset*, a set of short newswires and their topics, published by Reuters in 1986. It's a simple, widely used toy dataset for text classification. There are 46 different topics; some topics are more represented than others, but each topic has at least 10 examples in the training set.

Like IMDB and MNIST, the Reuters dataset comes packaged as part of Keras. Let's take a look.

Listing 3.12   Loading the Reuters dataset

```
from keras.datasets import reuters

(train_data, train_labels), (test_data, test_labels) = reuters.load_data(
    num_words=10000)
```

As with the IMDB dataset, the argument `num_words=10000` restricts the data to the 10,000 most frequently occurring words found in the data.

You have 8,982 training examples and 2,246 test examples:

```
>>> len(train_data)
8982
>>> len(test_data)
2246
```

As with the IMDB reviews, each example is a list of integers (word indices):

```
>>> train_data[10]
[1, 245, 273, 207, 156, 53, 74, 160, 26, 14, 46, 296, 26, 39, 74, 2979,
3554, 14, 46, 4689, 4329, 86, 61, 3499, 4795, 14, 61, 451, 4329, 17, 12]
```

Here's how you can decode it back to words, in case you're curious.

Listing 3.13   Decoding newswires back to text

```
word_index = reuters.get_word_index()
reverse_word_index = dict([(value, key) for (key, value) in word_index.items()])
decoded_newswire = ' '.join([reverse_word_index.get(i - 3, '?') for i in
    train_data[0]])
```

Note that the indices are offset by 3 because 0, 1, and 2 are reserved indices for "padding," "start of sequence," and "unknown."

The label associated with an example is an integer between 0 and 45—a topic index:

```
>>> train_labels[10]
3
```

3.5.2   Preparing the data

You can vectorize the data with the exact same code as in the previous example.

> **Listing 3.14   Encoding the data**

```
import numpy as np

def vectorize_sequences(sequences, dimension=10000):
    results = np.zeros((len(sequences), dimension))
    for i, sequence in enumerate(sequences):
        results[i, sequence] = 1.
    return results
x_train = vectorize_sequences(train_data)      ⟵┐ Vectorized training data
x_test = vectorize_sequences(test_data)      ⟵── Vectorized test data
```

To vectorize the labels, there are two possibilities: you can cast the label list as an integer tensor, or you can use one-hot encoding. One-hot encoding is a widely used format for categorical data, also called *categorical encoding*. For a more detailed explanation of one-hot encoding, see section 6.1. In this case, one-hot encoding of the labels consists of embedding each label as an all-zero vector with a 1 in the place of the label index. Here's an example:

```
def to_one_hot(labels, dimension=46):
    results = np.zeros((len(labels), dimension))
    for i, label in enumerate(labels):
        results[i, label] = 1.
    return results
one_hot_train_labels = to_one_hot(train_labels)      ⟵┐ Vectorized training labels
one_hot_test_labels = to_one_hot(test_labels)      ⟵── Vectorized test labels
```

Note that there is a built-in way to do this in Keras, which you've already seen in action in the MNIST example:

```
from keras.utils.np_utils import to_categorical

one_hot_train_labels = to_categorical(train_labels)
one_hot_test_labels = to_categorical(test_labels)
```

3.5.3   Building your network

This topic-classification problem looks similar to the previous movie-review classification problem: in both cases, you're trying to classify short snippets of text. But there is a new constraint here: the number of output classes has gone from 2 to 46. The dimensionality of the output space is much larger.

In a stack of Dense layers like that you've been using, each layer can only access information present in the output of the previous layer. If one layer drops some information relevant to the classification problem, this information can never be recovered by later layers: each layer can potentially become an information bottleneck. In the previous example, you used 16-dimensional intermediate layers, but a 16-dimensional space may be too limited to learn to separate 46 different classes: such small layers may act as information bottlenecks, permanently dropping relevant information.

For this reason you'll use larger layers. Let's go with 64 units.

Listing 3.15   Model definition

```
from keras import models
from keras import layers

model = models.Sequential()
model.add(layers.Dense(64, activation='relu', input_shape=(10000,)))
model.add(layers.Dense(64, activation='relu'))
model.add(layers.Dense(46, activation='softmax'))
```

There are two other things you should note about this architecture:

- You end the network with a Dense layer of size 46. This means for each input sample, the network will output a 46-dimensional vector. Each entry in this vector (each dimension) will encode a different output class.
- The last layer uses a softmax activation. You saw this pattern in the MNIST example. It means the network will output a *probability distribution* over the 46 different output classes—for every input sample, the network will produce a 46-dimensional output vector, where output[i] is the probability that the sample belongs to class i. The 46 scores will sum to 1.

The best loss function to use in this case is categorical_crossentropy. It measures the distance between two probability distributions: here, between the probability distribution output by the network and the true distribution of the labels. By minimizing the distance between these two distributions, you train the network to output something as close as possible to the true labels.

Listing 3.16   Compiling the model

```
model.compile(optimizer='rmsprop',
              loss='categorical_crossentropy',
              metrics=['accuracy'])
```

3.5.4   *Validating your approach*

Let's set apart 1,000 samples in the training data to use as a validation set.

Listing 3.17   Setting aside a validation set

```
x_val = x_train[:1000]
partial_x_train = x_train[1000:]

y_val = one_hot_train_labels[:1000]
partial_y_train = one_hot_train_labels[1000:]
```

Now, let's train the network for 20 epochs.

Listing 3.18 Training the model

```
history = model.fit(partial_x_train,
                     partial_y_train,
                     epochs=20,
                     batch_size=512,
                     validation_data=(x_val, y_val))
```

And finally, let's display its loss and accuracy curves (see figures 3.9 and 3.10).

Listing 3.19 Plotting the training and validation loss

```
import matplotlib.pyplot as plt

loss = history.history['loss']
val_loss = history.history['val_loss']

epochs = range(1, len(loss) + 1)

plt.plot(epochs, loss, 'bo', label='Training loss')
plt.plot(epochs, val_loss, 'b', label='Validation loss')
plt.title('Training and validation loss')
plt.xlabel('Epochs')
plt.ylabel('Loss')
plt.legend()

plt.show()
```

Listing 3.20 Plotting the training and validation accuracy

```
plt.clf()        ◁—— Clears the figure

acc = history.history['acc']
val_acc = history.history['val_acc']

plt.plot(epochs, acc, 'bo', label='Training acc')
plt.plot(epochs, val_acc, 'b', label='Validation acc')
plt.title('Training and validation accuracy')
plt.xlabel('Epochs')
plt.ylabel('Loss')
plt.legend()

plt.show()
```

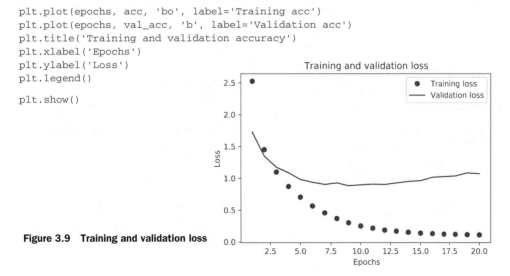

Figure 3.9 Training and validation loss

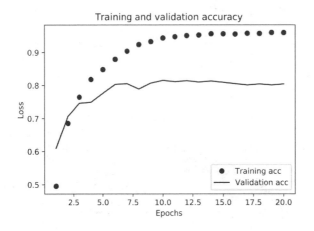

Training and validation accuracy

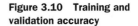

Figure 3.10   Training and validation accuracy

The network begins to overfit after nine epochs. Let's train a new network from scratch for nine epochs and then evaluate it on the test set.

Listing 3.21   Retraining a model from scratch

```
model = models.Sequential()
model.add(layers.Dense(64, activation='relu', input_shape=(10000,)))
model.add(layers.Dense(64, activation='relu'))
model.add(layers.Dense(46, activation='softmax'))

model.compile(optimizer='rmsprop',
              loss='categorical_crossentropy',
              metrics=['accuracy'])
model.fit(partial_x_train,
          partial_y_train,
          epochs=9,
          batch_size=512,
          validation_data=(x_val, y_val))
results = model.evaluate(x_test, one_hot_test_labels)
```

Here are the final results:

```
>>> results
[0.9565213431445807, 0.79697239536954589]
```

This approach reaches an accuracy of ~80%. With a balanced binary classification problem, the accuracy reached by a purely random classifier would be 50%. But in this case it's closer to 19%, so the results seem pretty good, at least when compared to a random baseline:

```
>>> import copy
>>> test_labels_copy = copy.copy(test_labels)
>>> np.random.shuffle(test_labels_copy)
>>> hits_array = np.array(test_labels) == np.array(test_labels_copy)
>>> float(np.sum(hits_array)) / len(test_labels)
0.18655387355298308
```

3.5.5 Generating predictions on new data

You can verify that the `predict` method of the model instance returns a probability distribution over all 46 topics. Let's generate topic predictions for all of the test data.

Listing 3.22 Generating predictions for new data

```
predictions = model.predict(x_test)
```

Each entry in `predictions` is a vector of length 46:

```
>>> predictions[0].shape
(46,)
```

The coefficients in this vector sum to 1:

```
>>> np.sum(predictions[0])
1.0
```

The largest entry is the predicted class—the class with the highest probability:

```
>>> np.argmax(predictions[0])
4
```

3.5.6 A different way to handle the labels and the loss

We mentioned earlier that another way to encode the labels would be to cast them as an integer tensor, like this:

```
y_train = np.array(train_labels)
y_test = np.array(test_labels)
```

The only thing this approach would change is the choice of the loss function. The loss function used in listing 3.21, `categorical_crossentropy`, expects the labels to follow a categorical encoding. With integer labels, you should use `sparse_categorical_crossentropy`:

```
model.compile(optimizer='rmsprop',
              loss='sparse_categorical_crossentropy',
              metrics=['acc'])
```

This new loss function is still mathematically the same as `categorical_crossentropy`; it just has a different interface.

3.5.7 The importance of having sufficiently large intermediate layers

We mentioned earlier that because the final outputs are 46-dimensional, you should avoid intermediate layers with many fewer than 46 hidden units. Now let's see what happens when you introduce an information bottleneck by having intermediate layers that are significantly less than 46-dimensional: for example, 4-dimensional.

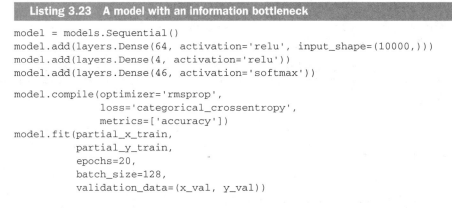

```
model = models.Sequential()
model.add(layers.Dense(64, activation='relu', input_shape=(10000,)))
model.add(layers.Dense(4, activation='relu'))
model.add(layers.Dense(46, activation='softmax'))

model.compile(optimizer='rmsprop',
              loss='categorical_crossentropy',
              metrics=['accuracy'])
model.fit(partial_x_train,
          partial_y_train,
          epochs=20,
          batch_size=128,
          validation_data=(x_val, y_val))
```

The network now peaks at ~71% validation accuracy, an 8% absolute drop. This drop is mostly due to the fact that you're trying to compress a lot of information (enough information to recover the separation hyperplanes of 46 classes) into an intermediate space that is too low-dimensional. The network is able to cram *most* of the necessary information into these eight-dimensional representations, but not all of it.

3.5.8 *Further experiments*

- Try using larger or smaller layers: 32 units, 128 units, and so on.
- You used two hidden layers. Now try using a single hidden layer, or three hidden layers.

3.5.9 *Wrapping up*

Here's what you should take away from this example:

- If you're trying to classify data points among N classes, your network should end with a Dense layer of size N.
- In a single-label, multiclass classification problem, your network should end with a softmax activation so that it will output a probability distribution over the N output classes.
- Categorical crossentropy is almost always the loss function you should use for such problems. It minimizes the distance between the probability distributions output by the network and the true distribution of the targets.
- There are two ways to handle labels in multiclass classification:
  - Encoding the labels via categorical encoding (also known as one-hot encoding) and using categorical_crossentropy as a loss function
  - Encoding the labels as integers and using the sparse_categorical_crossentropy loss function
- If you need to classify data into a large number of categories, you should avoid creating information bottlenecks in your network due to intermediate layers that are too small.

3.6   *Predicting house prices: a regression example*

The two previous examples were considered classification problems, where the goal was to predict a single discrete label of an input data point. Another common type of machine-learning problem is *regression*, which consists of predicting a continuous value instead of a discrete label: for instance, predicting the temperature tomorrow, given meteorological data; or predicting the time that a software project will take to complete, given its specifications.

> **NOTE** Don't confuse *regression* and the algorithm *logistic regression*. Confusingly, logistic regression isn't a regression algorithm—it's a classification algorithm.

3.6.1   *The Boston Housing Price dataset*

You'll attempt to predict the median price of homes in a given Boston suburb in the mid-1970s, given data points about the suburb at the time, such as the crime rate, the local property tax rate, and so on. The dataset you'll use has an interesting difference from the two previous examples. It has relatively few data points: only 506, split between 404 training samples and 102 test samples. And each *feature* in the input data (for example, the crime rate) has a different scale. For instance, some values are proportions, which take values between 0 and 1; others take values between 1 and 12, others between 0 and 100, and so on.

> **Listing 3.24   Loading the Boston housing dataset**

```
from keras.datasets import boston_housing

(train_data, train_targets), (test_data, test_targets) =
➥boston_housing.load_data()
```

Let's look at the data:

```
>>> train_data.shape
(404, 13)
>>> test_data.shape
(102, 13)
```

As you can see, you have 404 training samples and 102 test samples, each with 13 numerical features, such as per capita crime rate, average number of rooms per dwelling, accessibility to highways, and so on.

The targets are the median values of owner-occupied homes, in thousands of dollars:

```
>>> train_targets
[ 15.2,  42.3,  50. ...  19.4,  19.4,  29.1]
```

The prices are typically between $10,000 and $50,000. If that sounds cheap, remember that this was the mid-1970s, and these prices aren't adjusted for inflation.

3.6.2   *Preparing the data*

It would be problematic to feed into a neural network values that all take wildly different ranges. The network might be able to automatically adapt to such heterogeneous data, but it would definitely make learning more difficult. A widespread best practice to deal with such data is to do feature-wise normalization: for each feature in the input data (a column in the input data matrix), you subtract the mean of the feature and divide by the standard deviation, so that the feature is centered around 0 and has a unit standard deviation. This is easily done in Numpy.

Listing 3.25   Normalizing the data

```
mean = train_data.mean(axis=0)
train_data -= mean
std = train_data.std(axis=0)
train_data /= std

test_data -= mean
test_data /= std
```

Note that the quantities used for normalizing the test data are computed using the training data. You should never use in your workflow any quantity computed on the test data, even for something as simple as data normalization.

3.6.3   *Building your network*

Because so few samples are available, you'll use a very small network with two hidden layers, each with 64 units. In general, the less training data you have, the worse overfitting will be, and using a small network is one way to mitigate overfitting.

Listing 3.26   Model definition

```
from keras import models
from keras import layers

def build_model():
    model = models.Sequential()        ⟵
    model.add(layers.Dense(64, activation='relu',
                           input_shape=(train_data.shape[1],)))
    model.add(layers.Dense(64, activation='relu'))
    model.add(layers.Dense(1))
    model.compile(optimizer='rmsprop', loss='mse', metrics=['mae'])
    return model
```

Because you'll need to instantiate the same model multiple times, you use a function to construct it.

The network ends with a single unit and no activation (it will be a linear layer). This is a typical setup for scalar regression (a regression where you're trying to predict a single continuous value). Applying an activation function would constrain the range the output can take; for instance, if you applied a `sigmoid` activation function to the last layer, the network could only learn to predict values between 0 and 1. Here, because the last layer is purely linear, the network is free to learn to predict values in any range.

Note that you compile the network with the `mse` loss function—*mean squared error,* the square of the difference between the predictions and the targets. This is a widely used loss function for regression problems.

You're also monitoring a new metric during training: *mean absolute error* (MAE). It's the absolute value of the difference between the predictions and the targets. For instance, an MAE of 0.5 on this problem would mean your predictions are off by $500 on average.

3.6.4 *Validating your approach using K-fold validation*

To evaluate your network while you keep adjusting its parameters (such as the number of epochs used for training), you could split the data into a training set and a validation set, as you did in the previous examples. But because you have so few data points, the validation set would end up being very small (for instance, about 100 examples). As a consequence, the validation scores might change a lot depending on which data points you chose to use for validation and which you chose for training: the validation scores might have a high *variance* with regard to the validation split. This would prevent you from reliably evaluating your model.

The best practice in such situations is to use *K-fold* cross-validation (see figure 3.11). It consists of splitting the available data into *K* partitions (typically *K* = 4 or 5), instantiating *K* identical models, and training each one on *K* – 1 partitions while evaluating on the remaining partition. The validation score for the model used is then the average of the *K* validation scores obtained. In terms of code, this is straightforward.

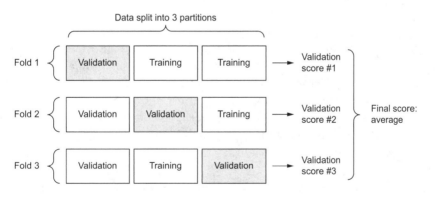

Figure 3.11   3-fold cross-validation

Listing 3.27   K-fold validation

```
import numpy as np

k = 4
num_val_samples = len(train_data) // k
num_epochs = 100
all_scores = []
```

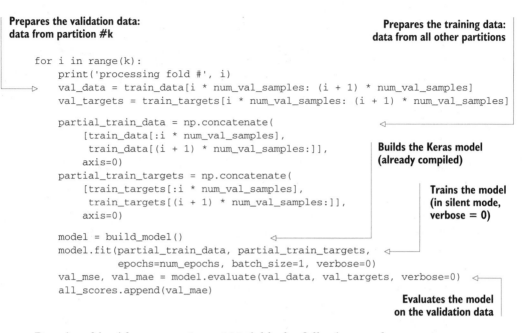

Prepares the validation data:
data from partition #k

Prepares the training data:
data from all other partitions

```
for i in range(k):
    print('processing fold #', i)
    val_data = train_data[i * num_val_samples: (i + 1) * num_val_samples]
    val_targets = train_targets[i * num_val_samples: (i + 1) * num_val_samples]

    partial_train_data = np.concatenate(
        [train_data[:i * num_val_samples],
         train_data[(i + 1) * num_val_samples:]],
        axis=0)
    partial_train_targets = np.concatenate(
        [train_targets[:i * num_val_samples],
         train_targets[(i + 1) * num_val_samples:]],
        axis=0)

    model = build_model()
    model.fit(partial_train_data, partial_train_targets,
              epochs=num_epochs, batch_size=1, verbose=0)
    val_mse, val_mae = model.evaluate(val_data, val_targets, verbose=0)
    all_scores.append(val_mae)
```

Builds the Keras model
(already compiled)

Trains the model
(in silent mode,
verbose = 0)

Evaluates the model
on the validation data

Running this with `num_epochs = 100` yields the following results:

```
>>> all_scores
[2.588258957792037, 3.1289568449719116, 3.1856116051248984, 3.0763342615401386]
>>> np.mean(all_scores)
2.9947904173572462
```

The different runs do indeed show rather different validation scores, from 2.6 to 3.2. The average (3.0) is a much more reliable metric than any single score—that's the entire point of K-fold cross-validation. In this case, you're off by $3,000 on average, which is significant considering that the prices range from $10,000 to $50,000.

Let's try training the network a bit longer: 500 epochs. To keep a record of how well the model does at each epoch, you'll modify the training loop to save the per-epoch validation score log.

Listing 3.28   Saving the validation logs at each fold

```
num_epochs = 500
all_mae_histories = []
for i in range(k):
    print('processing fold #', i)
    val_data = train_data[i * num_val_samples: (i + 1) * num_val_samples]
    val_targets = train_targets[i * num_val_samples: (i + 1) * num_val_samples]

    partial_train_data = np.concatenate(
        [train_data[:i * num_val_samples],
         train_data[(i + 1) * num_val_samples:]],
        axis=0)
```

Prepares the validation data:
data from partition #k

Prepares the training
data: data from all
other partitions

```
partial_train_targets = np.concatenate(
    [train_targets[:i * num_val_samples],
    .train_targets[(i + 1) * num_val_samples:]],
    axis=0)

model = build_model()                              ◁
history = model.fit(partial_train_data, partial_train_targets,   ◁
                    validation_data=(val_data, val_targets),
                    epochs=num_epochs, batch_size=1, verbose=0)
mae_history = history.history['val_mean_absolute_error']
all_mae_histories.append(mae_history)
```

Builds the Keras model (already compiled)

Trains the model (in silent mode, verbose=0)

You can then compute the average of the per-epoch MAE scores for all folds.

Listing 3.29 Building the history of successive mean K-fold validation scores

```
average_mae_history = [
    np.mean([x[i] for x in all_mae_histories]) for i in range(num_epochs)]
```

Let's plot this; see figure 3.12.

Listing 3.30 Plotting validation scores

```
import matplotlib.pyplot as plt

plt.plot(range(1, len(average_mae_history) + 1), average_mae_history)
plt.xlabel('Epochs')
plt.ylabel('Validation MAE')
plt.show()
```

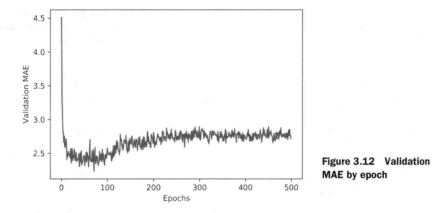

Figure 3.12   Validation MAE by epoch

It may be a little difficult to see the plot, due to scaling issues and relatively high variance. Let's do the following:

- Omit the first 10 data points, which are on a different scale than the rest of the curve.
- Replace each point with an exponential moving average of the previous points, to obtain a smooth curve.

The result is shown in figure 3.13.

Listing 3.31   Plotting validation scores, excluding the first 10 data points

```
def smooth_curve(points, factor=0.9):
  smoothed_points = []
  for point in points:
    if smoothed_points:
      previous = smoothed_points[-1]
      smoothed_points.append(previous * factor + point * (1 - factor))
    else:
      smoothed_points.append(point)
  return smoothed_points

smooth_mae_history = smooth_curve(average_mae_history[10:])

plt.plot(range(1, len(smooth_mae_history) + 1), smooth_mae_history)
plt.xlabel('Epochs')
plt.ylabel('Validation MAE')
plt.show()
```

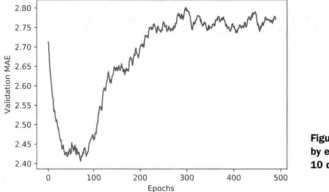

Figure 3.13   Validation MAE by epoch, excluding the first 10 data points

According to this plot, validation MAE stops improving significantly after 80 epochs. Past that point, you start overfitting.

Once you're finished tuning other parameters of the model (in addition to the number of epochs, you could also adjust the size of the hidden layers), you can train a final production model on all of the training data, with the best parameters, and then look at its performance on the test data.

Listing 3.32   Training the final model

Gets a fresh, compiled model

```
model = build_model()
model.fit(train_data, train_targets,
          epochs=80, batch_size=16, verbose=0)
test_mse_score, test_mae_score = model.evaluate(test_data, test_targets)
```

Trains it on the entirety of the data

Here's the final result:

```
>>> test_mae_score
2.5532484335057877
```

You're still off by about $2,550.

3.6.5 *Wrapping up*

Here's what you should take away from this example:

- Regression is done using different loss functions than what we used for classification. Mean squared error (MSE) is a loss function commonly used for regression.
- Similarly, evaluation metrics to be used for regression differ from those used for classification; naturally, the concept of accuracy doesn't apply for regression. A common regression metric is mean absolute error (MAE).
- When features in the input data have values in different ranges, each feature should be scaled independently as a preprocessing step.
- When there is little data available, using K-fold validation is a great way to reliably evaluate a model.
- When little training data is available, it's preferable to use a small network with few hidden layers (typically only one or two), in order to avoid severe overfitting.

Chapter summary

- You're now able to handle the most common kinds of machine-learning tasks on vector data: binary classification, multiclass classification, and scalar regression. The "Wrapping up" sections earlier in the chapter summarize the important points you've learned regarding these types of tasks.

- You'll usually need to preprocess raw data before feeding it into a neural network.

- When your data has features with different ranges, scale each feature independently as part of preprocessing.

- As training progresses, neural networks eventually begin to overfit and obtain worse results on never-before-seen data.

- If you don't have much training data, use a small network with only one or two hidden layers, to avoid severe overfitting.

- If your data is divided into many categories, you may cause information bottlenecks if you make the intermediate layers too small.

- Regression uses different loss functions and different evaluation metrics than classification.

- When you're working with little data, K-fold validation can help reliably evaluate your model.

Fundamentals of
machine learning

After the three practical examples in chapter 3, you should be starting to feel familiar with how to approach classification and regression problems using neural networks, and you've witnessed the central problem of machine learning: overfitting. This chapter will formalize some of your new intuition into a solid conceptual framework for attacking and solving deep-learning problems. We'll consolidate all of these concepts—model evaluation, data preprocessing and feature engineering, and tackling overfitting—into a detailed seven-step workflow for tackling any machine-learning task.

4.1   Four branches of machine learning

In our previous examples, you've become familiar with three specific types of machine-learning problems: binary classification, multiclass classification, and scalar regression. All three are instances of *supervised learning*, where the goal is to learn the relationship between training inputs and training targets.

Supervised learning is just the tip of the iceberg—machine learning is a vast field with a complex subfield taxonomy. Machine-learning algorithms generally fall into four broad categories, described in the following sections.

4.1.1   Supervised learning

This is by far the most common case. It consists of learning to map input data to known targets (also called *annotations*), given a set of examples (often annotated by humans). All four examples you've encountered in this book so far were canonical examples of supervised learning. Generally, almost all applications of deep learning that are in the spotlight these days belong in this category, such as optical character recognition, speech recognition, image classification, and language translation.

Although supervised learning mostly consists of classification and regression, there are more exotic variants as well, including the following (with examples):

- *Sequence generation*—Given a picture, predict a caption describing it. Sequence generation can sometimes be reformulated as a series of classification problems (such as repeatedly predicting a word or token in a sequence).
- *Syntax tree prediction*—Given a sentence, predict its decomposition into a syntax tree.
- *Object detection*—Given a picture, draw a bounding box around certain objects inside the picture. This can also be expressed as a classification problem (given many candidate bounding boxes, classify the contents of each one) or as a joint classification and regression problem, where the bounding-box coordinates are predicted via vector regression.
- *Image segmentation*—Given a picture, draw a pixel-level mask on a specific object.

4.1.2   Unsupervised learning

This branch of machine learning consists of finding interesting transformations of the input data without the help of any targets, for the purposes of data visualization, data compression, or data denoising, or to better understand the correlations present in the data at hand. Unsupervised learning is the bread and butter of data analytics, and it's often a necessary step in better understanding a dataset before attempting to solve a supervised-learning problem. *Dimensionality reduction* and *clustering* are well-known categories of unsupervised learning.

4.1.3   Self-supervised learning

This is a specific instance of supervised learning, but it's different enough that it deserves its own category. Self-supervised learning is supervised learning without human-annotated labels—you can think of it as supervised learning without any humans in the loop. There are still labels involved (because the learning has to be supervised by something), but they're generated from the input data, typically using a heuristic algorithm.

For instance, *autoencoders* are a well-known instance of self-supervised learning, where the generated targets are the input, unmodified. In the same way, trying to predict the next frame in a video, given past frames, or the next word in a text, given previous words, are instances of self-supervised learning (*temporally supervised learning*, in this case: supervision comes from future input data). Note that the distinction between supervised, self-supervised, and unsupervised learning can be blurry sometimes—these categories are more of a continuum without solid borders. Self-supervised learning can be reinterpreted as either supervised or unsupervised learning, depending on whether you pay attention to the learning mechanism or to the context of its application.

> **NOTE** In this book, we'll focus specifically on supervised learning, because it's by far the dominant form of deep learning today, with a wide range of industry applications. We'll also take a briefer look at self-supervised learning in later chapters.

4.1.4 *Reinforcement learning*

Long overlooked, this branch of machine learning recently started to get a lot of attention after Google DeepMind successfully applied it to learning to play Atari games (and, later, learning to play Go at the highest level). In reinforcement learning, an *agent* receives information about its environment and learns to choose actions that will maximize some reward. For instance, a neural network that "looks" at a video-game screen and outputs game actions in order to maximize its score can be trained via reinforcement learning.

Currently, reinforcement learning is mostly a research area and hasn't yet had significant practical successes beyond games. In time, however, we expect to see reinforcement learning take over an increasingly large range of real-world applications: self-driving cars, robotics, resource management, education, and so on. It's an idea whose time has come, or will come soon.

Classification and regression glossary

Classification and regression involve many specialized terms. You've come across some of them in earlier examples, and you'll see more of them in future chapters. They have precise, machine-learning-specific definitions, and you should be familiar with them:

- *Sample* or *input*—One data point that goes into your model.
- *Prediction* or *output*—What comes out of your model.
- *Target*—The truth. What your model should ideally have predicted, according to an external source of data.

(continued)

- *Prediction error* or *loss value*—A measure of the distance between your model's prediction and the target.
- *Classes*—A set of possible labels to choose from in a classification problem. For example, when classifying cat and dog pictures, "dog" and "cat" are the two classes.
- *Label*—A specific instance of a class annotation in a classification problem. For instance, if picture #1234 is annotated as containing the class "dog," then "dog" is a label of picture #1234.
- *Ground-truth* or *annotations*—All targets for a dataset, typically collected by humans.
- *Binary classification*—A classification task where each input sample should be categorized into two exclusive categories.
- *Multiclass classification*—A classification task where each input sample should be categorized into more than two categories: for instance, classifying handwritten digits.
- *Multilabel classification*—A classification task where each input sample can be assigned multiple labels. For instance, a given image may contain both a cat and a dog and should be annotated both with the "cat" label and the "dog" label. The number of labels per image is usually variable.
- *Scalar regression*—A task where the target is a continuous scalar value. Predicting house prices is a good example: the different target prices form a continuous space.
- *Vector regression*—A task where the target is a set of continuous values: for example, a continuous vector. If you're doing regression against multiple values (such as the coordinates of a bounding box in an image), then you're doing vector regression.
- *Mini-batch* or *batch*—A small set of samples (typically between 8 and 128) that are processed simultaneously by the model. The number of samples is often a power of 2, to facilitate memory allocation on GPU. When training, a mini-batch is used to compute a single gradient-descent update applied to the weights of the model.

4.2 Evaluating machine-learning models

In the three examples presented in chapter 3, we split the data into a training set, a validation set, and a test set. The reason not to evaluate the models on the same data they were trained on quickly became evident: after just a few epochs, all three models began to *overfit*. That is, their performance on never-before-seen data started stalling (or worsening) compared to their performance on the training data—which always improves as training progresses.

In machine learning, the goal is to achieve models that *generalize*—that perform well on never-before-seen data—and overfitting is the central obstacle. You can only control that which you can observe, so it's crucial to be able to reliably measure the generalization power of your model. The following sections look at strategies for mitigating overfitting and maximizing generalization. In this section, we'll focus on how to measure generalization: how to evaluate machine-learning models.

4.2.1 Training, validation, and test sets

Evaluating a model always boils down to splitting the available data into three sets: training, validation, and test. You train on the training data and evaluate your model on the validation data. Once your model is ready for prime time, you test it one final time on the test data.

You may ask, why not have two sets: a training set and a test set? You'd train on the training data and evaluate on the test data. Much simpler!

The reason is that developing a model always involves tuning its configuration: for example, choosing the number of layers or the size of the layers (called the *hyperparameters* of the model, to distinguish them from the *parameters*, which are the network's weights). You do this tuning by using as a feedback signal the performance of the model on the validation data. In essence, this tuning is a form of *learning*: a search for a good configuration in some parameter space. As a result, tuning the configuration of the model based on its performance on the validation set can quickly result in *overfitting to the validation set*, even though your model is never directly trained on it.

Central to this phenomenon is the notion of *information leaks*. Every time you tune a hyperparameter of your model based on the model's performance on the validation set, some information about the validation data leaks into the model. If you do this only once, for one parameter, then very few bits of information will leak, and your validation set will remain reliable to evaluate the model. But if you repeat this many times—running one experiment, evaluating on the validation set, and modifying your model as a result—then you'll leak an increasingly significant amount of information about the validation set into the model.

At the end of the day, you'll end up with a model that performs artificially well on the validation data, because that's what you optimized it for. You care about performance on completely new data, not the validation data, so you need to use a completely different, never-before-seen dataset to evaluate the model: the test dataset. Your model shouldn't have had access to *any* information about the test set, even indirectly.

If anything about the model has been tuned based on test set performance, then your measure of generalization will be flawed.

Splitting your data into training, validation, and test sets may seem straightforward, but there are a few advanced ways to do it that can come in handy when little data is available. Let's review three classic evaluation recipes: simple hold-out validation, K-fold validation, and iterated K-fold validation with shuffling.

SIMPLE HOLD-OUT VALIDATION

Set apart some fraction of your data as your test set. Train on the remaining data, and evaluate on the test set. As you saw in the previous sections, in order to prevent information leaks, you shouldn't tune your model based on the test set, and therefore you should *also* reserve a validation set.

Schematically, hold-out validation looks like figure 4.1. The following listing shows a simple implementation.

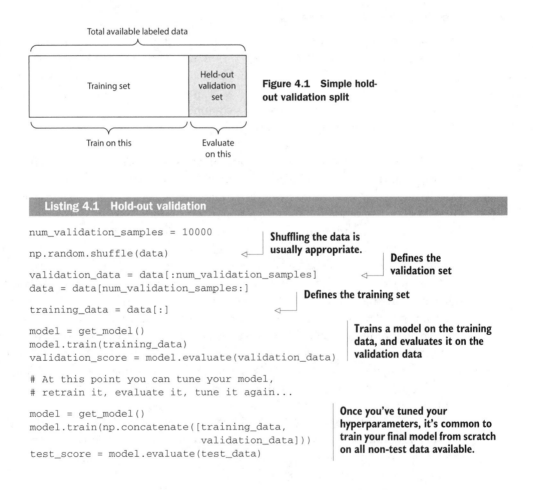

Figure 4.1   Simple hold-out validation split

Listing 4.1   Hold-out validation

```
num_validation_samples = 10000

np.random.shuffle(data)                         Shuffling the data is
                                                usually appropriate.

                                                         Defines the
                                                         validation set
validation_data = data[:num_validation_samples]
data = data[num_validation_samples:]

                                               Defines the training set
training_data = data[:]

model = get_model()                             Trains a model on the training
model.train(training_data)                      data, and evaluates it on the
validation_score = model.evaluate(validation_data)   validation data

# At this point you can tune your model,
# retrain it, evaluate it, tune it again...

model = get_model()                             Once you've tuned your
model.train(np.concatenate([training_data,      hyperparameters, it's common to
                            validation_data]))  train your final model from scratch
test_score = model.evaluate(test_data)          on all non-test data available.
```

This is the simplest evaluation protocol, and it suffers from one flaw: if little data is available, then your validation and test sets may contain too few samples to be statistically representative of the data at hand. This is easy to recognize: if different random shuffling rounds of the data before splitting end up yielding very different measures of model performance, then you're having this issue. K-fold validation and iterated K-fold validation are two ways to address this, as discussed next.

K-FOLD VALIDATION

With this approach, you split your data into K partitions of equal size. For each partition i, train a model on the remaining $K - 1$ partitions, and evaluate it on partition i. Your final score is then the averages of the K scores obtained. This method is helpful when the performance of your model shows significant variance based on your train-test split. Like hold-out validation, this method doesn't exempt you from using a distinct validation set for model calibration.

Schematically, K-fold cross-validation looks like figure 4.2. Listing 4.2 shows a simple implementation.

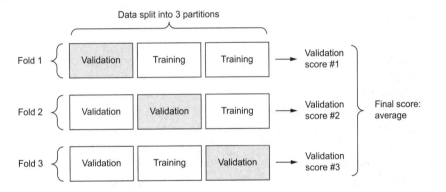

Figure 4.2   Three-fold validation

Listing 4.2   K-fold cross-validation

```
k = 4
num_validation_samples = len(data) // k

np.random.shuffle(data)

validation_scores = []
for fold in range(k):
    validation_data = data[num_validation_samples * fold:
      num_validation_samples * (fold + 1)]
    training_data = data[:num_validation_samples * fold] +
      data[num_validation_samples * (fold + 1):]

    model = get_model()
    model.train(training_data)
    validation_score = model.evaluate(validation_data)
    validation_scores.append(validation_score)
```

Selects the validation-data partition

Uses the remainder of the data as training data. Note that the + operator is list concatenation, not summation.

Creates a brand-new instance of the model (untrained)

```
validation_score = np.average(validation_scores)

model = get_model()
model.train(data)
test_score = model.evaluate(test_data)
```

> Validation score: average of the validation scores of the k folds

> Trains the final model on all non-test data available

ITERATED K-FOLD VALIDATION WITH SHUFFLING

This one is for situations in which you have relatively little data available and you need to evaluate your model as precisely as possible. I've found it to be extremely helpful in Kaggle competitions. It consists of applying K-fold validation multiple times, shuffling the data every time before splitting it K ways. The final score is the average of the scores obtained at each run of K-fold validation. Note that you end up training and evaluating $P \times K$ models (where P is the number of iterations you use), which can very expensive.

4.2.2   Things to keep in mind

Keep an eye out for the following when you're choosing an evaluation protocol:

- *Data representativeness*—You want both your training set and test set to be representative of the data at hand. For instance, if you're trying to classify images of digits, and you're starting from an array of samples where the samples are ordered by their class, taking the first 80% of the array as your training set and the remaining 20% as your test set will result in your training set containing only classes 0–7, whereas your test set contains only classes 8–9. This seems like a ridiculous mistake, but it's surprisingly common. For this reason, you usually should *randomly shuffle* your data before splitting it into training and test sets.

- *The arrow of time*—If you're trying to predict the future given the past (for example, tomorrow's weather, stock movements, and so on), you should *not* randomly shuffle your data before splitting it, because doing so will create a *temporal leak*: your model will effectively be trained on data from the future. In such situations, you should always make sure all data in your test set is *posterior* to the data in the training set.

- *Redundancy in your data*—If some data points in your data appear twice (fairly common with real-world data), then shuffling the data and splitting it into a training set and a validation set will result in redundancy between the training and validation sets. In effect, you'll be testing on part of your training data, which is the worst thing you can do! Make sure your training set and validation set are disjoint.

4.3 Data preprocessing, feature engineering, and feature learning

In addition to model evaluation, an important question we must tackle before we dive deeper into model development is the following: how do you prepare the input data and targets before feeding them into a neural network? Many data-preprocessing and feature-engineering techniques are domain specific (for example, specific to text data or image data); we'll cover those in the following chapters as we encounter them in practical examples. For now, we'll review the basics that are common to all data domains.

4.3.1 Data preprocessing for neural networks

Data preprocessing aims at making the raw data at hand more amenable to neural networks. This includes vectorization, normalization, handling missing values, and feature extraction.

VECTORIZATION

All inputs and targets in a neural network must be tensors of floating-point data (or, in specific cases, tensors of integers). Whatever data you need to process—sound, images, text—you must first turn into tensors, a step called *data vectorization*. For instance, in the two previous text-classification examples, we started from text represented as lists of integers (standing for sequences of words), and we used one-hot encoding to turn them into a tensor of `float32` data. In the examples of classifying digits and predicting house prices, the data already came in vectorized form, so you were able to skip this step.

VALUE NORMALIZATION

In the digit-classification example, you started from image data encoded as integers in the 0–255 range, encoding grayscale values. Before you fed this data into your network, you had to cast it to `float32` and divide by 255 so you'd end up with floating-point values in the 0–1 range. Similarly, when predicting house prices, you started from features that took a variety of ranges—some features had small floating-point values, others had fairly large integer values. Before you fed this data into your network, you had to normalize each feature independently so that it had a standard deviation of 1 and a mean of 0.

In general, it isn't safe to feed into a neural network data that takes relatively large values (for example, multidigit integers, which are much larger than the initial values taken by the weights of a network) or data that is heterogeneous (for example, data where one feature is in the range 0–1 and another is in the range 100–200). Doing so can trigger large gradient updates that will prevent the network from converging. To make learning easier for your network, your data should have the following characteristics:

- *Take small values*—Typically, most values should be in the 0–1 range.
- *Be homogenous*—That is, all features should take values in roughly the same range.

Additionally, the following stricter normalization practice is common and can help, although it isn't always necessary (for example, you didn't do this in the digit-classification example):

- Normalize each feature independently to have a mean of 0.
- Normalize each feature independently to have a standard deviation of 1.

This is easy to do with Numpy arrays:

```
x -= x.mean(axis=0)
x /= x.std(axis=0)
```

◁── **Assuming x is a 2D data matrix
of shape (samples, features)**

HANDLING MISSING VALUES

You may sometimes have missing values in your data. For instance, in the house-price example, the first feature (the column of index 0 in the data) was the per capita crime rate. What if this feature wasn't available for all samples? You'd then have missing values in the training or test data.

In general, with neural networks, it's safe to input missing values as 0, with the condition that 0 isn't already a meaningful value. The network will learn from exposure to the data that the value 0 means *missing data* and will start ignoring the value.

Note that if you're expecting missing values in the test data, but the network was trained on data without any missing values, the network won't have learned to ignore missing values! In this situation, you should artificially generate training samples with missing entries: copy some training samples several times, and drop some of the features that you expect are likely to be missing in the test data.

4.3.2 *Feature engineering*

Feature engineering is the process of using your own knowledge about the data and about the machine-learning algorithm at hand (in this case, a neural network) to make the algorithm work better by applying hardcoded (nonlearned) transformations to the data before it goes into the model. In many cases, it isn't reasonable to expect a machine-learning model to be able to learn from completely arbitrary data. The data needs to be presented to the model in a way that will make the model's job easier.

Let's look at an intuitive example. Suppose you're trying to develop a model that can take as input an image of a clock and can output the time of day (see figure 4.3).

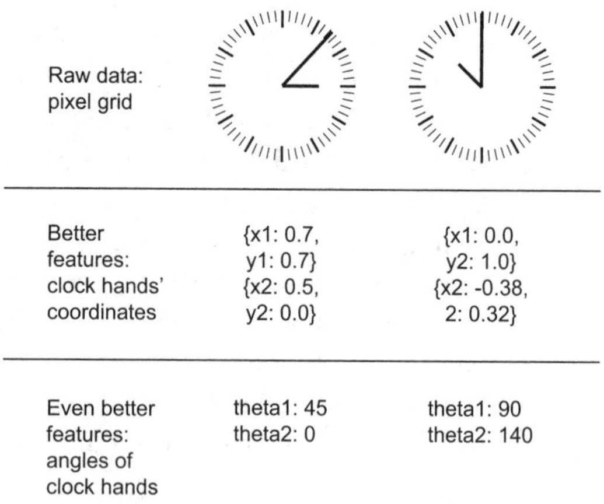

Raw data:
pixel grid		
Better
features:
clock hands'
coordinates	{x1: 0.7,
y1: 0.7}
{x2: 0.5,
y2: 0.0}	{x1: 0.0,
y2: 1.0}
{x2: -0.38,
2: 0.32}
Even better
features:
angles of
clock hands	theta1: 45
theta2: 0	theta1: 90
theta2: 140

Figure 4.3   Feature engineering for reading the time on a clock

If you choose to use the raw pixels of the image as input data, then you have a difficult machine-learning problem on your hands. You'll need a convolutional neural network to solve it, and you'll have to expend quite a bit of computational resources to train the network.

But if you already understand the problem at a high level (you understand how humans read time on a clock face), then you can come up with much better input features for a machine-learning algorithm: for instance, it's easy to write a five-line Python script to follow the black pixels of the clock hands and output the (x, y) coordinates of the tip of each hand. Then a simple machine-learning algorithm can learn to associate these coordinates with the appropriate time of day.

You can go even further: do a coordinate change, and express the (x, y) coordinates as polar coordinates with regard to the center of the image. Your input will become the angle `theta` of each clock hand. At this point, your features are making the problem so easy that no machine learning is required; a simple rounding operation and dictionary lookup are enough to recover the approximate time of day.

That's the essence of feature engineering: making a problem easier by expressing it in a simpler way. It usually requires understanding the problem in depth.

Before deep learning, feature engineering used to be critical, because classical shallow algorithms didn't have hypothesis spaces rich enough to learn useful features by themselves. The way you presented the data to the algorithm was essential to its success. For instance, before convolutional neural networks became successful on the MNIST digit-classification problem, solutions were typically based on hardcoded features such as the number of loops in a digit image, the height of each digit in an image, a histogram of pixel values, and so on.

Fortunately, modern deep learning removes the need for most feature engineering, because neural networks are capable of automatically extracting useful features from raw data. Does this mean you don't have to worry about feature engineering as long as you're using deep neural networks? No, for two reasons:

- Good features still allow you to solve problems more elegantly while using fewer resources. For instance, it would be ridiculous to solve the problem of reading a clock face using a convolutional neural network.
- Good features let you solve a problem with far less data. The ability of deep-learning models to learn features on their own relies on having lots of training data available; if you have only a few samples, then the information value in their features becomes critical.

4.4   Overfitting and underfitting

In all three examples in the previous chapter—predicting movie reviews, topic classification, and house-price regression—the performance of the model on the held-out validation data always peaked after a few epochs and then began to degrade: the model quickly started to *overfit* to the training data. Overfitting happens in every machine-learning problem. Learning how to deal with overfitting is essential to mastering machine learning.

The fundamental issue in machine learning is the tension between optimization and generalization. *Optimization* refers to the process of adjusting a model to get the best performance possible on the training data (the *learning* in *machine learning*), whereas *generalization* refers to how well the trained model performs on data it has never seen before. The goal of the game is to get good generalization, of course, but you don't control generalization; you can only adjust the model based on its training data.

At the beginning of training, optimization and generalization are correlated: the lower the loss on training data, the lower the loss on test data. While this is happening, your model is said to be *underfit*: there is still progress to be made; the network hasn't yet modeled all relevant patterns in the training data. But after a certain number of iterations on the training data, generalization stops improving, and validation metrics stall and then begin to degrade: the model is starting to overfit. That is, it's beginning to learn patterns that are specific to the training data but that are misleading or irrelevant when it comes to new data.

To prevent a model from learning misleading or irrelevant patterns found in the training data, *the best solution is to get more training data.* A model trained on more data will naturally generalize better. When that isn't possible, the next-best solution is to modulate the quantity of information that your model is allowed to store or to add constraints on what information it's allowed to store. If a network can only afford to memorize a small number of patterns, the optimization process will force it to focus on the most prominent patterns, which have a better chance of generalizing well.

The processing of fighting overfitting this way is called *regularization*. Let's review some of the most common regularization techniques and apply them in practice to improve the movie-classification model from section 3.4.

4.4.1   Reducing the network's size

The simplest way to prevent overfitting is to reduce the size of the model: the number of learnable parameters in the model (which is determined by the number of layers and the number of units per layer). In deep learning, the number of learnable parameters in a model is often referred to as the model's *capacity*. Intuitively, a model with more parameters has more *memorization capacity* and therefore can easily learn a perfect dictionary-like mapping between training samples and their targets—a mapping without any generalization power. For instance, a model with 500,000 binary parameters could easily be made to learn the class of every digit in the MNIST training set:

we'd need only 10 binary parameters for each of the 50,000 digits. But such a model would be useless for classifying new digit samples. Always keep this in mind: deep-learning models tend to be good at fitting to the training data, but the real challenge is generalization, not fitting.

On the other hand, if the network has limited memorization resources, it won't be able to learn this mapping as easily; thus, in order to minimize its loss, it will have to resort to learning compressed representations that have predictive power regarding the targets—precisely the type of representations we're interested in. At the same time, keep in mind that you should use models that have enough parameters that they don't underfit: your model shouldn't be starved for memorization resources. There is a compromise to be found between *too much capacity* and *not enough capacity*.

Unfortunately, there is no magical formula to determine the right number of layers or the right size for each layer. You must evaluate an array of different architectures (on your validation set, not on your test set, of course) in order to find the correct model size for your data. The general workflow to find an appropriate model size is to start with relatively few layers and parameters, and increase the size of the layers or add new layers until you see diminishing returns with regard to validation loss.

Let's try this on the movie-review classification network. The original network is shown next.

> **Listing 4.3 Original model**

```
from keras import models
from keras import layers

model = models.Sequential()
model.add(layers.Dense(16, activation='relu', input_shape=(10000,)))
model.add(layers.Dense(16, activation='relu'))
model.add(layers.Dense(1, activation='sigmoid'))
```

Now let's try to replace it with this smaller network.

> **Listing 4.4 Version of the model with lower capacity**

```
model = models.Sequential()
model.add(layers.Dense(4, activation='relu', input_shape=(10000,)))
model.add(layers.Dense(4, activation='relu'))
model.add(layers.Dense(1, activation='sigmoid'))
```

Figure 4.4 shows a comparison of the validation losses of the original network and the smaller network. The dots are the validation loss values of the smaller network, and the crosses are the initial network (remember, a lower validation loss signals a better model).

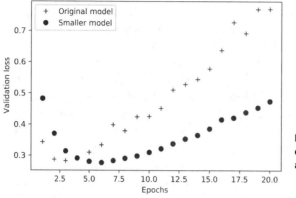

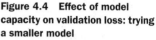

Figure 4.4   Effect of model capacity on validation loss: trying a smaller model

As you can see, the smaller network starts overfitting later than the reference network (after six epochs rather than four), and its performance degrades more slowly once it starts overfitting.

Now, for kicks, let's add to this benchmark a network that has much more capacity—far more than the problem warrants.

Listing 4.5   Version of the model with higher capacity

```
model = models.Sequential()
model.add(layers.Dense(512, activation='relu', input_shape=(10000,)))
model.add(layers.Dense(512, activation='relu'))
model.add(layers.Dense(1, activation='sigmoid'))
```

Figure 4.5 shows how the bigger network fares compared to the reference network. The dots are the validation loss values of the bigger network, and the crosses are the initial network.

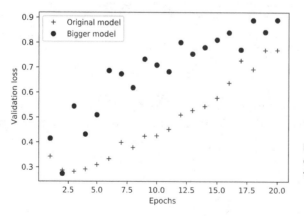

Figure 4.5   Effect of model capacity on validation loss: trying a bigger model

The bigger network starts overfitting almost immediately, after just one epoch, and it overfits much more severely. Its validation loss is also noisier.

Meanwhile, figure 4.6 shows the training losses for the two networks. As you can see, the bigger network gets its training loss near zero very quickly. The more capacity the network has, the more quickly it can model the training data (resulting in a low training loss), but the more susceptible it is to overfitting (resulting in a large difference between the training and validation loss).

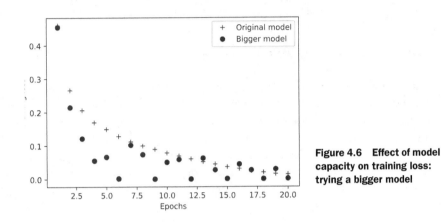

Figure 4.6 **Effect of model capacity on training loss: trying a bigger model**

4.4.2 Adding weight regularization

You may be familiar with the principle of *Occam's razor*: given two explanations for something, the explanation most likely to be correct is the simplest one—the one that makes fewer assumptions. This idea also applies to the models learned by neural networks: given some training data and a network architecture, multiple sets of weight values (multiple *models*) could explain the data. Simpler models are less likely to overfit than complex ones.

A *simple model* in this context is a model where the distribution of parameter values has less entropy (or a model with fewer parameters, as you saw in the previous section). Thus a common way to mitigate overfitting is to put constraints on the complexity of a network by forcing its weights to take only small values, which makes the distribution of weight values more *regular*. This is called *weight regularization*, and it's done by adding to the loss function of the network a *cost* associated with having large weights. This cost comes in two flavors:

- *L1 regularization*—The cost added is proportional to the *absolute value of the weight coefficients* (the *L1 norm* of the weights).
- *L2 regularization*—The cost added is proportional to the *square of the value of the weight coefficients* (the *L2 norm* of the weights). L2 regularization is also called *weight decay* in the context of neural networks. Don't let the different name confuse you: weight decay is mathematically the same as L2 regularization.

In Keras, weight regularization is added by passing *weight regularizer instances* to layers as keyword arguments. Let's add L2 weight regularization to the movie-review classification network.

Listing 4.6   Adding L2 weight regularization to the model

```
from keras import regularizers

model = models.Sequential()
model.add(layers.Dense(16, kernel_regularizer=regularizers.l2(0.001),
                       activation='relu', input_shape=(10000,)))
model.add(layers.Dense(16, kernel_regularizer=regularizers.l2(0.001),
                       activation='relu'))
model.add(layers.Dense(1, activation='sigmoid'))
```

`l2(0.001)` means every coefficient in the weight matrix of the layer will add `0.001 * weight_coefficient_value` to the total loss of the network. Note that because this penalty is *only added at training time*, the loss for this network will be much higher at training than at test time.

Figure 4.7 shows the impact of the L2 regularization penalty. As you can see, the model with L2 regularization (dots) has become much more resistant to overfitting than the reference model (crosses), even though both models have the same number of parameters.

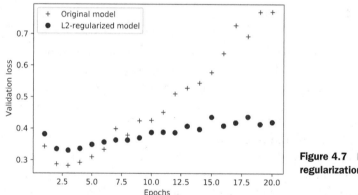

Figure 4.7   **Effect of L2 weight regularization on validation loss**

As an alternative to L2 regularization, you can use one of the following Keras weight regularizers.

Listing 4.7   Different weight regularizers available in Keras

```
from keras import regularizers

regularizers.l1(0.001)                 ◁——— L1 regularization

regularizers.l1_l2(l1=0.001, l2=0.001)       ◁—┐ Simultaneous L1 and
                                                │ L2 regularization
```
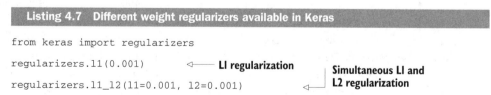

4.4.3   Adding dropout

Dropout is one of the most effective and most commonly used regularization techniques for neural networks, developed by Geoff Hinton and his students at the University of Toronto. Dropout, applied to a layer, consists of randomly *dropping out* (setting to zero) a number of output features of the layer during training. Let's say a given layer would normally return a vector [0.2, 0.5, 1.3, 0.8, 1.1] for a given input sample during training. After applying dropout, this vector will have a few zero entries distributed at random: for example, [0, 0.5, 1.3, 0, 1.1]. The *dropout rate* is the fraction of the features that are zeroed out; it's usually set between 0.2 and 0.5. At test time, no units are dropped out; instead, the layer's output values are scaled down by a factor equal to the dropout rate, to balance for the fact that more units are active than at training time.

Consider a Numpy matrix containing the output of a layer, `layer_output`, of shape (`batch_size`, `features`). At training time, we zero out at random a fraction of the values in the matrix:

```
layer_output *= np.random.randint(0, high=2, size=layer_output.shape)   ◁
```
At training time, drops out 50% of the units in the output

At test time, we scale down the output by the dropout rate. Here, we scale by 0.5 (because we previously dropped half the units):

```
layer_output *= 0.5   ◁——  At test time
```

Note that this process can be implemented by doing both operations at training time and leaving the output unchanged at test time, which is often the way it's implemented in practice (see figure 4.8):

```
layer_output *= np.random.randint(0, high=2, size=layer_output.shape)   ◁
layer_output /= 0.5   ◁
```
Note that we're scaling up rather scaling down in this case.   **At training time**

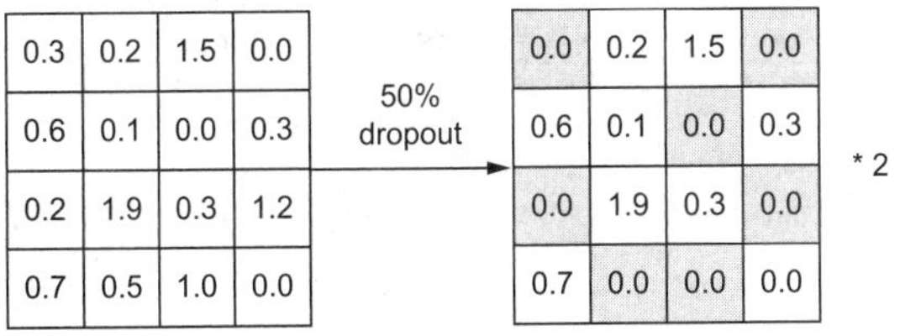

Figure 4.8   Dropout applied to an activation matrix at training time, with rescaling happening during training. At test time, the activation matrix is unchanged.

This technique may seem strange and arbitrary. Why would this help reduce overfitting? Hinton says he was inspired by, among other things, a fraud-prevention mechanism used by banks. In his own words, "I went to my bank. The tellers kept changing and I asked one of them why. He said he didn't know but they got moved around a lot.

I figured it must be because it would require cooperation between employees to successfully defraud the bank. This made me realize that randomly removing a different subset of neurons on each example would prevent conspiracies and thus reduce overfitting."[1] The core idea is that introducing noise in the output values of a layer can break up happenstance patterns that aren't significant (what Hinton refers to as *conspiracies*), which the network will start memorizing if no noise is present.

In Keras, you can introduce dropout in a network via the `Dropout` layer, which is applied to the output of the layer right before it:

```
model.add(layers.Dropout(0.5))
```

Let's add two `Dropout` layers in the IMDB network to see how well they do at reducing overfitting.

Listing 4.8   Adding dropout to the IMDB network

```
model = models.Sequential()
model.add(layers.Dense(16, activation='relu', input_shape=(10000,)))
model.add(layers.Dropout(0.5))
model.add(layers.Dense(16, activation='relu'))
model.add(layers.Dropout(0.5))
model.add(layers.Dense(1, activation='sigmoid'))
```

Figure 4.9 shows a plot of the results. Again, this is a clear improvement over the reference network.

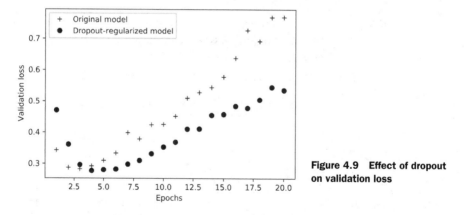

Figure 4.9   Effect of dropout on validation loss

To recap, these are the most common ways to prevent overfitting in neural networks:

- Get more training data.
- Reduce the capacity of the network.
- Add weight regularization.
- Add dropout.

---

[1] See the Reddit thread "AMA: We are the Google Brain team. We'd love to answer your questions about machine learning," http://mng.bz/XrsS.

4.5 *The universal workflow of machine learning*

In this section, we'll present a universal blueprint that you can use to attack and solve any machine-learning problem. The blueprint ties together the concepts you've learned about in this chapter: problem definition, evaluation, feature engineering, and fighting overfitting.

4.5.1 *Defining the problem and assembling a dataset*

First, you must define the problem at hand:

- What will your input data be? What are you trying to predict? You can only learn to predict something if you have available training data: for example, you can only learn to classify the sentiment of movie reviews if you have both movie reviews and sentiment annotations available. As such, data availability is usually the limiting factor at this stage (unless you have the means to pay people to collect data for you).
- What type of problem are you facing? Is it binary classification? Multiclass classification? Scalar regression? Vector regression? Multiclass, multilabel classification? Something else, like clustering, generation, or reinforcement learning? Identifying the problem type will guide your choice of model architecture, loss function, and so on.

You can't move to the next stage until you know what your inputs and outputs are, and what data you'll use. Be aware of the hypotheses you make at this stage:

- You hypothesize that your outputs can be predicted given your inputs.
- You hypothesize that your available data is sufficiently informative to learn the relationship between inputs and outputs.

Until you have a working model, these are merely hypotheses, waiting to be validated or invalidated. Not all problems can be solved; just because you've assembled examples of inputs X and targets Y doesn't mean X contains enough information to predict Y. For instance, if you're trying to predict the movements of a stock on the stock market given its recent price history, you're unlikely to succeed, because price history doesn't contain much predictive information.

One class of unsolvable problems you should be aware of is *nonstationary problems*. Suppose you're trying to build a recommendation engine for clothing, you're training it on one month of data (August), and you want to start generating recommendations in the winter. One big issue is that the kinds of clothes people buy change from season to season: clothes buying is a nonstationary phenomenon over the scale of a few months. What you're trying to model changes over time. In this case, the right move is to constantly retrain your model on data from the recent past, or gather data at a timescale where the problem is stationary. For a cyclical problem like clothes buying, a few years' worth of data will suffice to capture seasonal variation—but remember to make the time of the year an input of your model!

Keep in mind that machine learning can only be used to memorize patterns that are present in your training data. You can only recognize what you've seen before. Using machine learning trained on past data to predict the future is making the assumption that the future will behave like the past. That often isn't the case.

4.5.2   *Choosing a measure of success*

To control something, you need to be able to observe it. To achieve success, you must define what you mean by success—accuracy? Precision and recall? Customer-retention rate? Your metric for success will guide the choice of a loss function: what your model will optimize. It should directly align with your higher-level goals, such as the success of your business.

For balanced-classification problems, where every class is equally likely, accuracy and *area under the receiver operating characteristic curve* (ROC AUC) are common metrics. For class-imbalanced problems, you can use precision and recall. For ranking problems or multilabel classification, you can use mean average precision. And it isn't uncommon to have to define your own custom metric by which to measure success. To get a sense of the diversity of machine-learning success metrics and how they relate to different problem domains, it's helpful to browse the data science competitions on Kaggle (https://kaggle.com); they showcase a wide range of problems and evaluation metrics.

4.5.3   *Deciding on an evaluation protocol*

Once you know what you're aiming for, you must establish how you'll measure your current progress. We've previously reviewed three common evaluation protocols:

- *Maintaining a hold-out validation set*—The way to go when you have plenty of data
- *Doing K-fold cross-validation*—The right choice when you have too few samples for hold-out validation to be reliable
- *Doing iterated K-fold validation*—For performing highly accurate model evaluation when little data is available

Just pick one of these. In most cases, the first will work well enough.

4.5.4   *Preparing your data*

Once you know what you're training on, what you're optimizing for, and how to evaluate your approach, you're almost ready to begin training models. But first, you should format your data in a way that can be fed into a machine-learning model—here, we'll assume a deep neural network:

- As you saw previously, your data should be formatted as tensors.
- The values taken by these tensors should usually be scaled to small values: for example, in the [-1, 1] range or [0, 1] range.

- If different features take values in different ranges (heterogeneous data), then the data should be normalized.
- You may want to do some feature engineering, especially for small-data problems.

Once your tensors of input data and target data are ready, you can begin to train models.

4.5.5 *Developing a model that does better than a baseline*

Your goal at this stage is to achieve *statistical power*: that is, to develop a small model that is capable of beating a dumb baseline. In the MNIST digit-classification example, anything that achieves an accuracy greater than 0.1 can be said to have statistical power; in the IMDB example, it's anything with an accuracy greater than 0.5.

Note that it's not always possible to achieve statistical power. If you can't beat a random baseline after trying multiple reasonable architectures, it may be that the answer to the question you're asking isn't present in the input data. Remember that you make two hypotheses:

- You hypothesize that your outputs can be predicted given your inputs.
- You hypothesize that the available data is sufficiently informative to learn the relationship between inputs and outputs.

It may well be that these hypotheses are false, in which case you must go back to the drawing board.

Assuming that things go well, you need to make three key choices to build your first working model:

- *Last-layer activation*—This establishes useful constraints on the network's output. For instance, the IMDB classification example used `sigmoid` in the last layer; the regression example didn't use any last-layer activation; and so on.
- *Loss function*—This should match the type of problem you're trying to solve. For instance, the IMDB example used `binary_crossentropy`, the regression example used `mse`, and so on.
- *Optimization configuration*—What optimizer will you use? What will its learning rate be? In most cases, it's safe to go with `rmsprop` and its default learning rate.

Regarding the choice of a loss function, note that it isn't always possible to directly optimize for the metric that measures success on a problem. Sometimes there is no easy way to turn a metric into a loss function; loss functions, after all, need to be computable given only a mini-batch of data (ideally, a loss function should be computable for as little as a single data point) and must be differentiable (otherwise, you can't use backpropagation to train your network). For instance, the widely used classification metric ROC AUC can't be directly optimized. Hence, in classification tasks, it's common to optimize for a proxy metric of ROC AUC, such as crossentropy. In general, you can hope that the lower the crossentropy gets, the higher the ROC AUC will be.

Table 4.1 can help you choose a last-layer activation and a loss function for a few common problem types.

Table 4.1 **Choosing the right last-layer activation and loss function for your model**

Problem type	Last-layer activation	Loss function
Binary classification	`sigmoid`	`binary_crossentropy`
Multiclass, single-label classification	`softmax`	`categorical_crossentropy`
Multiclass, multilabel classification	`sigmoid`	`binary_crossentropy`
Regression to arbitrary values	None	`mse`
Regression to values between 0 and 1	`sigmoid`	`mse` or `binary_crossentropy`

4.5.6 *Scaling up: developing a model that overfits*

Once you've obtained a model that has statistical power, the question becomes, is your model sufficiently powerful? Does it have enough layers and parameters to properly model the problem at hand? For instance, a network with a single hidden layer with two units would have statistical power on MNIST but wouldn't be sufficient to solve the problem well. Remember that the universal tension in machine learning is between optimization and generalization; the ideal model is one that stands right at the border between underfitting and overfitting; between undercapacity and overcapacity. To figure out where this border lies, first you must cross it.

To figure out how big a model you'll need, you must develop a model that overfits. This is fairly easy:

1 Add layers.
2 Make the layers bigger.
3 Train for more epochs.

Always monitor the training loss and validation loss, as well as the training and validation values for any metrics you care about. When you see that the model's performance on the validation data begins to degrade, you've achieved overfitting.

The next stage is to start regularizing and tuning the model, to get as close as possible to the ideal model that neither underfits nor overfits.

4.5.7 *Regularizing your model and tuning your hyperparameters*

This step will take the most time: you'll repeatedly modify your model, train it, evaluate on your validation data (not the test data, at this point), modify it again, and repeat, until the model is as good as it can get. These are some things you should try:

- Add dropout.
- Try different architectures: add or remove layers.
- Add L1 and/or L2 regularization.

- Try different hyperparameters (such as the number of units per layer or the learning rate of the optimizer) to find the optimal configuration.
- Optionally, iterate on feature engineering: add new features, or remove features that don't seem to be informative.

Be mindful of the following: every time you use feedback from your validation process to tune your model, you leak information about the validation process into the model. Repeated just a few times, this is innocuous; but done systematically over many iterations, it will eventually cause your model to overfit to the validation process (even though no model is directly trained on any of the validation data). This makes the evaluation process less reliable.

Once you've developed a satisfactory model configuration, you can train your final production model on all the available data (training and validation) and evaluate it one last time on the test set. If it turns out that performance on the test set is significantly worse than the performance measured on the validation data, this may mean either that your validation procedure wasn't reliable after all, or that you began overfitting to the validation data while tuning the parameters of the model. In this case, you may want to switch to a more reliable evaluation protocol (such as iterated K-fold validation).

Chapter summary

- Define the problem at hand and the data on which you'll train. Collect this data, or annotate it with labels if need be.

- Choose how you'll measure success on your problem. Which metrics will you monitor on your validation data?

- Determine your evaluation protocol: hold-out validation? K-fold validation? Which portion of the data should you use for validation?

- Develop a first model that does better than a basic baseline: a model with statistical power.

- Develop a model that overfits.

- Regularize your model and tune its hyperparameters, based on performance on the validation data. A lot of machine-learning research tends to focus only on this step—but keep the big picture in mind.

Part 2

Deep learning in practice

Chapters 5–9 will help you gain practical intuition about how to solve real-world problems using deep learning, and will familiarize you with essential deep-learning best practices. Most of the code examples in the book are concentrated in this second half.

Deep learning
for computer vision

This chapter covers

- Understanding convolutional neural networks (convnets)
- Using data augmentation to mitigate overfitting
- Using a pretrained convnet to do feature extraction
- Fine-tuning a pretrained convnet
- Visualizing what convnets learn and how they make classification decisions

This chapter introduces convolutional neural networks, also known as *convnets*, a type of deep-learning model almost universally used in computer vision applications. You'll learn to apply convnets to image-classification problems—in particular those involving small training datasets, which are the most common use case if you aren't a large tech company.

5.1   *Introduction to convnets*

We're about to dive into the theory of what convnets are and why they have been so successful at computer vision tasks. But first, let's take a practical look at a simple convnet example. It uses a convnet to classify MNIST digits, a task we performed in chapter 2 using a densely connected network (our test accuracy then was 97.8%). Even though the convnet will be basic, its accuracy will blow out of the water that of the densely connected model from chapter 2.

The following lines of code show you what a basic convnet looks like. It's a stack of Conv2D and MaxPooling2D layers. You'll see in a minute exactly what they do.

Listing 5.1   Instantiating a small convnet

```
from keras import layers
from keras import models

model = models.Sequential()
model.add(layers.Conv2D(32, (3, 3), activation='relu', input_shape=(28, 28, 1)))
model.add(layers.MaxPooling2D((2, 2)))
model.add(layers.Conv2D(64, (3, 3), activation='relu'))
model.add(layers.MaxPooling2D((2, 2)))
model.add(layers.Conv2D(64, (3, 3), activation='relu'))
```

Importantly, a convnet takes as input tensors of shape (image_height, image_width, image_channels) (not including the batch dimension). In this case, we'll configure the convnet to process inputs of size (28, 28, 1), which is the format of MNIST images. We'll do this by passing the argument input_shape=(28, 28, 1) to the first layer.

Let's display the architecture of the convnet so far:

```
>>> model.summary()
```

```
Layer (type)                     Output Shape              Param #
=================================================================
conv2d_1 (Conv2D)                (None, 26, 26, 32)        320

maxpooling2d_1 (MaxPooling2D)    (None, 13, 13, 32)        0

conv2d_2 (Conv2D)                (None, 11, 11, 64)        18496

maxpooling2d_2 (MaxPooling2D)    (None, 5, 5, 64)          0

conv2d_3 (Conv2D)                (None, 3, 3, 64)          36928
=================================================================
Total params: 55,744
Trainable params: 55,744
Non-trainable params: 0
```

You can see that the output of every Conv2D and MaxPooling2D layer is a 3D tensor of shape (height, width, channels). The width and height dimensions tend to shrink as you go deeper in the network. The number of channels is controlled by the first argument passed to the Conv2D layers (32 or 64).

The next step is to feed the last output tensor (of shape (3, 3, 64)) into a densely connected classifier network like those you're already familiar with: a stack of Dense layers. These classifiers process vectors, which are 1D, whereas the current output is a 3D tensor. First we have to flatten the 3D outputs to 1D, and then add a few Dense layers on top.

> **Listing 5.2 Adding a classifier on top of the convnet**

```
model.add(layers.Flatten())
model.add(layers.Dense(64, activation='relu'))
model.add(layers.Dense(10, activation='softmax'))
```

We'll do 10-way classification, using a final layer with 10 outputs and a softmax activation. Here's what the network looks like now:

```
>>> model.summary()
```

Layer (type)	Output Shape	Param #
conv2d_1 (Conv2D)	(None, 26, 26, 32)	320
maxpooling2d_1 (MaxPooling2D)	(None, 13, 13, 32)	0
conv2d_2 (Conv2D)	(None, 11, 11, 64)	18496
maxpooling2d_2 (MaxPooling2D)	(None, 5, 5, 64)	0
conv2d_3 (Conv2D)	(None, 3, 3, 64)	36928
flatten_1 (Flatten)	(None, 576)	0
dense_1 (Dense)	(None, 64)	36928
dense_2 (Dense)	(None, 10)	650

```
Total params: 93,322
Trainable params: 93,322
Non-trainable params: 0
```

As you can see, the (3, 3, 64) outputs are flattened into vectors of shape (576,) before going through two Dense layers.

Now, let's train the convnet on the MNIST digits. We'll reuse a lot of the code from the MNIST example in chapter 2.

> **Listing 5.3 Training the convnet on MNIST images**

```
from keras.datasets import mnist
from keras.utils import to_categorical

(train_images, train_labels), (test_images, test_labels) = mnist.load_data()
```

```
train_images = train_images.reshape((60000, 28, 28, 1))
train_images = train_images.astype('float32') / 255

test_images = test_images.reshape((10000, 28, 28, 1))
test_images = test_images.astype('float32') / 255

train_labels = to_categorical(train_labels)
test_labels = to_categorical(test_labels)

model.compile(optimizer='rmsprop',
              loss='categorical_crossentropy',
              metrics=['accuracy'])
model.fit(train_images, train_labels, epochs=5, batch_size=64)
```

Let's evaluate the model on the test data:

```
>>> test_loss, test_acc = model.evaluate(test_images, test_labels)
>>> test_acc
0.99080000000000001
```

Whereas the densely connected network from chapter 2 had a test accuracy of 97.8%, the basic convnet has a test accuracy of 99.3%: we decreased the error rate by 68% (relative). Not bad!

But why does this simple convnet work so well, compared to a densely connected model? To answer this, let's dive into what the `Conv2D` and `MaxPooling2D` layers do.

5.1.1   *The convolution operation*

The fundamental difference between a densely connected layer and a convolution layer is this: `Dense` layers learn global patterns in their input feature space (for example, for a MNIST digit, patterns involving all pixels), whereas convolution layers learn local patterns (see figure 5.1): in the case of images, patterns found in small 2D windows of the inputs. In the previous example, these windows were all 3 × 3.

Figure 5.1   **Images can be broken into local patterns such as edges, textures, and so on.**

This key characteristic gives convnets two interesting properties:

- *The patterns they learn are translation invariant.* After learning a certain pattern in the lower-right corner of a picture, a convnet can recognize it anywhere: for example, in the upper-left corner. A densely connected network would have to learn the pattern anew if it appeared at a new location. This makes convnets data efficient when processing images (because *the visual world is fundamentally translation invariant*): they need fewer training samples to learn representations that have generalization power.

- *They can learn spatial hierarchies of patterns (see figure 5.2).* A first convolution layer will learn small local patterns such as edges, a second convolution layer will learn larger patterns made of the features of the first layers, and so on. This allows convnets to efficiently learn increasingly complex and abstract visual concepts (because *the visual world is fundamentally spatially hierarchical*).

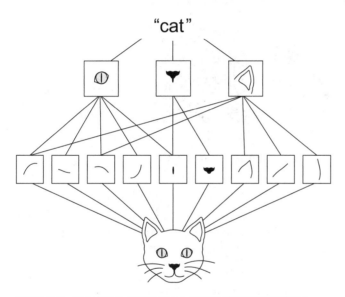

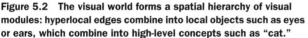

Figure 5.2 The visual world forms a spatial hierarchy of visual modules: hyperlocal edges combine into local objects such as eyes or ears, which combine into high-level concepts such as "cat."

Convolutions operate over 3D tensors, called *feature maps,* with two spatial axes (*height* and *width*) as well as a *depth* axis (also called the *channels* axis). For an RGB image, the dimension of the depth axis is 3, because the image has three color channels: red, green, and blue. For a black-and-white picture, like the MNIST digits, the depth is 1 (levels of gray). The convolution operation extracts patches from its input feature map and applies the same transformation to all of these patches, producing an *output feature map.* This output feature map is still a 3D tensor: it has a width and a height. Its depth can be arbitrary, because the output depth is a parameter of the layer, and the different channels in that depth axis no longer stand for specific colors as in RGB input; rather, they stand for *filters*. Filters encode specific aspects of the input data: at a high level, a single filter could encode the concept "presence of a face in the input," for instance.

In the MNIST example, the first convolution layer takes a feature map of size (28, 28, 1) and outputs a feature map of size (26, 26, 32): it computes 32 filters over its input. Each of these 32 output channels contains a 26 × 26 grid of values, which is a *response map* of the filter over the input, indicating the response of that filter pattern at different locations in the input (see figure 5.3). That is what the term *feature map* means: every dimension in the depth axis is a feature (or filter), and the 2D tensor output[:, :, n] is the 2D spatial *map* of the response of this filter over the input.

Original input

Single filter

Response map, quantifying the presence of the filter's pattern at different locations

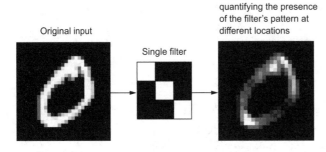

Figure 5.3   The concept of a *response map*: a 2D map of the presence of a pattern at different locations in an input

Convolutions are defined by two key parameters:

- *Size of the patches extracted from the inputs*—These are typically 3 × 3 or 5 × 5. In the example, they were 3 × 3, which is a common choice.
- *Depth of the output feature map*—The number of filters computed by the convolution. The example started with a depth of 32 and ended with a depth of 64.

In Keras Conv2D layers, these parameters are the first arguments passed to the layer: Conv2D(output_depth, (window_height, window_width)).

A convolution works by *sliding* these windows of size 3 × 3 or 5 × 5 over the 3D input feature map, stopping at every possible location, and extracting the 3D patch of surrounding features (shape (window_height, window_width, input_depth)). Each such 3D patch is then transformed (via a tensor product with the same learned weight matrix, called the *convolution kernel*) into a 1D vector of shape (output_depth,). All of these vectors are then spatially reassembled into a 3D output map of shape (height, width, output_depth). Every spatial location in the output feature map corresponds to the same location in the input feature map (for example, the lower-right corner of the output contains information about the lower-right corner of the input). For instance, with 3 × 3 windows, the vector output[i, j, :] comes from the 3D patch input[i-1:i+1, j-1:j+1, :]. The full process is detailed in figure 5.4.

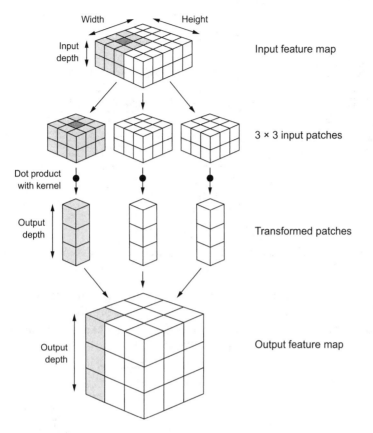

Figure 5.4   How convolution works

Note that the output width and height may differ from the input width and height. They may differ for two reasons:

- Border effects, which can be countered by padding the input feature map
- The use of *strides*, which I'll define in a second

Let's take a deeper look at these notions.

UNDERSTANDING BORDER EFFECTS AND PADDING

Consider a 5 × 5 feature map (25 tiles total). There are only 9 tiles around which you can center a 3 × 3 window, forming a 3 × 3 grid (see figure 5.5). Hence, the output feature map will be 3 × 3. It shrinks a little: by exactly two tiles alongside each dimension, in this case. You can see this border effect in action in the earlier example: you start with 28 × 28 inputs, which become 26 × 26 after the first convolution layer.

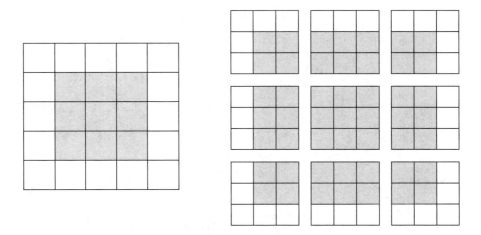

Figure 5.5   Valid locations of 3 × 3 patches in a 5 × 5 input feature map

If you want to get an output feature map with the same spatial dimensions as the input, you can use *padding*. Padding consists of adding an appropriate number of rows and columns on each side of the input feature map so as to make it possible to fit center convolution windows around every input tile. For a 3 × 3 window, you add one column on the right, one column on the left, one row at the top, and one row at the bottom. For a 5 × 5 window, you add two rows (see figure 5.6).

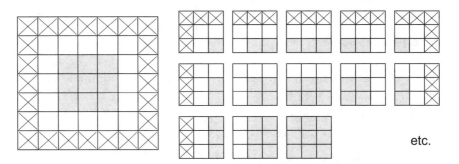

etc.

Figure 5.6   Padding a 5 × 5 input in order to be able to extract 25 3 × 3 patches

In Conv2D layers, padding is configurable via the padding argument, which takes two values: "valid", which means no padding (only valid window locations will be used); and "same", which means "pad in such a way as to have an output with the same width and height as the input." The padding argument defaults to "valid".

The other factor that can influence output size is the notion of *strides*. The description of convolution so far has assumed that the center tiles of the convolution windows are all contiguous. But the distance between two successive windows is a parameter of the convolution, called its *stride*, which defaults to 1. It's possible to have *strided convolutions*: convolutions with a stride higher than 1. In figure 5.7, you can see the patches extracted by a 3 × 3 convolution with stride 2 over a 5 × 5 input (without padding).

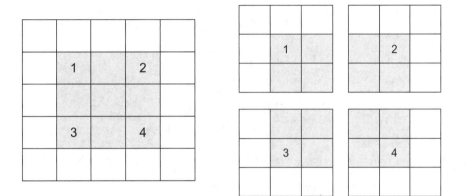

Figure 5.7   3 × 3 convolution patches with 2 × 2 strides

Using stride 2 means the width and height of the feature map are downsampled by a factor of 2 (in addition to any changes induced by border effects). Strided convolutions are rarely used in practice, although they can come in handy for some types of models; it's good to be familiar with the concept.

To downsample feature maps, instead of strides, we tend to use the *max-pooling* operation, which you saw in action in the first convnet example. Let's look at it in more depth.

5.1.2   *The max-pooling operation*

In the convnet example, you may have noticed that the size of the feature maps is halved after every `MaxPooling2D` layer. For instance, before the first `MaxPooling2D` layers, the feature map is 26 × 26, but the max-pooling operation halves it to 13 × 13. That's the role of max pooling: to aggressively downsample feature maps, much like strided convolutions.

Max pooling consists of extracting windows from the input feature maps and outputting the max value of each channel. It's conceptually similar to convolution, except that instead of transforming local patches via a learned linear transformation (the convolution kernel), they're transformed via a hardcoded `max` tensor operation. A big difference from convolution is that max pooling is usually done with 2 × 2 windows and stride 2, in order to downsample the feature maps by a factor of 2. On the other hand, convolution is typically done with 3×3 windows and no stride (stride 1).

Why downsample feature maps this way? Why not remove the max-pooling layers and keep fairly large feature maps all the way up? Let's look at this option. The convolutional base of the model would then look like this:

```
model_no_max_pool = models.Sequential()
model_no_max_pool.add(layers.Conv2D(32, (3, 3), activation='relu',
                      input_shape=(28, 28, 1)))
model_no_max_pool.add(layers.Conv2D(64, (3, 3), activation='relu'))
model_no_max_pool.add(layers.Conv2D(64, (3, 3), activation='relu'))
```

Here's a summary of the model:

```
>>> model_no_max_pool.summary()
```

```
Layer (type)                     Output Shape            Param #
=================================================================
conv2d_4 (Conv2D)                (None, 26, 26, 32)      320
_____
conv2d_5 (Conv2D)                (None, 24, 24, 64)      18496
_____
conv2d_6 (Conv2D)                (None, 22, 22, 64)      36928
=================================================================
Total params: 55,744
Trainable params: 55,744
Non-trainable params: 0
```

What's wrong with this setup? Two things:

- It isn't conducive to learning a spatial hierarchy of features. The 3×3 windows in the third layer will only contain information coming from 7×7 windows in the initial input. The high-level patterns learned by the convnet will still be very small with regard to the initial input, which may not be enough to learn to classify digits (try recognizing a digit by only looking at it through windows that are 7×7 pixels!). We need the features from the last convolution layer to contain information about the totality of the input.
- The final feature map has $22 \times 22 \times 64 = 30,976$ total coefficients per sample. This is huge. If you were to flatten it to stick a Dense layer of size 512 on top, that layer would have 15.8 million parameters. This is far too large for such a small model and would result in intense overfitting.

In short, the reason to use downsampling is to reduce the number of feature-map coefficients to process, as well as to induce spatial-filter hierarchies by making successive convolution layers look at increasingly large windows (in terms of the fraction of the original input they cover).

Note that max pooling isn't the only way you can achieve such downsampling. As you already know, you can also use strides in the prior convolution layer. And you can use average pooling instead of max pooling, where each local input patch is transformed by taking the average value of each channel over the patch, rather than the max. But max pooling tends to work better than these alternative solutions. In a nutshell, the reason is that features tend to encode the spatial presence of some pattern or concept over the different tiles of the feature map (hence, the term *feature map*), and it's more informative to look at the *maximal presence* of different features than at their *average presence*. So the most reasonable subsampling strategy is to first produce dense maps of features (via unstrided convolutions) and then look at the maximal activation of the features over small patches, rather than looking at sparser windows of the inputs (via strided convolutions) or averaging input patches, which could cause you to miss or dilute feature-presence information.

At this point, you should understand the basics of convnets—feature maps, convolution, and max pooling—and you know how to build a small convnet to solve a toy problem such as MNIST digits classification. Now let's move on to more useful, practical applications.

5.2   *Training a convnet from scratch on a small dataset*

Having to train an image-classification model using very little data is a common situation, which you'll likely encounter in practice if you ever do computer vision in a professional context. A "few" samples can mean anywhere from a few hundred to a few tens of thousands of images. As a practical example, we'll focus on classifying images as dogs or cats, in a dataset containing 4,000 pictures of cats and dogs (2,000 cats, 2,000 dogs). We'll use 2,000 pictures for training—1,000 for validation, and 1,000 for testing.

In this section, we'll review one basic strategy to tackle this problem: training a new model from scratch using what little data you have. You'll start by naively training a small convnet on the 2,000 training samples, without any regularization, to set a baseline for what can be achieved. This will get you to a classification accuracy of 71%. At that point, the main issue will be overfitting. Then we'll introduce *data augmentation*, a powerful technique for mitigating overfitting in computer vision. By using data augmentation, you'll improve the network to reach an accuracy of 82%.

In the next section, we'll review two more essential techniques for applying deep learning to small datasets: *feature extraction with a pretrained network* (which will get you to an accuracy of 90% to 96%) and *fine-tuning a pretrained network* (this will get you to a final accuracy of 97%). Together, these three strategies—training a small model from scratch, doing feature extraction using a pretrained model, and fine-tuning a pretrained model—will constitute your future toolbox for tackling the problem of performing image classification with small datasets.

5.2.1   *The relevance of deep learning for small-data problems*

You'll sometimes hear that deep learning only works when lots of data is available. This is valid in part: one fundamental characteristic of deep learning is that it can find interesting features in the training data on its own, without any need for manual feature engineering, and this can only be achieved when lots of training examples are available. This is especially true for problems where the input samples are very high-dimensional, like images.

But what constitutes lots of samples is relative—relative to the size and depth of the network you're trying to train, for starters. It isn't possible to train a convnet to solve a complex problem with just a few tens of samples, but a few hundred can potentially suffice if the model is small and well regularized and the task is simple. Because convnets learn local, translation-invariant features, they're highly data efficient on perceptual problems. Training a convnet from scratch on a very small image dataset will still yield reasonable results despite a relative lack of data, without the need for any custom feature engineering. You'll see this in action in this section.

What's more, deep-learning models are by nature highly repurposable: you can take, say, an image-classification or speech-to-text model trained on a large-scale dataset and reuse it on a significantly different problem with only minor changes. Specifically, in the case of computer vision, many pretrained models (usually trained on the Image-Net dataset) are now publicly available for download and can be used to bootstrap powerful vision models out of very little data. That's what you'll do in the next section. Let's start by getting your hands on the data.

5.2.2 Downloading the data

The Dogs vs. Cats dataset that you'll use isn't packaged with Keras. It was made available by Kaggle as part of a computer-vision competition in late 2013, back when convnets weren't mainstream. You can download the original dataset from www.kaggle .com/c/dogs-vs-cats/data (you'll need to create a Kaggle account if you don't already have one—don't worry, the process is painless).

The pictures are medium-resolution color JPEGs. Figure 5.8 shows some examples.

Figure 5.8 Samples from the Dogs vs. Cats dataset. Sizes weren't modified: the samples are heterogeneous in size, appearance, and so on.

Unsurprisingly, the dogs-versus-cats Kaggle competition in 2013 was won by entrants who used convnets. The best entries achieved up to 95% accuracy. In this example, you'll get fairly close to this accuracy (in the next section), even though you'll train your models on less than 10% of the data that was available to the competitors.

This dataset contains 25,000 images of dogs and cats (12,500 from each class) and is 543 MB (compressed). After downloading and uncompressing it, you'll create a new dataset containing three subsets: a training set with 1,000 samples of each class, a validation set with 500 samples of each class, and a test set with 500 samples of each class.

Following is the code to do this.

Listing 5.4 Copying images to training, validation, and test directories

Path to the directory where the original dataset was uncompressed

Directory where you'll store your smaller dataset

```
import os, shutil

original_dataset_dir = '/Users/fchollet/Downloads/kaggle_original_data'

base_dir = '/Users/fchollet/Downloads/cats_and_dogs_small'
os.mkdir(base_dir)

train_dir = os.path.join(base_dir, 'train')
os.mkdir(train_dir)
validation_dir = os.path.join(base_dir, 'validation')
os.mkdir(validation_dir)
test_dir = os.path.join(base_dir, 'test')
os.mkdir(test_dir)

train_cats_dir = os.path.join(train_dir, 'cats')
os.mkdir(train_cats_dir)

train_dogs_dir = os.path.join(train_dir, 'dogs')
os.mkdir(train_dogs_dir)

validation_cats_dir = os.path.join(validation_dir, 'cats')
os.mkdir(validation_cats_dir)

validation_dogs_dir = os.path.join(validation_dir, 'dogs')
os.mkdir(validation_dogs_dir)

test_cats_dir = os.path.join(test_dir, 'cats')
os.mkdir(test_cats_dir)

test_dogs_dir = os.path.join(test_dir, 'dogs')
os.mkdir(test_dogs_dir)

fnames = ['cat.{}.jpg'.format(i) for i in range(1000)]
for fname in fnames:
    src = os.path.join(original_dataset_dir, fname)
    dst = os.path.join(train_cats_dir, fname)
    shutil.copyfile(src, dst)

fnames = ['cat.{}.jpg'.format(i) for i in range(1000, 1500)]
for fname in fnames:
    src = os.path.join(original_dataset_dir, fname)
    dst = os.path.join(validation_cats_dir, fname)
    shutil.copyfile(src, dst)

fnames = ['cat.{}.jpg'.format(i) for i in range(1500, 2000)]
for fname in fnames:
    src = os.path.join(original_dataset_dir, fname)
    dst = os.path.join(test_cats_dir, fname)
    shutil.copyfile(src, dst)
```

Directories for the training, validation, and test splits

Directory with training cat pictures

Directory with training dog pictures

Directory with validation cat pictures

Directory with validation dog pictures

Directory with test cat pictures

Directory with test dog pictures

Copies the first 1,000 cat images to train_cats_dir

Copies the next 500 cat images to validation_cats_dir

Copies the next 500 cat images to test_cats_dir

```
fnames = ['dog.{}.jpg'.format(i) for i in range(1000)]
for fname in fnames:
    src = os.path.join(original_dataset_dir, fname)
    dst = os.path.join(train_dogs_dir, fname)
    shutil.copyfile(src, dst)
```

Copies the first 1,000 dog images to train_dogs_dir

```
fnames = ['dog.{}.jpg'.format(i) for i in range(1000, 1500)]
for fname in fnames:
    src = os.path.join(original_dataset_dir, fname)
    dst = os.path.join(validation_dogs_dir, fname)
    shutil.copyfile(src, dst)
```

Copies the next 500 dog images to validation_dogs_dir

```
fnames = ['dog.{}.jpg'.format(i) for i in range(1500, 2000)]
for fname in fnames:
    src = os.path.join(original_dataset_dir, fname)
    dst = os.path.join(test_dogs_dir, fname)
    shutil.copyfile(src, dst)
```

Copies the next 500 dog images to test_dogs_dir

As a sanity check, let's count how many pictures are in each training split (train/validation/test):

```
>>> print('total training cat images:', len(os.listdir(train_cats_dir)))
total training cat images: 1000
>>> print('total training dog images:', len(os.listdir(train_dogs_dir)))
total training dog images: 1000
>>> print('total validation cat images:', len(os.listdir(validation_cats_dir)))
total validation cat images: 500
>>> print('total validation dog images:', len(os.listdir(validation_dogs_dir)))
total validation dog images: 500
>>> print('total test cat images:', len(os.listdir(test_cats_dir)))
total test cat images: 500
>>> print('total test dog images:', len(os.listdir(test_dogs_dir)))
total test dog images: 500
```

So you do indeed have 2,000 training images, 1,000 validation images, and 1,000 test images. Each split contains the same number of samples from each class: this is a balanced binary-classification problem, which means classification accuracy will be an appropriate measure of success.

5.2.3   *Building your network*

You built a small convnet for MNIST in the previous example, so you should be familiar with such convnets. You'll reuse the same general structure: the convnet will be a stack of alternated Conv2D (with relu activation) and MaxPooling2D layers.

But because you're dealing with bigger images and a more complex problem, you'll make your network larger, accordingly: it will have one more Conv2D + MaxPooling2D stage. This serves both to augment the capacity of the network and to further reduce the size of the feature maps so they aren't overly large when you reach the Flatten layer. Here, because you start from inputs of size 150 × 150 (a somewhat arbitrary choice), you end up with feature maps of size 7 × 7 just before the Flatten layer.

NOTE The depth of the feature maps progressively increases in the network (from 32 to 128), whereas the size of the feature maps decreases (from 148 × 148 to 7 × 7). This is a pattern you'll see in almost all convnets.

Because you're attacking a binary-classification problem, you'll end the network with a single unit (a Dense layer of size 1) and a sigmoid activation. This unit will encode the probability that the network is looking at one class or the other.

Listing 5.5   Instantiating a small convnet for dogs vs. cats classification

```
from keras import layers
from keras import models

model = models.Sequential()
model.add(layers.Conv2D(32, (3, 3), activation='relu',
                        input_shape=(150, 150, 3)))
model.add(layers.MaxPooling2D((2, 2)))
model.add(layers.Conv2D(64, (3, 3), activation='relu'))
model.add(layers.MaxPooling2D((2, 2)))
model.add(layers.Conv2D(128, (3, 3), activation='relu'))
model.add(layers.MaxPooling2D((2, 2)))
model.add(layers.Conv2D(128, (3, 3), activation='relu'))
model.add(layers.MaxPooling2D((2, 2)))
model.add(layers.Flatten())
model.add(layers.Dense(512, activation='relu'))
model.add(layers.Dense(1, activation='sigmoid'))
```

Let's look at how the dimensions of the feature maps change with every successive layer:

```
>>> model.summary()
```

Layer (type)	Output Shape	Param #
conv2d_1 (Conv2D)	(None, 148, 148, 32)	896
maxpooling2d_1 (MaxPooling2D)	(None, 74, 74, 32)	0
conv2d_2 (Conv2D)	(None, 72, 72, 64)	18496
maxpooling2d_2 (MaxPooling2D)	(None, 36, 36, 64)	0
conv2d_3 (Conv2D)	(None, 34, 34, 128)	73856
maxpooling2d_3 (MaxPooling2D)	(None, 17, 17, 128)	0
conv2d_4 (Conv2D)	(None, 15, 15, 128)	147584
maxpooling2d_4 (MaxPooling2D)	(None, 7, 7, 128)	0
flatten_1 (Flatten)	(None, 6272)	0
dense_1 (Dense)	(None, 512)	3211776

```
dense_2 (Dense)                   (None, 1)                513
================================================================
Total params: 3,453,121
Trainable params: 3,453,121
Non-trainable params: 0
```

For the compilation step, you'll go with the RMSprop optimizer, as usual. Because you ended the network with a single sigmoid unit, you'll use binary crossentropy as the loss (as a reminder, check out table 4.1 for a cheatsheet on what loss function to use in various situations).

Listing 5.6   Configuring the model for training

```
from keras import optimizers

model.compile(loss='binary_crossentropy',
              optimizer=optimizers.RMSprop(lr=1e-4),
              metrics=['acc'])
```

5.2.4   *Data preprocessing*

As you know by now, data should be formatted into appropriately preprocessed floating-point tensors before being fed into the network. Currently, the data sits on a drive as JPEG files, so the steps for getting it into the network are roughly as follows:

1 Read the picture files.
2 Decode the JPEG content to RGB grids of pixels.
3 Convert these into floating-point tensors.
4 Rescale the pixel values (between 0 and 255) to the [0, 1] interval (as you know, neural networks prefer to deal with small input values).

It may seem a bit daunting, but fortunately Keras has utilities to take care of these steps automatically. Keras has a module with image-processing helper tools, located at keras.preprocessing.image. In particular, it contains the class ImageDataGenerator, which lets you quickly set up Python generators that can automatically turn image files on disk into batches of preprocessed tensors. This is what you'll use here.

Listing 5.7   Using ImageDataGenerator to read images from directories

```
from keras.preprocessing.image import ImageDataGenerator

train_datagen = ImageDataGenerator(rescale=1./255)          Rescales all images by 1/255
test_datagen = ImageDataGenerator(rescale=1./255)

train_generator = train_datagen.flow_from_directory(
        train_dir,
        target_size=(150, 150)      ◁── Resizes all images to 150 × 150
        batch_size=20,
        class_mode='binary')        ◁─────────────────
validation_generator = test_datagen.flow_from_directory(
        validation_dir,
```

Target directory

Because you use binary_crossentropy loss, you need binary labels.

```
        target_size=(150, 150),
        batch_size=20,
        class_mode='binary')
```

Understanding Python generators

A *Python generator* is an object that acts as an iterator: it's an object you can use with the `for ... in` operator. Generators are built using the `yield` operator.

Here is an example of a generator that yields integers:

```
def generator():
    i = 0
    while True:
        i += 1
        yield i

for item in generator():
    print(item)
    if item > 4:
        break
```

It prints this:

```
1
2
3
4
5
```

Let's look at the output of one of these generators: it yields batches of 150 × 150 RGB images (shape `(20, 150, 150, 3)`) and binary labels (shape `(20,)`). There are 20 samples in each batch (the batch size). Note that the generator yields these batches indefinitely: it loops endlessly over the images in the target folder. For this reason, you need to `break` the iteration loop at some point:

```
>>> for data_batch, labels_batch in train_generator:
>>>     print('data batch shape:', data_batch.shape)
>>>     print('labels batch shape:', labels_batch.shape)
>>>     break
data batch shape: (20, 150, 150, 3)
labels batch shape: (20,)
```

Let's fit the model to the data using the generator. You do so using the `fit_generator` method, the equivalent of `fit` for data generators like this one. It expects as its first argument a Python generator that will yield batches of inputs and targets indefinitely, like this one does. Because the data is being generated endlessly, the Keras model needs to know how many samples to draw from the generator before declaring an epoch over. This is the role of the `steps_per_epoch` argument: after having drawn `steps_per_epoch` batches from the generator—that is, after having run for steps_per_epoch gradient descent steps—the fitting process will go to the next epoch. In this case, batches are 20 samples, so it will take 100 batches until you see your target of 2,000 samples.

When using fit_generator, you can pass a validation_data argument, much as with the fit method. It's important to note that this argument is allowed to be a data generator, but it could also be a tuple of Numpy arrays. If you pass a generator as validation_data, then this generator is expected to yield batches of validation data endlessly; thus you should also specify the validation_steps argument, which tells the process how many batches to draw from the validation generator for evaluation.

Listing 5.8 Fitting the model using a batch generator

```
history = model.fit_generator(
    train_generator,
    steps_per_epoch=100,
    epochs=30,
    validation_data=validation_generator,
    validation_steps=50)
```

It's good practice to always save your models after training.

Listing 5.9 Saving the model

```
model.save('cats_and_dogs_small_1.h5')
```

Let's plot the loss and accuracy of the model over the training and validation data during training (see figures 5.9 and 5.10).

Listing 5.10 Displaying curves of loss and accuracy during training

```
import matplotlib.pyplot as plt

acc = history.history['acc']
val_acc = history.history['val_acc']
loss = history.history['loss']
val_loss = history.history['val_loss']

epochs = range(1, len(acc) + 1)

plt.plot(epochs, acc, 'bo', label='Training acc')
plt.plot(epochs, val_acc, 'b', label='Validation acc')
plt.title('Training and validation accuracy')
plt.legend()

plt.figure()

plt.plot(epochs, loss, 'bo', label='Training loss')
plt.plot(epochs, val_loss, 'b', label='Validation loss')
plt.title('Training and validation loss')
plt.legend()

plt.show()
```

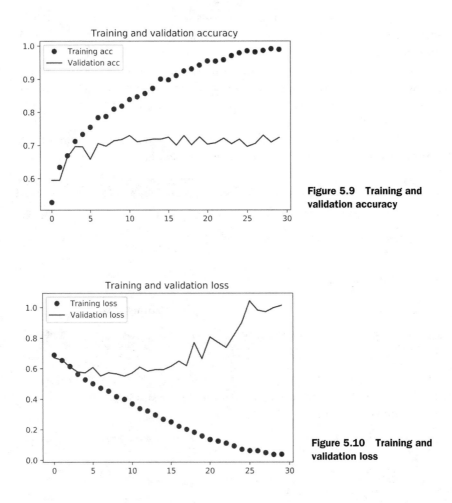

Figure 5.9   Training and validation accuracy

Figure 5.10   Training and validation loss

These plots are characteristic of overfitting. The training accuracy increases linearly over time, until it reaches nearly 100%, whereas the validation accuracy stalls at 70–72%. The validation loss reaches its minimum after only five epochs and then stalls, whereas the training loss keeps decreasing linearly until it reaches nearly 0.

Because you have relatively few training samples (2,000), overfitting will be your number-one concern. You already know about a number of techniques that can help mitigate overfitting, such as dropout and weight decay (L2 regularization). We're now going to work with a new one, specific to computer vision and used almost universally when processing images with deep-learning models: *data augmentation*.

5.2.5   *Using data augmentation*

Overfitting is caused by having too few samples to learn from, rendering you unable to train a model that can generalize to new data. Given infinite data, your model would be exposed to every possible aspect of the data distribution at hand: you would never overfit. Data augmentation takes the approach of generating more training data from existing training samples, by *augmenting* the samples via a number of random transformations that yield believable-looking images. The goal is that at training time, your model will never see the exact same picture twice. This helps expose the model to more aspects of the data and generalize better.

In Keras, this can be done by configuring a number of random transformations to be performed on the images read by the `ImageDataGenerator` instance. Let's get started with an example.

Listing 5.11 Setting up a data augmentation configuration via `ImageDataGenerator`

```
datagen = ImageDataGenerator(
      rotation_range=40,
      width_shift_range=0.2,
      height_shift_range=0.2,
      shear_range=0.2,
      zoom_range=0.2,
      horizontal_flip=True,
      fill_mode='nearest')
```

These are just a few of the options available (for more, see the Keras documentation). Let's quickly go over this code:

- `rotation_range` is a value in degrees (0–180), a range within which to randomly rotate pictures.
- `width_shift` and `height_shift` are ranges (as a fraction of total width or height) within which to randomly translate pictures vertically or horizontally.
- `shear_range` is for randomly applying shearing transformations.
- `zoom_range` is for randomly zooming inside pictures.
- `horizontal_flip` is for randomly flipping half the images horizontally—relevant when there are no assumptions of horizontal asymmetry (for example, real-world pictures).
- `fill_mode` is the strategy used for filling in newly created pixels, which can appear after a rotation or a width/height shift.

Let's look at the augmented images (see figure 5.11).

Listing 5.12 Displaying some randomly augmented training images

```
from keras.preprocessing import image          ⬅— Module with image-
                                                    preprocessing utilities
fnames = [os.path.join(train_cats_dir, fname) for
      fname in os.listdir(train_cats_dir)]

img_path = fnames[3]          ⬅—— Chooses one image to augment

img = image.load_img(img_path, target_size=(150, 150))    ⬅— Reads the image
                                                              and resizes it
```

```
x = image.img_to_array(img)        ◁─── Converts it to a Numpy array with shape (150, 150, 3)

x = x.reshape((1,) + x.shape)         ◁─── Reshapes it to (1, 150, 150, 3)

i = 0
for batch in datagen.flow(x, batch_size=1):
    plt.figure(i)
    imgplot = plt.imshow(image.array_to_img(batch[0]))
    i += 1
    if i % 4 == 0:
        break

plt.show()
```

Generates batches of
randomly transformed
images. Loops indefinitely,
so you need to break the
loop at some point!

Figure 5.11   Generation of cat pictures via random data augmentation

If you train a new network using this data-augmentation configuration, the network will never see the same input twice. But the inputs it sees are still heavily intercorrelated, because they come from a small number of original images—you can't produce new information, you can only remix existing information. As such, this may not be enough to completely get rid of overfitting. To further fight overfitting, you'll also add a Dropout layer to your model, right before the densely connected classifier.

Listing 5.13 Defining a new convnet that includes dropout

```
model = models.Sequential()
model.add(layers.Conv2D(32, (3, 3), activation='relu',
                        input_shape=(150, 150, 3)))
model.add(layers.MaxPooling2D((2, 2)))
model.add(layers.Conv2D(64, (3, 3), activation='relu'))
model.add(layers.MaxPooling2D((2, 2)))
model.add(layers.Conv2D(128, (3, 3), activation='relu'))
model.add(layers.MaxPooling2D((2, 2)))
model.add(layers.Conv2D(128, (3, 3), activation='relu'))
model.add(layers.MaxPooling2D((2, 2)))
model.add(layers.Flatten())
model.add(layers.Dropout(0.5))
model.add(layers.Dense(512, activation='relu'))
model.add(layers.Dense(1, activation='sigmoid'))

model.compile(loss='binary_crossentropy',
              optimizer=optimizers.RMSprop(lr=1e-4),
              metrics=['acc'])
```

Let's train the network using data augmentation and dropout.

Listing 5.14 Training the convnet using data-augmentation generators

```
train_datagen = ImageDataGenerator(
    rescale=1./255,
    rotation_range=40,
    width_shift_range=0.2,
    height_shift_range=0.2,
    shear_range=0.2,
    zoom_range=0.2,
    horizontal_flip=True,)

test_datagen = ImageDataGenerator(rescale=1./255)     ◁── Note that the
                                                          validation data
                                                          shouldn't be
                                                          augmented!

train_generator = train_datagen.flow_from_directory(
        train_dir,
        target_size=(150, 150),    ◁── Resizes all images to 150 × 150
        batch_size=32,
        class_mode='binary')       ◁─────────────── Because you use
                                                    binary_crossentropy
validation_generator = test_datagen.flow_from_directory(    loss, you need binary
        validation_dir,                                     labels.
        target_size=(150, 150),
        batch_size=32,
        class_mode='binary')

history = model.fit_generator(
        train_generator,
        steps_per_epoch=100,
        epochs=100,
        validation_data=validation_generator,
        validation_steps=50)
```

Target directory (annotation pointing to `train_dir`)

Let's save the model—you'll use it in section 5.4.

Listing 5.15   Saving the model

```
model.save('cats_and_dogs_small_2.h5')
```

And let's plot the results again: see figures 5.12 and 5.13. Thanks to data augmentation and dropout, you're no longer overfitting: the training curves are closely tracking the validation curves. You now reach an accuracy of 82%, a 15% relative improvement over the non-regularized model.

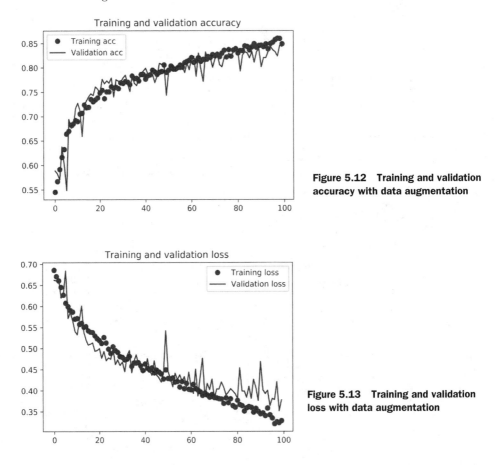

Figure 5.12   **Training and validation accuracy with data augmentation**

Figure 5.13   **Training and validation loss with data augmentation**

By using regularization techniques even further, and by tuning the network's parameters (such as the number of filters per convolution layer, or the number of layers in the network), you may be able to get an even better accuracy, likely up to 86% or 87%. But it would prove difficult to go any higher just by training your own convnet from scratch, because you have so little data to work with. As a next step to improve your accuracy on this problem, you'll have to use a pretrained model, which is the focus of the next two sections.

5.3 *Using a pretrained convnet*

A common and highly effective approach to deep learning on small image datasets is to use a pretrained network. A *pretrained network* is a saved network that was previously trained on a large dataset, typically on a large-scale image-classification task. If this original dataset is large enough and general enough, then the spatial hierarchy of features learned by the pretrained network can effectively act as a generic model of the visual world, and hence its features can prove useful for many different computer-vision problems, even though these new problems may involve completely different classes than those of the original task. For instance, you might train a network on ImageNet (where classes are mostly animals and everyday objects) and then repurpose this trained network for something as remote as identifying furniture items in images. Such portability of learned features across different problems is a key advantage of deep learning compared to many older, shallow-learning approaches, and it makes deep learning very effective for small-data problems.

In this case, let's consider a large convnet trained on the ImageNet dataset (1.4 million labeled images and 1,000 different classes). ImageNet contains many animal classes, including different species of cats and dogs, and you can thus expect to perform well on the dogs-versus-cats classification problem.

You'll use the VGG16 architecture, developed by Karen Simonyan and Andrew Zisserman in 2014; it's a simple and widely used convnet architecture for ImageNet.[1] Although it's an older model, far from the current state of the art and somewhat heavier than many other recent models, I chose it because its architecture is similar to what you're already familiar with and is easy to understand without introducing any new concepts. This may be your first encounter with one of these cutesy model names—VGG, ResNet, Inception, Inception-ResNet, Xception, and so on; you'll get used to them, because they will come up frequently if you keep doing deep learning for computer vision.

There are two ways to use a pretrained network: *feature extraction* and *fine-tuning*. We'll cover both of them. Let's start with feature extraction.

5.3.1 *Feature extraction*

Feature extraction consists of using the representations learned by a previous network to extract interesting features from new samples. These features are then run through a new classifier, which is trained from scratch.

As you saw previously, convnets used for image classification comprise two parts: they start with a series of pooling and convolution layers, and they end with a densely connected classifier. The first part is called the *convolutional base* of the model. In the case of convnets, feature extraction consists of taking the convolutional base of a

---

[1] Karen Simonyan and Andrew Zisserman, "Very Deep Convolutional Networks for Large-Scale Image Recognition," arXiv (2014), https://arxiv.org/abs/1409.1556.

previously trained network, running the new data through it, and training a new classifier on top of the output (see figure 5.14).

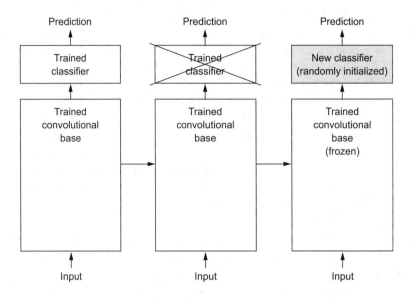

Figure 5.14   Swapping classifiers while keeping the same convolutional base

Why only reuse the convolutional base? Could you reuse the densely connected classifier as well? In general, doing so should be avoided. The reason is that the representations learned by the convolutional base are likely to be more generic and therefore more reusable: the feature maps of a convnet are presence maps of generic concepts over a picture, which is likely to be useful regardless of the computer-vision problem at hand. But the representations learned by the classifier will necessarily be specific to the set of classes on which the model was trained—they will only contain information about the presence probability of this or that class in the entire picture. Additionally, representations found in densely connected layers no longer contain any information about *where* objects are located in the input image: these layers get rid of the notion of space, whereas the object location is still described by convolutional feature maps. For problems where object location matters, densely connected features are largely useless.

Note that the level of generality (and therefore reusability) of the representations extracted by specific convolution layers depends on the depth of the layer in the model. Layers that come earlier in the model extract local, highly generic feature maps (such as visual edges, colors, and textures), whereas layers that are higher up extract more-abstract concepts (such as "cat ear" or "dog eye"). So if your new dataset differs a lot from the dataset on which the original model was trained, you may be better off using only the first few layers of the model to do feature extraction, rather than using the entire convolutional base.

In this case, because the ImageNet class set contains multiple dog and cat classes, it's likely to be beneficial to reuse the information contained in the densely connected layers of the original model. But we'll choose not to, in order to cover the more general case where the class set of the new problem doesn't overlap the class set of the original model. Let's put this in practice by using the convolutional base of the VGG16 network, trained on ImageNet, to extract interesting features from cat and dog images, and then train a dogs-versus-cats classifier on top of these features.

The VGG16 model, among others, comes prepackaged with Keras. You can import it from the `keras.applications` module. Here's the list of image-classification models (all pretrained on the ImageNet dataset) that are available as part of `keras .applications`:

- Xception
- Inception V3
- ResNet50
- VGG16
- VGG19
- MobileNet

Let's instantiate the VGG16 model.

Listing 5.16 Instantiating the VGG16 convolutional base

```
from keras.applications import VGG16

conv_base = VGG16(weights='imagenet',
                  include_top=False,
                  input_shape=(150, 150, 3))
```

You pass three arguments to the constructor:

- `weights` specifies the weight checkpoint from which to initialize the model.
- `include_top` refers to including (or not) the densely connected classifier on top of the network. By default, this densely connected classifier corresponds to the 1,000 classes from ImageNet. Because you intend to use your own densely connected classifier (with only two classes: `cat` and `dog`), you don't need to include it.
- `input_shape` is the shape of the image tensors that you'll feed to the network. This argument is purely optional: if you don't pass it, the network will be able to process inputs of any size.

Here's the detail of the architecture of the VGG16 convolutional base. It's similar to the simple convnets you're already familiar with:

```
>>> conv_base.summary()

Layer (type)                 Output Shape              Param #
=================================================================
input_1 (InputLayer)         (None, 150, 150, 3)       0
```

block1_conv1 (Convolution2D)	(None, 150, 150, 64)	1792
block1_conv2 (Convolution2D)	(None, 150, 150, 64)	36928
block1_pool (MaxPooling2D)	(None, 75, 75, 64)	0
block2_conv1 (Convolution2D)	(None, 75, 75, 128)	73856
block2_conv2 (Convolution2D)	(None, 75, 75, 128)	147584
block2_pool (MaxPooling2D)	(None, 37, 37, 128)	0
block3_conv1 (Convolution2D)	(None, 37, 37, 256)	295168
block3_conv2 (Convolution2D)	(None, 37, 37, 256)	590080
block3_conv3 (Convolution2D)	(None, 37, 37, 256)	590080
block3_pool (MaxPooling2D)	(None, 18, 18, 256)	0
block4_conv1 (Convolution2D)	(None, 18, 18, 512)	1180160
block4_conv2 (Convolution2D)	(None, 18, 18, 512)	2359808
block4_conv3 (Convolution2D)	(None, 18, 18, 512)	2359808
block4_pool (MaxPooling2D)	(None, 9, 9, 512)	0
block5_conv1 (Convolution2D)	(None, 9, 9, 512)	2359808
block5_conv2 (Convolution2D)	(None, 9, 9, 512)	2359808
block5_conv3 (Convolution2D)	(None, 9, 9, 512)	2359808
block5_pool (MaxPooling2D)	(None, 4, 4, 512)	0

```
===============================================================
Total params: 14,714,688
Trainable params: 14,714,688
Non-trainable params: 0
```

The final feature map has shape (4, 4, 512). That's the feature on top of which you'll stick a densely connected classifier.

At this point, there are two ways you could proceed:

- Running the convolutional base over your dataset, recording its output to a Numpy array on disk, and then using this data as input to a standalone, densely connected classifier similar to those you saw in part 1 of this book. This solution is fast and cheap to run, because it only requires running the convolutional base once for every input image, and the convolutional base is by far the most expensive part of the pipeline. But for the same reason, this technique won't allow you to use data augmentation.

- Extending the model you have (conv_base) by adding Dense layers on top, and running the whole thing end to end on the input data. This will allow you to use data augmentation, because every input image goes through the convolutional base every time it's seen by the model. But for the same reason, this technique is far more expensive than the first.

We'll cover both techniques. Let's walk through the code required to set up the first one: recording the output of conv_base on your data and using these outputs as inputs to a new model.

FAST FEATURE EXTRACTION WITHOUT DATA AUGMENTATION

You'll start by running instances of the previously introduced ImageDataGenerator to extract images as Numpy arrays as well as their labels. You'll extract features from these images by calling the predict method of the conv_base model.

> **Listing 5.17 Extracting features using the pretrained convolutional base**

```
import os
import numpy as np
from keras.preprocessing.image import ImageDataGenerator

base_dir = '/Users/fchollet/Downloads/cats_and_dogs_small'
train_dir = os.path.join(base_dir, 'train')
validation_dir = os.path.join(base_dir, 'validation')
test_dir = os.path.join(base_dir, 'test')

datagen = ImageDataGenerator(rescale=1./255)
batch_size = 20

def extract_features(directory, sample_count):
    features = np.zeros(shape=(sample_count, 4, 4, 512))
    labels = np.zeros(shape=(sample_count))
    generator = datagen.flow_from_directory(          Note that because generators
        directory,                                    yield data indefinitely in a loop,
        target_size=(150, 150),                       you must break after every
        batch_size=batch_size,                        image has been seen once.
        class_mode='binary')
    i = 0
    for inputs_batch, labels_batch in generator:
        features_batch = conv_base.predict(inputs_batch)
        features[i * batch_size : (i + 1) * batch_size] = features_batch
        labels[i * batch_size : (i + 1) * batch_size] = labels_batch
        i += 1
        if i * batch_size >= sample_count:
            break        ◁
    return features, labels

train_features, train_labels = extract_features(train_dir, 2000)
validation_features, validation_labels = extract_features(validation_dir, 1000)
test_features, test_labels = extract_features(test_dir, 1000)
```

The extracted features are currently of shape (samples, 4, 4, 512). You'll feed them to a densely connected classifier, so first you must flatten them to (samples, 8192):

```
train_features = np.reshape(train_features, (2000, 4 * 4 * 512))
validation_features = np.reshape(validation_features, (1000, 4 * 4 * 512))
test_features = np.reshape(test_features, (1000, 4 * 4 * 512))
```

At this point, you can define your densely connected classifier (note the use of dropout for regularization) and train it on the data and labels that you just recorded.

Listing 5.18   Defining and training the densely connected classifier

```
from keras import models
from keras import layers
from keras import optimizers

model = models.Sequential()
model.add(layers.Dense(256, activation='relu', input_dim=4 * 4 * 512))
model.add(layers.Dropout(0.5))
model.add(layers.Dense(1, activation='sigmoid'))

model.compile(optimizer=optimizers.RMSprop(lr=2e-5),
              loss='binary_crossentropy',
              metrics=['acc'])

history = model.fit(train_features, train_labels,
                    epochs=30,
                    batch_size=20,
                    validation_data=(validation_features, validation_labels))
```

Training is very fast, because you only have to deal with two Dense layers—an epoch takes less than one second even on CPU.

Let's look at the loss and accuracy curves during training (see figures 5.15 and 5.16).

Listing 5.19   Plotting the results

```
import matplotlib.pyplot as plt

acc = history.history['acc']
val_acc = history.history['val_acc']
loss = history.history['loss']
val_loss = history.history['val_loss']

epochs = range(1, len(acc) + 1)

plt.plot(epochs, acc, 'bo', label='Training acc')
plt.plot(epochs, val_acc, 'b', label='Validation acc')
plt.title('Training and validation accuracy')
plt.legend()

plt.figure()

plt.plot(epochs, loss, 'bo', label='Training loss')
plt.plot(epochs, val_loss, 'b', label='Validation loss')
plt.title('Training and validation loss')
plt.legend()

plt.show()
```

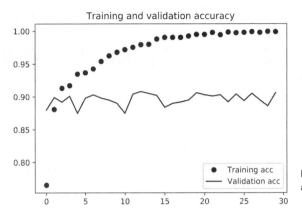

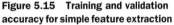

Figure 5.15   **Training and validation accuracy for simple feature extraction**

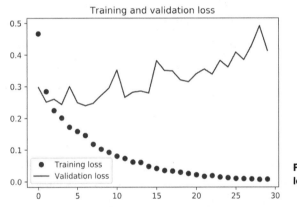

Figure 5.16   **Training and validation loss for simple feature extraction**

You reach a validation accuracy of about 90%—much better than you achieved in the previous section with the small model trained from scratch. But the plots also indicate that you're overfitting almost from the start—despite using dropout with a fairly large rate. That's because this technique doesn't use data augmentation, which is essential for preventing overfitting with small image datasets.

FEATURE EXTRACTION WITH DATA AUGMENTATION

Now, let's review the second technique I mentioned for doing feature extraction, which is much slower and more expensive, but which allows you to use data augmentation during training: extending the conv_base model and running it end to end on the inputs.

> **NOTE**   This technique is so expensive that you should only attempt it if you have access to a GPU—it's absolutely intractable on CPU. If you can't run your code on GPU, then the previous technique is the way to go.

Because models behave just like layers, you can add a model (like conv_base) to a Sequential model just like you would add a layer.

Listing 5.20   Adding a densely connected classifier on top of the convolutional base

```
from keras import models
from keras import layers

model = models.Sequential()
model.add(conv_base)
model.add(layers.Flatten())
model.add(layers.Dense(256, activation='relu'))
model.add(layers.Dense(1, activation='sigmoid'))
```

This is what the model looks like now:

```
>>> model.summary()

Layer (type)                     Output Shape           Param #
=================================================================
vgg16 (Model)                    (None, 4, 4, 512)      14714688
_____
flatten_1 (Flatten)              (None, 8192)           0
_____
dense_1 (Dense)                  (None, 256)            2097408
_____
dense_2 (Dense)                  (None, 1)              257
=================================================================
Total params: 16,812,353
Trainable params: 16,812,353
Non-trainable params: 0
```

As you can see, the convolutional base of VGG16 has 14,714,688 parameters, which is very large. The classifier you're adding on top has 2 million parameters.

Before you compile and train the model, it's very important to freeze the convolutional base. *Freezing* a layer or set of layers means preventing their weights from being updated during training. If you don't do this, then the representations that were previously learned by the convolutional base will be modified during training. Because the Dense layers on top are randomly initialized, very large weight updates would be propagated through the network, effectively destroying the representations previously learned.

In Keras, you freeze a network by setting its trainable attribute to False:

```
>>> print('This is the number of trainable weights '
          'before freezing the conv base:', len(model.trainable_weights))
This is the number of trainable weights before freezing the conv base: 30
>>> conv_base.trainable = False
>>> print('This is the number of trainable weights '
          'after freezing the conv base:', len(model.trainable_weights))
This is the number of trainable weights after freezing the conv base: 4
```

With this setup, only the weights from the two Dense layers that you added will be trained. That's a total of four weight tensors: two per layer (the main weight matrix and the bias vector). Note that in order for these changes to take effect, you must first compile the model. If you ever modify weight trainability after compilation, you should then recompile the model, or these changes will be ignored.

Now you can start training your model, with the same data-augmentation configuration that you used in the previous example.

> **Listing 5.21 Training the model end to end with a frozen convolutional base**

```
from keras.preprocessing.image import ImageDataGenerator
from keras import optimizers

train_datagen = ImageDataGenerator(
        rescale=1./255,
        rotation_range=40,
        width_shift_range=0.2,
        height_shift_range=0.2,
        shear_range=0.2,
        zoom_range=0.2,
        horizontal_flip=True,
        fill_mode='nearest')

test_datagen = ImageDataGenerator(rescale=1./255)

train_generator = train_datagen.flow_from_directory(
        train_dir,
        target_size=(150, 150),
        batch_size=20,
        class_mode='binary')

validation_generator = test_datagen.flow_from_directory(
        validation_dir,
        target_size=(150, 150),
        batch_size=20,
        class_mode='binary')

model.compile(loss='binary_crossentropy',
              optimizer=optimizers.RMSprop(lr=2e-5),
              metrics=['acc'])

history = model.fit_generator(
        train_generator,
        steps_per_epoch=100,
        epochs=30,
        validation_data=validation_generator,
        validation_steps=50)
```

Note that the validation data shouldn't be augmented!

Target directory

Resizes all images to 150 × 150

Because you use binary_crossentropy loss, you need binary labels.

Let's plot the results again (see figures 5.17 and 5.18). As you can see, you reach a validation accuracy of about 96%. This is much better than you achieved with the small convnet trained from scratch.

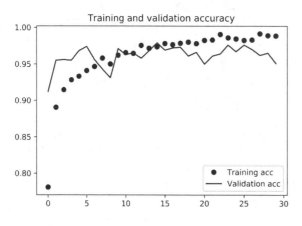

Figure 5.17   Training and validation accuracy for feature extraction with data augmentation

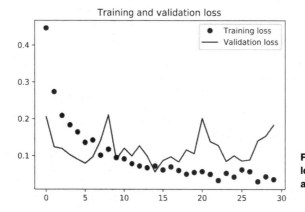

Figure 5.18   Training and validation loss for feature extraction with data augmentation

5.3.2   *Fine-tuning*

Another widely used technique for model reuse, complementary to feature extraction, is *fine-tuning* (see figure 5.19). Fine-tuning consists of unfreezing a few of the top layers of a frozen model base used for feature extraction, and jointly training both the newly added part of the model (in this case, the fully connected classifier) and these top layers. This is called *fine-tuning* because it slightly adjusts the more abstract representations of the model being reused, in order to make them more relevant for the problem at hand.

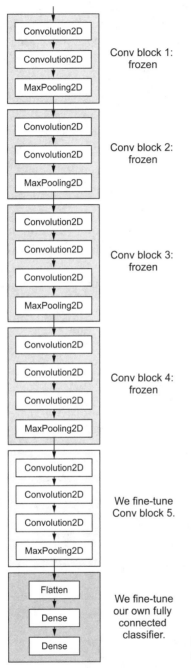

Conv block 1: frozen

Conv block 2: frozen

Conv block 3: frozen

Conv block 4: frozen

We fine-tune Conv block 5.

We fine-tune our own fully connected classifier.

Figure 5.19 Fine-tuning the last convolutional block of the VGG16 network

I stated earlier that it's necessary to freeze the convolution base of VGG16 in order to be able to train a randomly initialized classifier on top. For the same reason, it's only possible to fine-tune the top layers of the convolutional base once the classifier on top has already been trained. If the classifier isn't already trained, then the error signal propagating through the network during training will be too large, and the representations previously learned by the layers being fine-tuned will be destroyed. Thus the steps for fine-tuning a network are as follow:

1. Add your custom network on top of an already-trained base network.
2. Freeze the base network.
3. Train the part you added.
4. Unfreeze some layers in the base network.
5. Jointly train both these layers and the part you added.

You already completed the first three steps when doing feature extraction. Let's proceed with step 4: you'll unfreeze your conv_base and then freeze individual layers inside it.

As a reminder, this is what your convolutional base looks like:

```
>>> conv_base.summary()
```

Layer (type)	Output Shape	Param #
input_1 (InputLayer)	(None, 150, 150, 3)	0
block1_conv1 (Convolution2D)	(None, 150, 150, 64)	1792
block1_conv2 (Convolution2D)	(None, 150, 150, 64)	36928
block1_pool (MaxPooling2D)	(None, 75, 75, 64)	0
block2_conv1 (Convolution2D)	(None, 75, 75, 128)	73856
block2_conv2 (Convolution2D)	(None, 75, 75, 128)	147584
block2_pool (MaxPooling2D)	(None, 37, 37, 128)	0
block3_conv1 (Convolution2D)	(None, 37, 37, 256)	295168
block3_conv2 (Convolution2D)	(None, 37, 37, 256)	590080
block3_conv3 (Convolution2D)	(None, 37, 37, 256)	590080
block3_pool (MaxPooling2D)	(None, 18, 18, 256)	0
block4_conv1 (Convolution2D)	(None, 18, 18, 512)	1180160
block4_conv2 (Convolution2D)	(None, 18, 18, 512)	2359808
block4_conv3 (Convolution2D)	(None, 18, 18, 512)	2359808
block4_pool (MaxPooling2D)	(None, 9, 9, 512)	0

block5_conv1 (Convolution2D)	(None, 9, 9, 512)	2359808
block5_conv2 (Convolution2D)	(None, 9, 9, 512)	2359808
block5_conv3 (Convolution2D)	(None, 9, 9, 512)	2359808
block5_pool (MaxPooling2D)	(None, 4, 4, 512)	0

```
=================================================================
Total params: 14714688
```

You'll fine-tune the last three convolutional layers, which means all layers up to `block4_pool` should be frozen, and the layers `block5_conv1`, `block5_conv2`, and `block5_conv3` should be trainable.

Why not fine-tune more layers? Why not fine-tune the entire convolutional base? You could. But you need to consider the following:

- Earlier layers in the convolutional base encode more-generic, reusable features, whereas layers higher up encode more-specialized features. It's more useful to fine-tune the more specialized features, because these are the ones that need to be repurposed on your new problem. There would be fast-decreasing returns in fine-tuning lower layers.
- The more parameters you're training, the more you're at risk of overfitting. The convolutional base has 15 million parameters, so it would be risky to attempt to train it on your small dataset.

Thus, in this situation, it's a good strategy to fine-tune only the top two or three layers in the convolutional base. Let's set this up, starting from where you left off in the previous example.

Listing 5.22 Freezing all layers up to a specific one

```
conv_base.trainable = True

set_trainable = False
for layer in conv_base.layers:
    if layer.name == 'block5_conv1':
        set_trainable = True
    if set_trainable:
        layer.trainable = True
    else:
        layer.trainable = False
```

Now you can begin fine-tuning the network. You'll do this with the RMSProp optimizer, using a very low learning rate. The reason for using a low learning rate is that you want to limit the magnitude of the modifications you make to the representations of the three layers you're fine-tuning. Updates that are too large may harm these representations.

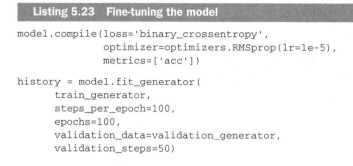

Listing 5.23   Fine-tuning the model

```
model.compile(loss='binary_crossentropy',
              optimizer=optimizers.RMSprop(lr=1e-5),
              metrics=['acc'])

history = model.fit_generator(
    train_generator,
    steps_per_epoch=100,
    epochs=100,
    validation_data=validation_generator,
    validation_steps=50)
```

Let's plot the results using the same plotting code as before (see figures 5.20 and 5.21).

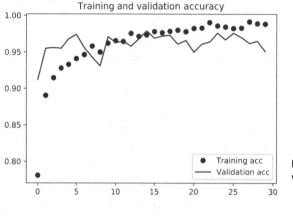

Figure 5.20   Training and validation accuracy for fine-tuning

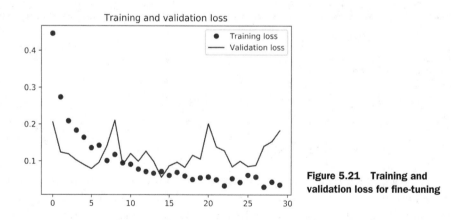

Figure 5.21   Training and validation loss for fine-tuning

These curves look noisy. To make them more readable, you can smooth them by replacing every loss and accuracy with exponential moving averages of these quantities. Here's a trivial utility function to do this (see figures 5.22 and 5.23).

Listing 5.24 Smoothing the plots

```
def smooth_curve(points, factor=0.8):
  smoothed_points = []
  for point in points:
    if smoothed_points:
      previous = smoothed_points[-1]
      smoothed_points.append(previous * factor + point * (1 - factor))
    else:
      smoothed_points.append(point)
  return smoothed_points

plt.plot(epochs,
         smooth_curve(acc), 'bo', label='Smoothed training acc')
plt.plot(epochs,
         smooth_curve(val_acc), 'b', label='Smoothed validation acc')
plt.title('Training and validation accuracy')
plt.legend()

plt.figure()

plt.plot(epochs,
         smooth_curve(loss), 'bo', label='Smoothed training loss')
plt.plot(epochs,
         smooth_curve(val_loss), 'b', label='Smoothed validation loss')
plt.title('Training and validation loss')
plt.legend()

plt.show()
```

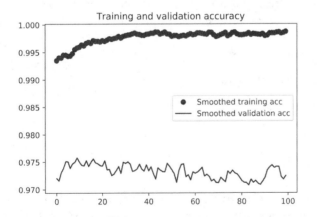

Figure 5.22 Smoothed curves for training and validation accuracy for fine-tuning

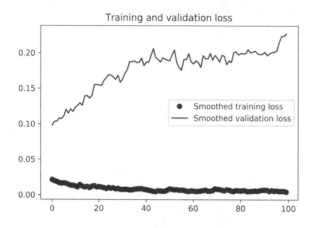

Figure 5.23   Smoothed curves for training and validation loss for fine-tuning

The validation accuracy curve look much cleaner. You're seeing a nice 1% absolute improvement in accuracy, from about 96% to above 97%.

Note that the loss curve doesn't show any real improvement (in fact, it's deteriorating). You may wonder, how could accuracy stay stable or improve if the loss isn't decreasing? The answer is simple: what you display is an average of pointwise loss values; but what matters for accuracy is the distribution of the loss values, not their average, because accuracy is the result of a binary thresholding of the class probability predicted by the model. The model may still be improving even if this isn't reflected in the average loss.

You can now finally evaluate this model on the test data:

```
test_generator = test_datagen.flow_from_directory(
        test_dir,
        target_size=(150, 150),
        batch_size=20,
        class_mode='binary')

test_loss, test_acc = model.evaluate_generator(test_generator, steps=50)
print('test acc:', test_acc)
```

Here you get a test accuracy of 97%. In the original Kaggle competition around this dataset, this would have been one of the top results. But using modern deep-learning techniques, you managed to reach this result using only a small fraction of the training data available (about 10%). There is a huge difference between being able to train on 20,000 samples compared to 2,000 samples!

5.3.3 *Wrapping up*

Here's what you should take away from the exercises in the past two sections:

- Convnets are the best type of machine-learning models for computer-vision tasks. It's possible to train one from scratch even on a very small dataset, with decent results.
- On a small dataset, overfitting will be the main issue. Data augmentation is a powerful way to fight overfitting when you're working with image data.
- It's easy to reuse an existing convnet on a new dataset via feature extraction. This is a valuable technique for working with small image datasets.
- As a complement to feature extraction, you can use fine-tuning, which adapts to a new problem some of the representations previously learned by an existing model. This pushes performance a bit further.

Now you have a solid set of tools for dealing with image-classification problems—in particular with small datasets.

5.4   *Visualizing what convnets learn*

It's often said that deep-learning models are "black boxes": learning representations that are difficult to extract and present in a human-readable form. Although this is partially true for certain types of deep-learning models, it's definitely not true for convnets. The representations learned by convnets are highly amenable to visualization, in large part because they're *representations of visual concepts*. Since 2013, a wide array of techniques have been developed for visualizing and interpreting these representations. We won't survey all of them, but we'll cover three of the most accessible and useful ones:

- *Visualizing intermediate convnet outputs (intermediate activations)*—Useful for understanding how successive convnet layers transform their input, and for getting a first idea of the meaning of individual convnet filters.
- *Visualizing convnets filters*—Useful for understanding precisely what visual pattern or concept each filter in a convnet is receptive to.
- *Visualizing heatmaps of class activation in an image*—Useful for understanding which parts of an image were identified as belonging to a given class, thus allowing you to localize objects in images.

For the first method—activation visualization—you'll use the small convnet that you trained from scratch on the dogs-versus-cats classification problem in section 5.2. For the next two methods, you'll use the VGG16 model introduced in section 5.3.

5.4.1   *Visualizing intermediate activations*

Visualizing intermediate activations consists of displaying the feature maps that are output by various convolution and pooling layers in a network, given a certain input (the output of a layer is often called its *activation*, the output of the activation function). This gives a view into how an input is decomposed into the different filters learned by the network. You want to visualize feature maps with three dimensions: width, height, and depth (channels). Each channel encodes relatively independent features, so the proper way to visualize these feature maps is by independently plotting the contents of every channel as a 2D image. Let's start by loading the model that you saved in section 5.2:

```
>>> from keras.models import load_model
>>> model = load_model('cats_and_dogs_small_2.h5')
>>> model.summary()   <1> As a reminder.
```

Layer (type)	Output Shape	Param #
conv2d_5 (Conv2D)	(None, 148, 148, 32)	896
maxpooling2d_5 (MaxPooling2D)	(None, 74, 74, 32)	0
conv2d_6 (Conv2D)	(None, 72, 72, 64)	18496
maxpooling2d_6 (MaxPooling2D)	(None, 36, 36, 64)	0

conv2d_7 (Conv2D)	(None, 34, 34, 128)	73856
maxpooling2d_7 (MaxPooling2D)	(None, 17, 17, 128)	0
conv2d_8 (Conv2D)	(None, 15, 15, 128)	147584
maxpooling2d_8 (MaxPooling2D)	(None, 7, 7, 128)	0
flatten_2 (Flatten)	(None, 6272)	0
dropout_1 (Dropout)	(None, 6272)	0
dense_3 (Dense)	(None, 512)	3211776
dense_4 (Dense)	(None, 1)	513

```
=================================================================
Total params: 3,453,121
Trainable params: 3,453,121
Non-trainable params: 0
```

Next, you'll get an input image—a picture of a cat, not part of the images the network was trained on.

Listing 5.25 Preprocessing a single image

```
img_path = '/Users/fchollet/Downloads/cats_and_dogs_small/test/cats/cat.1700.jpg'

from keras.preprocessing import image          ◁————  Preprocesses the image
import numpy as np                                      into a 4D tensor

img = image.load_img(img_path, target_size=(150, 150))
img_tensor = image.img_to_array(img)
img_tensor = np.expand_dims(img_tensor, axis=0)
img_tensor /= 255.          ◁————  Remember that the model
                                    was trained on inputs that
<1> Its shape is (1, 150, 150, 3)   were preprocessed this way.
print(img_tensor.shape)
```

Let's display the picture (see figure 5.24).

Listing 5.26 Displaying the test picture

```
import matplotlib.pyplot as plt

plt.imshow(img_tensor[0])
plt.show()
```

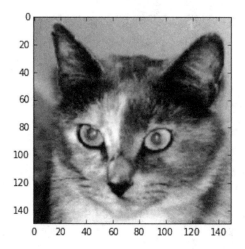

Figure 5.24   The test cat picture

In order to extract the feature maps you want to look at, you'll create a Keras model that takes batches of images as input, and outputs the activations of all convolution and pooling layers. To do this, you'll use the Keras class `Model`. A model is instantiated using two arguments: an input tensor (or list of input tensors) and an output tensor (or list of output tensors). The resulting class is a Keras model, just like the `Sequential` models you're familiar with, mapping the specified inputs to the specified outputs. What sets the `Model` class apart is that it allows for models with multiple outputs, unlike `Sequential`. For more information about the `Model` class, see section 7.1.

> **Listing 5.27   Instantiating a model from an input tensor and a list of output tensors**

```
from keras import models

layer_outputs = [layer.output for layer in model.layers[:8]]
activation_model = models.Model(inputs=model.input, outputs=layer_outputs)
```

**Extracts the outputs of
the top eight layers**

**Creates a model that will return these
outputs, given the model input**

When fed an image input, this model returns the values of the layer activations in the original model. This is the first time you've encountered a multi-output model in this book: until now, the models you've seen have had exactly one input and one output. In the general case, a model can have any number of inputs and outputs. This one has one input and eight outputs: one output per layer activation.

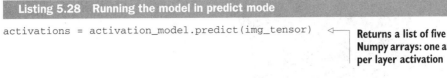

```
activations = activation_model.predict(img_tensor)
```

Returns a list of five
Numpy arrays: one array
per layer activation

For instance, this is the activation of the first convolution layer for the cat image input:

```
>>> first_layer_activation = activations[0]
>>> print(first_layer_activation.shape)
(1, 148, 148, 32)
```

It's a 148 × 148 feature map with 32 channels. Let's try plotting the fourth channel of the activation of the first layer of the original model (see figure 5.25).

Listing 5.29 Visualizing the fourth channel

```
import matplotlib.pyplot as plt

plt.matshow(first_layer_activation[0, :, :, 4], cmap='viridis')
```

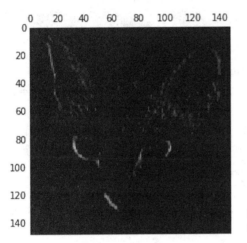

Figure 5.25   Fourth channel of the activation of the first layer on the test cat picture

This channel appears to encode a diagonal edge detector. Let's try the seventh channel (see figure 5.26)—but note that your own channels may vary, because the specific filters learned by convolution layers aren't deterministic.

Listing 5.30 Visualizing the seventh channel

```
plt.matshow(first_layer_activation[0, :, :, 7], cmap='viridis')
```

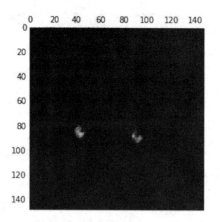

Figure 5.26   Seventh channel of the activation of the first layer on the test cat picture

This one looks like a "bright green dot" detector, useful to encode cat eyes. At this point, let's plot a complete visualization of all the activations in the network (see figure 5.27). You'll extract and plot every channel in each of the eight activation maps, and you'll stack the results in one big image tensor, with channels stacked side by side.

Listing 5.31   Visualizing every channel in every intermediate activation

```
layer_names = []                              Names of the layers, so you can
for layer in model.layers[:8]:                have them as part of your plot
    layer_names.append(layer.name)

images_per_row = 16                                        Displays the feature maps

for layer_name, layer_activation in zip(layer_names, activations):
    n_features = layer_activation.shape[-1]       The feature map has shape
                                                  (I, size, size, n_features).
    size = layer_activation.shape[1]

    n_cols = n_features // images_per_row
    display_grid = np.zeros((size * n_cols, images_per_row * size))

    for col in range(n_cols):                                 Tiles each filter into
        for row in range(images_per_row):                     a big horizontal grid
            channel_image = layer_activation[0,
                                             :, :,
                                             col * images_per_row + row]
            channel_image -= channel_image.mean()
            channel_image /= channel_image.std()
            channel_image *= 64
            channel_image += 128
            channel_image = np.clip(channel_image, 0, 255).astype('uint8')
            display_grid[col * size : (col + 1) * size,
                         row * size : (row + 1) * size] = channel_image

    scale = 1. / size                                        Displays the grid
    plt.figure(figsize=(scale * display_grid.shape[1],
                        scale * display_grid.shape[0]))
    plt.title(layer_name)
    plt.grid(False)
    plt.imshow(display_grid, aspect='auto', cmap='viridis')
```

Number of features in the feature map → n_features = layer_activation.shape[-1]

Tiles the activation channels in this matrix → n_cols = n_features // images_per_row

Post-processes the feature to make it visually palatable → channel_image -= channel_image.mean()

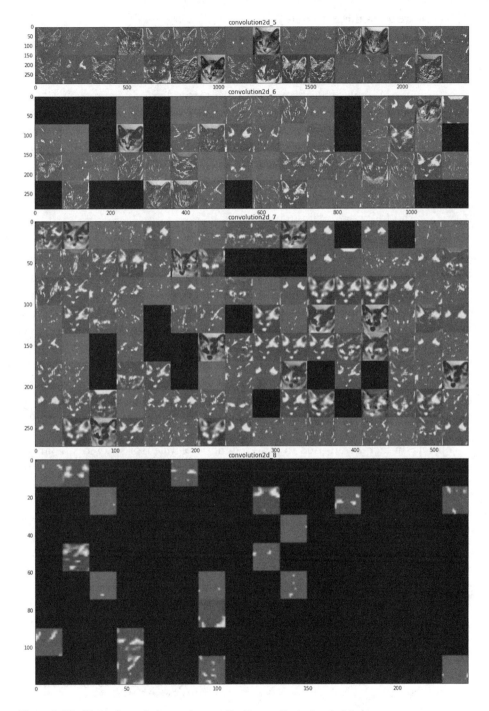

Figure 5.27 Every channel of every layer activation on the test cat picture

There are a few things to note here:

- The first layer acts as a collection of various edge detectors. At that stage, the activations retain almost all of the information present in the initial picture.
- As you go higher, the activations become increasingly abstract and less visually interpretable. They begin to encode higher-level concepts such as "cat ear" and "cat eye." Higher presentations carry increasingly less information about the visual contents of the image, and increasingly more information related to the class of the image.
- The sparsity of the activations increases with the depth of the layer: in the first layer, all filters are activated by the input image; but in the following layers, more and more filters are blank. This means the pattern encoded by the filter isn't found in the input image.

We have just evidenced an important universal characteristic of the representations learned by deep neural networks: the features extracted by a layer become increasingly abstract with the depth of the layer. The activations of higher layers carry less and less information about the specific input being seen, and more and more information about the target (in this case, the class of the image: cat or dog). A deep neural network effectively acts as an *information distillation pipeline*, with raw data going in (in this case, RGB pictures) and being repeatedly transformed so that irrelevant information is filtered out (for example, the specific visual appearance of the image), and useful information is magnified and refined (for example, the class of the image).

This is analogous to the way humans and animals perceive the world: after observing a scene for a few seconds, a human can remember which abstract objects were present in it (bicycle, tree) but can't remember the specific appearance of these objects. In fact, if you tried to draw a generic bicycle from memory, chances are you couldn't get it even remotely right, even though you've seen thousands of bicycles in your lifetime (see, for example, figure 5.28). Try it right now: this effect is absolutely real. You brain has learned to completely abstract its visual input—to transform it into high-level visual concepts while filtering out irrelevant visual details—making it tremendously difficult to remember how things around you look.

Figure 5.28 Left: attempts to draw a bicycle from memory. Right: what a schematic bicycle should look like.

5.4.2 Visualizing convnet filters

Another easy way to inspect the filters learned by convnets is to display the visual pattern that each filter is meant to respond to. This can be done with *gradient ascent in input space*: applying *gradient descent* to the value of the input image of a convnet so as to *maximize* the response of a specific filter, starting from a blank input image. The resulting input image will be one that the chosen filter is maximally responsive to.

The process is simple: you'll build a loss function that maximizes the value of a given filter in a given convolution layer, and then you'll use stochastic gradient descent to adjust the values of the input image so as to maximize this activation value. For instance, here's a loss for the activation of filter 0 in the layer `block3_conv1` of the VGG16 network, pretrained on ImageNet.

Listing 5.32 Defining the loss tensor for filter visualization

```
from keras.applications import VGG16
from keras import backend as K

model = VGG16(weights='imagenet',
              include_top=False)

layer_name = 'block3_conv1'
filter_index = 0

layer_output = model.get_layer(layer_name).output
loss = K.mean(layer_output[:, :, :, filter_index])
```

To implement gradient descent, you'll need the gradient of this loss with respect to the model's input. To do this, you'll use the `gradients` function packaged with the backend module of Keras.

Listing 5.33 Obtaining the gradient of the loss with regard to the input

```
grads = K.gradients(loss, model.input)[0]
```
⊲ **The call to gradients returns a list of tensors (of size 1 in this case). Hence, you keep only the first element— which is a tensor.**

A non-obvious trick to use to help the gradient-descent process go smoothly is to normalize the gradient tensor by dividing it by its L2 norm (the square root of the average of the square of the values in the tensor). This ensures that the magnitude of the updates done to the input image is always within the same range.

Listing 5.34 Gradient-normalization trick

```
grads /= (K.sqrt(K.mean(K.square(grads))) + 1e-5)
```
⊲ **Add 1e–5 before dividing to avoid accidentally dividing by 0.**

Now you need a way to compute the value of the loss tensor and the gradient tensor, given an input image. You can define a Keras backend function to do this: `iterate` is a function that takes a Numpy tensor (as a list of tensors of size 1) and returns a list of two Numpy tensors: the loss value and the gradient value.

Listing 5.35   Fetching Numpy output values given Numpy input values

```
iterate = K.function([model.input], [loss, grads])

import numpy as np
loss_value, grads_value = iterate([np.zeros((1, 150, 150, 3))])
```

At this point, you can define a Python loop to do stochastic gradient descent.

Listing 5.36   Loss maximization via stochastic gradient descent

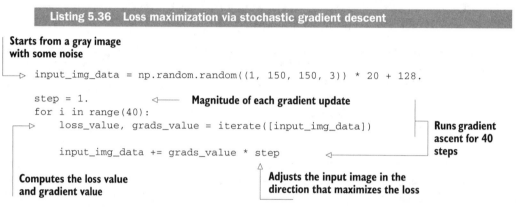

Starts from a gray image with some noise

```
input_img_data = np.random.random((1, 150, 150, 3)) * 20 + 128.

step = 1.          ◁——  Magnitude of each gradient update
for i in range(40):
    loss_value, grads_value = iterate([input_img_data])

    input_img_data += grads_value * step
```

Computes the loss value and gradient value

Runs gradient ascent for 40 steps

Adjusts the input image in the direction that maximizes the loss

The resulting image tensor is a floating-point tensor of shape (1, 150, 150, 3), with values that may not be integers within [0, 255]. Hence, you need to postprocess this tensor to turn it into a displayable image. You do so with the following straightforward utility function.

Listing 5.37   Utility function to convert a tensor into a valid image

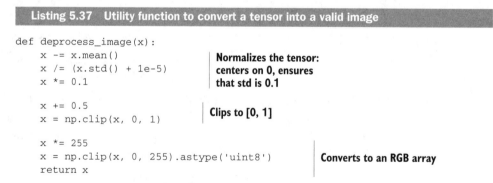

```
def deprocess_image(x):
    x -= x.mean()
    x /= (x.std() + 1e-5)
    x *= 0.1

    x += 0.5
    x = np.clip(x, 0, 1)

    x *= 255
    x = np.clip(x, 0, 255).astype('uint8')
    return x
```

Normalizes the tensor: centers on 0, ensures that std is 0.1

Clips to [0, 1]

Converts to an RGB array

Now you have all the pieces. Let's put them together into a Python function that takes as input a layer name and a filter index, and returns a valid image tensor representing the pattern that maximizes the activation of the specified filter.

Listing 5.38 Function to generate filter visualizations

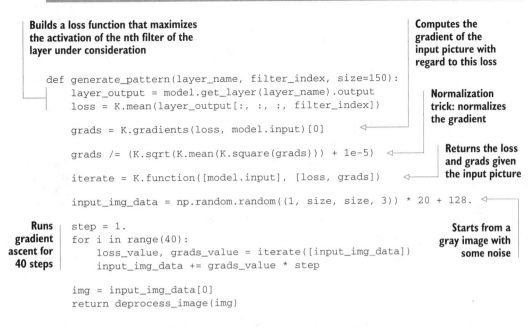

Builds a loss function that maximizes the activation of the nth filter of the layer under consideration

Computes the gradient of the input picture with regard to this loss

Normalization trick: normalizes the gradient

Returns the loss and grads given the input picture

Runs gradient ascent for 40 steps

Starts from a gray image with some noise

```
def generate_pattern(layer_name, filter_index, size=150):
    layer_output = model.get_layer(layer_name).output
    loss = K.mean(layer_output[:, :, :, filter_index])

    grads = K.gradients(loss, model.input)[0]

    grads /= (K.sqrt(K.mean(K.square(grads))) + 1e-5)

    iterate = K.function([model.input], [loss, grads])

    input_img_data = np.random.random((1, size, size, 3)) * 20 + 128.

    step = 1.
    for i in range(40):
        loss_value, grads_value = iterate([input_img_data])
        input_img_data += grads_value * step

    img = input_img_data[0]
    return deprocess_image(img)
```

Let's try it (see figure 5.29):

```
>>> plt.imshow(generate_pattern('block3_conv1', 0))
```

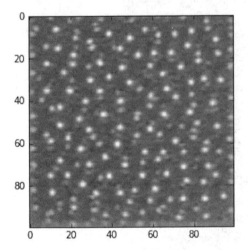

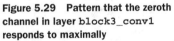

Figure 5.29 Pattern that the zeroth channel in layer `block3_conv1` responds to maximally

It seems that filter 0 in layer `block3_conv1` is responsive to a polka-dot pattern. Now the fun part: you can start visualizing every filter in every layer. For simplicity, you'll only look at the first 64 filters in each layer, and you'll only look at the first layer of each convolution block (`block1_conv1`, `block2_conv1`, `block3_conv1`, `block4_conv1`, `block5_conv1`). You'll arrange the outputs on an 8 × 8 grid of 64 × 64 filter patterns, with some black margins between each filter pattern (see figures 5.30–5.33).

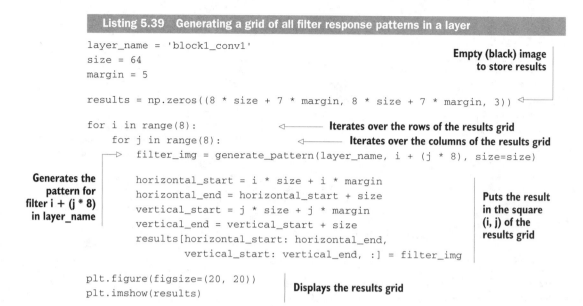

Listing 5.39 Generating a grid of all filter response patterns in a layer

```
layer_name = 'block1_conv1'
size = 64
margin = 5

results = np.zeros((8 * size + 7 * margin, 8 * size + 7 * margin, 3))

for i in range(8):
    for j in range(8):
        filter_img = generate_pattern(layer_name, i + (j * 8), size=size)

        horizontal_start = i * size + i * margin
        horizontal_end = horizontal_start + size
        vertical_start = j * size + j * margin
        vertical_end = vertical_start + size
        results[horizontal_start: horizontal_end,
                vertical_start: vertical_end, :] = filter_img

plt.figure(figsize=(20, 20))
plt.imshow(results)
```

Empty (black) image to store results

Iterates over the rows of the results grid

Iterates over the columns of the results grid

Generates the pattern for filter i + (j * 8) in layer_name

Puts the result in the square (i, j) of the results grid

Displays the results grid

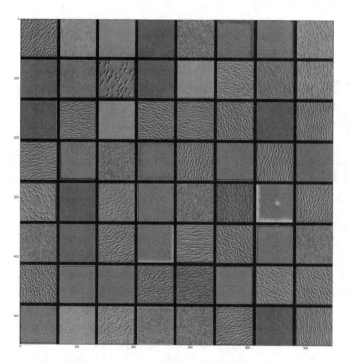

Figure 5.30 Filter patterns for layer `block1_conv1`

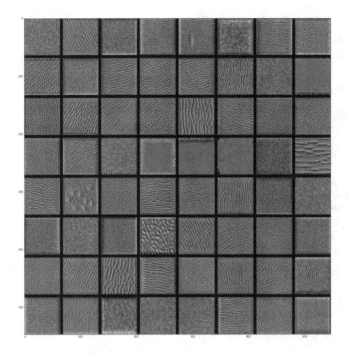

Figure 5.31 Filter patterns for layer `block2_conv1`

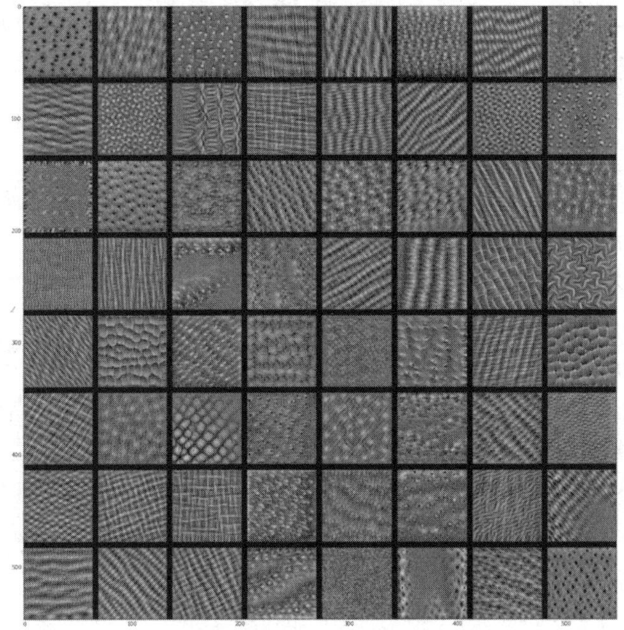

Figure 5.32 Filter patterns for layer `block3_conv1`

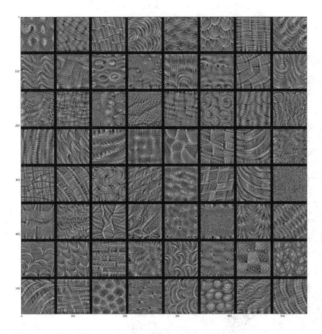

Figure 5.33   Filter patterns for layer `block4_conv1`

These filter visualizations tell you a lot about how convnet layers see the world: each layer in a convnet learns a collection of filters such that their inputs can be expressed as a combination of the filters. This is similar to how the Fourier transform decomposes signals onto a bank of cosine functions. The filters in these convnet filter banks get increasingly complex and refined as you go higher in the model:

- The filters from the first layer in the model (`block1_conv1`) encode simple directional edges and colors (or colored edges, in some cases).
- The filters from `block2_conv1` encode simple textures made from combinations of edges and colors.
- The filters in higher layers begin to resemble textures found in natural images: feathers, eyes, leaves, and so on.

5.4.3   *Visualizing heatmaps of class activation*

I'll introduce one more visualization technique: one that is useful for understanding which parts of a given image led a convnet to its final classification decision. This is helpful for debugging the decision process of a convnet, particularly in the case of a classification mistake. It also allows you to locate specific objects in an image.

This general category of techniques is called *class activation map* (CAM) visualization, and it consists of producing heatmaps of class activation over input images. A class activation heatmap is a 2D grid of scores associated with a specific output class, computed for every location in any input image, indicating how important each location is with respect to the class under consideration. For instance, given an image fed into a dogs-versus-cats convnet, CAM visualization allows you to generate a heatmap for the class "cat," indicating how cat-like different parts of the image are, and also a heatmap for the class "dog," indicating how dog-like parts of the image are.

The specific implementation you'll use is the one described in "Grad-CAM: Visual Explanations from Deep Networks via Gradient-based Localization."[2] It's very simple: it consists of taking the output feature map of a convolution layer, given an input image, and weighing every channel in that feature map by the gradient of the class with respect to the channel. Intuitively, one way to understand this trick is that you're weighting a spatial map of "how intensely the input image activates different channels" by "how important each channel is with regard to the class," resulting in a spatial map of "how intensely the input image activates the class."

We'll demonstrate this technique using the pretrained VGG16 network again.

Listing 5.40 Loading the VGG16 network with pretrained weights

```
from keras.applications.vgg16 import VGG16

model = VGG16(weights='imagenet')
```

> Note that you include the densely connected classifier on top; in all previous cases, you discarded it.

Consider the image of two African elephants shown in figure 5.34 (under a Creative Commons license), possibly a mother and her calf, strolling on the savanna. Let's convert this image into something the VGG16 model can read: the model was trained on images of size 224 × 244, preprocessed according to a few rules that are packaged in the utility function `keras.applications.vgg16.preprocess_input`. So you need to load the image, resize it to 224 × 224, convert it to a Numpy `float32` tensor, and apply these preprocessing rules.

Figure 5.34   Test picture of African elephants

---

[2] Ramprasaath R. Selvaraju et al., arXiv (2017), https://arxiv.org/abs/ 1610.02391.

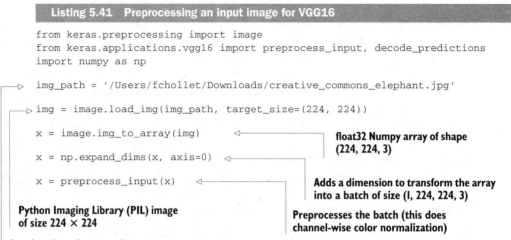

Listing 5.41 Preprocessing an input image for VGG16

```
from keras.preprocessing import image
from keras.applications.vgg16 import preprocess_input, decode_predictions
import numpy as np

img_path = '/Users/fchollet/Downloads/creative_commons_elephant.jpg'

img = image.load_img(img_path, target_size=(224, 224))

x = image.img_to_array(img)

x = np.expand_dims(x, axis=0)

x = preprocess_input(x)
```

float32 Numpy array of shape (224, 224, 3)

Adds a dimension to transform the array into a batch of size (I, 224, 224, 3)

Preprocesses the batch (this does channel-wise color normalization)

Python Imaging Library (PIL) image of size 224 × 224

Local path to the target image

You can now run the pretrained network on the image and decode its prediction vector back to a human-readable format:

```
>>> preds = model.predict(x)
>>> print('Predicted:', decode_predictions(preds, top=3)[0])
Predicted:', [(u'n02504458', u'African_elephant', 0.92546833),
(u'n01871265', u'tusker', 0.070257246),
(u'n02504013', u'Indian_elephant', 0.0042589349)]
```

The top three classes predicted for this image are as follows:

- African elephant (with 92.5% probability)
- Tusker (with 7% probability)
- Indian elephant (with 0.4% probability)

The network has recognized the image as containing an undetermined quantity of African elephants. The entry in the prediction vector that was maximally activated is the one corresponding to the "African elephant" class, at index 386:

```
>>> np.argmax(preds[0])
386
```

To visualize which parts of the image are the most African elephant–like, let's set up the Grad-CAM process.

Listing 5.42 Setting up the Grad-CAM algorithm

"African elephant" entry in the prediction vector

Output feature map of the block5_conv3 layer, the last convolutional layer in VGG16

```
african_e66lephant_output = model.output[:, 386]

last_conv_layer = model.get_layer('block5_conv3')
```

Gradient of the "African
elephant" class with regard to
the output feature map of
block5_conv3

Vector of shape (512,), where each entry
is the mean intensity of the gradient
over a specific feature-map channel

```
grads = K.gradients(african_elephant_output, last_conv_layer.output)[0]

pooled_grads = K.mean(grads, axis=(0, 1, 2))

iterate = K.function([model.input],
                     [pooled_grads, last_conv_layer.output[0]])

pooled_grads_value, conv_layer_output_value = iterate([x])

for i in range(512):
    conv_layer_output_value[:, :, i] *= pooled_grads_value[i]

heatmap = np.mean(conv_layer_output_value, axis=-1)
```

**Values of these two quantities, as
Numpy arrays, given the sample image
of two elephants**

**The channel-wise mean of
the resulting feature map
is the heatmap of the
class activation.**

**Multiplies each
channel in the
feature-map array
by "how
important this
channel is" with
regard to the
"elephant" class**

**Lets you access the values of the quantities
you just defined: pooled_grads and the
output feature map of block5_conv3, given
a sample image**

For visualization purposes, you'll also normalize the heatmap between 0 and 1. The result is shown in figure 5.35.

Listing 5.43 Heatmap post-processing

```
heatmap = np.maximum(heatmap, 0)
heatmap /= np.max(heatmap)
plt.matshow(heatmap)
```

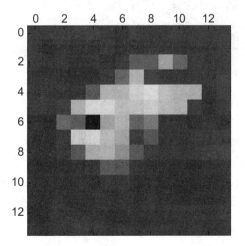

**Figure 5.35 African elephant class
activation heatmap over the test picture**

Finally, you'll use OpenCV to generate an image that superimposes the original image on the heatmap you just obtained (see figure 5.36).

Listing 5.44 Superimposing the heatmap with the original picture

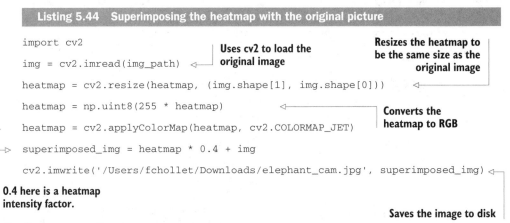

```
import cv2

img = cv2.imread(img_path)

heatmap = cv2.resize(heatmap, (img.shape[1], img.shape[0]))

heatmap = np.uint8(255 * heatmap)

heatmap = cv2.applyColorMap(heatmap, cv2.COLORMAP_JET)

superimposed_img = heatmap * 0.4 + img

cv2.imwrite('/Users/fchollet/Downloads/elephant_cam.jpg', superimposed_img)
```

Uses cv2 to load the original image

Resizes the heatmap to be the same size as the original image

Converts the heatmap to RGB

0.4 here is a heatmap intensity factor.

Applies the heatmap to the original image

Saves the image to disk

Figure 5.36 Superimposing the class activation heatmap on the original picture

This visualization technique answers two important questions:

- Why did the network think this image contained an African elephant?
- Where is the African elephant located in the picture?

In particular, it's interesting to note that the ears of the elephant calf are strongly activated: this is probably how the network can tell the difference between African and Indian elephants.

Chapter summary

- Convnets are the best tool for attacking visual-classification problems.

- Convnets work by learning a hierarchy of modular patterns and concepts to represent the visual world.

- The representations they learn are easy to inspect—convnets are the opposite of black boxes!

- You're now capable of training your own convnet from scratch to solve an image-classification problem.

- You understand how to use visual data augmentation to fight overfitting.

- You know how to use a pretrained convnet to do feature extraction and fine-tuning.

- You can generate visualizations of the filters learned by your convnets, as well as heatmaps of class activity.

Deep learning for
text and sequences

6

This chapter covers

- Preprocessing text data into useful representations
- Working with recurrent neural networks
- Using 1D convnets for sequence processing

This chapter explores deep-learning models that can process text (understood as sequences of word or sequences of characters), timeseries, and sequence data in general. The two fundamental deep-learning algorithms for sequence processing are *recurrent neural networks* and *1D convnets*, the one-dimensional version of the 2D convnets that we covered in the previous chapters. We'll discuss both of these approaches in this chapter.

Applications of these algorithms include the following:

- Document classification and timeseries classification, such as identifying the topic of an article or the author of a book
- Timeseries comparisons, such as estimating how closely related two documents or two stock tickers are

- Sequence-to-sequence learning, such as decoding an English sentence into French

- Sentiment analysis, such as classifying the sentiment of tweets or movie reviews as positive or negative

- Timeseries forecasting, such as predicting the future weather at a certain location, given recent weather data

This chapter's examples focus on two narrow tasks: sentiment analysis on the IMDB dataset, a task we approached earlier in the book, and temperature forecasting. But the techniques demonstrated for these two tasks are relevant to all the applications just listed, and many more.

6.1   *Working with text data*

Text is one of the most widespread forms of sequence data. It can be understood as either a sequence of characters or a sequence of words, but it's most common to work at the level of words. The deep-learning sequence-processing models introduced in the following sections can use text to produce a basic form of natural-language understanding, sufficient for applications including document classification, sentiment analysis, author identification, and even question-answering (QA) (in a constrained context). Of course, keep in mind throughout this chapter that none of these deep-learning models truly understand text in a human sense; rather, these models can map the statistical structure of written language, which is sufficient to solve many simple textual tasks. Deep learning for natural-language processing is pattern recognition applied to words, sentences, and paragraphs, in much the same way that computer vision is pattern recognition applied to pixels.

Like all other neural networks, deep-learning models don't take as input raw text: they only work with numeric tensors. *Vectorizing* text is the process of transforming text into numeric tensors. This can be done in multiple ways:

- Segment text into words, and transform each word into a vector.
- Segment text into characters, and transform each character into a vector.
- Extract n-grams of words or characters, and transform each n-gram into a vector. *N-grams* are overlapping groups of multiple consecutive words or characters.

Collectively, the different units into which you can break down text (words, characters, or n-grams) are called *tokens*, and breaking text into such tokens is called *tokenization*. All text-vectorization processes consist of applying some tokenization scheme and then associating numeric vectors with the generated tokens. These vectors, packed into sequence tensors, are fed into deep neural networks. There are multiple ways to associate a vector with a token. In this section, I'll present two major ones: *one-hot encoding* of tokens, and *token embedding* (typically used exclusively for words, and called *word embedding*). The remainder of this section explains these techniques and shows how to use them to go from raw text to a Numpy tensor that you can send to a Keras network.

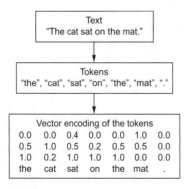

Figure 6.1   From text to tokens to vectors

Understanding n-grams and bag-of-words

Word n-grams are groups of *N* (or fewer) consecutive words that you can extract from a sentence. The same concept may also be applied to characters instead of words.

Here's a simple example. Consider the sentence "The cat sat on the mat." It may be decomposed into the following set of 2-grams:

```
{"The", "The cat", "cat", "cat sat", "sat",
  "sat on", "on", "on the", "the", "the mat", "mat"}
```

It may also be decomposed into the following set of 3-grams:

```
{"The", "The cat", "cat", "cat sat", "The cat sat",
  "sat", "sat on", "on", "cat sat on", "on the", "the",
  "sat on the", "the mat", "mat", "on the mat"}
```

Such a set is called a *bag-of-2-grams* or *bag-of-3-grams*, respectively. The term *bag* here refers to the fact that you're dealing with a *set* of tokens rather than a list or sequence: the tokens have no specific order. This family of tokenization methods is called *bag-of-words*.

Because bag-of-words isn't an order-preserving tokenization method (the tokens generated are understood as a set, not a sequence, and the general structure of the sentences is lost), it tends to be used in shallow language-processing models rather than in deep-learning models. Extracting n-grams is a form of feature engineering, and deep learning does away with this kind of rigid, brittle approach, replacing it with hierarchical feature learning. One-dimensional convnets and recurrent neural networks, introduced later in this chapter, are capable of learning representations for groups of words and characters without being explicitly told about the existence of such groups, by looking at continuous word or character sequences. For this reason, we won't cover n-grams any further in this book. But do keep in mind that they're a powerful, unavoidable feature-engineering tool when using lightweight, shallow text-processing models such as logistic regression and random forests.

6.1.1 One-hot encoding of words and characters

One-hot encoding is the most common, most basic way to turn a token into a vector. You saw it in action in the initial IMDB and Reuters examples in chapter 3 (done with words, in that case). It consists of associating a unique integer index with every word and then turning this integer index i into a binary vector of size N (the size of the vocabulary); the vector is all zeros except for the ith entry, which is 1.

Of course, one-hot encoding can be done at the character level, as well. To unambiguously drive home what one-hot encoding is and how to implement it, listings 6.1 and 6.2 show two toy examples: one for words, the other for characters.

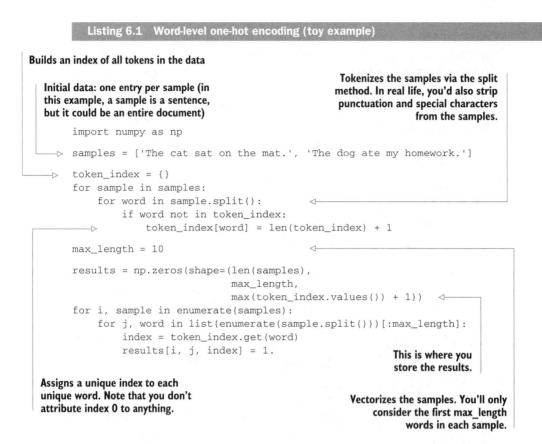

Listing 6.1 Word-level one-hot encoding (toy example)

Builds an index of all tokens in the data

Initial data: one entry per sample (in this example, a sample is a sentence, but it could be an entire document)

Tokenizes the samples via the split method. In real life, you'd also strip punctuation and special characters from the samples.

```
import numpy as np

samples = ['The cat sat on the mat.', 'The dog ate my homework.']

token_index = {}
for sample in samples:
    for word in sample.split():
        if word not in token_index:
            token_index[word] = len(token_index) + 1

max_length = 10

results = np.zeros(shape=(len(samples),
                          max_length,
                          max(token_index.values()) + 1))
for i, sample in enumerate(samples):
    for j, word in list(enumerate(sample.split()))[:max_length]:
        index = token_index.get(word)
        results[i, j, index] = 1.
```

This is where you store the results.

Assigns a unique index to each unique word. Note that you don't attribute index 0 to anything.

Vectorizes the samples. You'll only consider the first max_length words in each sample.

Listing 6.2 Character-level one-hot encoding (toy example)

```
import string

samples = ['The cat sat on the mat.', 'The dog ate my homework.']
characters = string.printable
token_index = dict(zip(range(1, len(characters) + 1), characters))

max_length = 50
results = np.zeros((len(samples), max_length, max(token_index.keys()) + 1))
for i, sample in enumerate(samples):
    for j, character in enumerate(sample):
        index = token_index.get(character)
        results[i, j, index] = 1.
```

All printable ASCII characters

Note that Keras has built-in utilities for doing one-hot encoding of text at the word level or character level, starting from raw text data. You should use these utilities, because they take care of a number of important features such as stripping special characters from strings and only taking into account the N most common words in your dataset (a common restriction, to avoid dealing with very large input vector spaces).

Listing 6.3   Using Keras for word-level one-hot encoding

Creates a tokenizer, configured
to only take into account the
1,000 most common words

```
from keras.preprocessing.text import Tokenizer

samples = ['The cat sat on the mat.', 'The dog ate my homework.']

tokenizer = Tokenizer(num_words=1000)
tokenizer.fit_on_texts(samples)
sequences = tokenizer.texts_to_sequences(samples)

one_hot_results = tokenizer.texts_to_matrix(samples, mode='binary')

word_index = tokenizer.word_index
print('Found %s unique tokens.' % len(word_index))
```

Builds
the
word
index

Turns strings into lists
of integer indices

You could also directly get the one-hot
binary representations. Vectorization
modes other than one-hot encoding
are supported by this tokenizer.

How you can recover
the word index that
was computed

A variant of one-hot encoding is the so-called *one-hot hashing trick*, which you can use when the number of unique tokens in your vocabulary is too large to handle explicitly. Instead of explicitly assigning an index to each word and keeping a reference of these indices in a dictionary, you can hash words into vectors of fixed size. This is typically done with a very lightweight hashing function. The main advantage of this method is that it does away with maintaining an explicit word index, which saves memory and allows online encoding of the data (you can generate token vectors right away, before you've seen all of the available data). The one drawback of this approach is that it's susceptible to *hash collisions*: two different words may end up with the same hash, and subsequently any machine-learning model looking at these hashes won't be able to tell the difference between these words. The likelihood of hash collisions decreases when the dimensionality of the hashing space is much larger than the total number of unique tokens being hashed.

Listing 6.4   Word-level one-hot encoding with hashing trick (toy example)

```
samples = ['The cat sat on the mat.', 'The dog ate my homework.']

dimensionality = 1000
max_length = 10

results = np.zeros((len(samples), max_length, dimensionality))
for i, sample in enumerate(samples):
    for j, word in list(enumerate(sample.split()))[:max_length]:
        index = abs(hash(word)) % dimensionality
        results[i, j, index] = 1.
```

Stores the words as vectors of size 1,000. If you have close
to 1,000 words (or more), you'll see many hash collisions,
which will decrease the accuracy of this encoding method.

Hashes the word into a
random integer index
between 0 and 1,000

6.1.2   Using word embeddings

Another popular and powerful way to associate a vector with a word is the use of dense *word vectors*, also called *word embeddings*. Whereas the vectors obtained through one-hot encoding are binary, sparse (mostly made of zeros), and very high-dimensional (same dimensionality as the number of words in the vocabulary), word embeddings are low-dimensional floating-point vectors (that is, dense vectors, as opposed to sparse vectors); see figure 6.2. Unlike the word vectors obtained via one-hot encoding, word embeddings are learned from data. It's common to see word embeddings that are 256-dimensional, 512-dimensional, or 1,024-dimensional when dealing with very large vocabularies. On the other hand, one-hot encoding words generally leads to vectors that are 20,000-dimensional or greater (capturing a vocabulary of 20,000 tokens, in this case). So, word embeddings pack more information into far fewer dimensions.

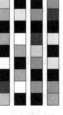

One-hot word vectors:
- Sparse
- High-dimensional
- Hardcoded

Word embeddings:
- Dense
- Lower-dimensional
- Learned from data

Figure 6.2   Whereas word representations obtained from one-hot encoding or hashing are sparse, high-dimensional, and hardcoded, word embeddings are dense, relatively low-dimensional, and learned from data.

There are two ways to obtain word embeddings:

- Learn word embeddings jointly with the main task you care about (such as document classification or sentiment prediction). In this setup, you start with random word vectors and then learn word vectors in the same way you learn the weights of a neural network.
- Load into your model word embeddings that were precomputed using a different machine-learning task than the one you're trying to solve. These are called *pretrained word embeddings*.

Let's look at both.

Learning word embeddings with the Embedding layer

The simplest way to associate a dense vector with a word is to choose the vector at random. The problem with this approach is that the resulting embedding space has no structure: for instance, the words *accurate* and *exact* may end up with completely different embeddings, even though they're interchangeable in most sentences. It's difficult for a deep neural network to make sense of such a noisy, unstructured embedding space.

To get a bit more abstract, the geometric relationships between word vectors should reflect the semantic relationships between these words. Word embeddings are meant to map human language into a geometric space. For instance, in a reasonable embedding space, you would expect synonyms to be embedded into similar word vectors; and in general, you would expect the geometric distance (such as L2 distance) between any two word vectors to relate to the semantic distance between the associated words (words meaning different things are embedded at points far away from each other, whereas related words are closer). In addition to distance, you may want specific *directions* in the embedding space to be meaningful. To make this clearer, let's look at a concrete example.

In figure 6.3, four words are embedded on a 2D plane: *cat, dog, wolf,* and *tiger.* With the vector representations we chose here, some semantic relationships between these words can be encoded as geometric transformations. For instance, the same vector allows us to go from *cat* to *tiger* and from *dog* to *wolf*: this vector could be interpreted as the "from pet to wild animal" vector. Similarly, another vector lets us go from *dog* to *cat* and from *wolf* to *tiger,* which could be interpreted as a "from canine to feline" vector.

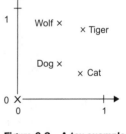

Figure 6.3 A toy example of a word-embedding space

In real-world word-embedding spaces, common examples of meaningful geometric transformations are "gender" vectors and "plural" vectors. For instance, by adding a "female" vector to the vector "king," we obtain the vector "queen." By adding a "plural" vector, we obtain "kings." Word-embedding spaces typically feature thousands of such interpretable and potentially useful vectors.

Is there some ideal word-embedding space that would perfectly map human language and could be used for any natural-language-processing task? Possibly, but we have yet to compute anything of the sort. Also, there is no such a thing as *human language*—there are many different languages, and they aren't isomorphic, because a language is the reflection of a specific culture and a specific context. But more pragmatically, what makes a good word-embedding space depends heavily on your task: the perfect word-embedding space for an English-language movie-review sentiment-analysis model may look different from the perfect embedding space for an English-language legal-document-classification model, because the importance of certain semantic relationships varies from task to task.

It's thus reasonable to *learn* a new embedding space with every new task. Fortunately, backpropagation makes this easy, and Keras makes it even easier. It's about learning the weights of a layer: the `Embedding` layer.

Listing 6.5   Instantiating an `Embedding` layer

```
from keras.layers import Embedding

embedding_layer = Embedding(1000, 64)
```
⊲ The Embedding layer takes at least two arguments: the number of possible tokens (here, 1,000: 1 + maximum word index) and the dimensionality of the embeddings (here, 64).

The `Embedding` layer is best understood as a dictionary that maps integer indices (which stand for specific words) to dense vectors. It takes integers as input, it looks up these integers in an internal dictionary, and it returns the associated vectors. It's effectively a dictionary lookup (see figure 6.4).

Word index ⟶ Embedding layer ⟶ Corresponding word vector

Figure 6.4   The `Embedding` layer

The `Embedding` layer takes as input a 2D tensor of integers, of shape (`samples,` `sequence_length`), where each entry is a sequence of integers. It can embed sequences of variable lengths: for instance, you could feed into the `Embedding` layer in the previous example batches with shapes (`32, 10`) (batch of 32 sequences of length 10) or (`64, 15`) (batch of 64 sequences of length 15). All sequences in a batch must have the same length, though (because you need to pack them into a single tensor), so sequences that are shorter than others should be padded with zeros, and sequences that are longer should be truncated.

This layer returns a 3D floating-point tensor of shape (`samples,` `sequence_length,` `embedding_dimensionality`). Such a 3D tensor can then be processed by an RNN layer or a 1D convolution layer (both will be introduced in the following sections).

When you instantiate an `Embedding` layer, its weights (its internal dictionary of token vectors) are initially random, just as with any other layer. During training, these word vectors are gradually adjusted via backpropagation, structuring the space into something the downstream model can exploit. Once fully trained, the embedding space will show a lot of structure—a kind of structure specialized for the specific problem for which you're training your model.

Let's apply this idea to the IMDB movie-review sentiment-prediction task that you're already familiar with. First, you'll quickly prepare the data. You'll restrict the movie reviews to the top 10,000 most common words (as you did the first time you worked with this dataset) and cut off the reviews after only 20 words. The network will learn 8-dimensional embeddings for each of the 10,000 words, turn the input integer sequences (2D integer tensor) into embedded sequences (3D float tensor), flatten the tensor to 2D, and train a single Dense layer on top for classification.

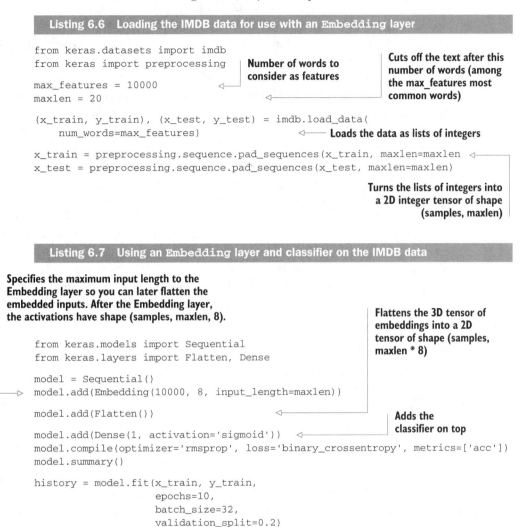

Listing 6.6 Loading the IMDB data for use with an Embedding layer

```
from keras.datasets import imdb
from keras import preprocessing

max_features = 10000
maxlen = 20

(x_train, y_train), (x_test, y_test) = imdb.load_data(
    num_words=max_features)

x_train = preprocessing.sequence.pad_sequences(x_train, maxlen=maxlen)
x_test = preprocessing.sequence.pad_sequences(x_test, maxlen=maxlen)
```

Number of words to consider as features

Cuts off the text after this number of words (among the max_features most common words)

Loads the data as lists of integers

Turns the lists of integers into a 2D integer tensor of shape (samples, maxlen)

Listing 6.7 Using an Embedding layer and classifier on the IMDB data

Specifies the maximum input length to the Embedding layer so you can later flatten the embedded inputs. After the Embedding layer, the activations have shape (samples, maxlen, 8).

Flattens the 3D tensor of embeddings into a 2D tensor of shape (samples, maxlen * 8)

```
from keras.models import Sequential
from keras.layers import Flatten, Dense

model = Sequential()
model.add(Embedding(10000, 8, input_length=maxlen))

model.add(Flatten())

model.add(Dense(1, activation='sigmoid'))
model.compile(optimizer='rmsprop', loss='binary_crossentropy', metrics=['acc'])
model.summary()

history = model.fit(x_train, y_train,
                    epochs=10,
                    batch_size=32,
                    validation_split=0.2)
```

Adds the classifier on top

You get to a validation accuracy of ~76%, which is pretty good considering that you're only looking at the first 20 words in every review. But note that merely flattening the embedded sequences and training a single Dense layer on top leads to a model that treats each word in the input sequence separately, without considering inter-word relationships and sentence structure (for example, this model would likely treat both "this movie is a bomb" and "this movie is the bomb" as being negative reviews). It's much better to add recurrent layers or 1D convolutional layers on top of the embedded sequences to learn features that take into account each sequence as a whole. That's what we'll focus on in the next few sections.

USING PRETRAINED WORD EMBEDDINGS

Sometimes, you have so little training data available that you can't use your data alone to learn an appropriate task-specific embedding of your vocabulary. What do you do then?

Instead of learning word embeddings jointly with the problem you want to solve, you can load embedding vectors from a precomputed embedding space that you know is highly structured and exhibits useful properties—that captures generic aspects of language structure. The rationale behind using pretrained word embeddings in natural-language processing is much the same as for using pretrained convnets in image classification: you don't have enough data available to learn truly powerful features on your own, but you expect the features that you need to be fairly generic—that is, common visual features or semantic features. In this case, it makes sense to reuse features learned on a different problem.

Such word embeddings are generally computed using word-occurrence statistics (observations about what words co-occur in sentences or documents), using a variety of techniques, some involving neural networks, others not. The idea of a dense, low-dimensional embedding space for words, computed in an unsupervised way, was initially explored by Bengio et al. in the early 2000s,[1] but it only started to take off in research and industry applications after the release of one of the most famous and successful word-embedding schemes: the Word2vec algorithm (https://code.google.com/archive/p/word2vec), developed by Tomas Mikolov at Google in 2013. Word2vec dimensions capture specific semantic properties, such as gender.

There are various precomputed databases of word embeddings that you can download and use in a Keras `Embedding` layer. Word2vec is one of them. Another popular one is called Global Vectors for Word Representation (GloVe, https://nlp.stanford.edu/projects/glove), which was developed by Stanford researchers in 2014. This embedding technique is based on factorizing a matrix of word co-occurrence statistics. Its developers have made available precomputed embeddings for millions of English tokens, obtained from Wikipedia data and Common Crawl data.

Let's look at how you can get started using GloVe embeddings in a Keras model. The same method is valid for Word2vec embeddings or any other word-embedding database. You'll also use this example to refresh the text-tokenization techniques introduced a few paragraphs ago: you'll start from raw text and work your way up.

6.1.3   *Putting it all together: from raw text to word embeddings*

You'll use a model similar to the one we just went over: embedding sentences in sequences of vectors, flattening them, and training a `Dense` layer on top. But you'll do so using pretrained word embeddings; and instead of using the pretokenized IMDB data packaged in Keras, you'll start from scratch by downloading the original text data.

---

[1]   Yoshua Bengio et al., *Neural Probabilistic Language Models* (Springer, 2003).

DOWNLOADING THE IMDB DATA AS RAW TEXT

First, head to http://mng.bz/0tIo and download the raw IMDB dataset. Uncompress it.

Now, let's collect the individual training reviews into a list of strings, one string per review. You'll also collect the review labels (positive/negative) into a `labels` list.

Listing 6.8 Processing the labels of the raw IMDB data

```
import os

imdb_dir = '/Users/fchollet/Downloads/aclImdb'
train_dir = os.path.join(imdb_dir, 'train')

labels = []
texts = []

for label_type in ['neg', 'pos']:
    dir_name = os.path.join(train_dir, label_type)
    for fname in os.listdir(dir_name):
        if fname[-4:] == '.txt':
            f = open(os.path.join(dir_name, fname))
            texts.append(f.read())
            f.close()
            if label_type == 'neg':
                labels.append(0)
            else:
                labels.append(1)
```

TOKENIZING THE DATA

Let's vectorize the text and prepare a training and validation split, using the concepts introduced earlier in this section. Because pretrained word embeddings are meant to be particularly useful on problems where little training data is available (otherwise, task-specific embeddings are likely to outperform them), we'll add the following twist: restricting the training data to the first 200 samples. So you'll learn to classify movie reviews after looking at just 200 examples.

Listing 6.9 Tokenizing the text of the raw IMDB data

```
from keras.preprocessing.text import Tokenizer
from keras.preprocessing.sequence import pad_sequences
import numpy as np

maxlen = 100                        ◁——— Cuts off reviews after 100 words
training_samples = 200              ◁——— Trains on 200 samples
validation_samples = 10000          ◁——— Validates on 10,000 samples
max_words = 10000                   ◁———┐
                                         │ Considers only the top
tokenizer = Tokenizer(num_words=max_words)  │ 10,000 words in the dataset
tokenizer.fit_on_texts(texts)
sequences = tokenizer.texts_to_sequences(texts)
```

```
word_index = tokenizer.word_index
print('Found %s unique tokens.' % len(word_index))

data = pad_sequences(sequences, maxlen=maxlen)

labels = np.asarray(labels)
print('Shape of data tensor:', data.shape)
print('Shape of label tensor:', labels.shape)

indices = np.arange(data.shape[0])
np.random.shuffle(indices)
data = data[indices]
labels = labels[indices]

x_train = data[:training_samples]
y_train = labels[:training_samples]
x_val = data[training_samples: training_samples + validation_samples]
y_val = labels[training_samples: training_samples + validation_samples]
```

> Splits the data into a training set and a validation set, but first shuffles the data, because you're starting with data in which samples are ordered (all negative first, then all positive)

DOWNLOADING THE GLOVE WORD EMBEDDINGS

Go to https://nlp.stanford.edu/projects/glove, and download the precomputed embeddings from 2014 English Wikipedia. It's an 822 MB zip file called glove.6B.zip, containing 100-dimensional embedding vectors for 400,000 words (or nonword tokens). Unzip it.

PREPROCESSING THE EMBEDDINGS

Let's parse the unzipped file (a .txt file) to build an index that maps words (as strings) to their vector representation (as number vectors).

Listing 6.10 Parsing the GloVe word-embeddings file

```
glove_dir = '/Users/fchollet/Downloads/glove.6B'

embeddings_index = {}
f = open(os.path.join(glove_dir, 'glove.6B.100d.txt'))
for line in f:
    values = line.split()
    word = values[0]
    coefs = np.asarray(values[1:], dtype='float32')
    embeddings_index[word] = coefs
f.close()

print('Found %s word vectors.' % len(embeddings_index))
```

Next, you'll build an embedding matrix that you can load into an Embedding layer. It must be a matrix of shape (max_words, embedding_dim), where each entry *i* contains the embedding_dim-dimensional vector for the word of index *i* in the reference word index (built during tokenization). Note that index 0 isn't supposed to stand for any word or token—it's a placeholder.

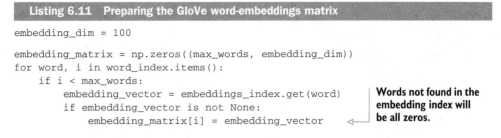

Listing 6.11 Preparing the GloVe word-embeddings matrix

```
embedding_dim = 100

embedding_matrix = np.zeros((max_words, embedding_dim))
for word, i in word_index.items():
    if i < max_words:
        embedding_vector = embeddings_index.get(word)
        if embedding_vector is not None:
            embedding_matrix[i] = embedding_vector
```

> Words not found in the embedding index will be all zeros.

DEFINING A MODEL

You'll use the same model architecture as before.

Listing 6.12 Model definition

```
from keras.models import Sequential
from keras.layers import Embedding, Flatten, Dense

model = Sequential()
model.add(Embedding(max_words, embedding_dim, input_length=maxlen))
model.add(Flatten())
model.add(Dense(32, activation='relu'))
model.add(Dense(1, activation='sigmoid'))
model.summary()
```

LOADING THE GLOVE EMBEDDINGS IN THE MODEL

The `Embedding` layer has a single weight matrix: a 2D float matrix where each entry *i* is the word vector meant to be associated with index *i*. Simple enough. Load the GloVe matrix you prepared into the `Embedding` layer, the first layer in the model.

Listing 6.13 Loading pretrained word embeddings into the `Embedding` layer

```
model.layers[0].set_weights([embedding_matrix])
model.layers[0].trainable = False
```

Additionally, you'll freeze the `Embedding` layer (set its `trainable` attribute to `False`), following the same rationale you're already familiar with in the context of pretrained convnet features: when parts of a model are pretrained (like your `Embedding` layer) and parts are randomly initialized (like your classifier), the pretrained parts shouldn't be updated during training, to avoid forgetting what they already know. The large gradient updates triggered by the randomly initialized layers would be disruptive to the already-learned features.

TRAINING AND EVALUATING THE MODEL

Compile and train the model.

Listing 6.14   Training and evaluation

```
model.compile(optimizer='rmsprop',
              loss='binary_crossentropy',
              metrics=['acc'])
history = model.fit(x_train, y_train,
                    epochs=10,
                    batch_size=32,
                    validation_data=(x_val, y_val))
model.save_weights('pre_trained_glove_model.h5')
```

Now, plot the model's performance over time (see figures 6.5 and 6.6).

Listing 6.15   Plotting the results

```
import matplotlib.pyplot as plt

acc = history.history['acc']
val_acc = history.history['val_acc']
loss = history.history['loss']
val_loss = history.history['val_loss']

epochs = range(1, len(acc) + 1)

plt.plot(epochs, acc, 'bo', label='Training acc')
plt.plot(epochs, val_acc, 'b', label='Validation acc')
plt.title('Training and validation accuracy')
plt.legend()

plt.figure()

plt.plot(epochs, loss, 'bo', label='Training loss')
plt.plot(epochs, val_loss, 'b', label='Validation loss')
plt.title('Training and validation loss')
plt.legend()

plt.show()
```

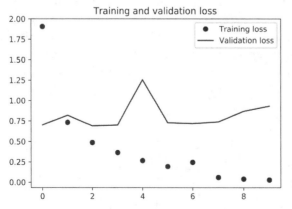

Figure 6.5   Training and validation loss when using pretrained word embeddings

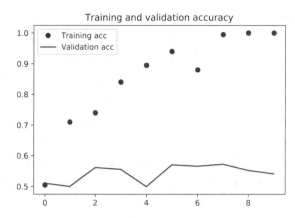

Training and validation accuracy

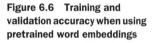

Figure 6.6 Training and validation accuracy when using pretrained word embeddings

The model quickly starts overfitting, which is unsurprising given the small number of training samples. Validation accuracy has high variance for the same reason, but it seems to reach the high 50s.

Note that your mileage may vary: because you have so few training samples, performance is heavily dependent on exactly which 200 samples you choose—and you're choosing them at random. If this works poorly for you, try choosing a different random set of 200 samples, for the sake of the exercise (in real life, you don't get to choose your training data).

You can also train the same model without loading the pretrained word embeddings and without freezing the embedding layer. In that case, you'll learn a task-specific embedding of the input tokens, which is generally more powerful than pretrained word embeddings when lots of data is available. But in this case, you have only 200 training samples. Let's try it (see figures 6.7 and 6.8).

Listing 6.16 Training the same model without pretrained word embeddings

```
from keras.models import Sequential
from keras.layers import Embedding, Flatten, Dense

model = Sequential()
model.add(Embedding(max_words, embedding_dim, input_length=maxlen))
model.add(Flatten())
model.add(Dense(32, activation='relu'))
model.add(Dense(1, activation='sigmoid'))
model.summary()

model.compile(optimizer='rmsprop',
              loss='binary_crossentropy',
              metrics=['acc'])
history = model.fit(x_train, y_train,
                    epochs=10,
                    batch_size=32,
                    validation_data=(x_val, y_val))
```

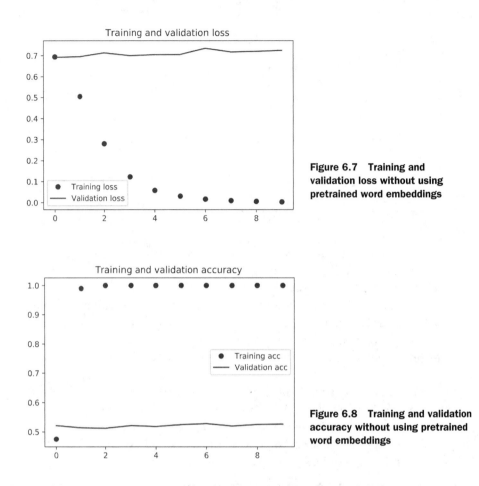

Figure 6.7   Training and validation loss without using pretrained word embeddings

Figure 6.8   Training and validation accuracy without using pretrained word embeddings

Validation accuracy stalls in the low 50s. So in this case, pretrained word embeddings outperform jointly learned embeddings. If you increase the number of training samples, this will quickly stop being the case—try it as an exercise.

Finally, let's evaluate the model on the test data. First, you need to tokenize the test data.

Listing 6.17   Tokenizing the data of the test set

```
test_dir = os.path.join(imdb_dir, 'test')

labels = []
texts = []

for label_type in ['neg', 'pos']:
    dir_name = os.path.join(test_dir, label_type)
    for fname in sorted(os.listdir(dir_name)):
        if fname[-4:] == '.txt':
            f = open(os.path.join(dir_name, fname))
            texts.append(f.read())
```

```
            f.close()
            if label_type == 'neg':
                labels.append(0)
            else:
                labels.append(1)
sequences = tokenizer.texts_to_sequences(texts)
x_test = pad_sequences(sequences, maxlen=maxlen)
y_test = np.asarray(labels)
```

Next, load and evaluate the first model.

Listing 6.18   Evaluating the model on the test set

```
model.load_weights('pre_trained_glove_model.h5')
model.evaluate(x_test, y_test)
```

You get an appalling test accuracy of 56%. Working with just a handful of training samples is difficult!

6.1.4 Wrapping up

Now you're able to do the following:

- Turn raw text into something a neural network can process
- Use the Embedding layer in a Keras model to learn task-specific token embeddings
- Use pretrained word embeddings to get an extra boost on small natural-language-processing problems

6.2   *Understanding recurrent neural networks*

A major characteristic of all neural networks you've seen so far, such as densely connected networks and convnets, is that they have no memory. Each input shown to them is processed independently, with no state kept in between inputs. With such networks, in order to process a sequence or a temporal series of data points, you have to show the entire sequence to the network at once: turn it into a single data point. For instance, this is what you did in the IMDB example: an entire movie review was transformed into a single large vector and processed in one go. Such networks are called *feedforward networks*.

In contrast, as you're reading the present sentence, you're processing it word by word—or rather, eye saccade by eye saccade—while keeping memories of what came before; this gives you a fluid representation of the meaning conveyed by this sentence. Biological intelligence processes information incrementally while maintaining an internal model of what it's processing, built from past information and constantly updated as new information comes in.

A *recurrent neural network* (RNN) adopts the same principle, albeit in an extremely simplified version: it processes sequences by iterating through the sequence elements and maintaining a *state* containing information relative to what it has seen so far. In effect, an RNN is a type of neural network that has an internal loop (see figure 6.9). The state of the RNN is reset between processing two different, independent sequences (such as two different IMDB reviews), so you still consider one sequence a single data point: a single input to the network. What changes is that this data point is no longer processed in a single step; rather, the network internally loops over sequence elements.

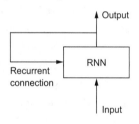

Figure 6.9   A recurrent network: a network with a loop

To make these notions of *loop* and *state* clear, let's implement the forward pass of a toy RNN in Numpy. This RNN takes as input a sequence of vectors, which you'll encode as a 2D tensor of size (timesteps, input_features). It loops over timesteps, and at each timestep, it considers its current state at t and the input at t (of shape (input_features,), and combines them to obtain the output at t. You'll then set the state for the next step to be this previous output. For the first timestep, the previous output isn't defined; hence, there is no current state. So, you'll initialize the state as an all-zero vector called the *initial state* of the network.

In pseudocode, this is the RNN.

Listing 6.19   Pseudocode RNN

```
state_t = 0                          ⟵── The state at t
for input_t in input_sequence:       ⟵── Iterates over sequence elements
    output_t = f(input_t, state_t)
    state_t = output_t    ⟵── The previous output becomes the state for the next iteration.
```

You can even flesh out the function f: the transformation of the input and state into an output will be parameterized by two matrices, W and U, and a bias vector. It's similar to the transformation operated by a densely connected layer in a feedforward network.

Listing 6.20 More detailed pseudocode for the RNN

```
state_t = 0
for input_t in input_sequence:
    output_t = activation(dot(W, input_t) + dot(U, state_t) + b)
    state_t = output_t
```

To make these notions absolutely unambiguous, let's write a naive Numpy implementation of the forward pass of the simple RNN.

Listing 6.21 Numpy implementation of a simple RNN

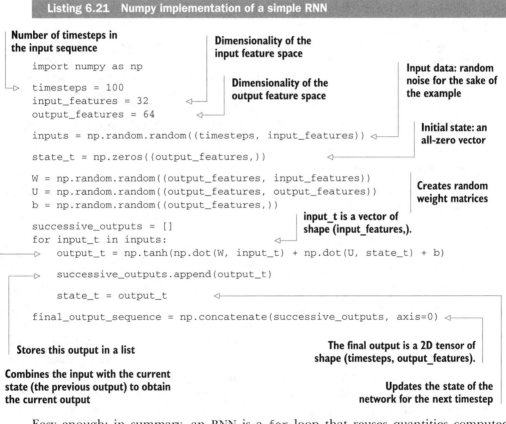

Number of timesteps in the input sequence

Dimensionality of the input feature space

Dimensionality of the output feature space

Input data: random noise for the sake of the example

```
import numpy as np

timesteps = 100
input_features = 32
output_features = 64

inputs = np.random.random((timesteps, input_features))

state_t = np.zeros((output_features,))

W = np.random.random((output_features, input_features))
U = np.random.random((output_features, output_features))
b = np.random.random((output_features,))

successive_outputs = []
for input_t in inputs:
    output_t = np.tanh(np.dot(W, input_t) + np.dot(U, state_t) + b)

    successive_outputs.append(output_t)

    state_t = output_t

final_output_sequence = np.concatenate(successive_outputs, axis=0)
```

Initial state: an all-zero vector

Creates random weight matrices

input_t is a vector of shape (input_features,).

Stores this output in a list

The final output is a 2D tensor of shape (timesteps, output_features).

Combines the input with the current state (the previous output) to obtain the current output

Updates the state of the network for the next timestep

Easy enough: in summary, an RNN is a for loop that reuses quantities computed during the previous iteration of the loop, nothing more. Of course, there are many different RNNs fitting this definition that you could build—this example is one of the simplest RNN formulations. RNNs are characterized by their step function, such as the following function in this case (see figure 6.10):

```
output_t = np.tanh(np.dot(W, input_t) + np.dot(U, state_t) + b)
```

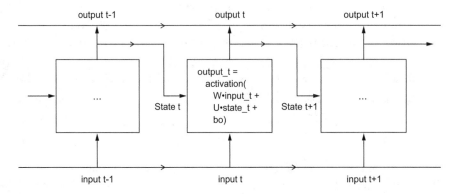

Figure 6.10   A simple RNN, unrolled over time

> **NOTE**   In this example, the final output is a 2D tensor of shape (timesteps, output_features), where each timestep is the output of the loop at time t. Each timestep t in the output tensor contains information about timesteps 0 to t in the input sequence—about the entire past. For this reason, in many cases, you don't need this full sequence of outputs; you just need the last output (output_t at the end of the loop), because it already contains information about the entire sequence.

6.2.1   A recurrent layer in Keras

The process you just naively implemented in Numpy corresponds to an actual Keras layer—the SimpleRNN layer:

```
from keras.layers import SimpleRNN
```

There is one minor difference: SimpleRNN processes batches of sequences, like all other Keras layers, not a single sequence as in the Numpy example. This means it takes inputs of shape (batch_size, timesteps, input_features), rather than (timesteps, input_features).

Like all recurrent layers in Keras, SimpleRNN can be run in two different modes: it can return either the full sequences of successive outputs for each timestep (a 3D tensor of shape (batch_size, timesteps, output_features)) or only the last output for each input sequence (a 2D tensor of shape (batch_size, output_features)). These two modes are controlled by the return_sequences constructor argument. Let's look at an example that uses SimpleRNN and returns only the output at the last timestep:

```
>>> from keras.models import Sequential
>>> from keras.layers import Embedding, SimpleRNN
>>> model = Sequential()
>>> model.add(Embedding(10000, 32))
>>> model.add(SimpleRNN(32))
>>> model.summary()
```

```
Layer (type)                    Output Shape            Param #
=================================================================
embedding_22 (Embedding)        (None, None, 32)        320000
_____
simplernn_10 (SimpleRNN)        (None, 32)              2080
=================================================================
Total params: 322,080
Trainable params: 322,080
Non-trainable params: 0
```

The following example returns the full state sequence:

```
>>> model = Sequential()
>>> model.add(Embedding(10000, 32))
>>> model.add(SimpleRNN(32, return_sequences=True))
>>> model.summary()
```

```
Layer (type)                    Output Shape            Param #
=================================================================
embedding_23 (Embedding)        (None, None, 32)        320000
_____
simplernn_11 (SimpleRNN)        (None, None, 32)        2080
=================================================================
Total params: 322,080
Trainable params: 322,080
Non-trainable params: 0
```

It's sometimes useful to stack several recurrent layers one after the other in order to increase the representational power of a network. In such a setup, you have to get all of the intermediate layers to return full sequence of outputs:

```
>>> model = Sequential()
>>> model.add(Embedding(10000, 32))
>>> model.add(SimpleRNN(32, return_sequences=True))
>>> model.add(SimpleRNN(32, return_sequences=True))
>>> model.add(SimpleRNN(32, return_sequences=True))     Last layer only returns
>>> model.add(SimpleRNN(32))                            the last output
>>> model.summary()
```

```
Layer (type)                    Output Shape            Param #
=================================================================
embedding_24 (Embedding)        (None, None, 32)        320000
_____
simplernn_12 (SimpleRNN)        (None, None, 32)        2080
_____
simplernn_13 (SimpleRNN)        (None, None, 32)        2080
_____
simplernn_14 (SimpleRNN)        (None, None, 32)        2080
_____
simplernn_15 (SimpleRNN)        (None, 32)              2080
=================================================================
Total params: 328,320
Trainable params: 328,320
Non-trainable params: 0
```

Now, let's use such a model on the IMDB movie-review-classification problem. First, preprocess the data.

Listing 6.22   Preparing the IMDB data

```
from keras.datasets import imdb
from keras.preprocessing import sequence

max_features = 10000
maxlen = 500
batch_size = 32

print('Loading data...')
(input_train, y_train), (input_test, y_test) = imdb.load_data(
    num_words=max_features)
print(len(input_train), 'train sequences')
print(len(input_test), 'test sequences')

print('Pad sequences (samples x time)')
input_train = sequence.pad_sequences(input_train, maxlen=maxlen)
input_test = sequence.pad_sequences(input_test, maxlen=maxlen)
print('input_train shape:', input_train.shape)
print('input_test shape:', input_test.shape)
```

Number of words to consider as features

Cuts off texts after this many words (among the max_features most common words)

Let's train a simple recurrent network using an `Embedding` layer and a `SimpleRNN` layer.

Listing 6.23   Training the model with `Embedding` and `SimpleRNN` layers

```
from keras.layers import Dense

model = Sequential()
model.add(Embedding(max_features, 32))
model.add(SimpleRNN(32))
model.add(Dense(1, activation='sigmoid'))

model.compile(optimizer='rmsprop', loss='binary_crossentropy', metrics=['acc'])
history = model.fit(input_train, y_train,
                    epochs=10,
                    batch_size=128,
                    validation_split=0.2)
```

Now, let's display the training and validation loss and accuracy (see figures 6.11 and 6.12).

Listing 6.24   Plotting results

```
import matplotlib.pyplot as plt

acc = history.history['acc']
val_acc = history.history['val_acc']
loss = history.history['loss']
val_loss = history.history['val_loss']

epochs = range(1, len(acc) + 1)

plt.plot(epochs, acc, 'bo', label='Training acc')
plt.plot(epochs, val_acc, 'b', label='Validation acc')
```

```
plt.title('Training and validation accuracy')
plt.legend()

plt.figure()

plt.plot(epochs, loss, 'bo', label='Training loss')
plt.plot(epochs, val_loss, 'b', label='Validation loss')
plt.title('Training and validation loss')
plt.legend()

plt.show()
```

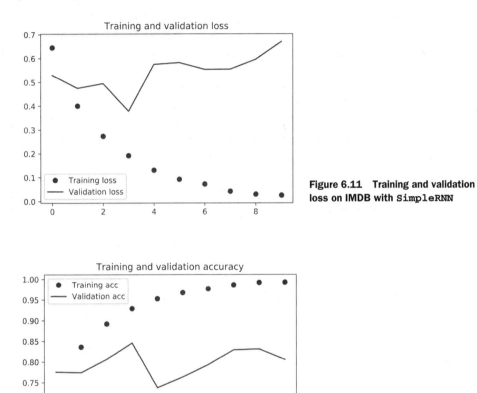

Figure 6.11 Training and validation loss on IMDB with `SimpleRNN`

Figure 6.12 Training and validation accuracy on IMDB with `SimpleRNN`

As a reminder, in chapter 3, the first naive approach to this dataset got you to a test accuracy of 88%. Unfortunately, this small recurrent network doesn't perform well compared to this baseline (only 85% validation accuracy). Part of the problem is that your inputs only consider the first 500 words, rather than full sequences—hence, the RNN has access to less information than the earlier baseline model. The remainder of the problem is that `SimpleRNN` isn't good at processing long sequences, such as text.

Other types of recurrent layers perform much better. Let's look at some more-advanced layers.

6.2.2 Understanding the LSTM and GRU layers

SimpleRNN isn't the only recurrent layer available in Keras. There are two others: LSTM and GRU. In practice, you'll always use one of these, because SimpleRNN is generally too simplistic to be of real use. SimpleRNN has a major issue: although it should theoretically be able to retain at time t information about inputs seen many timesteps before, in practice, such long-term dependencies are impossible to learn. This is due to the *vanishing gradient problem*, an effect that is similar to what is observed with non-recurrent networks (feedforward networks) that are many layers deep: as you keep adding layers to a network, the network eventually becomes untrainable. The theoretical reasons for this effect were studied by Hochreiter, Schmidhuber, and Bengio in the early 1990s.[2] The LSTM and GRU layers are designed to solve this problem.

Let's consider the LSTM layer. The underlying Long Short-Term Memory (LSTM) algorithm was developed by Hochreiter and Schmidhuber in 1997;[3] it was the culmination of their research on the vanishing gradient problem.

This layer is a variant of the SimpleRNN layer you already know about; it adds a way to carry information across many timesteps. Imagine a conveyor belt running parallel to the sequence you're processing. Information from the sequence can jump onto the conveyor belt at any point, be transported to a later timestep, and jump off, intact, when you need it. This is essentially what LSTM does: it saves information for later, thus preventing older signals from gradually vanishing during processing.

To understand this in detail, let's start from the SimpleRNN cell (see figure 6.13). Because you'll have a lot of weight matrices, index the W and U matrices in the cell with the letter o (Wo and Uo) for *output.*

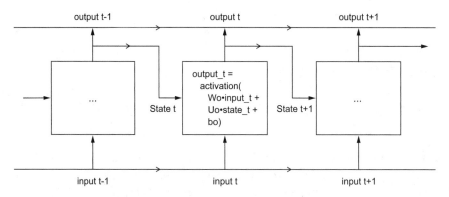

Figure 6.13   The starting point of an LSTM layer: a SimpleRNN

---

[2]   See, for example, Yoshua Bengio, Patrice Simard, and Paolo Frasconi, "Learning Long-Term Dependencies with Gradient Descent Is Difficult," *IEEE Transactions on Neural Networks* 5, no. 2 (1994).

[3]   Sepp Hochreiter and Jürgen Schmidhuber, "Long Short-Term Memory," *Neural Computation* 9, no. 8 (1997).

Let's add to this picture an additional data flow that carries information across time-steps. Call its values at different timesteps Ct, where *C* stands for *carry*. This information will have the following impact on the cell: it will be combined with the input connection and the recurrent connection (via a dense transformation: a dot product with a weight matrix followed by a bias add and the application of an activation function), and it will affect the state being sent to the next timestep (via an activation function an a multiplication operation). Conceptually, the carry dataflow is a way to modulate the next output and the next state (see figure 6.14). Simple so far.

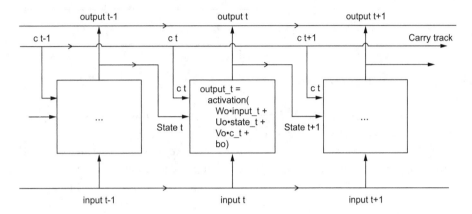

Figure 6.14 Going from a `SimpleRNN` to an `LSTM`: adding a carry track

Now the subtlety: the way the next value of the carry dataflow is computed. It involves three distinct transformations. All three have the form of a `SimpleRNN` cell:

```
y = activation(dot(state_t, U) + dot(input_t, W) + b)
```

But all three transformations have their own weight matrices, which you'll index with the letters i, f, and k. Here's what you have so far (it may seem a bit arbitrary, but bear with me).

Listing 6.25 Pseudocode details of the LSTM architecture (1/2)

```
output_t = activation(dot(state_t, Uo) + dot(input_t, Wo) + dot(C_t, Vo) + bo)

i_t = activation(dot(state_t, Ui) + dot(input_t, Wi) + bi)
f_t = activation(dot(state_t, Uf) + dot(input_t, Wf) + bf)
k_t = activation(dot(state_t, Uk) + dot(input_t, Wk) + bk)
```

You obtain the new carry state (the next c_t) by combining i_t, f_t, and k_t.

Listing 6.26 Pseudocode details of the LSTM architecture (2/2)

```
c_t+1 = i_t * k_t + c_t * f_t
```

Add this as shown in figure 6.15. And that's it. Not so complicated—merely a tad complex.

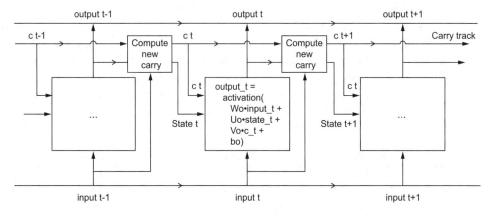

Figure 6.15 Anatomy of an LSTM

If you want to get philosophical, you can interpret what each of these operations is meant to do. For instance, you can say that multiplying c_t and f_t is a way to deliberately forget irrelevant information in the carry dataflow. Meanwhile, i_t and k_t provide information about the present, updating the carry track with new information. But at the end of the day, these interpretations don't mean much, because what these operations *actually* do is determined by the contents of the weights parameterizing them; and the weights are learned in an end-to-end fashion, starting over with each training round, making it impossible to credit this or that operation with a specific purpose. The specification of an RNN cell (as just described) determines your hypothesis space—the space in which you'll search for a good model configuration during training—but it doesn't determine what the cell does; that is up to the cell weights. The same cell with different weights can be doing very different things. So the combination of operations making up an RNN cell is better interpreted as a set of *constraints* on your search, not as a *design* in an engineering sense.

To a researcher, it seems that the choice of such constraints—the question of how to implement RNN cells—is better left to optimization algorithms (like genetic algorithms or reinforcement learning processes) than to human engineers. And in the future, that's how we'll build networks. In summary: you don't need to understand anything about the specific architecture of an LSTM cell; as a human, it shouldn't be your job to understand it. Just keep in mind what the LSTM cell is meant to do: allow past information to be reinjected at a later time, thus fighting the vanishing-gradient problem.

6.2.3 *A concrete LSTM example in Keras*

Now let's switch to more practical concerns: you'll set up a model using an LSTM layer and train it on the IMDB data (see figures 6.16 and 6.17). The network is similar to the one with SimpleRNN that was just presented. You only specify the output dimensionality of the LSTM layer; leave every other argument (there are many) at the Keras defaults. Keras has good defaults, and things will almost always "just work" without you having to spend time tuning parameters by hand.

Listing 6.27 Using the `LSTM` layer in Keras

```
from keras.layers import LSTM

model = Sequential()
model.add(Embedding(max_features, 32))
model.add(LSTM(32))
model.add(Dense(1, activation='sigmoid'))

model.compile(optimizer='rmsprop',
              loss='binary_crossentropy',
              metrics=['acc'])
history = model.fit(input_train, y_train,
                    epochs=10,
                    batch_size=128,
                    validation_split=0.2)
```

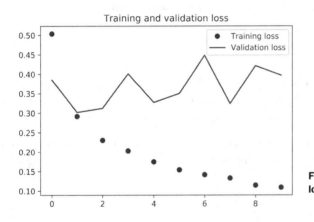

Figure 6.16 Training and validation loss on IMDB with LSTM

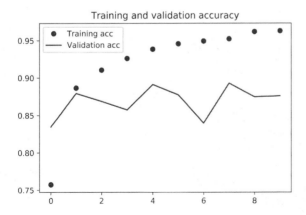

Figure 6.17 Training and validation accuracy on IMDB with LSTM

This time, you achieve up to 89% validation accuracy. Not bad: certainly much better than the SimpleRNN network—that's largely because LSTM suffers much less from the vanishing-gradient problem—and slightly better than the fully connected approach from chapter 3, even though you're looking at less data than you were in chapter 3. You're truncating sequences after 500 timesteps, whereas in chapter 3, you were considering full sequences.

But this result isn't groundbreaking for such a computationally intensive approach. Why isn't LSTM performing better? One reason is that you made no effort to tune hyperparameters such as the embeddings dimensionality or the LSTM output dimensionality. Another may be lack of regularization. But honestly, the primary reason is that analyzing the global, long-term structure of the reviews (what LSTM is good at) isn't helpful for a sentiment-analysis problem. Such a basic problem is well solved by looking at what words occur in each review, and at what frequency. That's what the first fully connected approach looked at. But there are far more difficult natural-language-processing problems out there, where the strength of LSTM will become apparent: in particular, question-answering and machine translation.

6.2.4 *Wrapping up*

Now you understand the following:

- What RNNs are and how they work
- What LSTM is, and why it works better on long sequences than a naive RNN
- How to use Keras RNN layers to process sequence data

Next, we'll review a number of more advanced features of RNNs, which can help you get the most out of your deep-learning sequence models.

6.3 *Advanced use of recurrent neural networks*

In this section, we'll review three advanced techniques for improving the performance and generalization power of recurrent neural networks. By the end of the section, you'll know most of what there is to know about using recurrent networks with Keras. We'll demonstrate all three concepts on a temperature-forecasting problem, where you have access to a timeseries of data points coming from sensors installed on the roof of a building, such as temperature, air pressure, and humidity, which you use to predict what the temperature will be 24 hours after the last data point. This is a fairly challenging problem that exemplifies many common difficulties encountered when working with timeseries.

We'll cover the following techniques:

- *Recurrent dropout*—This is a specific, built-in way to use dropout to fight overfitting in recurrent layers.
- *Stacking recurrent layers*—This increases the representational power of the network (at the cost of higher computational loads).
- *Bidirectional recurrent layers*—These present the same information to a recurrent network in different ways, increasing accuracy and mitigating forgetting issues.

6.3.1 *A temperature-forecasting problem*

Until now, the only sequence data we've covered has been text data, such as the IMDB dataset and the Reuters dataset. But sequence data is found in many more problems than just language processing. In all the examples in this section, you'll play with a weather timeseries dataset recorded at the Weather Station at the Max Planck Institute for Biogeochemistry in Jena, Germany.[4]

In this dataset, 14 different quantities (such air temperature, atmospheric pressure, humidity, wind direction, and so on) were recorded every 10 minutes, over several years. The original data goes back to 2003, but this example is limited to data from 2009–2016. This dataset is perfect for learning to work with numerical timeseries. You'll use it to build a model that takes as input some data from the recent past (a few days' worth of data points) and predicts the air temperature 24 hours in the future.

Download and uncompress the data as follows:

```
cd ~/Downloads
mkdir jena_climate
cd jena_climate
wget https://s3.amazonaws.com/keras-datasets/jena_climate_2009_2016.csv.zip
unzip jena_climate_2009_2016.csv.zip
```

Let's look at the data.

---

[4] Olaf Kolle, www.bgc-jena.mpg.de/wetter.

Listing 6.28   Inspecting the data of the Jena weather dataset

```
import os

data_dir = '/users/fchollet/Downloads/jena_climate'
fname = os.path.join(data_dir, 'jena_climate_2009_2016.csv')

f = open(fname)
data = f.read()
f.close()

lines = data.split('\n')
header = lines[0].split(',')
lines = lines[1:]

print(header)
print(len(lines))
```

This outputs a count of 420,551 lines of data (each line is a timestep: a record of a date and 14 weather-related values), as well as the following header:

```
["Date Time",
 "p (mbar)",
 "T (degC)",
 "Tpot (K)",
 "Tdew (degC)",
 "rh (%)",
 "VPmax (mbar)",
 "VPact (mbar)",
 "VPdef (mbar)",
 "sh (g/kg)",
 "H2OC (mmol/mol)",
 "rho (g/m**3)",
 "wv (m/s)",
 "max. wv (m/s)",
 "wd (deg)"]
```

Now, convert all 420,551 lines of data into a Numpy array.

Listing 6.29   Parsing the data

```
import numpy as np

float_data = np.zeros((len(lines), len(header) - 1))
for i, line in enumerate(lines):
    values = [float(x) for x in line.split(',')[1:]]
    float_data[i, :] = values
```

For instance, here is the plot of temperature (in degrees Celsius) over time (see figure 6.18). On this plot, you can clearly see the yearly periodicity of temperature.

Listing 6.30   Plotting the temperature timeseries

```
from matplotlib import pyplot as plt

temp = float_data[:, 1]   <1> temperature (in degrees Celsius)
plt.plot(range(len(temp)), temp)
```

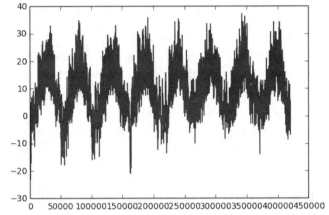

Figure 6.18   Temperature over the full temporal range of the dataset (°C)

Here is a more narrow plot of the first 10 days of temperature data (see figure 6.19). Because the data is recorded every 10 minutes, you get 144 data points per day.

Listing 6.31   Plotting the first 10 days of the temperature timeseries

```
plt.plot(range(1440), temp[:1440])
```

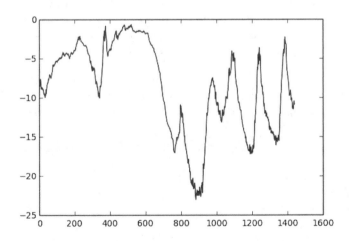

Figure 6.19   Temperature over the first 10 days of the dataset (°C)

On this plot, you can see daily periodicity, especially evident for the last 4 days. Also note that this 10-day period must be coming from a fairly cold winter month.

If you were trying to predict average temperature for the next month given a few months of past data, the problem would be easy, due to the reliable year-scale periodicity of the data. But looking at the data over a scale of days, the temperature looks a lot more chaotic. Is this timeseries predictable at a daily scale? Let's find out.

6.3.2 Preparing the data

The exact formulation of the problem will be as follows: given data going as far back as `lookback` timesteps (a timestep is 10 minutes) and sampled every `steps` timesteps, can you predict the temperature in `delay` timesteps? You'll use the following parameter values:

- `lookback = 720`—Observations will go back 5 days.
- `steps = 6`—Observations will be sampled at one data point per hour.
- `delay = 144`—Targets will be 24 hours in the future.

To get started, you need to do two things:

- Preprocess the data to a format a neural network can ingest. This is easy: the data is already numerical, so you don't need to do any vectorization. But each timeseries in the data is on a different scale (for example, temperature is typically between -20 and +30, but atmospheric pressure, measured in mbar, is around 1,000). You'll normalize each timeseries independently so that they all take small values on a similar scale.
- Write a Python generator that takes the current array of float data and yields batches of data from the recent past, along with a target temperature in the future. Because the samples in the dataset are highly redundant (sample *N* and sample *N* + 1 will have most of their timesteps in common), it would be wasteful to explicitly allocate every sample. Instead, you'll generate the samples on the fly using the original data.

You'll preprocess the data by subtracting the mean of each timeseries and dividing by the standard deviation. You're going to use the first 200,000 timesteps as training data, so compute the mean and standard deviation only on this fraction of the data.

Listing 6.32   Normalizing the data

```
mean = float_data[:200000].mean(axis=0)
float_data -= mean
std = float_data[:200000].std(axis=0)
float_data /= std
```

Listing 6.33 shows the data generator you'll use. It yields a tuple (`samples`, `targets`), where `samples` is one batch of input data and `targets` is the corresponding array of target temperatures. It takes the following arguments:

- data—The original array of floating-point data, which you normalized in listing 6.32.
- lookback—How many timesteps back the input data should go.
- delay—How many timesteps in the future the target should be.
- min_index and max_index—Indices in the data array that delimit which time-steps to draw from. This is useful for keeping a segment of the data for valida-tion and another for testing.
- shuffle—Whether to shuffle the samples or draw them in chronological order.
- batch_size—The number of samples per batch.
- step—The period, in timesteps, at which you sample data. You'll set it to 6 in order to draw one data point every hour.

Listing 6.33   Generator yielding timeseries samples and their targets

```
def generator(data, lookback, delay, min_index, max_index,
              shuffle=False, batch_size=128, step=6):
    if max_index is None:
        max_index = len(data) - delay - 1
    i = min_index + lookback
    while 1:
        if shuffle:
            rows = np.random.randint(
                min_index + lookback, max_index, size=batch_size)
        else:
            if i + batch_size >= max_index:
                i = min_index + lookback
            rows = np.arange(i, min(i + batch_size, max_index))
            i += len(rows)

        samples = np.zeros((len(rows),
                           lookback // step,
                           data.shape[-1]))
        targets = np.zeros((len(rows),))
        for j, row in enumerate(rows):
            indices = range(rows[j] - lookback, rows[j], step)
            samples[j] = data[indices]
            targets[j] = data[rows[j] + delay][1]
        yield samples, targets
```

Now, let's use the abstract generator function to instantiate three generators: one for training, one for validation, and one for testing. Each will look at different temporal segments of the original data: the training generator looks at the first 200,000 time-steps, the validation generator looks at the following 100,000, and the test generator looks at the remainder.

Listing 6.34   Preparing the training, validation, and test generators

```
lookback = 1440
step = 6
delay = 144
batch_size = 128
```

```
train_gen = generator(float_data,
                      lookback=lookback,
                      delay=delay,
                      min_index=0,
                      max_index=200000,
                      shuffle=True,
                      step=step,
                      batch_size=batch_size)
val_gen = generator(float_data,
                    lookback=lookback,
                    delay=delay,
                    min_index=200001,
                    max_index=300000,
                    step=step,
                    batch_size=batch_size)
test_gen = generator(float_data,
                     lookback=lookback,
                     delay=delay,
                     min_index=300001,
                     max_index=None,
                     step=step,
                     batch_size=batch_size)

val_steps = (300000 - 200001 - lookback)

test_steps = (len(float_data) - 300001 - lookback)
```

How many steps to draw from val_gen in order to see the entire validation set

How many steps to draw from test_gen in order to see the entire test set

6.3.3 *A common-sense, non-machine-learning baseline*

Before you start using black-box deep-learning models to solve the temperature-prediction problem, let's try a simple, common-sense approach. It will serve as a sanity check, and it will establish a baseline that you'll have to beat in order to demonstrate the usefulness of more-advanced machine-learning models. Such common-sense baselines can be useful when you're approaching a new problem for which there is no known solution (yet). A classic example is that of unbalanced classification tasks, where some classes are much more common than others. If your dataset contains 90% instances of class A and 10% instances of class B, then a common-sense approach to the classification task is to always predict "A" when presented with a new sample. Such a classifier is 90% accurate overall, and any learning-based approach should therefore beat this 90% score in order to demonstrate usefulness. Sometimes, such elementary baselines can prove surprisingly hard to beat.

In this case, the temperature timeseries can safely be assumed to be continuous (the temperatures tomorrow are likely to be close to the temperatures today) as well as periodical with a daily period. Thus a common-sense approach is to always predict that the temperature 24 hours from now will be equal to the temperature right now. Let's evaluate this approach, using the mean absolute error (MAE) metric:

```
np.mean(np.abs(preds - targets))
```

Here's the evaluation loop.

Listing 6.35   **Computing the common-sense baseline MAE**

```
def evaluate_naive_method():
    batch_maes = []
    for step in range(val_steps):
        samples, targets = next(val_gen)
        preds = samples[:, -1, 1]
        mae = np.mean(np.abs(preds - targets))
        batch_maes.append(mae)
    print(np.mean(batch_maes))

evaluate_naive_method()
```

This yields an MAE of 0.29. Because the temperature data has been normalized to be centered on 0 and have a standard deviation of 1, this number isn't immediately interpretable. It translates to an average absolute error of 0.29 × `temperature_std` degrees Celsius: 2.57°C.

Listing 6.36   **Converting the MAE back to a Celsius error**

```
celsius_mae = 0.29 * std[1]
```

That's a fairly large average absolute error. Now the game is to use your knowledge of deep learning to do better.

6.3.4   *A basic machine-learning approach*

In the same way that it's useful to establish a common-sense baseline before trying machine-learning approaches, it's useful to try simple, cheap machine-learning models (such as small, densely connected networks) before looking into complicated and computationally expensive models such as RNNs. This is the best way to make sure any further complexity you throw at the problem is legitimate and delivers real benefits.

The following listing shows a fully connected model that starts by flattening the data and then runs it through two Dense layers. Note the lack of activation function on the last Dense layer, which is typical for a regression problem. You use MAE as the loss. Because you evaluate on the exact same data and with the exact same metric you did with the common-sense approach, the results will be directly comparable.

Listing 6.37   **Training and evaluating a densely connected model**

```
from keras.models import Sequential
from keras import layers
from keras.optimizers import RMSprop

model = Sequential()
model.add(layers.Flatten(input_shape=(lookback // step, float_data.shape[-1])))
model.add(layers.Dense(32, activation='relu'))
model.add(layers.Dense(1))
```

```
model.compile(optimizer=RMSprop(), loss='mae')
history = model.fit_generator(train_gen,
                              steps_per_epoch=500,
                              epochs=20,
                              validation_data=val_gen,
                              validation_steps=val_steps)
```

Let's display the loss curves for validation and training (see figure 6.20).

Listing 6.38   Plotting results

```
import matplotlib.pyplot as plt

loss = history.history['loss']
val_loss = history.history['val_loss']

epochs = range(1, len(loss) + 1)

plt.figure()

plt.plot(epochs, loss, 'bo', label='Training loss')
plt.plot(epochs, val_loss, 'b', label='Validation loss')
plt.title('Training and validation loss')
plt.legend()

plt.show()
```

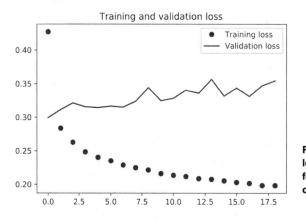

Figure 6.20   Training and validation loss on the Jena temperature-forecasting task with a simple, densely connected network

Some of the validation losses are close to the no-learning baseline, but not reliably. This goes to show the merit of having this baseline in the first place: it turns out to be not easy to outperform. Your common sense contains a lot of valuable information that a machine-learning model doesn't have access to.

You may wonder, if a simple, well-performing model exists to go from the data to the targets (the common-sense baseline), why doesn't the model you're training find it and improve on it? Because this simple solution isn't what your training setup is looking for. The space of models in which you're searching for a solution—that is, your hypothesis space—is the space of all possible two-layer networks with the configuration you defined. These networks are already fairly complicated. When you're looking for a solution with a space of complicated models, the simple, well-performing baseline may be unlearnable, even if it's technically part of the hypothesis space. That is a pretty significant limitation of machine learning in general: unless the learning algorithm is hardcoded to look for a specific kind of simple model, parameter learning can sometimes fail to find a simple solution to a simple problem.

6.3.5 *A first recurrent baseline*

The first fully connected approach didn't do well, but that doesn't mean machine learning isn't applicable to this problem. The previous approach first flattened the timeseries, which removed the notion of time from the input data. Let's instead look at the data as what it is: a sequence, where causality and order matter. You'll try a recurrent-sequence processing model—it should be the perfect fit for such sequence data, precisely because it exploits the temporal ordering of data points, unlike the first approach.

Instead of the LSTM layer introduced in the previous section, you'll use the GRU layer, developed by Chung et al. in 2014.[5] Gated recurrent unit (GRU) layers work using the same principle as LSTM, but they're somewhat streamlined and thus cheaper to run (although they may not have as much representational power as LSTM). This trade-off between computational expensiveness and representational power is seen everywhere in machine learning.

Listing 6.39 Training and evaluating a GRU-based model

```
from keras.models import Sequential
from keras import layers
from keras.optimizers import RMSprop

model = Sequential()
model.add(layers.GRU(32, input_shape=(None, float_data.shape[-1])))
model.add(layers.Dense(1))

model.compile(optimizer=RMSprop(), loss='mae')
history = model.fit_generator(train_gen,
                              steps_per_epoch=500,
                              epochs=20,
                              validation_data=val_gen,
                              validation_steps=val_steps)
```

Figure 6.21 shows the results. Much better! You can significantly beat the common-sense baseline, demonstrating the value of machine learning as well as the superiority of recurrent networks compared to sequence-flattening dense networks on this type of task.

---

[5] Junyoung Chung et al., "Empirical Evaluation of Gated Recurrent Neural Networks on Sequence Modeling," Conference on Neural Information Processing Systems (2014), https://arxiv.org/abs/1412.3555.

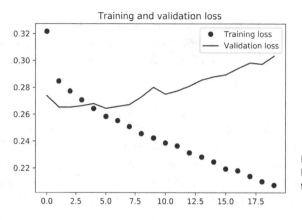

Training and validation loss

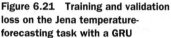

Figure 6.21   Training and validation loss on the Jena temperature-forecasting task with a GRU

The new validation MAE of ~0.265 (before you start significantly overfitting) translates to a mean absolute error of 2.35°C after denormalization. That's a solid gain on the initial error of 2.57°C, but you probably still have a bit of a margin for improvement.

6.3.6   *Using recurrent dropout to fight overfitting*

It's evident from the training and validation curves that the model is overfitting: the training and validation losses start to diverge considerably after a few epochs. You're already familiar with a classic technique for fighting this phenomenon: dropout, which randomly zeros out input units of a layer in order to break happenstance correlations in the training data that the layer is exposed to. But how to correctly apply dropout in recurrent networks isn't a trivial question. It has long been known that applying dropout before a recurrent layer hinders learning rather than helping with regularization. In 2015, Yarin Gal, as part of his PhD thesis on Bayesian deep learning,[6] determined the proper way to use dropout with a recurrent network: the same dropout mask (the same pattern of dropped units) should be applied at every time-step, instead of a dropout mask that varies randomly from timestep to timestep. What's more, in order to regularize the representations formed by the recurrent gates of layers such as GRU and LSTM, a temporally constant dropout mask should be applied to the inner recurrent activations of the layer (a *recurrent* dropout mask). Using the same dropout mask at every timestep allows the network to properly propagate its learning error through time; a temporally random dropout mask would disrupt this error signal and be harmful to the learning process.

Yarin Gal did his research using Keras and helped build this mechanism directly into Keras recurrent layers. Every recurrent layer in Keras has two dropout-related arguments: dropout, a float specifying the dropout rate for input units of the layer,

---

[6]   See Yarin Gal, "Uncertainty in Deep Learning (PhD Thesis)," October 13, 2016, http://mlg.eng.cam.ac.uk/yarin/blog_2248.html.

and `recurrent_dropout`, specifying the dropout rate of the recurrent units. Let's add dropout and recurrent dropout to the GRU layer and see how doing so impacts overfitting. Because networks being regularized with dropout always take longer to fully converge, you'll train the network for twice as many epochs.

Listing 6.40 Training and evaluating a dropout-regularized GRU-based model

```
from keras.models import Sequential
from keras import layers
from keras.optimizers import RMSprop

model = Sequential()
model.add(layers.GRU(32,
                     dropout=0.2,
                     recurrent_dropout=0.2,
                     input_shape=(None, float_data.shape[-1])))
model.add(layers.Dense(1))

model.compile(optimizer=RMSprop(), loss='mae')
history = model.fit_generator(train_gen,
                              steps_per_epoch=500,
                              epochs=40,
                              validation_data=val_gen,
                              validation_steps=val_steps)
```

Figure 6.22 shows the results. Success! You're no longer overfitting during the first 30 epochs. But although you have more stable evaluation scores, your best scores aren't much lower than they were previously.

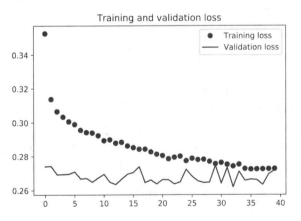

Figure 6.22 Training and validation loss on the Jena temperature-forecasting task with a dropout-regularized GRU

6.3.7 Stacking recurrent layers

Because you're no longer overfitting but seem to have hit a performance bottleneck, you should consider increasing the capacity of the network. Recall the description of the universal machine-learning workflow: it's generally a good idea to increase the capacity of your network until overfitting becomes the primary obstacle (assuming you're already taking basic steps to mitigate overfitting, such as using dropout). As long as you aren't overfitting too badly, you're likely under capacity.

Increasing network capacity is typically done by increasing the number of units in the layers or adding more layers. Recurrent layer stacking is a classic way to build more-powerful recurrent networks: for instance, what currently powers the Google Translate algorithm is a stack of seven large LSTM layers—that's huge.

To stack recurrent layers on top of each other in Keras, all intermediate layers should return their full sequence of outputs (a 3D tensor) rather than their output at the last timestep. This is done by specifying return_sequences=True.

> **Listing 6.41   Training and evaluating a dropout-regularized, stacked GRU model**

```
from keras.models import Sequential
from keras import layers
from keras.optimizers import RMSprop

model = Sequential()
model.add(layers.GRU(32,
                     dropout=0.1,
                     recurrent_dropout=0.5,
                     return_sequences=True,
                     input_shape=(None, float_data.shape[-1])))
model.add(layers.GRU(64, activation='relu',
                     dropout=0.1,
                     recurrent_dropout=0.5))
model.add(layers.Dense(1))

model.compile(optimizer=RMSprop(), loss='mae')
history = model.fit_generator(train_gen,
                              steps_per_epoch=500,
                              epochs=40,
                              validation_data=val_gen,
                              validation_steps=val_steps)
```

Figure 6.23 shows the results. You can see that the added layer does improve the results a bit, though not significantly. You can draw two conclusions:

- Because you're still not overfitting too badly, you could safely increase the size of your layers in a quest for validation-loss improvement. This has a non-negligible computational cost, though.
- Adding a layer didn't help by a significant factor, so you may be seeing diminishing returns from increasing network capacity at this point.

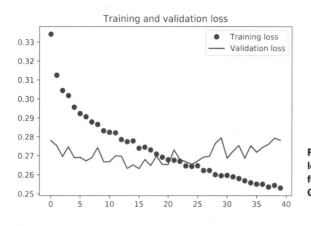

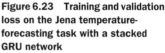

Figure 6.23   Training and validation loss on the Jena temperature-forecasting task with a stacked GRU network

6.3.8   *Using bidirectional RNNs*

The last technique introduced in this section is called *bidirectional RNNs*. A bidirectional RNN is a common RNN variant that can offer greater performance than a regular RNN on certain tasks. It's frequently used in natural-language processing—you could call it the Swiss Army knife of deep learning for natural-language processing.

RNNs are notably order dependent, or time dependent: they process the timesteps of their input sequences in order, and shuffling or reversing the timesteps can completely change the representations the RNN extracts from the sequence. This is precisely the reason they perform well on problems where order is meaningful, such as the temperature-forecasting problem. A bidirectional RNN exploits the order sensitivity of RNNs: it consists of using two regular RNNs, such as the GRU and LSTM layers you're already familiar with, each of which processes the input sequence in one direction (chronologically and antichronologically), and then merging their representations. By processing a sequence both ways, a bidirectional RNN can catch patterns that may be overlooked by a unidirectional RNN.

Remarkably, the fact that the RNN layers in this section have processed sequences in chronological order (older timesteps first) may have been an arbitrary decision. At least, it's a decision we made no attempt to question so far. Could the RNNs have performed well enough if they processed input sequences in antichronological order, for instance (newer timesteps first)? Let's try this in practice and see what happens. All you need to do is write a variant of the data generator where the input sequences are reverted along the time dimension (replace the last line with `yield samples[:, ::-1, :], targets`). Training the same one-GRU-layer network that you used in the first experiment in this section, you get the results shown in figure 6.24.

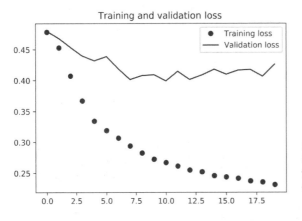

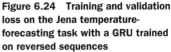

Figure 6.24 **Training and validation loss on the Jena temperature-forecasting task with a GRU trained on reversed sequences**

The reversed-order GRU strongly underperforms even the common-sense baseline, indicating that in this case, chronological processing is important to the success of your approach. This makes perfect sense: the underlying GRU layer will typically be better at remembering the recent past than the distant past, and naturally the more recent weather data points are more predictive than older data points for the problem (that's what makes the common-sense baseline fairly strong). Thus the chronological version of the layer is bound to outperform the reversed-order version. Importantly, this isn't true for many other problems, including natural language: intuitively, the importance of a word in understanding a sentence isn't usually dependent on its position in the sentence. Let's try the same trick on the LSTM IMDB example from section 6.2.

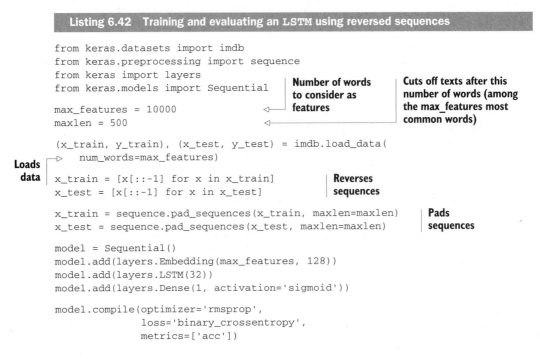

Listing 6.42 **Training and evaluating an LSTM using reversed sequences**

```
from keras.datasets import imdb
from keras.preprocessing import sequence
from keras import layers
from keras.models import Sequential        Number of words      Cuts off texts after this
                                           to consider as       number of words (among
max_features = 10000                   ◁── features            the max_features most
maxlen = 500                          ◁────────────────────    common words)

(x_train, y_train), (x_test, y_test) = imdb.load_data(
         num_words=max_features)
x_train = [x[::-1] for x in x_train]            Reverses
x_test = [x[::-1] for x in x_test]              sequences

x_train = sequence.pad_sequences(x_train, maxlen=maxlen)     Pads
x_test = sequence.pad_sequences(x_test, maxlen=maxlen)       sequences

model = Sequential()
model.add(layers.Embedding(max_features, 128))
model.add(layers.LSTM(32))
model.add(layers.Dense(1, activation='sigmoid'))

model.compile(optimizer='rmsprop',
              loss='binary_crossentropy',
              metrics=['acc'])
```

Loads
data

```
history = model.fit(x_train, y_train,
                    epochs=10,
                    batch_size=128,
                    validation_split=0.2)
```

You get performance nearly identical to that of the chronological-order LSTM. Remarkably, on such a text dataset, reversed-order processing works just as well as chronological processing, confirming the hypothesis that, although word order *does* matter in understanding language, *which* order you use isn't crucial. Importantly, an RNN trained on reversed sequences will learn different representations than one trained on the original sequences, much as you would have different mental models if time flowed backward in the real world—if you lived a life where you died on your first day and were born on your last day. In machine learning, representations that are *different* yet *useful* are always worth exploiting, and the more they differ, the better: they offer a new angle from which to look at your data, capturing aspects of the data that were missed by other approaches, and thus they can help boost performance on a task. This is the intuition behind *ensembling*, a concept we'll explore in chapter 7.

A bidirectional RNN exploits this idea to improve on the performance of chronological-order RNNs. It looks at its input sequence both ways (see figure 6.25), obtaining potentially richer representations and capturing patterns that may have been missed by the chronological-order version alone.

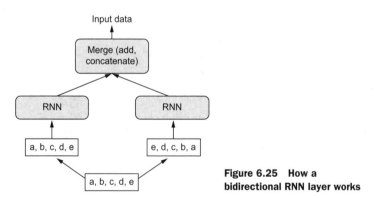

Figure 6.25   How a bidirectional RNN layer works

To instantiate a bidirectional RNN in Keras, you use the `Bidirectional` layer, which takes as its first argument a recurrent layer instance. `Bidirectional` creates a second, separate instance of this recurrent layer and uses one instance for processing the input sequences in chronological order and the other instance for processing the input sequences in reversed order. Let's try it on the IMDB sentiment-analysis task.

Listing 6.43   Training and evaluating a bidirectional LSTM

```
model = Sequential()
model.add(layers.Embedding(max_features, 32))
model.add(layers.Bidirectional(layers.LSTM(32)))
model.add(layers.Dense(1, activation='sigmoid'))
```

```
model.compile(optimizer='rmsprop', loss='binary_crossentropy', metrics=['acc'])
history = model.fit(x_train, y_train,
                    epochs=10,
                    batch_size=128,
                    validation_split=0.2)
```

It performs slightly better than the regular LSTM you tried in the previous section, achieving over 89% validation accuracy. It also seems to overfit more quickly, which is unsurprising because a bidirectional layer has twice as many parameters as a chronological LSTM. With some regularization, the bidirectional approach would likely be a strong performer on this task.

Now let's try the same approach on the temperature-prediction task.

Listing 6.44 Training a bidirectional GRU

```
from keras.models import Sequential
from keras import layers
from keras.optimizers import RMSprop

model = Sequential()
model.add(layers.Bidirectional(
    layers.GRU(32), input_shape=(None, float_data.shape[-1])))
model.add(layers.Dense(1))

model.compile(optimizer=RMSprop(), loss='mae')
history = model.fit_generator(train_gen,
                              steps_per_epoch=500,
                              epochs=40,
                              validation_data=val_gen,
                              validation_steps=val_steps)
```

This performs about as well as the regular GRU layer. It's easy to understand why: all the predictive capacity must come from the chronological half of the network, because the antichronological half is known to be severely underperforming on this task (again, because the recent past matters much more than the distant past in this case).

6.3.9 *Going even further*

There are many other things you could try, in order to improve performance on the temperature-forecasting problem:

- Adjust the number of units in each recurrent layer in the stacked setup. The current choices are largely arbitrary and thus probably suboptimal.
- Adjust the learning rate used by the RMSprop optimizer.
- Try using LSTM layers instead of GRU layers.
- Try using a bigger densely connected regressor on top of the recurrent layers: that is, a bigger Dense layer or even a stack of Dense layers.
- Don't forget to eventually run the best-performing models (in terms of validation MAE) on the test set! Otherwise, you'll develop architectures that are overfitting to the validation set.

As always, deep learning is more an art than a science. We can provide guidelines that suggest what is likely to work or not work on a given problem, but, ultimately, every problem is unique; you'll have to evaluate different strategies empirically. There is currently no theory that will tell you in advance precisely what you should do to optimally solve a problem. You must iterate.

6.3.10 *Wrapping up*

Here's what you should take away from this section:

- As you first learned in chapter 4, when approaching a new problem, it's good to first establish common-sense baselines for your metric of choice. If you don't have a baseline to beat, you can't tell whether you're making real progress.
- Try simple models before expensive ones, to justify the additional expense. Sometimes a simple model will turn out to be your best option.
- When you have data where temporal ordering matters, recurrent networks are a great fit and easily outperform models that first flatten the temporal data.
- To use dropout with recurrent networks, you should use a time-constant dropout mask and recurrent dropout mask. These are built into Keras recurrent layers, so all you have to do is use the `dropout` and `recurrent_dropout` arguments of recurrent layers.
- Stacked RNNs provide more representational power than a single RNN layer. They're also much more expensive and thus not always worth it. Although they offer clear gains on complex problems (such as machine translation), they may not always be relevant to smaller, simpler problems.
- Bidirectional RNNs, which look at a sequence both ways, are useful on natural-language processing problems. But they aren't strong performers on sequence data where the recent past is much more informative than the beginning of the sequence.

NOTE There are two important concepts we won't cover in detail here: recurrent attention and sequence masking. Both tend to be especially relevant for natural-language processing, and they aren't particularly applicable to the temperature-forecasting problem. We'll leave them for future study outside of this book.

Markets and machine learning

Some readers are bound to want to take the techniques we've introduced here and try them on the problem of forecasting the future price of securities on the stock market (or currency exchange rates, and so on). Markets have *very different statistical characteristics* than natural phenomena such as weather patterns. Trying to use machine learning to beat markets, when you only have access to publicly available data, is a difficult endeavor, and you're likely to waste your time and resources with nothing to show for it.

Always remember that when it comes to markets, past performance is *not* a good predictor of future returns—looking in the rear-view mirror is a bad way to drive. Machine learning, on the other hand, is applicable to datasets where the past *is* a good predictor of the future.

6.4 Sequence processing with convnets

In chapter 5, you learned about convolutional neural networks (convnets) and how they perform particularly well on computer vision problems, due to their ability to operate *convolutionally*, extracting features from local input patches and allowing for representation modularity and data efficiency. The same properties that make convnets excel at computer vision also make them highly relevant to sequence processing. Time can be treated as a spatial dimension, like the height or width of a 2D image.

Such 1D convnets can be competitive with RNNs on certain sequence-processing problems, usually at a considerably cheaper computational cost. Recently, 1D convnets, typically used with dilated kernels, have been used with great success for audio generation and machine translation. In addition to these specific successes, it has long been known that small 1D convnets can offer a fast alternative to RNNs for simple tasks such as text classification and timeseries forecasting.

6.4.1 Understanding 1D convolution for sequence data

The convolution layers introduced previously were 2D convolutions, extracting 2D patches from image tensors and applying an identical transformation to every patch. In the same way, you can use 1D convolutions, extracting local 1D patches (subsequences) from sequences (see figure 6.26).

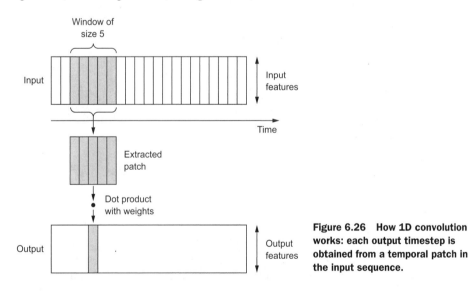

Figure 6.26 How 1D convolution works: each output timestep is obtained from a temporal patch in the input sequence.

Such 1D convolution layers can recognize local patterns in a sequence. Because the same input transformation is performed on every patch, a pattern learned at a certain position in a sentence can later be recognized at a different position, making 1D convnets translation invariant (for temporal translations). For instance, a 1D convnet processing sequences of characters using convolution windows of size 5 should be able to learn words or word fragments of length 5 or less, and it should be able to recognize these words in any context in an input sequence. A character-level 1D convnet is thus able to learn about word morphology.

6.4.2 1D pooling for sequence data

You're already familiar with 2D pooling operations, such as 2D average pooling and max pooling, used in convnets to spatially downsample image tensors. The 2D pooling operation has a 1D equivalent: extracting 1D patches (subsequences) from an input and outputting the maximum value (max pooling) or average value (average pooling). Just as with 2D convnets, this is used for reducing the length of 1D inputs (*subsampling*).

6.4.3 Implementing a 1D convnet

In Keras, you use a 1D convnet via the `Conv1D` layer, which has an interface similar to `Conv2D`. It takes as input 3D tensors with shape (samples, time, features) and returns similarly shaped 3D tensors. The convolution window is a 1D window on the temporal axis: axis 1 in the input tensor.

Let's build a simple two-layer 1D convnet and apply it to the IMDB sentiment-classification task you're already familiar with. As a reminder, this is the code for obtaining and preprocessing the data.

Listing 6.45 Preparing the IMDB data

```
from keras.datasets import imdb
from keras.preprocessing import sequence

max_features = 10000
max_len = 500

print('Loading data...')
(x_train, y_train), (x_test, y_test) = imdb.load_data(num_words=max_features)
print(len(x_train), 'train sequences')
print(len(x_test), 'test sequences')

print('Pad sequences (samples x time)')
x_train = sequence.pad_sequences(x_train, maxlen=max_len)
x_test = sequence.pad_sequences(x_test, maxlen=max_len)
print('x_train shape:', x_train.shape)
print('x_test shape:', x_test.shape)
```

1D convnets are structured in the same way as their 2D counterparts, which you used in chapter 5: they consist of a stack of `Conv1D` and `MaxPooling1D` layers, ending in either a global pooling layer or a `Flatten` layer, that turn the 3D outputs into 2D outputs, allowing you to add one or more `Dense` layers to the model for classification or regression.

One difference, though, is the fact that you can afford to use larger convolution windows with 1D convnets. With a 2D convolution layer, a 3 × 3 convolution window contains 3 × 3 = 9 feature vectors; but with a 1D convolution layer, a convolution window of size 3 contains only 3 feature vectors. You can thus easily afford 1D convolution windows of size 7 or 9.

This is the example 1D convnet for the IMDB dataset.

Listing 6.46 Training and evaluating a simple 1D convnet on the IMDB data

```
from keras.models import Sequential
from keras import layers
from keras.optimizers import RMSprop

model = Sequential()
model.add(layers.Embedding(max_features, 128, input_length=max_len))
model.add(layers.Conv1D(32, 7, activation='relu'))
model.add(layers.MaxPooling1D(5))
model.add(layers.Conv1D(32, 7, activation='relu'))
model.add(layers.GlobalMaxPooling1D())
model.add(layers.Dense(1))

model.summary()

model.compile(optimizer=RMSprop(lr=1e-4),
              loss='binary_crossentropy',
              metrics=['acc'])
history = model.fit(x_train, y_train,
                    epochs=10,
                    batch_size=128,
                    validation_split=0.2)
```

Figures 6.27 and 6.28 show the training and validation results. Validation accuracy is somewhat less than that of the LSTM, but runtime is faster on both CPU and GPU (the exact increase in speed will vary greatly depending on your exact configuration). At this point, you could retrain this model for the right number of epochs (eight) and run it on the test set. This is a convincing demonstration that a 1D convnet can offer a fast, cheap alternative to a recurrent network on a word-level sentiment-classification task.

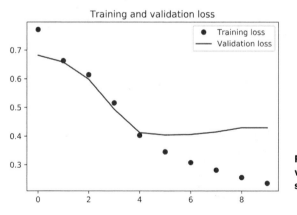

Figure 6.27 Training and validation loss on IMDB with a simple 1D convnet

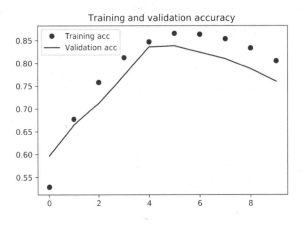

Figure 6.28   **Training and validation accuracy on IMDB with a simple 1D convnet**

6.4.4   Combining CNNs and RNNs to process long sequences

Because 1D convnets process input patches independently, they aren't sensitive to the order of the timesteps (beyond a local scale, the size of the convolution windows), unlike RNNs. Of course, to recognize longer-term patterns, you can stack many convolution layers and pooling layers, resulting in upper layers that will see long chunks of the original inputs—but that's still a fairly weak way to induce order sensitivity. One way to evidence this weakness is to try 1D convnets on the temperature-forecasting problem, where order-sensitivity is key to producing good predictions. The following example reuses the following variables defined previously: `float_data`, `train_gen`, `val_gen`, and `val_steps`.

Listing 6.47   Training and evaluating a simple 1D convnet on the Jena data

```
from keras.models import Sequential
from keras import layers
from keras.optimizers import RMSprop

model = Sequential()
model.add(layers.Conv1D(32, 5, activation='relu',
                        input_shape=(None, float_data.shape[-1])))
model.add(layers.MaxPooling1D(3))
model.add(layers.Conv1D(32, 5, activation='relu'))
model.add(layers.MaxPooling1D(3))
model.add(layers.Conv1D(32, 5, activation='relu'))
model.add(layers.GlobalMaxPooling1D())
model.add(layers.Dense(1))

model.compile(optimizer=RMSprop(), loss='mae')
history = model.fit_generator(train_gen,
                              steps_per_epoch=500,
                              epochs=20,
                              validation_data=val_gen,
                              validation_steps=val_steps)
```

Figure 6.29 shows the training and validation MAEs.

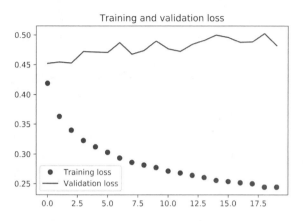

Training and validation loss

Figure 6.29 Training and validation loss on the Jena temperature-forecasting task with a simple 1D convnet

The validation MAE stays in the 0.40s: you can't even beat the common-sense baseline using the small convnet. Again, this is because the convnet looks for patterns any-where in the input timeseries and has no knowledge of the temporal position of a pat-tern it sees (toward the beginning, toward the end, and so on). Because more recent data points should be interpreted differently from older data points in the case of this specific forecasting problem, the convnet fails at producing meaningful results. This limitation of convnets isn't an issue with the IMDB data, because patterns of keywords associated with a positive or negative sentiment are informative independently of where they're found in the input sentences.

One strategy to combine the speed and lightness of convnets with the order-sensitivity of RNNs is to use a 1D convnet as a preprocessing step before an RNN (see figure 6.30). This is especially beneficial when you're deal-ing with sequences that are so long they can't realistically be processed with RNNs, such as sequences with thousands of steps. The conv-net will turn the long input sequence into much shorter (downsampled) sequences of higher-level features. This sequence of extracted features then becomes the input to the RNN part of the network.

This technique isn't seen often in research papers and practical applications, possibly because it isn't well known. It's effec-tive and ought to be more common. Let's try it on the temperature-forecasting dataset. Because this strategy allows you to manipu-late much longer sequences, you can either

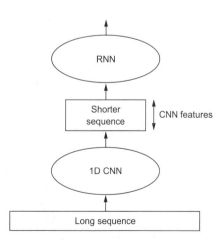

Figure 6.30 Combining a 1D convnet and an RNN for processing long sequences

look at data from longer ago (by increasing the `lookback` parameter of the data generator) or look at high-resolution timeseries (by decreasing the `step` parameter of the generator). Here, somewhat arbitrarily, you'll use a `step` that's half as large, resulting in a timeseries twice as long, where the temperature data is sampled at a rate of 1 point per 30 minutes. The example reuses the `generator` function defined earlier.

Listing 6.48   Preparing higher-resolution data generators for the Jena dataset

```
step = 3                                    Previously set to 6 (1 point per hour);
lookback = 720                              now 3 (1 point per 30 min)
delay = 144

train_gen = generator(float_data,
                      lookback=lookback,
                      delay=delay,
                      min_index=0,
                      max_index=200000,
                      shuffle=True,
                      step=step)
val_gen = generator(float_data,
                    lookback=lookback,
                    delay=delay,
                    min_index=200001,
                    max_index=300000,
                    step=step)
test_gen = generator(float_data,
                     lookback=lookback,
                     delay=delay,
                     min_index=300001,
                     max_index=None,
                     step=step)
val_steps = (300000 - 200001 - lookback) // 128
test_steps = (len(float_data) - 300001 - lookback) // 128
```

(margin label) **Unchanged**

This is the model, starting with two `Conv1D` layers and following up with a `GRU` layer. Figure 6.31 shows the results.

Listing 6.49   Model combining a 1D convolutional base and a `GRU` layer

```
from keras.models import Sequential
from keras import layers
from keras.optimizers import RMSprop

model = Sequential()
model.add(layers.Conv1D(32, 5, activation='relu',
                        input_shape=(None, float_data.shape[-1])))
model.add(layers.MaxPooling1D(3))
model.add(layers.Conv1D(32, 5, activation='relu'))
model.add(layers.GRU(32, dropout=0.1, recurrent_dropout=0.5))
model.add(layers.Dense(1))

model.summary()

model.compile(optimizer=RMSprop(), loss='mae')
```

```
history = model.fit_generator(train_gen,
                              steps_per_epoch=500,
                              epochs=20,
                              validation_data=val_gen,
                              validation_steps=val_steps)
```

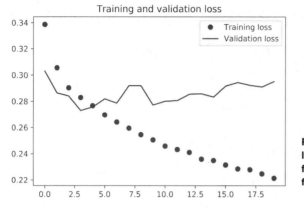

Training and validation loss

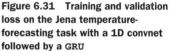

Figure 6.31 Training and validation loss on the Jena temperature-forecasting task with a 1D convnet followed by a GRU

Judging from the validation loss, this setup isn't as good as the regularized GRU alone, but it's significantly faster. It looks at twice as much data, which in this case doesn't appear to be hugely helpful but may be important for other datasets.

6.4.5 *Wrapping up*

Here's what you should take away from this section:

- In the same way that 2D convnets perform well for processing visual patterns in 2D space, 1D convnets perform well for processing temporal patterns. They offer a faster alternative to RNNs on some problems, in particular natural-language processing tasks.
- Typically, 1D convnets are structured much like their 2D equivalents from the world of computer vision: they consist of stacks of Conv1D layers and Max-Pooling1D layers, ending in a global pooling operation or flattening operation.
- Because RNNs are extremely expensive for processing very long sequences, but 1D convnets are cheap, it can be a good idea to use a 1D convnet as a preprocessing step before an RNN, shortening the sequence and extracting useful representations for the RNN to process.

Chapter summary

- In this chapter, you learned the following techniques, which are widely applicable to any dataset of sequence data, from text to timeseries:
  - How to tokenize text
  - What word embeddings are, and how to use them
  - What recurrent networks are, and how to use them
  - How to stack RNN layers and use bidirectional RNNs to build more-powerful sequence-processing models
  - How to use 1D convnets for sequence processing
  - How to combine 1D convnets and RNNs to process long sequences

- You can use RNNs for timeseries regression ("predicting the future"), timeseries classification, anomaly detection in timeseries, and sequence labeling (such as identifying names or dates in sentences).

- Similarly, you can use 1D convnets for machine translation (sequence-to-sequence convolutional models, like SliceNet[a]), document classification, and spelling correction.

- If *global order matters* in your sequence data, then it's preferable to use a recurrent network to process it. This is typically the case for timeseries, where the recent past is likely to be more informative than the distant past.

- If *global ordering isn't fundamentally meaningful*, then 1D convnets will turn out to work at least as well and are cheaper. This is often the case for text data, where a keyword found at the beginning of a sentence is just as meaningful as a keyword found at the end.

[a] See https://arxiv.org/abs/1706.03059.

Advanced deep-learning best practices

This chapter explores a number of powerful tools that will bring you closer to being able to develop state-of-the-art models on difficult problems. Using the Keras functional API, you can build graph-like models, share a layer across different inputs, and use Keras models just like Python functions. Keras callbacks and the TensorBoard browser-based visualization tool let you monitor models during training. We'll also discuss several other best practices including batch normalization, residual connections, hyperparameter optimization, and model ensembling.

7.1 Going beyond the Sequential model: the Keras functional API

Until now, all neural networks introduced in this book have been implemented using the Sequential model. The Sequential model makes the assumption that the network has exactly one input and exactly one output, and that it consists of a linear stack of layers (see figure 7.1).

This is a commonly verified assumption; the configuration is so common that we've been able to cover many topics and practical applications in these pages so far using only the Sequential model class. But this set of assumptions is too inflexible in a number of cases. Some networks require several independent inputs, others require multiple outputs, and some networks have internal branching between layers that makes them look like *graphs* of layers rather than linear stacks of layers.

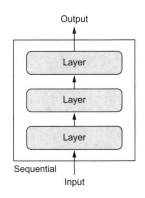

Figure 7.1 A Sequential model: a linear stack of layers

Some tasks, for instance, require *multimodal* inputs: they merge data coming from different input sources, processing each type of data using different kinds of neural layers. Imagine a deep-learning model trying to predict the most likely market price of a second-hand piece of clothing, using the following inputs: user-provided metadata (such as the item's brand, age, and so on), a user-provided text description, and a picture of the item. If you had only the metadata available, you could one-hot encode it and use a densely connected network to predict the price. If you had only the text description available, you could use an RNN or a 1D convnet. If you had only the picture, you could use a 2D convnet. But how can you use all three at the same time? A naive approach would be to train three separate models and then do a weighted average of their predictions. But this may be suboptimal, because the information extracted by the models may be redundant. A better way is to *jointly* learn a more accurate model of the data by using a model that can see all available input modalities simultaneously: a model with three input branches (see figure 7.2).

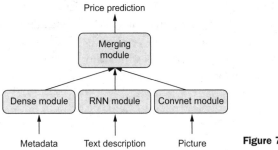

Figure 7.2 A multi-input model

Similarly, some tasks need to predict multiple target attributes of input data. Given the text of a novel or short story, you might want to automatically classify it by genre (such as romance or thriller) but also predict the approximate date it was written. Of course, you could train two separate models: one for the genre and one for the date. But because these attributes aren't statistically independent, you could build a better model by learning to jointly predict both genre and date at the same time. Such a joint model would then have two outputs, or *heads* (see figure 7.3). Due to correlations between genre and date, knowing the date of a novel would help the model learn rich, accurate representations of the space of novel genres, and vice versa.

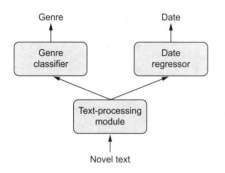

Figure 7.3   A multi-output (or multihead) model

Additionally, many recently developed neural architectures require nonlinear network topology: networks structured as directed acyclic graphs. The Inception family of networks (developed by Szegedy et al. at Google),[1] for instance, relies on *Inception modules*, where the input is processed by several parallel convolutional branches whose outputs are then merged back into a single tensor (see figure 7.4). There's also the recent trend of adding *residual connections* to a model, which started with the ResNet family of networks (developed by He et al. at Microsoft).[2] A residual connection consists of reinjecting previous representations into the downstream flow of data by adding a past output tensor to a later output tensor (see figure 7.5), which helps prevent information loss along the data-processing flow. There are many other examples of such graph-like networks.

---

[1] Christian Szegedy et al., "Going Deeper with Convolutions," Conference on Computer Vision and Pattern Recognition (2014), https://arxiv.org/abs/1409.4842.

[2] Kaiming He et al., "Deep Residual Learning for Image Recognition," Conference on Computer Vision and Pattern Recognition (2015), https://arxiv.org/abs/1512.03385.

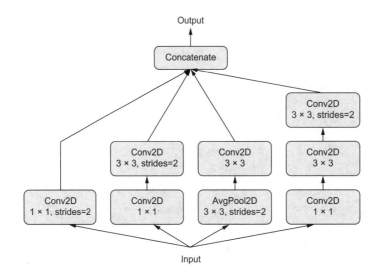

Figure 7.4   An Inception module: a subgraph of layers with several parallel convolutional branches

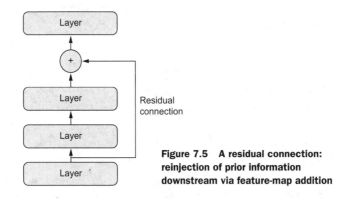

Figure 7.5   A residual connection: reinjection of prior information downstream via feature-map addition

These three important use cases—multi-input models, multi-output models, and graph-like models—aren't possible when using only the Sequential model class in Keras. But there's another far more general and flexible way to use Keras: the *functional API*. This section explains in detail what it is, what it can do, and how to use it.

7.1.1   Introduction to the functional API

In the functional API, you directly manipulate tensors, and you use layers as *functions* that take tensors and return tensors (hence, the name *functional API*):

```
from keras import Input, layers

input_tensor = Input(shape=(32,))          ◁——— A tensor
```

```
dense = layers.Dense(32, activation='relu')      ◁——— A layer is a function.

output_tensor = dense(input_tensor)      ◁——┐ A layer may be called on a
                                              tensor, and it returns a tensor.
```

Let's start with a minimal example that shows side by side a simple `Sequential` model and its equivalent in the functional API:

```
from keras.models import Sequential, Model
from keras import layers
from keras import Input                       ┐ Sequential model, which
                                              ┘ you already know about
seq_model = Sequential()                  ◁——┘
seq_model.add(layers.Dense(32, activation='relu', input_shape=(64,)))
seq_model.add(layers.Dense(32, activation='relu'))
seq_model.add(layers.Dense(10, activation='softmax'))

input_tensor = Input(shape=(64,))
x = layers.Dense(32, activation='relu')(input_tensor)   ┐ Its functional
x = layers.Dense(32, activation='relu')(x)              ┘ equivalent
output_tensor = layers.Dense(10, activation='softmax')(x)

model = Model(input_tensor, output_tensor)   ◁——┐ The Model class turns an input tensor
                                                 and output tensor into a model.
model.summary()   ◁——— Let's look at it!
```

This is what the call to `model.summary()` displays:

```
Layer (type)                   Output Shape              Param #
=================================================================
input_1 (InputLayer)           (None, 64)                0
_____
dense_1 (Dense)                (None, 32)                2080
_____
dense_2 (Dense)                (None, 32)                1056
_____
dense_3 (Dense)                (None, 10)                330
=================================================================
Total params: 3,466
Trainable params: 3,466
Non-trainable params: 0
_____
```

The only part that may seem a bit magical at this point is instantiating a `Model` object using only an input tensor and an output tensor. Behind the scenes, Keras retrieves every layer involved in going from `input_tensor` to `output_tensor`, bringing them together into a graph-like data structure—a `Model`. Of course, the reason it works is that `output_tensor` was obtained by repeatedly transforming `input_tensor`. If you tried to build a model from inputs and outputs that weren't related, you'd get a `RuntimeError`:

```
>>> unrelated_input = Input(shape=(32,))
>>> bad_model = model = Model(unrelated_input, output_tensor)
```

```
RuntimeError: Graph disconnected: cannot
obtain value for tensor
➡Tensor("input_1:0", shape=(?, 64), dtype=float32) at layer "input_1".
```

This error tells you, in essence, that Keras couldn't reach `input_1` from the provided output tensor.

When it comes to compiling, training, or evaluating such an instance of `Model`, the API is the same as that of `Sequential`:

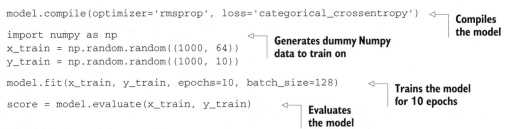

```
model.compile(optimizer='rmsprop', loss='categorical_crossentropy')        Compiles
                                                                           the model

import numpy as np                                  Generates dummy Numpy
x_train = np.random.random((1000, 64))              data to train on
y_train = np.random.random((1000, 10))

model.fit(x_train, y_train, epochs=10, batch_size=128)       Trains the model
                                                             for 10 epochs
score = model.evaluate(x_train, y_train)      Evaluates
                                              the model
```

7.1.2   *Multi-input models*

The functional API can be used to build models that have multiple inputs. Typically, such models at some point merge their different input branches using a layer that can combine several tensors: by adding them, concatenating them, and so on. This is usually done via a Keras merge operation such as `keras.layers.add`, `keras.layers.concatenate`, and so on. Let's look at a very simple example of a multi-input model: a question-answering model.

A typical question-answering model has two inputs: a natural-language question and a text snippet (such as a news article) providing information to be used for answering the question. The model must then produce an answer: in the simplest possible setup, this is a one-word answer obtained via a softmax over some predefined vocabulary (see figure 7.6).

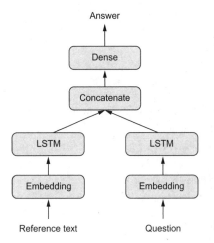

Figure 7.6   A question-answering model

Following is an example of how you can build such a model with the functional API. You set up two independent branches, encoding the text input and the question input as representation vectors; then, concatenate these vectors; and finally, add a softmax classifier on top of the concatenated representations.

Listing 7.1 Functional API implementation of a two-input question-answering model

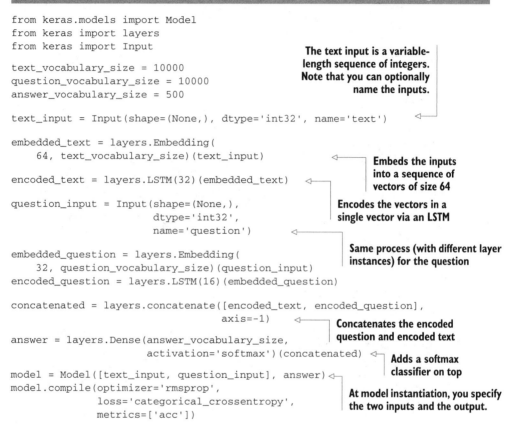

```
from keras.models import Model
from keras import layers
from keras import Input

text_vocabulary_size = 10000
question_vocabulary_size = 10000
answer_vocabulary_size = 500

text_input = Input(shape=(None,), dtype='int32', name='text')

embedded_text = layers.Embedding(
    64, text_vocabulary_size)(text_input)

encoded_text = layers.LSTM(32)(embedded_text)

question_input = Input(shape=(None,),
                       dtype='int32',
                       name='question')

embedded_question = layers.Embedding(
    32, question_vocabulary_size)(question_input)
encoded_question = layers.LSTM(16)(embedded_question)

concatenated = layers.concatenate([encoded_text, encoded_question],
                       axis=-1)

answer = layers.Dense(answer_vocabulary_size,
                      activation='softmax')(concatenated)

model = Model([text_input, question_input], answer)
model.compile(optimizer='rmsprop',
              loss='categorical_crossentropy',
              metrics=['acc'])
```

The text input is a variable-length sequence of integers. Note that you can optionally name the inputs.

Embeds the inputs into a sequence of vectors of size 64

Encodes the vectors in a single vector via an LSTM

Same process (with different layer instances) for the question

Concatenates the encoded question and encoded text

Adds a softmax classifier on top

At model instantiation, you specify the two inputs and the output.

Now, how do you train this two-input model? There are two possible APIs: you can feed the model a list of Numpy arrays as inputs, or you can feed it a dictionary that maps input names to Numpy arrays. Naturally, the latter option is available only if you give names to your inputs.

Listing 7.2 Feeding data to a multi-input model

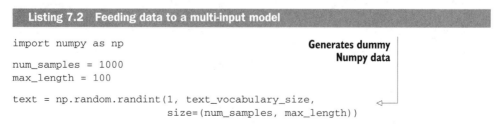

```
import numpy as np

num_samples = 1000
max_length = 100

text = np.random.randint(1, text_vocabulary_size,
                         size=(num_samples, max_length))
```

Generates dummy Numpy data

```
question = np.random.randint(1, question_vocabulary_size,
                             size=(num_samples, max_length))
answers = np.random.randint(0, 1,
                            size=(num_samples, answer_vocabulary_size))
```
Answers are one-hot encoded, not integers

```
model.fit([text, question], answers, epochs=10, batch_size=128)

model.fit({'text': text, 'question': question}, answers,
          epochs=10, batch_size=128)
```

Fitting using a list of inputs   **Fitting using a dictionary of inputs (only if inputs are named)**

7.1.3   Multi-output models

In the same way, you can use the functional API to build models with multiple outputs (or multiple *heads*). A simple example is a network that attempts to simultaneously predict different properties of the data, such as a network that takes as input a series of social media posts from a single anonymous person and tries to predict attributes of that person, such as age, gender, and income level (see figure 7.7).

Listing 7.3   Functional API implementation of a three-output model

```
from keras import layers
from keras import Input
from keras.models import Model

vocabulary_size = 50000
num_income_groups = 10

posts_input = Input(shape=(None,), dtype='int32', name='posts')
embedded_posts = layers.Embedding(256, vocabulary_size)(posts_input)
x = layers.Conv1D(128, 5, activation='relu')(embedded_posts)
x = layers.MaxPooling1D(5)(x)
x = layers.Conv1D(256, 5, activation='relu')(x)
x = layers.Conv1D(256, 5, activation='relu')(x)
x = layers.MaxPooling1D(5)(x)
x = layers.Conv1D(256, 5, activation='relu')(x)
x = layers.Conv1D(256, 5, activation='relu')(x)
x = layers.GlobalMaxPooling1D()(x)
x = layers.Dense(128, activation='relu')(x)

age_prediction = layers.Dense(1, name='age')(x)
income_prediction = layers.Dense(num_income_groups,
                                 activation='softmax',
                                 name='income')(x)
gender_prediction = layers.Dense(1, activation='sigmoid', name='gender')(x)

model = Model(posts_input,
              [age_prediction, income_prediction, gender_prediction])
```

Note that the output layers are given names.

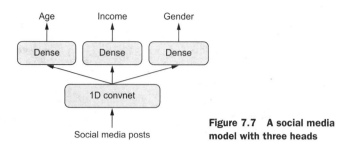

Figure 7.7   A social media model with three heads

Importantly, training such a model requires the ability to specify different loss functions for different heads of the network: for instance, age prediction is a scalar regression task, but gender prediction is a binary classification task, requiring a different training procedure. But because gradient descent requires you to minimize a *scalar*, you must combine these losses into a single value in order to train the model. The simplest way to combine different losses is to sum them all. In Keras, you can use either a list or a dictionary of losses in `compile` to specify different objects for different outputs; the resulting loss values are summed into a global loss, which is minimized during training.

Listing 7.4   Compilation options of a multi-output model: multiple losses

```
model.compile(optimizer='rmsprop',
              loss=['mse', 'categorical_crossentropy', 'binary_crossentropy'])

model.compile(optimizer='rmsprop',
              loss={'age': 'mse',
                    'income': 'categorical_crossentropy',
                    'gender': 'binary_crossentropy'})
```

Equivalent (possible only if you give names to the output layers)

Note that very imbalanced loss contributions will cause the model representations to be optimized preferentially for the task with the largest individual loss, at the expense of the other tasks. To remedy this, you can assign different levels of importance to the loss values in their contribution to the final loss. This is useful in particular if the losses' values use different scales. For instance, the mean squared error (MSE) loss used for the age-regression task typically takes a value around 3–5, whereas the crossentropy loss used for the gender-classification task can be as low as 0.1. In such a situation, to balance the contribution of the different losses, you can assign a weight of 10 to the crossentropy loss and a weight of 0.25 to the MSE loss.

Listing 7.5   Compilation options of a multi-output model: loss weighting

```
model.compile(optimizer='rmsprop',
              loss=['mse', 'categorical_crossentropy', 'binary_crossentropy'],
              loss_weights=[0.25, 1., 10.])
```

```
model.compile(optimizer='rmsprop',
              loss={'age': 'mse',
                    'income': 'categorical_crossentropy',
                    'gender': 'binary_crossentropy'},
              loss_weights={'age': 0.25,
                            'income': 1.,
                            'gender': 10.})
```

Equivalent (possible only if you give names to the output layers)

Much as in the case of multi-input models, you can pass Numpy data to the model for training either via a list of arrays or via a dictionary of arrays.

Listing 7.6   Feeding data to a multi-output model

```
model.fit(posts, [age_targets, income_targets, gender_targets],
          epochs=10, batch_size=64)

model.fit(posts, {'age': age_targets,
                  'income': income_targets,
                  'gender': gender_targets},
          epochs=10, batch_size=64)
```

Equivalent (possible only if you give names to the output layers)

age_targets, income_targets, and gender_targets are assumed to be Numpy arrays.

7.1.4 *Directed acyclic graphs of layers*

With the functional API, not only can you build models with multiple inputs and multiple outputs, but you can also implement networks with a complex internal topology. Neural networks in Keras are allowed to be arbitrary *directed acyclic graphs* of layers. The qualifier *acyclic* is important: these graphs can't have cycles. It's impossible for a tensor x to become the input of one of the layers that generated x. The only processing *loops* that are allowed (that is, recurrent connections) are those internal to recurrent layers.

Several common neural-network components are implemented as graphs. Two notable ones are Inception modules and residual connections. To better understand how the functional API can be used to build graphs of layers, let's take a look at how you can implement both of them in Keras.

INCEPTION MODULES

Inception[3] is a popular type of network architecture for convolutional neural networks; it was developed by Christian Szegedy and his colleagues at Google in 2013–2014, inspired by the earlier *network-in-network* architecture.[4] It consists of a stack of modules that themselves look like small independent networks, split into several parallel branches. The most basic form of an Inception module has three to four branches starting with a 1 × 1 convolution, followed by a 3 × 3 convolution, and ending with the concatenation of the resulting features. This setup helps the network separately learn

---

[3] https://arxiv.org/abs/1409.4842.
[4] Min Lin, Qiang Chen, and Shuicheng Yan, "Network in Network," International Conference on Learning Representations (2013), https://arxiv.org/abs/1312.4400.

spatial features and channel-wise features, which is more efficient than learning them jointly. More-complex versions of an Inception module are also possible, typically involving pooling operations, different spatial convolution sizes (for example, 5 × 5 instead of 3 × 3 on some branches), and branches without a spatial convolution (only a 1 × 1 convolution). An example of such a module, taken from Inception V3, is shown in figure 7.8.

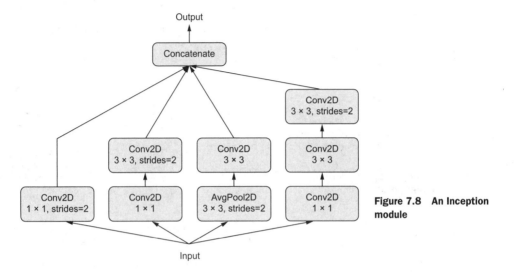

Figure 7.8 An Inception module

The purpose of 1 × 1 convolutions

You already know that convolutions extract spatial patches around every tile in an input tensor and apply the same transformation to each patch. An edge case is when the patches extracted consist of a single tile. The convolution operation then becomes equivalent to running each tile vector through a Dense layer: it will compute features that mix together information from the channels of the input tensor, but it won't mix information across space (because it's looking at one tile at a time). Such 1 × 1 convolutions (also called *pointwise convolutions*) are featured in Inception modules, where they contribute to factoring out channel-wise feature learning and space-wise feature learning—a reasonable thing to do if you assume that each channel is highly autocorrelated across space, but different channels may not be highly correlated with each other.

Here's how you'd implement the module featured in figure 7.8 using the functional API. This example assumes the existence of a 4D input tensor x:

Every branch has the same stride value (2), which is necessary to keep all branch outputs the same size so you can concatenate them.

In this branch, the striding occurs in the spatial convolution layer.

```
from keras import layers

branch_a = layers.Conv2D(128, 1,
                         activation='relu', strides=2)(x)
branch_b = layers.Conv2D(128, 1, activation='relu')(x)
branch_b = layers.Conv2D(128, 3, activation='relu', strides=2)(branch_b)

branch_c = layers.AveragePooling2D(3, strides=2)(x)
branch_c = layers.Conv2D(128, 3, activation='relu')(branch_c)

branch_d = layers.Conv2D(128, 1, activation='relu')(x)
branch_d = layers.Conv2D(128, 3, activation='relu')(branch_d)
branch_d = layers.Conv2D(128, 3, activation='relu', strides=2)(branch_d)

output = layers.concatenate(
    [branch_a, branch_b, branch_c, branch_d], axis=-1)
```

In this branch, the striding occurs in the average pooling layer.

Concatenates the branch outputs to obtain the module output

Note that the full Inception V3 architecture is available in Keras as `keras.applications.inception_v3.InceptionV3`, including weights pretrained on the ImageNet dataset. Another closely related model available as part of the Keras applications module is *Xception*.[5] Xception, which stands for *extreme inception*, is a convnet architecture loosely inspired by Inception. It takes the idea of separating the learning of channel-wise and space-wise features to its logical extreme, and replaces Inception modules with depthwise separable convolutions consisting of a depthwise convolution (a spatial convolution where every input channel is handled separately) followed by a pointwise convolution (a 1 × 1 convolution)—effectively, an extreme form of an Inception module, where spatial features and channel-wise features are fully separated. Xception has roughly the same number of parameters as Inception V3, but it shows better runtime performance and higher accuracy on ImageNet as well as other large-scale datasets, due to a more efficient use of model parameters.

RESIDUAL CONNECTIONS

Residual connections are a common graph-like network component found in many post-2015 network architectures, including Xception. They were introduced by He et al. from Microsoft in their winning entry in the ILSVRC ImageNet challenge in late 2015.[6] They tackle two common problems that plague any large-scale deep-learning model: vanishing gradients and representational bottlenecks. In general, adding residual connections to any model that has more than 10 layers is likely to be beneficial.

---

[5] François Chollet, "Xception: Deep Learning with Depthwise Separable Convolutions," Conference on Computer Vision and Pattern Recognition (2017), https://arxiv.org/abs/1610.02357.

[6] He et al., "Deep Residual Learning for Image Recognition," https://arxiv.org/abs/1512.03385.

A residual connection consists of making the output of an earlier layer available as input to a later layer, effectively creating a shortcut in a sequential network. Rather than being concatenated to the later activation, the earlier output is summed with the later activation, which assumes that both activations are the same size. If they're different sizes, you can use a linear transformation to reshape the earlier activation into the target shape (for example, a `Dense` layer without an activation or, for convolutional feature maps, a 1 × 1 convolution without an activation).

Here's how to implement a residual connection in Keras when the feature-map sizes are the same, using identity residual connections. This example assumes the existence of a 4D input tensor x:

```
from keras import layers                                    Applies a transformation to x

x = ...
y = layers.Conv2D(128, 3, activation='relu', padding='same')(x)   ◁
y = layers.Conv2D(128, 3, activation='relu', padding='same')(y)
y = layers.Conv2D(128, 3, activation='relu', padding='same')(y)

y = layers.add([y, x])        ◁        Adds the original x back to
                                       the output features
```

And the following implements a residual connection when the feature-map sizes differ, using a linear residual connection (again, assuming the existence of a 4D input tensor x):

```
                                        Uses a 1 × 1 convolution to
                                        linearly downsample the original
from keras import layers                x tensor to the same shape as y

x = ...
y = layers.Conv2D(128, 3, activation='relu', padding='same')(x)
y = layers.Conv2D(128, 3, activation='relu', padding='same')(y)
y = layers.MaxPooling2D(2, strides=2)(y)

residual = layers.Conv2D(128, 1, strides=2, padding='same')(x)   ◁

y = layers.add([y, residual])     ◁        Adds the residual tensor
                                           back to the output features
```

Representational bottlenecks in deep learning

In a `Sequential` model, each successive representation layer is built on top of the previous one, which means it only has access to information contained in the activation of the previous layer. If one layer is too small (for example, it has features that are too low-dimensional), then the model will be constrained by how much information can be crammed into the activations of this layer.

(continued)

You can grasp this concept with a signal-processing analogy: if you have an audio-processing pipeline that consists of a series of operations, each of which takes as input the output of the previous operation, then if one operation crops your signal to a low-frequency range (for example, 0–15 kHz), the operations downstream will never be able to recover the dropped frequencies. Any loss of information is permanent. Residual connections, by reinjecting earlier information downstream, partially solve this issue for deep-learning models.

Vanishing gradients in deep learning

Backpropagation, the master algorithm used to train deep neural networks, works by propagating a feedback signal from the output loss down to earlier layers. If this feedback signal has to be propagated through a deep stack of layers, the signal may become tenuous or even be lost entirely, rendering the network untrainable. This issue is known as *vanishing gradients*.

This problem occurs both with deep networks and with recurrent networks over very long sequences—in both cases, a feedback signal must be propagated through a long series of operations. You're already familiar with the solution that the LSTM layer uses to address this problem in recurrent networks: it introduces a *carry track* that propagates information parallel to the main processing track. Residual connections work in a similar way in feedforward deep networks, but they're even simpler: they introduce a purely linear information carry track parallel to the main layer stack, thus helping to propagate gradients through arbitrarily deep stacks of layers.

7.1.5 *Layer weight sharing*

One more important feature of the functional API is the ability to reuse a layer instance several times. When you call a layer instance twice, instead of instantiating a new layer for each call, you reuse the same weights with every call. This allows you to build models that have shared branches—several branches that all share the same knowledge and perform the same operations. That is, they share the same representations and learn these representations simultaneously for different sets of inputs.

For example, consider a model that attempts to assess the semantic similarity between two sentences. The model has two inputs (the two sentences to compare) and outputs a score between 0 and 1, where 0 means unrelated sentences and 1 means sentences that are either identical or reformulations of each other. Such a model could be useful in many applications, including deduplicating natural-language queries in a dialog system.

In this setup, the two input sentences are interchangeable, because semantic similarity is a symmetrical relationship: the similarity of A to B is identical to the similarity of B to A. For this reason, it wouldn't make sense to learn two independent models for processing each input sentence. Rather, you want to process both with a single LSTM layer. The representations of this LSTM layer (its weights) are learned based on both inputs simultaneously. This is what we call a *Siamese LSTM* model or a *shared LSTM*.

Here's how to implement such a model using layer sharing (layer reuse) in the Keras functional API:

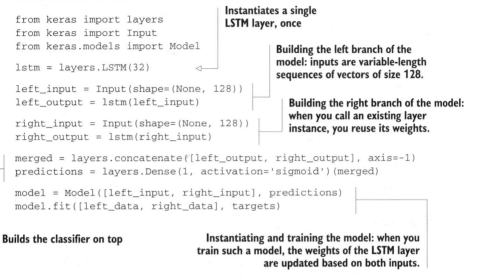

```
from keras import layers
from keras import Input
from keras.models import Model

lstm = layers.LSTM(32)

left_input = Input(shape=(None, 128))
left_output = lstm(left_input)

right_input = Input(shape=(None, 128))
right_output = lstm(right_input)

merged = layers.concatenate([left_output, right_output], axis=-1)
predictions = layers.Dense(1, activation='sigmoid')(merged)

model = Model([left_input, right_input], predictions)
model.fit([left_data, right_data], targets)
```

Instantiates a single LSTM layer, once

Building the left branch of the model: inputs are variable-length sequences of vectors of size 128.

Building the right branch of the model: when you call an existing layer instance, you reuse its weights.

Builds the classifier on top

Instantiating and training the model: when you train such a model, the weights of the LSTM layer are updated based on both inputs.

Naturally, a layer instance may be used more than once—it can be called arbitrarily many times, reusing the same set of weights every time.

7.1.6 *Models as layers*

Importantly, in the functional API, models can be used as you'd use layers—effectively, you can think of a model as a "bigger layer." This is true of both the Sequential and Model classes. This means you can call a model on an input tensor and retrieve an output tensor:

```
y = model(x)
```

If the model has multiple input tensors and multiple output tensors, it should be called with a list of tensors:

```
y1, y2 = model([x1, x2])
```

When you call a model instance, you're reusing the weights of the model—exactly like what happens when you call a layer instance. Calling an instance, whether it's a layer instance or a model instance, will always reuse the existing learned representations of the instance—which is intuitive.

One simple practical example of what you can build by reusing a model instance is a vision model that uses a dual camera as its input: two parallel cameras, a few centimeters (one inch) apart. Such a model can perceive depth, which can be useful in many applications. You shouldn't need two independent models to extract visual features from the left camera and the right camera before merging the two feeds. Such low-level processing can be shared across the two inputs: that is, done via layers that use the same weights and thus share the same representations. Here's how you'd implement a Siamese vision model (shared convolutional base) in Keras:

```
from keras import layers
from keras import applications
from keras import Input

xception_base = applications.Xception(weights=None,
                                      include_top=False)

left_input = Input(shape=(250, 250, 3))
right_input = Input(shape=(250, 250, 3))

left_features = xception_base(left_input)
right_input = xception_base(right_input)

merged_features = layers.concatenate(
    [left_features, right_input], axis=-1)
```

The base image-processing model is the Xception network (convolutional base only).

The inputs are 250 × 250 RGB images.

Calls the same vision model twice

The merged features contain information from the right visual feed and the left visual feed.

7.1.7 *Wrapping up*

This concludes our introduction to the Keras functional API—an essential tool for building advanced deep neural network architectures. Now you know the following:

- To step out of the `Sequential` API whenever you need anything more than a linear stack of layers
- How to build Keras models with several inputs, several outputs, and complex internal network topology, using the Keras functional API
- How to reuse the weights of a layer or model across different processing branches, by calling the same layer or model instance several times

7.2 Inspecting and monitoring deep-learning models using Keras callbacks and TensorBoard

In this section, we'll review ways to gain greater access to and control over what goes on inside your model during training. Launching a training run on a large dataset for tens of epochs using `model.fit()` or `model.fit_generator()` can be a bit like launching a paper airplane: past the initial impulse, you don't have any control over its trajectory or its landing spot. If you want to avoid bad outcomes (and thus wasted paper airplanes), it's smarter to use not a paper plane, but a drone that can sense its environment, send data back to its operator, and automatically make steering decisions based on its current state. The techniques we present here will transform the call to `model.fit()` from a paper airplane into a smart, autonomous drone that can self-introspect and dynamically take action.

7.2.1 Using callbacks to act on a model during training

When you're training a model, there are many things you can't predict from the start. In particular, you can't tell how many epochs will be needed to get to an optimal validation loss. The examples so far have adopted the strategy of training for enough epochs that you begin overfitting, using the first run to figure out the proper number of epochs to train for, and then finally launching a new training run from scratch using this optimal number. Of course, this approach is wasteful.

A much better way to handle this is to stop training when you measure that the validation loss in no longer improving. This can be achieved using a Keras callback. A *callback* is an object (a class instance implementing specific methods) that is passed to the model in the call to `fit` and that is called by the model at various points during training. It has access to all the available data about the state of the model and its performance, and it can take action: interrupt training, save a model, load a different weight set, or otherwise alter the state of the model.

Here are some examples of ways you can use callbacks:

- *Model checkpointing*—Saving the current weights of the model at different points during training.
- *Early stopping*—Interrupting training when the validation loss is no longer improving (and of course, saving the best model obtained during training).
- *Dynamically adjusting the value of certain parameters during training*—Such as the learning rate of the optimizer.
- *Logging training and validation metrics during training, or visualizing the representations learned by the model as they're updated*—The Keras progress bar that you're familiar with is a callback!

The `keras.callbacks` module includes a number of built-in callbacks (this is not an exhaustive list):

```
keras.callbacks.ModelCheckpoint
keras.callbacks.EarlyStopping
```

```
keras.callbacks.LearningRateScheduler
keras.callbacks.ReduceLROnPlateau
keras.callbacks.CSVLogger
```

Let's review a few of them to give you an idea of how to use them: `ModelCheckpoint`, `EarlyStopping`, and `ReduceLROnPlateau`.

THE MODELCHECKPOINT AND EARLYSTOPPING CALLBACKS

You can use the `EarlyStopping` callback to interrupt training once a target metric being monitored has stopped improving for a fixed number of epochs. For instance, this callback allows you to interrupt training as soon as you start overfitting, thus avoiding having to retrain your model for a smaller number of epochs. This callback is typically used in combination with `ModelCheckpoint`, which lets you continually save the model during training (and, optionally, save only the current best model so far: the version of the model that achieved the best performance at the end of an epoch):

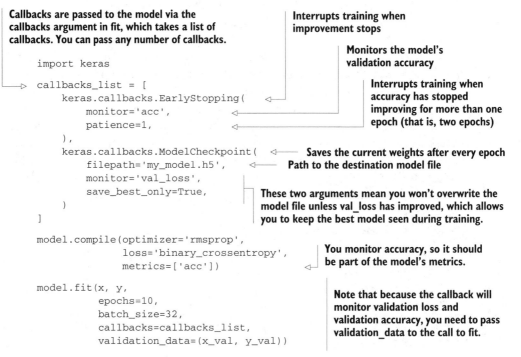

Callbacks are passed to the model via the callbacks argument in fit, which takes a list of callbacks. You can pass any number of callbacks.

Interrupts training when improvement stops

Monitors the model's validation accuracy

Interrupts training when accuracy has stopped improving for more than one epoch (that is, two epochs)

```
import keras

callbacks_list = [
    keras.callbacks.EarlyStopping(
        monitor='acc',
        patience=1,
    ),
    keras.callbacks.ModelCheckpoint(
        filepath='my_model.h5',
        monitor='val_loss',
        save_best_only=True,
    )
]

model.compile(optimizer='rmsprop',
              loss='binary_crossentropy',
              metrics=['acc'])

model.fit(x, y,
          epochs=10,
          batch_size=32,
          callbacks=callbacks_list,
          validation_data=(x_val, y_val))
```

Saves the current weights after every epoch
Path to the destination model file

These two arguments mean you won't overwrite the model file unless val_loss has improved, which allows you to keep the best model seen during training.

You monitor accuracy, so it should be part of the model's metrics.

Note that because the callback will monitor validation loss and validation accuracy, you need to pass validation_data to the call to fit.

THE REDUCELRONPLATEAU CALLBACK

You can use this callback to reduce the learning rate when the validation loss has stopped improving. Reducing or increasing the learning rate in case of a *loss plateau* is is an effective strategy to get out of local minima during training. The following example uses the `ReduceLROnPlateau` callback:

```
callbacks_list = [
    keras.callbacks.ReduceLROnPlateau(
        monitor='val_loss'
        factor=0.1,
        patience=10,
    )
]
```

Monitors the model's validation loss

Divides the learning rate by 10 when triggered

The callback is triggered after the validation loss has stopped improving for 10 epochs.

```
model.fit(x, y,
          epochs=10,
          batch_size=32,
          callbacks=callbacks_list,
          validation_data=(x_val, y_val))
```

Because the callback will monitor the validation loss, you need to pass validation_data to the call to fit.

WRITING YOUR OWN CALLBACK

If you need to take a specific action during training that isn't covered by one of the built-in callbacks, you can write your own callback. Callbacks are implemented by subclassing the class `keras.callbacks.Callback`. You can then implement any number of the following transparently named methods, which are called at various points during training:

```
on_epoch_begin        Called at the start of every epoch
on_epoch_end          Called at the end of every epoch

on_batch_begin        Called right before processing each batch
on_batch_end          Called right after processing each batch

on_train_begin        Called at the start of training
on_train_end          Called at the end of training
```

These methods all are called with a `logs` argument, which is a dictionary containing information about the previous batch, epoch, or training run: training and validation metrics, and so on. Additionally, the callback has access to the following attributes:

- `self.model`—The model instance from which the callback is being called
- `self.validation_data`—The value of what was passed to `fit` as validation data

Here's a simple example of a custom callback that saves to disk (as Numpy arrays) the activations of every layer of the model at the end of every epoch, computed on the first sample of the validation set:

```
import keras
import numpy as np

class ActivationLogger(keras.callbacks.Callback):

    def set_model(self, model):
        self.model = model
        layer_outputs = [layer.output for layer in model.layers]
        self.activations_model = keras.models.Model(model.input,
                                                    layer_outputs)

    def on_epoch_end(self, epoch, logs=None):
        if self.validation_data is None:
            raise RuntimeError('Requires validation_data.')
```

Called by the parent model before training, to inform the callback of what model will be calling it

Model instance that returns the activations of every layer

```
validation_sample = self.validation_data[0][0:1]
activations = self.activations_model.predict(validation_sample)
f = open('activations_at_epoch_' + str(epoch) + '.npz', 'w')
np.savez(f, activations)
f.close()
```

**Obtains the first input sample
of the validation data**   **Saves arrays to disk**

This is all you need to know about callbacks—the rest is technical details, which you can easily look up. Now you're equipped to perform any sort of logging or preprogrammed intervention on a Keras model during training.

7.2.2   Introduction to TensorBoard: the TensorFlow visualization framework

To do good research or develop good models, you need rich, frequent feedback about what's going on inside your models during your experiments. That's the point of running experiments: to get information about how well a model performs—as much information as possible. Making progress is an iterative process, or loop: you start with an idea and express it as an experiment, attempting to validate or invalidate your idea. You run this experiment and process the information it generates. This inspires your next idea. The more iterations of this loop you're able to run, the more refined and powerful your ideas become. Keras helps you go from idea to experiment in the least possible time, and fast GPUs can help you get from experiment to result as quickly as possible. But what about processing the experiment results? That's where TensorBoard comes in.

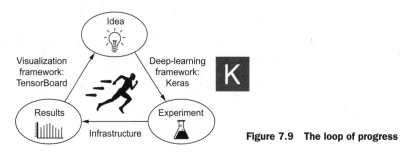

Figure 7.9   The loop of progress

This section introduces TensorBoard, a browser-based visualization tool that comes packaged with TensorFlow. Note that it's only available for Keras models when you're using Keras with the TensorFlow backend.

The key purpose of TensorBoard is to help you visually monitor everything that goes on inside your model during training. If you're monitoring more information than just the model's final loss, you can develop a clearer vision of what the model does and doesn't do, and you can make progress more quickly. TensorBoard gives you access to several neat features, all in your browser:

- Visually monitoring metrics during training
- Visualizing your model architecture
- Visualizing histograms of activations and gradients
- Exploring embeddings in 3D

Let's demonstrate these features on a simple example. You'll train a 1D convnet on the IMDB sentiment-analysis task.

The model is similar to the one you saw in the last section of chapter 6. You'll consider only the top 2,000 words in the IMDB vocabulary, to make visualizing word embeddings more tractable.

Listing 7.7 Text-classification model to use with TensorBoard

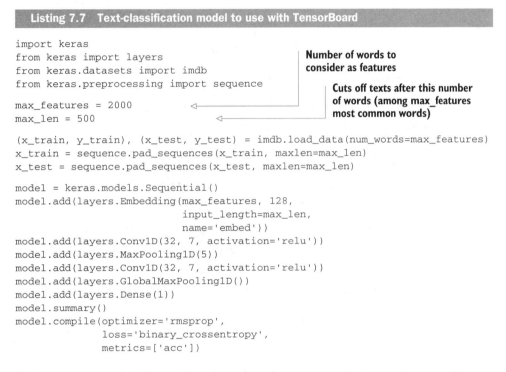

```
import keras
from keras import layers                          Number of words to
from keras.datasets import imdb                    consider as features
from keras.preprocessing import sequence
                                                   Cuts off texts after this number
max_features = 2000        ◁                       of words (among max_features
max_len = 500                          ◁           most common words)

(x_train, y_train), (x_test, y_test) = imdb.load_data(num_words=max_features)
x_train = sequence.pad_sequences(x_train, maxlen=max_len)
x_test = sequence.pad_sequences(x_test, maxlen=max_len)

model = keras.models.Sequential()
model.add(layers.Embedding(max_features, 128,
                           input_length=max_len,
                           name='embed'))
model.add(layers.Conv1D(32, 7, activation='relu'))
model.add(layers.MaxPooling1D(5))
model.add(layers.Conv1D(32, 7, activation='relu'))
model.add(layers.GlobalMaxPooling1D())
model.add(layers.Dense(1))
model.summary()
model.compile(optimizer='rmsprop',
              loss='binary_crossentropy',
              metrics=['acc'])
```

Before you start using TensorBoard, you need to create a directory where you'll store the log files it generates.

Listing 7.8 Creating a directory for TensorBoard log files

```
$ mkdir my_log_dir
```

Let's launch the training with a `TensorBoard` callback instance. This callback will write log events to disk at the specified location.

Listing 7.9   Training the model with a `TensorBoard` callback

```
callbacks = [
    keras.callbacks.TensorBoard(
        log_dir='my_log_dir',
        histogram_freq=1,
        embeddings_freq=1,
    )
]
history = model.fit(x_train, y_train,
                    epochs=20,
                    batch_size=128,
                    validation_split=0.2,
                    callbacks=callbacks)
```

Log files will be written at this location.

Records activation histograms every 1 epoch

Records embedding data every 1 epoch

At this point, you can launch the TensorBoard server from the command line, instructing it to read the logs the callback is currently writing. The `tensorboard` utility should have been automatically installed on your machine the moment you installed TensorFlow (for example, via `pip`):

```
$ tensorboard --logdir=my_log_dir
```

You can then browse to http://localhost:6006 and look at your model training (see figure 7.10). In addition to live graphs of the training and validation metrics, you get access to the Histograms tab, where you can find pretty visualizations of histograms of activation values taken by your layers (see figure 7.11).

Figure 7.10   TensorBoard: metrics monitoring

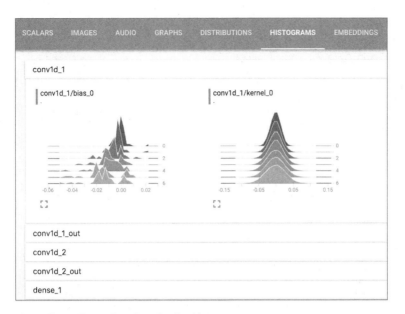

Figure 7.11   TensorBoard: activation histograms

The Embeddings tab gives you a way to inspect the embedding locations and spatial relationships of the 10,000 words in the input vocabulary, as learned by the initial `Embedding` layer. Because the embedding space is 128-dimensional, TensorBoard automatically reduces it to 2D or 3D using a dimensionality-reduction algorithm of your choice: either principal component analysis (PCA) or t-distributed stochastic neighbor embedding (t-SNE). In figure 7.12, in the point cloud, you can clearly see two clusters: words with a positive connotation and words with a negative connotation. The visualization makes it immediately obvious that embeddings trained jointly with a specific objective result in models that are completely specific to the underlying task—that's the reason using pretrained generic word embeddings is rarely a good idea.

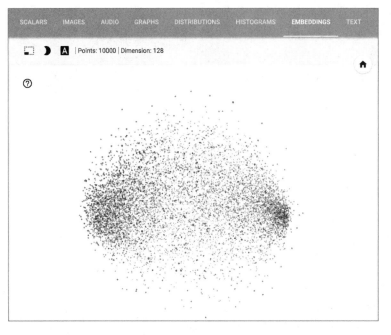

Figure 7.12 TensorBoard: interactive 3D word-embedding visualization

The Graphs tab shows an interactive visualization of the graph of low-level TensorFlow operations underlying your Keras model (see figure 7.13). As you can see, there's a lot more going on than you would expect. The model you just built may look simple when defined in Keras—a small stack of basic layers—but under the hood, you need to construct a fairly complex graph structure to make it work. A lot of it is related to the gradient-descent process. This complexity differential between what you see and what you're manipulating is the key motivation for using Keras as your way of building models, instead of working with raw TensorFlow to define everything from scratch. Keras makes your workflow dramatically simpler.

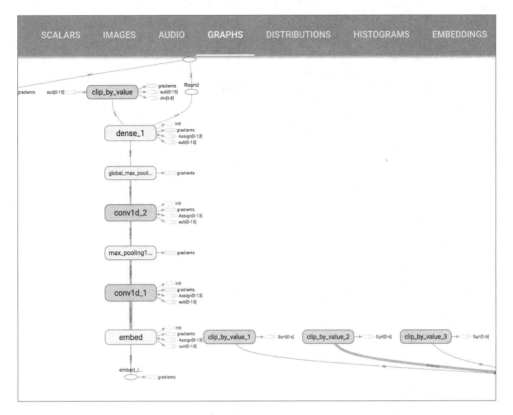

Figure 7.13 TensorBoard: TensorFlow graph visualization

Note that Keras also provides another, cleaner way to plot models as graphs of layers rather than graphs of TensorFlow operations: the utility `keras.utils.plot_model`. Using it requires that you've installed the Python `pydot` and `pydot-ng` libraries as well as the `graphviz` library. Let's take a quick look:

```
from keras.utils import plot_model

plot_model(model, to_file='model.png')
```

This creates the PNG image shown in figure 7.14.

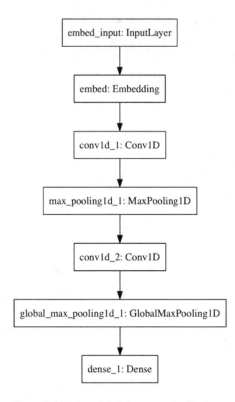

Figure 7.14   A model plot as a graph of layers, generated with `plot_model`

You also have the option of displaying shape information in the graph of layers. This example visualizes model topology using `plot_model` and the `show_shapes` option (see figure 7.15):

```
from keras.utils import plot_model

plot_model(model, show_shapes=True, to_file='model.png')
```

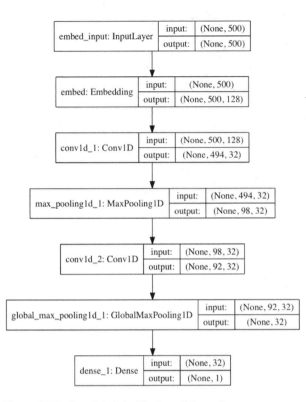

Figure 7.15   A model plot with shape information

7.2.3   *Wrapping up*

- Keras callbacks provide a simple way to monitor models during training and automatically take action based on the state of the model.
- When you're using TensorFlow, TensorBoard is a great way to visualize model activity in your browser. You can use it in Keras models via the `TensorBoard` callback.

7.3   *Getting the most out of your models*

Trying out architectures blindly works well enough if you just need something that works okay. In this section, we'll go beyond "works okay" to "works great and wins machine-learning competitions" by offering you a quick guide to a set of must-know techniques for building state-of-the-art deep-learning models.

7.3.1   *Advanced architecture patterns*

We covered one important design pattern in detail in the previous section: residual connections. There are two more design patterns you should know about: normalization and depthwise separable convolution. These patterns are especially relevant when you're building high-performing deep convnets, but they're commonly found in many other types of architectures as well.

BATCH NORMALIZATION

Normalization is a broad category of methods that seek to make different samples seen by a machine-learning model more similar to each other, which helps the model learn and generalize well to new data. The most common form of data normalization is one you've seen several times in this book already: centering the data on 0 by subtracting the mean from the data, and giving the data a unit standard deviation by dividing the data by its standard deviation. In effect, this makes the assumption that the data follows a normal (or Gaussian) distribution and makes sure this distribution is centered and scaled to unit variance:

```
normalized_data = (data - np.mean(data, axis=...)) / np.std(data, axis=...)
```

Previous examples normalized data before feeding it into models. But data normalization should be a concern after every transformation operated by the network: even if the data entering a `Dense` or `Conv2D` network has a 0 mean and unit variance, there's no reason to expect a priori that this will be the case for the data coming out.

Batch normalization is a type of layer (`BatchNormalization` in Keras) introduced in 2015 by Ioffe and Szegedy;[7] it can adaptively normalize data even as the mean and variance change over time during training. It works by internally maintaining an exponential moving average of the batch-wise mean and variance of the data seen during training. The main effect of batch normalization is that it helps with gradient propagation—much like residual connections—and thus allows for deeper networks. Some very deep networks can only be trained if they include multiple `BatchNormalization` layers. For instance, `BatchNormalization` is used liberally in many of the advanced convnet architectures that come packaged with Keras, such as ResNet50, Inception V3, and Xception.

---

[7] Sergey Ioffe and Christian Szegedy, "Batch Normalization: Accelerating Deep Network Training by Reducing Internal Covariate Shift," *Proceedings of the 32nd International Conference on Machine Learning* (2015), https://arxiv.org/abs/1502.03167.

The `BatchNormalization` layer is typically used after a convolutional or densely connected layer:

```
conv_model.add(layers.Conv2D(32, 3, activation='relu'))    ◁─── After a Conv layer
conv_model.add(layers.BatchNormalization())

dense_model.add(layers.Dense(32, activation='relu'))    ◁─── After a Dense layer
dense_model.add(layers.BatchNormalization())
```

The `BatchNormalization` layer takes an `axis` argument, which specifies the feature axis that should be normalized. This argument defaults to -1, the last axis in the input tensor. This is the correct value when using `Dense` layers, `Conv1D` layers, RNN layers, and `Conv2D` layers with `data_format` set to `"channels_last"`. But in the niche use case of `Conv2D` layers with `data_format` set to `"channels_first"`, the features axis is axis 1; the `axis` argument in `BatchNormalization` should accordingly be set to 1.

Batch renormalization

A recent improvement over regular batch normalization is *batch renormalization*, introduced by Ioffe in 2017.[a] It offers clears benefits over batch normalization, at no apparent cost. At the time of writing, it's too early to tell whether it will supplant batch normalization—but I think it's likely. Even more recently, Klambauer et al. introduced *self-normalizing neural networks*,[b] which manage to keep data normalized after going through any `Dense` layer by using a specific activation function (`selu`) and a specific initializer (`lecun_normal`). This scheme, although highly interesting, is limited to densely connected networks for now, and its usefulness hasn't yet been broadly replicated.

[a] Sergey Ioffe, "Batch Renormalization: Towards Reducing Minibatch Dependence in Batch-Normalized Models" (2017), https://arxiv.org/abs/1702.03275.
[b] Günter Klambauer et al., "Self-Normalizing Neural Networks," Conference on Neural Information Processing Systems (2017), https://arxiv.org/abs/1706.02515.

DEPTHWISE SEPARABLE CONVOLUTION

What if I told you that there's a layer you can use as a drop-in replacement for `Conv2D` that will make your model lighter (fewer trainable weight parameters) and faster (fewer floating-point operations) and cause it to perform a few percentage points better on its task? That is precisely what the *depthwise separable convolution* layer does (`SeparableConv2D`). This layer performs a spatial convolution on each channel of its input, independently, before mixing output channels via a pointwise convolution (a 1 × 1 convolution), as shown in figure 7.16. This is equivalent to separating the learning of spatial features and the learning of channel-wise features, which makes a lot of sense if you assume that spatial locations in the input are highly correlated, but different channels are fairly independent. It requires significantly fewer parameters and involves fewer computations, thus resulting in smaller, speedier models. And because it's a more representationally efficient way to perform convolution, it tends to learn better representations using less data, resulting in better-performing models.

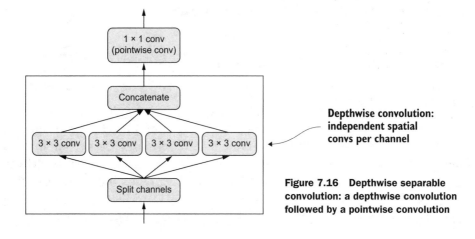

Figure 7.16 Depthwise separable convolution: a depthwise convolution followed by a pointwise convolution

These advantages become especially important when you're training small models from scratch on limited data. For instance, here's how you can build a lightweight, depthwise separable convnet for an image-classification task (softmax categorical classification) on a small dataset:

```
from keras.models import Sequential, Model
from keras import layers

height = 64
width = 64
channels = 3
num_classes = 10

model = Sequential()
model.add(layers.SeparableConv2D(32, 3,
                                 activation='relu',
                                 input_shape=(height, width, channels,)))
model.add(layers.SeparableConv2D(64, 3, activation='relu'))
model.add(layers.MaxPooling2D(2))

model.add(layers.SeparableConv2D(64, 3, activation='relu'))
model.add(layers.SeparableConv2D(128, 3, activation='relu'))
model.add(layers.MaxPooling2D(2))

model.add(layers.SeparableConv2D(64, 3, activation='relu'))
model.add(layers.SeparableConv2D(128, 3, activation='relu'))
model.add(layers.GlobalAveragePooling2D())

model.add(layers.Dense(32, activation='relu'))
model.add(layers.Dense(num_classes, activation='softmax'))

model.compile(optimizer='rmsprop', loss='categorical_crossentropy')
```

When it comes to larger-scale models, depthwise separable convolutions are the basis of the Xception architecture, a high-performing convnet that comes packaged with Keras. You can read more about the theoretical grounding for depthwise separable convolutions and Xception in my paper "Xception: Deep Learning with Depthwise Separable Convolutions."[8]

7.3.2 *Hyperparameter optimization*

When building a deep-learning model, you have to make many seemingly arbitrary decisions: How many layers should you stack? How many units or filters should go in each layer? Should you use `relu` as activation, or a different function? Should you use `BatchNormalization` after a given layer? How much dropout should you use? And so on. These architecture-level parameters are called *hyperparameters* to distinguish them from the parameters of a model, which are trained via backpropagation.

In practice, experienced machine-learning engineers and researchers build intuition over time as to what works and what doesn't when it comes to these choices—they develop hyperparameter-tuning skills. But there are no formal rules. If you want to get to the very limit of what can be achieved on a given task, you can't be content with arbitrary choices made by a fallible human. Your initial decisions are almost always suboptimal, even if you have good intuition. You can refine your choices by tweaking them by hand and retraining the model repeatedly—that's what machine-learning engineers and researchers spend most of their time doing. But it shouldn't be your job as a human to fiddle with hyperparameters all day—that is better left to a machine.

Thus you need to explore the space of possible decisions automatically, systematically, in a principled way. You need to search the architecture space and find the best-performing ones empirically. That's what the field of automatic hyperparameter optimization is about: it's an entire field of research, and an important one.

The process of optimizing hyperparameters typically looks like this:

1 Choose a set of hyperparameters (automatically).
2 Build the corresponding model.
3 Fit it to your training data, and measure the final performance on the validation data.
4 Choose the next set of hyperparameters to try (automatically).
5 Repeat.
6 Eventually, measure performance on your test data.

The key to this process is the algorithm that uses this history of validation performance, given various sets of hyperparameters, to choose the next set of hyperparameters to evaluate. Many different techniques are possible: Bayesian optimization, genetic algorithms, simple random search, and so on.

Training the weights of a model is relatively easy: you compute a loss function on a mini-batch of data and then use the Backpropagation algorithm to move the weights

---

[8] See note 5 above.

in the right direction. Updating hyperparameters, on the other hand, is extremely challenging. Consider the following:

- Computing the feedback signal (does this set of hyperparameters lead to a high-performing model on this task?) can be extremely expensive: it requires creating and training a new model from scratch on your dataset.
- The hyperparameter space is typically made of discrete decisions and thus isn't continuous or differentiable. Hence, you typically can't do gradient descent in hyperparameter space. Instead, you must rely on gradient-free optimization techniques, which naturally are far less efficient than gradient descent.

Because these challenges are difficult and the field is still young, we currently only have access to very limited tools to optimize models. Often, it turns out that random search (choosing hyperparameters to evaluate at random, repeatedly) is the best solution, despite being the most naive one. But one tool I have found reliably better than random search is Hyperopt (https://github.com/hyperopt/hyperopt), a Python library for hyperparameter optimization that internally uses trees of Parzen estimators to predict sets of hyperparameters that are likely to work well. Another library called Hyperas (https://github.com/maxpumperla/hyperas) integrates Hyperopt for use with Keras models. Do check it out.

> **NOTE**   One important issue to keep in mind when doing automatic hyperparameter optimization at scale is validation-set overfitting. Because you're updating hyperparameters based on a signal that is computed using your validation data, you're effectively training them on the validation data, and thus they will quickly overfit to the validation data. Always keep this in mind.

Overall, hyperparameter optimization is a powerful technique that is an absolute requirement to get to state-of-the-art models on any task or to win machine-learning competitions. Think about it: once upon a time, people handcrafted the features that went into shallow machine-learning models. That was very much suboptimal. Now, deep learning automates the task of hierarchical feature engineering—features are learned using a feedback signal, not hand-tuned, and that's the way it should be. In the same way, you shouldn't handcraft your model architectures; you should optimize them in a principled way. At the time of writing, the field of automatic hyperparameter optimization is very young and immature, as deep learning was some years ago, but I expect it to boom in the next few years.

7.3.3   *Model ensembling*

Another powerful technique for obtaining the best possible results on a task is *model ensembling*. Ensembling consists of pooling together the predictions of a set of different models, to produce better predictions. If you look at machine-learning competitions, in particular on Kaggle, you'll see that the winners use very large ensembles of models that inevitably beat any single model, no matter how good.

Ensembling relies on the assumption that different good models trained independently are likely to be good for *different reasons*: each model looks at slightly different aspects of the data to make its predictions, getting part of the "truth" but not all of it. You may be familiar with the ancient parable of the blind men and the elephant: a group of blind men come across an elephant for the first time and try to understand what the elephant is by touching it. Each man touches a different part of the elephant's body—just one part, such as the trunk or a leg. Then the men describe to each other what an elephant is: "It's like a snake," "Like a pillar or a tree," and so on. The blind men are essentially machine-learning models trying to understand the manifold of the training data, each from its own perspective, using its own assumptions (provided by the unique architecture of the model and the unique random weight initialization). Each of them gets part of the truth of the data, but not the whole truth. By pooling their perspectives together, you can get a far more accurate description of the data. The elephant is a combination of parts: not any single blind man gets it quite right, but, interviewed together, they can tell a fairly accurate story.

Let's use classification as an example. The easiest way to pool the predictions of a set of classifiers (to *ensemble the classifiers*) is to average their predictions at inference time:

Use four different models to compute initial predictions.

```
preds_a = model_a.predict(x_val)
preds_b = model_b.predict(x_val)
preds_c = model_c.predict(x_val)
preds_d = model_d.predict(x_val)

final_preds = 0.25 * (preds_a + preds_b + preds_c + preds_d)
```

This new prediction array should be more accurate than any of the initial ones.

This will work only if the classifiers are more or less equally good. If one of them is significantly worse than the others, the final predictions may not be as good as the best classifier of the group.

A smarter way to ensemble classifiers is to do a weighted average, where the weights are learned on the validation data—typically, the better classifiers are given a higher weight, and the worse classifiers are given a lower weight. To search for a good set of ensembling weights, you can use random search or a simple optimization algorithm such as Nelder-Mead:

```
preds_a = model_a.predict(x_val)
preds_b = model_b.predict(x_val)
preds_c = model_c.predict(x_val)
preds_d = model_d.predict(x_val)

final_preds = 0.5 * preds_a + 0.25 * preds_b + 0.1 * preds_c + 0.15 * preds_d
```

These weights (0.5, 0.25, 0.1, 0.15) are assumed to be learned empirically.

There are many possible variants: you can do an average of an exponential of the predictions, for instance. In general, a simple weighted average with weights optimized on the validation data provides a very strong baseline.

The key to making ensembling work is the *diversity* of the set of classifiers. Diversity is strength. If all the blind men only touched the elephant's trunk, they would agree that elephants are like snakes, and they would forever stay ignorant of the truth of the elephant. Diversity is what makes ensembling work. In machine-learning terms, if all of your models are biased in the same way, then your ensemble will retain this same bias. If your models are *biased in different ways*, the biases will cancel each other out, and the ensemble will be more robust and more accurate.

For this reason, you should ensemble models that are *as good as possible* while being *as different as possible*. This typically means using very different architectures or even different brands of machine-learning approaches. One thing that is largely *not* worth doing is ensembling the same network trained several times independently, from different random initializations. If the only difference between your models is their random initialization and the order in which they were exposed to the training data, then your ensemble will be low-diversity and will provide only a tiny improvement over any single model.

One thing I have found to work well in practice—but that doesn't generalize to every problem domain—is the use of an ensemble of tree-based methods (such as random forests or gradient-boosted trees) and deep neural networks. In 2014, partner Andrei Kolev and I took fourth place in the Higgs Boson decay detection challenge on Kaggle (www.kaggle.com/c/higgs-boson) using an ensemble of various tree models and deep neural networks. Remarkably, one of the models in the ensemble originated from a different method than the others (it was a regularized greedy forest) and had a significantly worse score than the others. Unsurprisingly, it was assigned a small weight in the ensemble. But to our surprise, it turned out to improve the overall ensemble by a large factor, because it was so different from every other model: it provided information that the other models didn't have access to. That's precisely the point of ensembling. It's not so much about how good your best model is; it's about the diversity of your set of candidate models.

In recent times, one style of basic ensemble that has been very successful in practice is the *wide and deep* category of models, blending deep learning with shallow learning. Such models consist of jointly training a deep neural network with a large linear model. The joint training of a family of diverse models is yet another option to achieve model ensembling.

7.3.4   *Wrapping up*

- When building high-performing deep convnets, you'll need to use residual connections, batch normalization, and depthwise separable convolutions. In the future, it's likely that depthwise separable convolutions will completely replace regular convolutions, whether for 1D, 2D, or 3D applications, due to their higher representational efficiency.

- Building deep networks requires making many small hyperparameter and architecture choices, which together define how good your model will be. Rather than basing these choices on intuition or random chance, it's better to systematically search hyperparameter space to find optimal choices. At this time, the process is expensive, and the tools to do it aren't very good. But the Hyperopt and Hyperas libraries may be able to help you. When doing hyperparameter optimization, be mindful of validation-set overfitting!

- Winning machine-learning competitions or otherwise obtaining the best possible results on a task can only be done with large ensembles of models. Ensembling via a well-optimized weighted average is usually good enough. Remember: diversity is strength. It's largely pointless to ensemble very similar models; the best ensembles are sets of models that are as dissimilar as possible (while having as much predictive power as possible, naturally).

Chapter summary

- In this chapter, you learned the following:
  - How to build models as arbitrary graphs of layers, reuse layers (layer weight sharing), and use models as Python functions (model templating).
  - You can use Keras callbacks to monitor your models during training and take action based on model state.
  - TensorBoard allows you to visualize metrics, activation histograms, and even embedding spaces.
  - What batch normalization, depthwise separable convolution, and residual connections are.
  - Why you should use hyperparameter optimization and model ensembling.

- With these new tools, you're better equipped to use deep learning in the real world and start building highly competitive deep-learning models.

Generative deep learning

8

This chapter covers

- Text generation with LSTM
- Implementing DeepDream
- Performing neural style transfer
- Variational autoencoders
- Understanding generative adversarial networks

The potential of artificial intelligence to emulate human thought processes goes beyond passive tasks such as object recognition and mostly reactive tasks such as driving a car. It extends well into creative activities. When I first made the claim that in a not-so-distant future, most of the cultural content that we consume will be created with substantial help from AIs, I was met with utter disbelief, even from long-time machine-learning practitioners. That was in 2014. Fast-forward three years, and the disbelief has receded—at an incredible speed. In the summer of 2015, we were entertained by Google's DeepDream algorithm turning an image into a psychedelic mess of dog eyes and pareidolic artifacts; in 2016, we used the Prisma application to turn photos into paintings of various styles. In the summer of 2016, an experimental short movie, *Sunspring*, was directed using a script written by a Long Short-Term Memory (LSTM) algorithm—complete with dialogue. Maybe you've recently listened to music that was tentatively generated by a neural network.

Granted, the artistic productions we've seen from AI so far have been fairly low quality. AI isn't anywhere close to rivaling human screenwriters, painters, and composers. But replacing humans was always beside the point: artificial intelligence isn't about replacing our own intelligence with something else, it's about bringing into our lives and work *more* intelligence—intelligence of a different kind. In many fields, but especially in creative ones, AI will be used by humans as a tool to augment their own capabilities: more *augmented* intelligence than *artificial* intelligence.

A large part of artistic creation consists of simple pattern recognition and technical skill. And that's precisely the part of the process that many find less attractive or even dispensable. That's where AI comes in. Our perceptual modalities, our language, and our artwork all have statistical structure. Learning this structure is what deep-learning algorithms excel at. Machine-learning models can learn the statistical *latent space* of images, music, and stories, and they can then *sample* from this space, creating new artworks with characteristics similar to those the model has seen in its training data. Naturally, such sampling is hardly an act of artistic creation in itself. It's a mere mathematical operation: the algorithm has no grounding in human life, human emotions, or our experience of the world; instead, it learns from an experience that has little in common with ours. It's only our interpretation, as human spectators, that will give meaning to what the model generates. But in the hands of a skilled artist, algorithmic generation can be steered to become meaningful—and beautiful. Latent space sampling can become a brush that empowers the artist, augments our creative affordances, and expands the space of what we can imagine. What's more, it can make artistic creation more accessible by eliminating the need for technical skill and practice—setting up a new medium of pure expression, factoring art apart from craft.

Iannis Xenakis, a visionary pioneer of electronic and algorithmic music, beautifully expressed this same idea in the 1960s, in the context of the application of automation technology to music composition:[1]

> *Freed from tedious calculations, the composer is able to devote himself to the general problems that the new musical form poses and to explore the nooks and crannies of this form while modifying the values of the input data. For example, he may test all instrumental combinations from soloists to chamber orchestras, to large orchestras. With the aid of electronic computers the composer becomes a sort of pilot: he presses the buttons, introduces coordinates, and supervises the controls of a cosmic vessel sailing in the space of sound, across sonic constellations and galaxies that he could formerly glimpse only as a distant dream.*

In this chapter, we'll explore from various angles the potential of deep learning to augment artistic creation. We'll review sequence data generation (which can be used to generate text or music), DeepDream, and image generation using both variational autoencoders and generative adversarial networks. We'll get your computer to dream up content never seen before; and maybe we'll get you to dream, too, about the fantastic possibilities that lie at the intersection of technology and art. Let's get started.

---

[1] Iannis Xenakis, "Musiques formelles: nouveaux principes formels de composition musicale," special issue of *La Revue musicale*, nos. 253 -254 (1963).

8.1 Text generation with LSTM

In this section, we'll explore how recurrent neural networks can be used to generate sequence data. We'll use text generation as an example, but the exact same techniques can be generalized to any kind of sequence data: you could apply it to sequences of musical notes in order to generate new music, to timeseries of brush-stroke data (for example, recorded while an artist paints on an iPad) to generate paintings stroke by stroke, and so on.

Sequence data generation is in no way limited to artistic content generation. It has been successfully applied to speech synthesis and to dialogue generation for chatbots. The Smart Reply feature that Google released in 2016, capable of automatically generating a selection of quick replies to emails or text messages, is powered by similar techniques.

8.1.1 A brief history of generative recurrent networks

In late 2014, few people had ever seen the initials LSTM, even in the machine-learning community. Successful applications of sequence data generation with recurrent networks only began to appear in the mainstream in 2016. But these techniques have a fairly long history, starting with the development of the LSTM algorithm in 1997.[2] This new algorithm was used early on to generate text character by character.

In 2002, Douglas Eck, then at Schmidhuber's lab in Switzerland, applied LSTM to music generation for the first time, with promising results. Eck is now a researcher at Google Brain, and in 2016 he started a new research group there, called Magenta, focused on applying modern deep-learning techniques to produce engaging music. Sometimes, good ideas take 15 years to get started.

In the late 2000s and early 2010s, Alex Graves did important pioneering work on using recurrent networks for sequence data generation. In particular, his 2013 work on applying recurrent mixture density networks to generate human-like handwriting using timeseries of pen positions is seen by some as a turning point.[3] This specific application of neural networks at that specific moment in time captured for me the notion of *machines that dream* and was a significant inspiration around the time I started developing Keras. Graves left a similar commented-out remark hidden in a 2013 LaTeX file uploaded to the preprint server arXiv: "generating sequential data is the closest computers get to dreaming." Several years later, we take a lot of these developments for granted; but at the time, it was difficult to watch Graves's demonstrations and not walk away awe-inspired by the possibilities.

Since then, recurrent neural networks have been successfully used for music generation, dialogue generation, image generation, speech synthesis, and molecule design. They were even used to produce a movie script that was then cast with live actors.

---

[2] Sepp Hochreiter and Jürgen Schmidhuber, "Long Short-Term Memory," *Neural Computation* 9, no. 8 (1997).

[3] Alex Graves, "Generating Sequences With Recurrent Neural Networks," arXiv (2013), https://arxiv.org/abs/1308.0850.

8.1.2   *How do you generate sequence data?*

The universal way to generate sequence data in deep learning is to train a network (usually an RNN or a convnet) to predict the next token or next few tokens in a sequence, using the previous tokens as input. For instance, given the input "the cat is on the ma," the network is trained to predict the target *t*, the next character. As usual when working with text data, *tokens* are typically words or characters, and any network that can model the probability of the next token given the previous ones is called a *language model*. A language model captures the *latent space* of language: its statistical structure.

Once you have such a trained language model, you can *sample* from it (generate new sequences): you feed it an initial string of text (called *conditioning data*), ask it to generate the next character or the next word (you can even generate several tokens at once), add the generated output back to the input data, and repeat the process many times (see figure 8.1). This loop allows you to generate sequences of arbitrary length that reflect the structure of the data on which the model was trained: sequences that look *almost* like human-written sentences. In the example we present in this section, you'll take a LSTM layer, feed it strings of *N* characters extracted from a text corpus, and train it to predict character *N* + 1. The output of the model will be a softmax over all possible characters: a probability distribution for the next character. This LSTM is called a *character-level neural language model*.

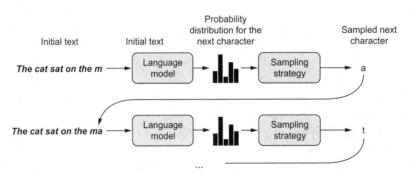

Figure 8.1   The process of character-by-character text generation using a language model

8.1.3   *The importance of the sampling strategy*

When generating text, the way you choose the next character is crucially important. A naive approach is *greedy sampling*, consisting of always choosing the most likely next character. But such an approach results in repetitive, predictable strings that don't look like coherent language. A more interesting approach makes slightly more surprising choices: it introduces randomness in the sampling process, by sampling from the probability distribution for the next character. This is called *stochastic sampling* (recall that *stochasticity* is what we call *randomness* in this field). In such a setup, if *e* has a probability 0.3 of being the next character, according to the model, you'll choose it

30% of the time. Note that greedy sampling can be also cast as sampling from a probability distribution: one where a certain character has probability 1 and all others have probability 0.

Sampling probabilistically from the softmax output of the model is neat: it allows even unlikely characters to be sampled some of the time, generating more interesting-looking sentences and sometimes showing creativity by coming up with new, realistic-sounding words that didn't occur in the training data. But there's one issue with this strategy: it doesn't offer a way to *control the amount of randomness* in the sampling process.

Why would you want more or less randomness? Consider an extreme case: pure random sampling, where you draw the next character from a uniform probability distribution, and every character is equally likely. This scheme has maximum randomness; in other words, this probability distribution has maximum entropy. Naturally, it won't produce anything interesting. At the other extreme, greedy sampling doesn't produce anything interesting, either, and has no randomness: the corresponding probability distribution has minimum entropy. Sampling from the "real" probability distribution—the distribution that is output by the model's softmax function—constitutes an intermediate point between these two extremes. But there are many other intermediate points of higher or lower entropy that you may want to explore. Less entropy will give the generated sequences a more predictable structure (and thus they will potentially be more realistic looking), whereas more entropy will result in more surprising and creative sequences. When sampling from generative models, it's always good to explore different amounts of randomness in the generation process. Because we—humans—are the ultimate judges of how interesting the generated data is, interestingness is highly subjective, and there's no telling in advance where the point of optimal entropy lies.

In order to control the amount of stochasticity in the sampling process, we'll introduce a parameter called the *softmax temperature* that characterizes the entropy of the probability distribution used for sampling: it characterizes how surprising or predictable the choice of the next character will be. Given a `temperature` value, a new probability distribution is computed from the original one (the softmax output of the model) by reweighting it in the following way.

Listing 8.1   Reweighting a probability distribution to a different temperature

```python
import numpy as np

def reweight_distribution(original_distribution, temperature=0.5):
    distribution = np.log(original_distribution) / temperature
    distribution = np.exp(distribution)
    return distribution / np.sum(distribution)
```

original_distribution is a 1D Numpy array of probability values that must sum to 1. temperature is a factor quantifying the entropy of the output distribution.

Returns a reweighted version of the original distribution. The sum of the distribution may no longer be 1, so you divide it by its sum to obtain the new distribution.

Higher temperatures result in sampling distributions of higher entropy that will generate more surprising and unstructured generated data, whereas a lower temperature will result in less randomness and much more predictable generated data (see figure 8.2).

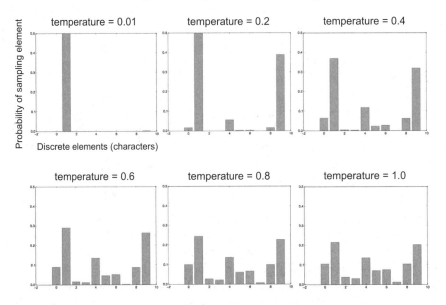

Figure 8.2   Different reweightings of one probability distribution. Low temperature = more deterministic, high temperature = more random.

8.1.4   Implementing character-level LSTM text generation

Let's put these ideas into practice in a Keras implementation. The first thing you need is a lot of text data that you can use to learn a language model. You can use any sufficiently large text file or set of text files—Wikipedia, *The Lord of the Rings*, and so on. In this example, you'll use some of the writings of Nietzsche, the late-nineteenth century German philosopher (translated into English). The language model you'll learn will thus be specifically a model of Nietzsche's writing style and topics of choice, rather than a more generic model of the English language.

PREPARING THE DATA

Let's start by downloading the corpus and converting it to lowercase.

Listing 8.2   Downloading and parsing the initial text file

```
import keras
import numpy as np

path = keras.utils.get_file(
    'nietzsche.txt',
    origin='https://s3.amazonaws.com/text-datasets/nietzsche.txt')
text = open(path).read().lower()
print('Corpus length:', len(text))
```

Next, you'll extract partially overlapping sequences of length `maxlen`, one-hot encode them, and pack them in a 3D Numpy array `x` of shape `(sequences, maxlen, unique_characters)`. Simultaneously, you'll prepare an array `y` containing the corresponding targets: the one-hot-encoded characters that come after each extracted sequence.

Listing 8.3   Vectorizing sequences of characters

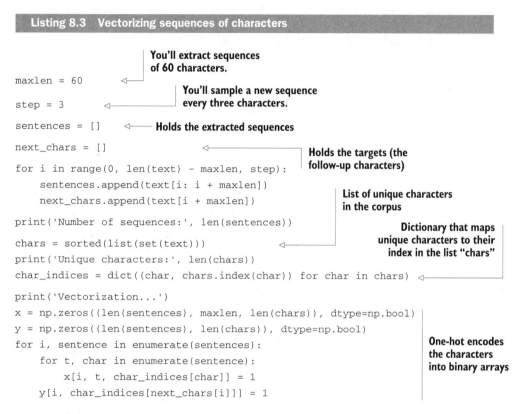

```
maxlen = 60              ◁──────   You'll extract sequences
                                   of 60 characters.

step = 3          ◁──────────────  You'll sample a new sequence
                                   every three characters.

sentences = []    ◁──────  Holds the extracted sequences

next_chars = []              ◁─────────────  Holds the targets (the
                                             follow-up characters)
for i in range(0, len(text) - maxlen, step):
    sentences.append(text[i: i + maxlen])
    next_chars.append(text[i + maxlen])              List of unique characters
                                                     in the corpus
print('Number of sequences:', len(sentences))
                                                          Dictionary that maps
chars = sorted(list(set(text)))           ◁──────    unique characters to their
print('Unique characters:', len(chars))                 index in the list "chars"
char_indices = dict((char, chars.index(char)) for char in chars)  ◁──────

print('Vectorization...')
x = np.zeros((len(sentences), maxlen, len(chars)), dtype=np.bool)
y = np.zeros((len(sentences), len(chars)), dtype=np.bool)
for i, sentence in enumerate(sentences):                   One-hot encodes
    for t, char in enumerate(sentence):                    the characters
        x[i, t, char_indices[char]] = 1                    into binary arrays
    y[i, char_indices[next_chars[i]]] = 1
```

BUILDING THE NETWORK

This network is a single `LSTM` layer followed by a `Dense` classifier and softmax over all possible characters. But note that recurrent neural networks aren't the only way to do sequence data generation; 1D convnets also have proven extremely successful at this task in recent times.

Listing 8.4   Single-layer LSTM model for next-character prediction

```
from keras import layers

model = keras.models.Sequential()
model.add(layers.LSTM(128, input_shape=(maxlen, len(chars))))
model.add(layers.Dense(len(chars), activation='softmax'))
```

Because your targets are one-hot encoded, you'll use `categorical_crossentropy` as the loss to train the model.

Listing 8.5   Model compilation configuration

```
optimizer = keras.optimizers.RMSprop(lr=0.01)
model.compile(loss='categorical_crossentropy', optimizer=optimizer)
```

TRAINING THE LANGUAGE MODEL AND SAMPLING FROM IT

Given a trained model and a seed text snippet, you can generate new text by doing the following repeatedly:

1. Draw from the model a probability distribution for the next character, given the generated text available so far.
2. Reweight the distribution to a certain temperature.
3. Sample the next character at random according to the reweighted distribution.
4. Add the new character at the end of the available text.

This is the code you use to reweight the original probability distribution coming out of the model and draw a character index from it (the *sampling function*).

Listing 8.6   Function to sample the next character given the model's predictions

```
def sample(preds, temperature=1.0):
    preds = np.asarray(preds).astype('float64')
    preds = np.log(preds) / temperature
    exp_preds = np.exp(preds)
    preds = exp_preds / np.sum(exp_preds)
    probas = np.random.multinomial(1, preds, 1)
    return np.argmax(probas)
```

Finally, the following loop repeatedly trains and generates text. You begin generating text using a range of different temperatures after every epoch. This allows you to see how the generated text evolves as the model begins to converge, as well as the impact of temperature in the sampling strategy.

Listing 8.7   Text-generation loop

```
import random
import sys                          Trains the model for 60 epochs

for epoch in range(1, 60):          ◄──┘
    print('epoch', epoch)                          Fits the model for one iteration
    model.fit(x, y, batch_size=128, epochs=1)  ◄── on the data
    start_index = random.randint(0, len(text) - maxlen - 1)     Selects a text
    generated_text = text[start_index: start_index + maxlen]    seed at
    print('--- Generating with seed: "' + generated_text + '"') random

    for temperature in [0.2, 0.5, 1.0, 1.2]:    ◄──  Tries a range of different
        print('------ temperature:', temperature)     sampling temperatures
        sys.stdout.write(generated_text)
```

<table>
<tr><td>

Generates 400
characters,
starting from
the seed text
</td><td>

```
for i in range(400):
    sampled = np.zeros((1, maxlen, len(chars)))
    for t, char in enumerate(generated_text):
        sampled[0, t, char_indices[char]] = 1.

    preds = model.predict(sampled, verbose=0)[0]
    next_index = sample(preds, temperature)
    next_char = chars[next_index]

    generated_text += next_char
    generated_text = generated_text[1:]

    sys.stdout.write(next_char)
```
</td><td>

One-hot encodes
the characters
generated so far

Samples
the next
character
</td></tr>
</table>

Here, we used the random seed text "new faculty, and the jubilation reached its climax when kant." Here's what you get at epoch 20, long before the model has fully converged, with `temperature=0.2`:

```
new faculty, and the jubilation reached its climax when kant and such a man
in the same time the spirit of the surely and the such the such
as a man is the sunligh and subject the present to the superiority of the
special pain the most man and strange the subjection of the
special conscience the special and nature and such men the subjection of the
special men, the most surely the subjection of the special
intellect of the subjection of the same things and
```

Here's the result with `temperature=0.5`:

```
new faculty, and the jubilation reached its climax when kant in the eterned
and such man as it's also become himself the condition of the
experience of off the basis the superiory and the special morty of the
strength, in the langus, as which the same time life and "even who
discless the mankind, with a subject and fact all you have to be the stand
and lave no comes a troveration of the man and surely the
conscience the superiority, and when one must be w
```

And here's what you get with `temperature=1.0`:

```
new faculty, and the jubilation reached its climax when kant, as a
periliting of manner to all definites and transpects it it so
hicable and ont him artiar resull
too such as if ever the proping to makes as cnecience. to been juden,
all every could coldiciousnike hother aw passife, the plies like
which might thiod was account, indifferent germin, that everythery
certain destrution, intellect into the deteriorablen origin of moralian,
and a lessority o
```

At epoch 60, the model has mostly converged, and the text starts to look significantly more coherent. Here's the result with `temperature=0.2`:

```
cheerfulness, friendliness and kindness of a heart are the sense of the
spirit is a man with the sense of the sense of the world of the
self-end and self-concerning the subjection of the strengthorixes--the
```

```
subjection of the subjection of the subjection of the
self-concerning the feelings in the superiority in the subjection of the
subjection of the spirit isn't to be a man of the sense of the
subjection and said to the strength of the sense of the
```

Here's temperature=0.5:

```
cheerfulness, friendliness and kindness of a heart are the part of the soul
who have been the art of the philosophers, and which the one
won't say, which is it the higher the and with religion of the frences.
the life of the spirit among the most continuess of the
strengther of the sense the conscience of men of precisely before enough
presumption, and can mankind, and something the conceptions, the
subjection of the sense and suffering and the
```

And here's temperature=1.0:

```
cheerfulness, friendliness and kindness of a heart are spiritual by the
ciuture for the
entalled is, he astraged, or errors to our you idstood--and it needs,
to think by spars to whole the amvives of the newoatly, prefectly
raals! it was
name, for example but voludd atu-especity"--or rank onee, or even all
"solett increessic of the world and
implussional tragedy experience, transf, or insiderar,--must hast
if desires of the strubction is be stronges
```

As you can see, a low temperature value results in extremely repetitive and predictable text, but local structure is highly realistic: in particular, all words (a *word* being a local pattern of characters) are real English words. With higher temperatures, the generated text becomes more interesting, surprising, even creative; it sometimes invents completely new words that sound somewhat plausible (such as *eterned* and *troveration*). With a high temperature, the local structure starts to break down, and most words look like semi-random strings of characters. Without a doubt, 0.5 is the most interesting temperature for text generation in this specific setup. Always experiment with multiple sampling strategies! A clever balance between learned structure and randomness is what makes generation interesting.

Note that by training a bigger model, longer, on more data, you can achieve generated samples that look much more coherent and realistic than this one. But, of course, don't expect to ever generate any meaningful text, other than by random chance: all you're doing is sampling data from a statistical model of which characters come after which characters. Language is a communication channel, and there's a distinction between what communications are about and the statistical structure of the messages in which communications are encoded. To evidence this distinction, here's a thought experiment: what if human language did a better job of compressing communications, much like computers do with most digital communications? Language would be no less meaningful, but it would lack any intrinsic statistical structure, thus making it impossible to learn a language model as you just did.

8.1.5 Wrapping up

- You can generate discrete sequence data by training a model to predict the next tokens(s), given previous tokens.
- In the case of text, such a model is called a *language model*. It can be based on either words or characters.
- Sampling the next token requires balance between adhering to what the model judges likely, and introducing randomness.
- One way to handle this is the notion of softmax temperature. Always experiment with different temperatures to find the right one.

8.2   *DeepDream*

DeepDream is an artistic image-modification technique that uses the representations learned by convolutional neural networks. It was first released by Google in the summer of 2015, as an implementation written using the Caffe deep-learning library (this was several months before the first public release of TensorFlow).[4] It quickly became an internet sensation thanks to the trippy pictures it could generate (see, for example, figure 8.3), full of algorithmic pareidolia artifacts, bird feathers, and dog eyes—a byproduct of the fact that the DeepDream convnet was trained on ImageNet, where dog breeds and bird species are vastly overrepresented.

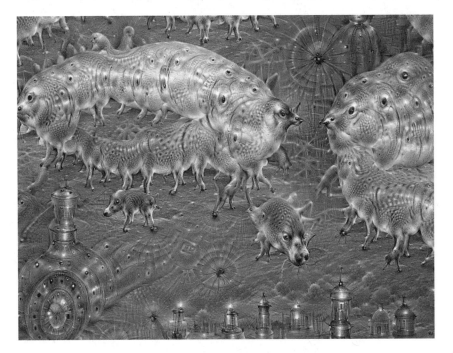

Figure 8.3   Example of a DeepDream output image

The DeepDream algorithm is almost identical to the convnet filter-visualization technique introduced in chapter 5, consisting of running a convnet in reverse: doing gradient ascent on the input to the convnet in order to maximize the activation of a specific filter in an upper layer of the convnet. DeepDream uses this same idea, with a few simple differences:

- With DeepDream, you try to maximize the activation of entire layers rather than that of a specific filter, thus mixing together visualizations of large numbers of features at once.

---

[4] Alexander Mordvintsev, Christopher Olah, and Mike Tyka, "DeepDream: A Code Example for Visualizing Neural Networks," *Google Research Blog,* July 1, 2015, http://mng.bz/xXlM.

- You start not from blank, slightly noisy input, but rather from an existing image—thus the resulting effects latch on to preexisting visual patterns, distorting elements of the image in a somewhat artistic fashion.
- The input images are processed at different scales (called *octaves*), which improves the quality of the visualizations.

Let's make some DeepDreams.

8.2.1 Implementing DeepDream in Keras

You'll start from a convnet pretrained on ImageNet. In Keras, many such convnets are available: VGG16, VGG19, Xception, ResNet50, and so on. You can implement Deep-Dream with any of them, but your convnet of choice will naturally affect your visualizations, because different convnet architectures result in different learned features. The convnet used in the original DeepDream release was an Inception model, and in practice Inception is known to produce nice-looking DeepDreams, so you'll use the Inception V3 model that comes with Keras.

Listing 8.8 Loading the pretrained Inception V3 model

```
from keras.applications import inception_v3
from keras import backend as K

K.set_learning_phase(0)

model = inception_v3.InceptionV3(weights='imagenet',
                                 include_top=False)
```

You won't be training the model, so this command disables all training-specific operations.

Builds the Inception V3 network, without its convolutional base. The model will be loaded with pretrained ImageNet weights.

Next, you'll compute the *loss*: the quantity you'll seek to maximize during the gradient-ascent process. In chapter 5, for filter visualization, you tried to maximize the value of a specific filter in a specific layer. Here, you'll simultaneously maximize the activation of all filters in a number of layers. Specifically, you'll maximize a weighted sum of the L2 norm of the activations of a set of high-level layers. The exact set of layers you choose (as well as their contribution to the final loss) has a major influence on the visuals you'll be able to produce, so you want to make these parameters easily configurable. Lower layers result in geometric patterns, whereas higher layers result in visuals in which you can recognize some classes from ImageNet (for example, birds or dogs). You'll start from a somewhat arbitrary configuration involving four layers—but you'll definitely want to explore many different configurations later.

Listing 8.9 Setting up the DeepDream configuration

```
layer_contributions = {
    'mixed2': 0.2,
    'mixed3': 3.,
    'mixed4': 2.,
    'mixed5': 1.5,
}
```

Dictionary mapping layer names to a coefficient quantifying how much the layer's activation contributes to the loss you'll seek to maximize. Note that the layer names are hardcoded in the built-in Inception V3 application. You can list all layer names using model.summary().

Now, let's define a tensor that contains the loss: the weighted sum of the L2 norm of the activations of the layers in listing 8.9.

Listing 8.10   Defining the loss to be maximized

Creates a dictionary that maps layer names to layer instances

```
layer_dict = dict([(layer.name, layer) for layer in model.layers])

loss = K.variable(0.)
for layer_name in layer_contributions:
    coeff = layer_contributions[layer_name]
    activation = layer_dict[layer_name].output

    scaling = K.prod(K.cast(K.shape(activation), 'float32'))
    loss += coeff * K.sum(K.square(activation[:, 2: -2, 2: -2, :])) / scaling
```

You'll define the loss by adding layer contributions to this scalar variable.

Retrieves the layer's output

Adds the L2 norm of the features of a layer to the loss. You avoid border artifacts by only involving nonborder pixels in the loss.

Next, you can set up the gradient-ascent process.

Listing 8.11   Gradient-ascent process

This tensor holds the generated image: the dream.

Computes the gradients of the dream with regard to the loss

```
dream = model.input

grads = K.gradients(loss, dream)[0]

grads /= K.maximum(K.mean(K.abs(grads)), 1e-7)

outputs = [loss, grads]
fetch_loss_and_grads = K.function([dream], outputs)

def eval_loss_and_grads(x):
    outs = fetch_loss_and_grads([x])
    loss_value = outs[0]
    grad_values = outs[1]
    return loss_value, grad_values

def gradient_ascent(x, iterations, step, max_loss=None):
    for i in range(iterations):
        loss_value, grad_values = eval_loss_and_grads(x)
        if max_loss is not None and loss_value > max_loss:
            break
        print('...Loss value at', i, ':', loss_value)
        x += step * grad_values
    return x
```

Normalizes the gradients (important trick)

Sets up a Keras function to retrieve the value of the loss and gradients, given an input image

This function runs gradient ascent for a number of iterations.

Finally: the actual DeepDream algorithm. First, you define a list of *scales* (also called *octaves*) at which to process the images. Each successive scale is larger than the previous one by a factor of 1.4 (it's 40% larger): you start by processing a small image and then increasingly scale it up (see figure 8.4).

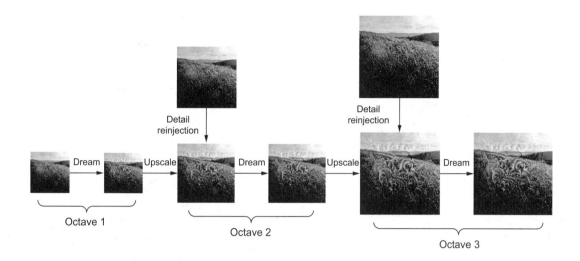

Figure 8.4 The DeepDream process: successive scales of spatial processing (octaves) and detail reinjection upon upscaling

For each successive scale, from the smallest to the largest, you run gradient ascent to maximize the loss you previously defined, at that scale. After each gradient ascent run, you upscale the resulting image by 40%.

To avoid losing a lot of image detail after each successive scale-up (resulting in increasingly blurry or pixelated images), you can use a simple trick: after each scale-up, you'll reinject the lost details back into the image, which is possible because you know what the original image should look like at the larger scale. Given a small image size *S* and a larger image size *L*, you can compute the difference between the original image resized to size *L* and the original resized to size *S*—this difference quantifies the details lost when going from *S* to *L*.

Listing 8.12 Running gradient ascent over different successive scales

Playing with these hyperparameters will let you achieve new effects.

Gradient ascent step size

Number of scales at which to run gradient ascent

Size ratio between scales

Number of ascent steps to run at each scale

If the loss grows larger than 10, you'll interrupt the gradient-ascent process to avoid ugly artifacts.

```
import numpy as np

step = 0.01
num_octave = 3
octave_scale = 1.4
iterations = 20

max_loss = 10.

base_image_path = '...'

img = preprocess_image(base_image_path)
```

Fill this with the path to the image you want to use.

Loads the base image into a Numpy array (function is defined in listing 8.13)

```
original_shape = img.shape[1:3]
successive_shapes = [original_shape]
for i in range(1, num_octave):
    shape = tuple([int(dim / (octave_scale ** i))
        for dim in original_shape])
    successive_shapes.append(shape)

successive_shapes = successive_shapes[::-1]

original_img = np.copy(img)
shrunk_original_img = resize_img(img, successive_shapes[0])

for shape in successive_shapes:
    print('Processing image shape', shape)
    img = resize_img(img, shape)
    img = gradient_ascent(img,
                          iterations=iterations,
                          step=step,
                          max_loss=max_loss)
    upscaled_shrunk_original_img = resize_img(shrunk_original_img, shape)
    same_size_original = resize_img(original_img, shape)
    lost_detail = same_size_original - upscaled_shrunk_original_img

    img += lost_detail
    shrunk_original_img = resize_img(original_img, shape)
    save_img(img, fname='dream_at_scale_' + str(shape) + '.png')

save_img(img, fname='final_dream.png')
```

Prepares a list of shape tuples defining the different scales at which to run gradient ascent

Reverses the list of shapes so they're in increasing order

Scales up the dream image

Resizes the Numpy array of the image to the smallest scale

Runs gradient ascent, altering the dream

Scales up the smaller version of the original image: it will be pixellated.

Reinjects lost detail into the dream

Computes the high-quality version of the original image at this size

The difference between the two is the detail that was lost when scaling up.

Note that this code uses the following straightforward auxiliary Numpy functions, which all do as their names suggest. They require that you have SciPy installed.

Listing 8.13 Auxiliary functions

```
import scipy
from keras.preprocessing import image

def resize_img(img, size):
    img = np.copy(img)
    factors = (1,
               float(size[0]) / img.shape[1],
               float(size[1]) / img.shape[2],
               1)
    return scipy.ndimage.zoom(img, factors, order=1)

def save_img(img, fname):
    pil_img = deprocess_image(np.copy(img))
    scipy.misc.imsave(fname, pil_img)

def preprocess_image(image_path):
    img = image.load_img(image_path)
    img = image.img_to_array(img)
```

Util function to open, resize, and format pictures into tensors that Inception V3 can process

```
    img = np.expand_dims(img, axis=0)
    img = inception_v3.preprocess_input(img)
    return img

def deprocess_image(x):
    if K.image_data_format() == 'channels_first':
        x = x.reshape((3, x.shape[2], x.shape[3]))
        x = x.transpose((1, 2, 0))
    else:
        x = x.reshape((x.shape[1], x.shape[2], 3))
    x /= 2.
    x += 0.5
    x *= 255.
    x = np.clip(x, 0, 255).astype('uint8')
    return x
```

Util function to convert a tensor into a valid image

Undoes preprocessing that was performed by inception_v3.preprocess_input

NOTE Because the original Inception V3 network was trained to recognize concepts in images of size 299 × 299, and given that the process involves scaling the images down by a reasonable factor, the DeepDream implementation produces much better results on images that are somewhere between 300 × 300 and 400 × 400. Regardless, you can run the same code on images of any size and any ratio.

Starting from a photograph taken in the small hills between San Francisco Bay and the Google campus, we obtained the DeepDream shown in figure 8.5.

Figure 8.5 Running the DeepDream code on an example image

We strongly suggest that you explore what you can do by adjusting which layers you use in your loss. Layers that are lower in the network contain more-local, less-abstract representations and lead to dream patterns that look more geometric. Layers that are higher up lead to more-recognizable visual patterns based on the most common objects found in ImageNet, such as dog eyes, bird feathers, and so on. You can use random generation of the parameters in the `layer_contributions` dictionary to quickly explore many different layer combinations. Figure 8.6 shows a range of results obtained using different layer configurations, from an image of a delicious home-made pastry.

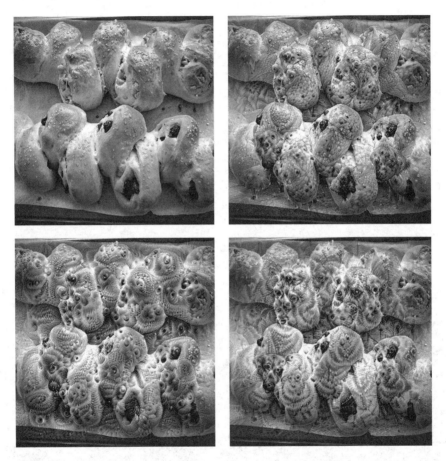

Figure 8.6   Trying a range of DeepDream configurations on an example image

8.2.2   *Wrapping up*

- DeepDream consists of running a convnet in reverse to generate inputs based on the representations learned by the network.
- The results produced are fun and somewhat similar to the visual artifacts induced in humans by the disruption of the visual cortex via psychedelics.
- Note that the process isn't specific to image models or even to convnets. It can be done for speech, music, and more.

8.3 *Neural style transfer*

In addition to DeepDream, another major development in deep-learning-driven image modification is *neural style transfer*, introduced by Leon Gatys et al. in the summer of 2015.[5] The neural style transfer algorithm has undergone many refinements and spawned many variations since its original introduction, and it has made its way into many smartphone photo apps. For simplicity, this section focuses on the formulation described in the original paper.

Neural style transfer consists of applying the style of a reference image to a target image while conserving the content of the target image. Figure 8.7 shows an example.

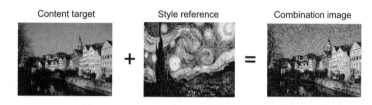

Figure 8.7 A style transfer example

In this context, *style* essentially means textures, colors, and visual patterns in the image, at various spatial scales; and the *content* is the higher-level macrostructure of the image. For instance, blue-and-yellow circular brushstrokes are considered to be the style in figure 8.7 (using *Starry Night* by Vincent Van Gogh), and the buildings in the Tübingen photograph are considered to be the content.

The idea of style transfer, which is tightly related to that of texture generation, has had a long history in the image-processing community prior to the development of neural style transfer in 2015. But as it turns out, the deep-learning-based implementations of style transfer offer results unparalleled by what had been previously achieved with classical computer-vision techniques, and they triggered an amazing renaissance in creative applications of computer vision.

The key notion behind implementing style transfer is the same idea that's central to all deep-learning algorithms: you define a loss function to specify what you want to achieve, and you minimize this loss. You know what you want to achieve: conserving the content of the original image while adopting the style of the reference image. If we were able to mathematically define *content* and *style*, then an appropriate loss function to minimize would be the following:

```
loss = distance(style(reference_image) - style(generated_image)) +
       distance(content(original_image) - content(generated_image))
```

[5] Leon A. Gatys, Alexander S. Ecker, and Matthias Bethge, "A Neural Algorithm of Artistic Style," arXiv (2015), https://arxiv.org/abs/1508.06576.

Here, `distance` is a norm function such as the L2 norm, `content` is a function that takes an image and computes a representation of its content, and `style` is a function that takes an image and computes a representation of its style. Minimizing this loss causes `style(generated_image)` to be close to `style(reference_image)`, and `content(generated_image)` is close to `content(generated_image)`, thus achieving style transfer as we defined it.

A fundamental observation made by Gatys et al. was that deep convolutional neural networks offer a way to mathematically define the `style` and `content` functions. Let's see how.

8.3.1   *The content loss*

As you already know, activations from earlier layers in a network contain *local* information about the image, whereas activations from higher layers contain increasingly *global, abstract* information. Formulated in a different way, the activations of the different layers of a convnet provide a decomposition of the contents of an image over different spatial scales. Therefore, you'd expect the content of an image, which is more global and abstract, to be captured by the representations of the upper layers in a convnet.

A good candidate for content loss is thus the L2 norm between the activations of an upper layer in a pretrained convnet, computed over the target image, and the activations of the same layer computed over the generated image. This guarantees that, as seen from the upper layer, the generated image will look similar to the original target image. Assuming that what the upper layers of a convnet see is really the content of their input images, then this works as a way to preserve image content.

8.3.2   *The style loss*

The content loss only uses a single upper layer, but the style loss as defined by Gatys et al. uses multiple layers of a convnet: you try to capture the appearance of the style-reference image at all spatial scales extracted by the convnet, not just a single scale. For the style loss, Gatys et al. use the *Gram matrix* of a layer's activations: the inner product of the feature maps of a given layer. This inner product can be understood as representing a map of the correlations between the layer's features. These feature correlations capture the statistics of the patterns of a particular spatial scale, which empirically correspond to the appearance of the textures found at this scale.

Hence, the style loss aims to preserve similar internal correlations within the activations of different layers, across the style-reference image and the generated image. In turn, this guarantees that the textures found at different spatial scales look similar across the style-reference image and the generated image.

In short, you can use a pretrained convnet to define a loss that will do the following:

- Preserve content by maintaining similar high-level layer activations between the target content image and the generated image. The convnet should "see" both the target image and the generated image as containing the same things.

- Preserve style by maintaining similar *correlations* within activations for both low-level layers and high-level layers. Feature correlations capture *textures*: the generated image and the style-reference image should share the same textures at different spatial scales.

Now, let's look at a Keras implementation of the original 2015 neural style transfer algorithm. As you'll see, it shares many similarities with the DeepDream implementation developed in the previous section.

8.3.3 *Neural style transfer in Keras*

Neural style transfer can be implemented using any pretrained convnet. Here, you'll use the VGG19 network used by Gatys et al. VGG19 is a simple variant of the VGG16 network introduced in chapter 5, with three more convolutional layers.

This is the general process:

1 Set up a network that computes VGG19 layer activations for the style-reference image, the target image, and the generated image at the same time.
2 Use the layer activations computed over these three images to define the loss function described earlier, which you'll minimize in order to achieve style transfer.
3 Set up a gradient-descent process to minimize this loss function.

Let's start by defining the paths to the style-reference image and the target image. To make sure that the processed images are a similar size (widely different sizes make style transfer more difficult), you'll later resize them all to a shared height of 400 px.

Listing 8.14 Defining initial variables

```
from keras.preprocessing.image import load_img, img_to_array

target_image_path = 'img/portrait.jpg'
style_reference_image_path = 'img/transfer_style_reference.jpg'

width, height = load_img(target_image_path).size
img_height = 400
img_width = int(width * img_height / height)
```

Path to the image you want to transform

Path to the style image

Dimensions of the generated picture

You need some auxiliary functions for loading, preprocessing, and postprocessing the images that go in and out of the VGG19 convnet.

Listing 8.15 Auxiliary functions

```
import numpy as np
from keras.applications import vgg19

def preprocess_image(image_path):
    img = load_img(image_path, target_size=(img_height, img_width))
    img = img_to_array(img)
    img = np.expand_dims(img, axis=0)
    img = vgg19.preprocess_input(img)
    return img
```

```
def deprocess_image(x):
    x[:, :, 0] += 103.939
    x[:, :, 1] += 116.779
    x[:, :, 2] += 123.68
    x = x[:, :, ::-1]
    x = np.clip(x, 0, 255).astype('uint8')
    return x
```

Zero-centering by removing the mean pixel value from ImageNet. This reverses a transformation done by vgg19.preprocess_input.

Converts images from 'BGR' to 'RGB'. This is also part of the reversal of vgg19.preprocess_input.

Let's set up the VGG19 network. It takes as input a batch of three images: the style-reference image, the target image, and a placeholder that will contain the generated image. A placeholder is a symbolic tensor, the values of which are provided externally via Numpy arrays. The style-reference and target image are static and thus defined using K.constant, whereas the values contained in the placeholder of the generated image will change over time.

Listing 8.16 Loading the pretrained VGG19 network and applying it to the three images

Placeholder that will contain the generated image

```
from keras import backend as K

target_image = K.constant(preprocess_image(target_image_path))
style_reference_image = K.constant(preprocess_image(style_reference_image_path))
combination_image = K.placeholder((1, img_height, img_width, 3))

input_tensor = K.concatenate([target_image,
                              style_reference_image,
                              combination_image], axis=0)

model = vgg19.VGG19(input_tensor=input_tensor,
                    weights='imagenet',
                    include_top=False)
print('Model loaded.')
```

Combines the three images in a single batch

Builds the VGG19 network with the batch of three images as input. The model will be loaded with pretrained ImageNet weights.

Let's define the content loss, which will make sure the top layer of the VGG19 convnet has a similar view of the target image and the generated image.

Listing 8.17 Content loss

```
def content_loss(base, combination):
    return K.sum(K.square(combination - base))
```

Next is the style loss. It uses an auxiliary function to compute the Gram matrix of an input matrix: a map of the correlations found in the original feature matrix.

Listing 8.18 Style loss

```
def gram_matrix(x):
    features = K.batch_flatten(K.permute_dimensions(x, (2, 0, 1)))
    gram = K.dot(features, K.transpose(features))
    return gram
```

```
def style_loss(style, combination):
    S = gram_matrix(style)
    C = gram_matrix(combination)
    channels = 3
    size = img_height * img_width
    return K.sum(K.square(S - C)) / (4. * (channels ** 2) * (size ** 2))
```

To these two loss components, you add a third: the *total variation loss*, which operates on the pixels of the generated combination image. It encourages spatial continuity in the generated image, thus avoiding overly pixelated results. You can interpret it as a regularization loss.

Listing 8.19 Total variation loss

```
def total_variation_loss(x):
    a = K.square(
        x[:, :img_height - 1, :img_width - 1, :] -
        x[:, 1:, :img_width - 1, :])
    b = K.square(
        x[:, :img_height - 1, :img_width - 1, :] -
        x[:, :img_height - 1, 1:, :])
    return K.sum(K.pow(a + b, 1.25))
```

The loss that you minimize is a weighted average of these three losses. To compute the content loss, you use only one upper layer—the `block5_conv2` layer—whereas for the style loss, you use a list of layers than spans both low-level and high-level layers. You add the total variation loss at the end.

Depending on the style-reference image and content image you're using, you'll likely want to tune the `content_weight` coefficient (the contribution of the content loss to the total loss). A higher `content_weight` means the target content will be more recognizable in the generated image.

Listing 8.20 Defining the final loss that you'll minimize

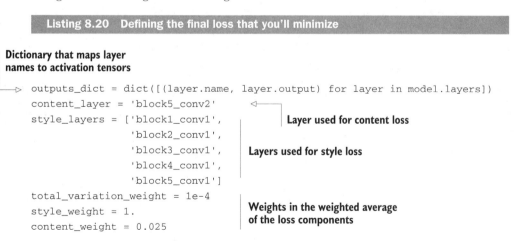

Dictionary that maps layer names to activation tensors

```
outputs_dict = dict([(layer.name, layer.output) for layer in model.layers])
content_layer = 'block5_conv2'
style_layers = ['block1_conv1',
                'block2_conv1',
                'block3_conv1',
                'block4_conv1',
                'block5_conv1']
total_variation_weight = 1e-4
style_weight = 1.
content_weight = 0.025
```

Layer used for content loss

Layers used for style loss

Weights in the weighted average of the loss components

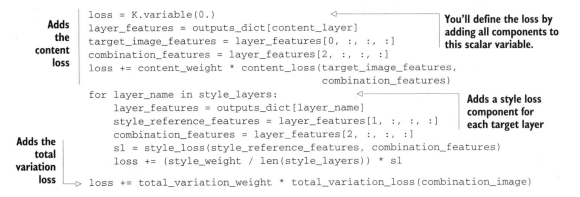

Adds the content loss

```
loss = K.variable(0.)
layer_features = outputs_dict[content_layer]
target_image_features = layer_features[0, :, :, :]
combination_features = layer_features[2, :, :, :]
loss += content_weight * content_loss(target_image_features,
                                      combination_features)
```

You'll define the loss by adding all components to this scalar variable.

```
for layer_name in style_layers:
    layer_features = outputs_dict[layer_name]
    style_reference_features = layer_features[1, :, :, :]
    combination_features = layer_features[2, :, :, :]
    sl = style_loss(style_reference_features, combination_features)
    loss += (style_weight / len(style_layers)) * sl
```

Adds a style loss component for each target layer

Adds the total variation loss

```
loss += total_variation_weight * total_variation_loss(combination_image)
```

Finally, you'll set up the gradient-descent process. In the original Gatys et al. paper, optimization is performed using the L-BFGS algorithm, so that's what you'll use here. This is a key difference from the DeepDream example in section 8.2. The L-BFGS algorithm comes packaged with SciPy, but there are two slight limitations with the SciPy implementation:

- It requires that you pass the value of the loss function and the value of the gradients as two separate functions.
- It can only be applied to flat vectors, whereas you have a 3D image array.

It would be inefficient to compute the value of the loss function and the value of the gradients independently, because doing so would lead to a lot of redundant computation between the two; the process would be almost twice as slow as computing them jointly. To bypass this, you'll set up a Python class named `Evaluator` that computes both the loss value and the gradients value at once, returns the loss value when called the first time, and caches the gradients for the next call.

> **Listing 8.21 Setting up the gradient-descent process**

Gets the gradients of the generated image with regard to the loss

```
grads = K.gradients(loss, combination_image)[0]

fetch_loss_and_grads = K.function([combination_image], [loss, grads])

class Evaluator(object):

    def __init__(self):
        self.loss_value = None
        self.grads_values = None

    def loss(self, x):
        assert self.loss_value is None
        x = x.reshape((1, img_height, img_width, 3))
        outs = fetch_loss_and_grads([x])
```

Function to fetch the values of the current loss and the current gradients

This class wraps fetch_loss_and_grads in a way that lets you retrieve the losses and gradients via two separate method calls, which is required by the SciPy optimizer you'll use.

```
    loss_value = outs[0]
    grad_values = outs[1].flatten().astype('float64')
    self.loss_value = loss_value
    self.grad_values = grad_values
    return self.loss_value

def grads(self, x):
    assert self.loss_value is not None
    grad_values = np.copy(self.grad_values)
    self.loss_value = None
    self.grad_values = None
    return grad_values

evaluator = Evaluator()
```

Finally, you can run the gradient-ascent process using SciPy's L-BFGS algorithm, saving the current generated image at each iteration of the algorithm (here, a single iteration represents 20 steps of gradient ascent).

Listing 8.22 Style-transfer loop

```
from scipy.optimize import fmin_l_bfgs_b
from scipy.misc import imsave
import time

result_prefix = 'my_result'
iterations = 20

x = preprocess_image(target_image_path)
x = x.flatten()
for i in range(iterations):
    print('Start of iteration', i)
    start_time = time.time()
    x, min_val, info = fmin_l_bfgs_b(evaluator.loss,
                                     x,
                                     fprime=evaluator.grads,
                                     maxfun=20)
    print('Current loss value:', min_val)
    img = x.copy().reshape((img_height, img_width, 3))
    img = deprocess_image(img)
    fname = result_prefix + '_at_iteration_%d.png' % i
    imsave(fname, img)
    print('Image saved as', fname)
    end_time = time.time()
    print('Iteration %d completed in %ds' % (i, end_time - start_time))
```

This is the initial state: the target image.

You flatten the image because scipy.optimize.fmin_l_bfgs_b can only process flat vectors.

Runs L-BFGS optimization over the pixels of the generated image to minimize the neural style loss. Note that you have to pass the function that computes the loss and the function that computes the gradients as two separate arguments.

Saves the current generated image.

Figure 8.8 shows what you get. Keep in mind that what this technique achieves is merely a form of image retexturing, or texture transfer. It works best with style-reference images that are strongly textured and highly self-similar, and with content targets that don't require high levels of detail in order to be recognizable. It typically can't achieve fairly abstract feats such as transferring the style of one portrait to another. The algorithm is closer to classical signal processing than to AI, so don't expect it to work like magic!

Figure 8.8   Some example results

Additionally, note that running this style-transfer algorithm is slow. But the transformation operated by the setup is simple enough that it can be learned by a small, fast feedforward convnet as well—as long as you have appropriate training data available. Fast style transfer can thus be achieved by first spending a lot of compute cycles to generate input-output training examples for a fixed style-reference image, using the method outlined here, and then training a simple convnet to learn this style-specific transformation. Once that's done, stylizing a given image is instantaneous: it's just a forward pass of this small convnet.

8.3.4 Wrapping up

- Style transfer consists of creating a new image that preserves the contents of a target image while also capturing the style of a reference image.
- Content can be captured by the high-level activations of a convnet.
- Style can be captured by the internal correlations of the activations of different layers of a convnet.
- Hence, deep learning allows style transfer to be formulated as an optimization process using a loss defined with a pretrained convnet.
- Starting from this basic idea, many variants and refinements are possible.

8.4   *Generating images with variational autoencoders*

Sampling from a latent space of images to create entirely new images or edit existing ones is currently the most popular and successful application of creative AI. In this section and the next, we'll review some high-level concepts pertaining to image generation, alongside implementations details relative to the two main techniques in this domain: *variational autoencoders* (VAEs) and *generative adversarial networks* (GANs). The techniques we present here aren't specific to images—you could develop latent spaces of sound, music, or even text, using GANs and VAEs—but in practice, the most interesting results have been obtained with pictures, and that's what we focus on here.

8.4.1   *Sampling from latent spaces of images*

The key idea of image generation is to develop a low-dimensional *latent space* of representations (which naturally is a vector space) where any point can be mapped to a realistic-looking image. The module capable of realizing this mapping, taking as input a latent point and outputting an image (a grid of pixels), is called a *generator* (in the case of GANs) or a *decoder* (in the case of VAEs). Once such a latent space has been developed, you can sample points from it, either deliberately or at random, and, by mapping them to image space, generate images that have never been seen before (see figure 8.9).

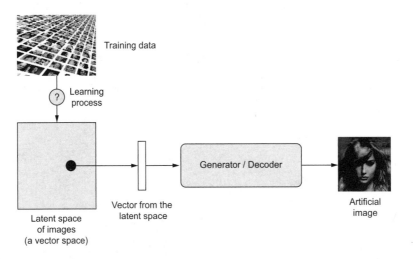

Figure 8.9   Learning a latent vector space of images, and using it to sample new images

GANs and VAEs are two different strategies for learning such latent spaces of image representations, each with its own characteristics. VAEs are great for learning latent spaces that are well structured, where specific directions encode a meaningful axis of variation in the data. GANs generate images that can potentially be highly realistic, but the latent space they come from may not have as much structure and continuity.

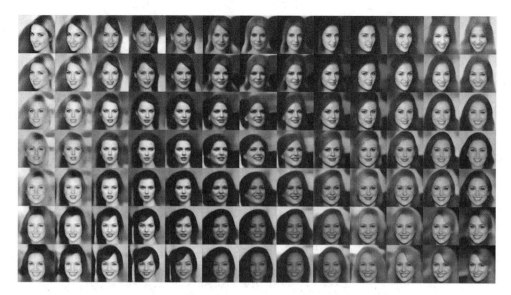

Figure 8.10   A continuous space of faces generated by Tom White using VAEs

8.4.2   *Concept vectors for image editing*

We already hinted at the idea of a *concept vector* when we covered word embeddings in chapter 6. The idea is still the same: given a latent space of representations, or an embedding space, certain directions in the space may encode interesting axes of variation in the original data. In a latent space of images of faces, for instance, there may be a *smile vectors*, such that if latent point z is the embedded representation of a certain face, then latent point z + s is the embedded representation of the same face, smiling. Once you've identified such a vector, it then becomes possible to edit images by projecting them into the latent space, moving their representation in a meaningful way, and then decoding them back to image space. There are concept vectors for essentially any independent dimension of variation in image space—in the case of faces, you may discover vectors for adding sunglasses to a face, removing glasses, turning a male face into as female face, and so on. Figure 8.11 is an example of a smile vector, a concept vector discovered by Tom White from the Victoria University School of Design in New Zealand, using VAEs trained on a dataset of faces of celebrities (the CelebA dataset).

Figure 8.11   The smile vector

8.4.3   *Variational autoencoders*

Variational autoencoders, simultaneously discovered by Kingma and Welling in December 2013[6] and Rezende, Mohamed, and Wierstra in January 2014,[7] are a kind of generative model that's especially appropriate for the task of image editing via concept vectors. They're a modern take on autoencoders—a type of network that aims to encode an input to a low-dimensional latent space and then decode it back—that mixes ideas from deep learning with Bayesian inference.

A classical image autoencoder takes an image, maps it to a latent vector space via an encoder module, and then decodes it back to an output with the same dimensions as the original image, via a decoder module (see figure 8.12). It's then trained by using as target data the *same images* as the input images, meaning the autoencoder learns to reconstruct the original inputs. By imposing various constraints on the code (the output of the encoder), you can get the autoencoder to learn more-or-less interesting latent representations of the data. Most commonly, you'll constrain the code to be low-dimensional and sparse (mostly zeros), in which case the encoder acts as a way to compress the input data into fewer bits of information.

---

[6] Diederik P. Kingma and Max Welling, "Auto-Encoding Variational Bayes, arXiv (2013), https://arxiv.org/abs/1312.6114.

[7] Danilo Jimenez Rezende, Shakir Mohamed, and Daan Wierstra, "Stochastic Backpropagation and Approximate Inference in Deep Generative Models," arXiv (2014), https://arxiv.org/abs/1401.4082.

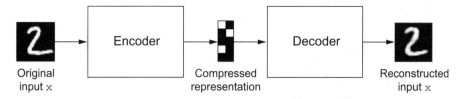

Figure 8.12   An autoencoder: mapping an input x to a compressed representation and then decoding it back as x'

In practice, such classical autoencoders don't lead to particularly useful or nicely structured latent spaces. They're not much good at compression, either. For these reasons, they have largely fallen out of fashion. VAEs, however, augment autoencoders with a little bit of statistical magic that forces them to learn continuous, highly structured latent spaces. They have turned out to be a powerful tool for image generation.

A VAE, instead of compressing its input image into a fixed code in the latent space, turns the image into the parameters of a statistical distribution: a mean and a variance. Essentially, this means you're assuming the input image has been generated by a statistical process, and that the randomness of this process should be taken into accounting during encoding and decoding. The VAE then uses the mean and variance parameters to randomly sample one element of the distribution, and decodes that element back to the original input (see figure 8.13). The stochasticity of this process improves robustness and forces the latent space to encode meaningful representations everywhere: every point sampled in the latent space is decoded to a valid output.

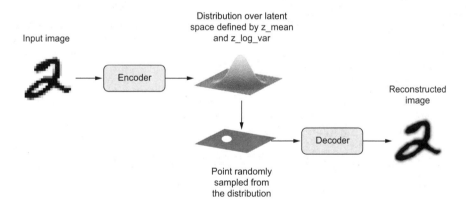

Figure 8.13   A VAE maps an image to two vectors, z_mean and z_log_sigma, which define a probability distribution over the latent space, used to sample a latent point to decode.

In technical terms, here's how a VAE works:

1   An encoder module turns the input samples input_img into two parameters in a latent space of representations, z_mean and z_log_variance.

2   You randomly sample a point z from the latent normal distribution that's assumed to generate the input image, via z = z_mean + exp(z_log_variance) * epsilon, where epsilon is a random tensor of small values.

3   A decoder module maps this point in the latent space back to the original input image.

Because epsilon is random, the process ensures that every point that's close to the latent location where you encoded input_img (z-mean) can be decoded to something similar to input_img, thus forcing the latent space to be continuously meaningful. Any two close points in the latent space will decode to highly similar images. Continuity, combined with the low dimensionality of the latent space, forces every direction in the latent space to encode a meaningful axis of variation of the data, making the latent space very structured and thus highly suitable to manipulation via concept vectors.

The parameters of a VAE are trained via two loss functions: a *reconstruction loss* that forces the decoded samples to match the initial inputs, and a *regularization loss* that helps learn well-formed latent spaces and reduce overfitting to the training data. Let's quickly go over a Keras implementation of a VAE. Schematically, it looks like this:

```
z_mean, z_log_variance = encoder(input_img)        ← Encodes the input into a
                                                      mean and variance parameter
z = z_mean + exp(z_log_variance) * epsilon         ← Draws a latent point using
                                                      a small random epsilon
reconstructed_img = decoder(z)     ← Decodes z back to an image

model = Model(input_img, reconstructed_img)        ← Instantiates the autoencoder
                                                      model, which maps an input image
                                                      to its reconstruction
```

You can then train the model using the reconstruction loss and the regularization loss.

The following listing shows the encoder network you'll use, mapping images to the parameters of a probability distribution over the latent space. It's a simple convnet that maps the input image x to two vectors, z_mean and z_log_var.

Listing 8.23   VAE encoder network

```
import keras
from keras import layers
from keras import backend as K
from keras.models import Model
import numpy as np

img_shape = (28, 28, 1)
batch_size = 16
latent_dim = 2        ← Dimensionality of the
                         latent space: a 2D plane

input_img = keras.Input(shape=img_shape)
```

```
x = layers.Conv2D(32, 3,
                   padding='same', activation='relu')(input_img)
x = layers.Conv2D(64, 3,
                   padding='same', activation='relu',
                   strides=(2, 2))(x)
x = layers.Conv2D(64, 3,
                   padding='same', activation='relu')(x)
x = layers.Conv2D(64, 3,
                   padding='same', activation='relu')(x)
shape_before_flattening = K.int_shape(x)

x = layers.Flatten()(x)
x = layers.Dense(32, activation='relu')(x)

z_mean = layers.Dense(latent_dim)(x)
z_log_var = layers.Dense(latent_dim)(x)
```

The input image ends up being encoded into these two parameters.

Next is the code for using z_mean and z_log_var, the parameters of the statistical distribution assumed to have produced input_img, to generate a latent space point z. Here, you wrap some arbitrary code (built on top of Keras backend primitives) into a Lambda layer. In Keras, everything needs to be a layer, so code that isn't part of a built-in layer should be wrapped in a Lambda (or in a custom layer).

Listing 8.24 Latent-space-sampling function

```
def sampling(args):
    z_mean, z_log_var = args
    epsilon = K.random_normal(shape=(K.shape(z_mean)[0], latent_dim),
                              mean=0., stddev=1.)
    return z_mean + K.exp(z_log_var) * epsilon

z = layers.Lambda(sampling)([z_mean, z_log_var])
```

The following listing shows the decoder implementation. You reshape the vector z to the dimensions of an image and then use a few convolution layers to obtain a final image output that has the same dimensions as the original input_img.

Listing 8.25 VAE decoder network, mapping latent space points to images

```
decoder_input = layers.Input(K.int_shape(z)[1:])        ← Input where you'll feed z

x = layers.Dense(np.prod(shape_before_flattening[1:]),
                 activation='relu')(decoder_input)       Upsamples the input

x = layers.Reshape(shape_before_flattening[1:])(x)

x = layers.Conv2DTranspose(32, 3,
                           padding='same',
                           activation='relu',
                           strides=(2, 2))(x)
x = layers.Conv2D(1, 3,
                  padding='same',
                  activation='sigmoid')(x)
```

Uses a Conv2DTranspose layer and Conv2D layer to decode z into a feature map the same size as the original image input

Reshapes z into a feature map of the same shape as the feature map just before the last Flatten layer in the encoder model

```
decoder = Model(decoder_input, x)
```
> Instantiates the decoder model, which turns "decoder_input" into the decoded image

```
z_decoded = decoder(z)
```
> Applies it to z to recover the decoded z

The dual loss of a VAE doesn't fit the traditional expectation of a sample-wise function of the form loss(input, target). Thus, you'll set up the loss by writing a custom layer that internally uses the built-in add_loss layer method to create an arbitrary loss.

Listing 8.26   Custom layer used to compute the VAE loss

```
class CustomVariationalLayer(keras.layers.Layer):

    def vae_loss(self, x, z_decoded):
        x = K.flatten(x)
        z_decoded = K.flatten(z_decoded)
        xent_loss = keras.metrics.binary_crossentropy(x, z_decoded)
        kl_loss = -5e-4 * K.mean(
            1 + z_log_var - K.square(z_mean) - K.exp(z_log_var), axis=-1)
        return K.mean(xent_loss + kl_loss)

    def call(self, inputs):
        x = inputs[0]
        z_decoded = inputs[1]
        loss = self.vae_loss(x, z_decoded)
        self.add_loss(loss, inputs=inputs)
        return x

y = CustomVariationalLayer()([input_img, z_decoded])
```
> You implement custom layers by writing a call method.

> You don't use this output, but the layer must return something.

> Calls the custom layer on the input and the decoded output to obtain the final model output

Finally, you're ready to instantiate and train the model. Because the loss is taken care of in the custom layer, you don't specify an external loss at compile time (loss=None), which in turn means you won't pass target data during training (as you can see, you only pass x_train to the model in fit).

Listing 8.27   Training the VAE

```
from keras.datasets import mnist

vae = Model(input_img, y)
vae.compile(optimizer='rmsprop', loss=None)
vae.summary()

(x_train, _), (x_test, y_test) = mnist.load_data()

x_train = x_train.astype('float32') / 255.
x_train = x_train.reshape(x_train.shape + (1,))
x_test = x_test.astype('float32') / 255.
x_test = x_test.reshape(x_test.shape + (1,))

vae.fit(x=x_train, y=None,
        shuffle=True,
        epochs=10,
        batch_size=batch_size,
        validation_data=(x_test, None))
```

Once such a model is trained—on MNIST, in this case—you can use the `decoder` network to turn arbitrary latent space vectors into images.

> **Listing 8.28　Sampling a grid of points from the 2D latent space and decoding them to images**

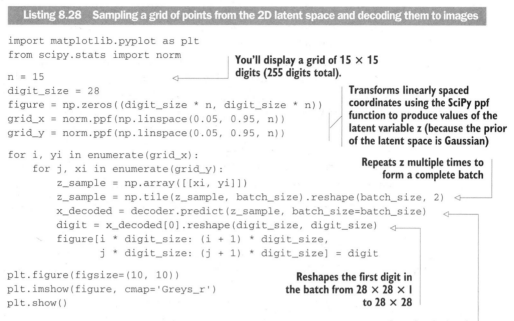

```
import matplotlib.pyplot as plt
from scipy.stats import norm

n = 15
digit_size = 28
figure = np.zeros((digit_size * n, digit_size * n))
grid_x = norm.ppf(np.linspace(0.05, 0.95, n))
grid_y = norm.ppf(np.linspace(0.05, 0.95, n))

for i, yi in enumerate(grid_x):
    for j, xi in enumerate(grid_y):
        z_sample = np.array([[xi, yi]])
        z_sample = np.tile(z_sample, batch_size).reshape(batch_size, 2)
        x_decoded = decoder.predict(z_sample, batch_size=batch_size)
        digit = x_decoded[0].reshape(digit_size, digit_size)
        figure[i * digit_size: (i + 1) * digit_size,
               j * digit_size: (j + 1) * digit_size] = digit

plt.figure(figsize=(10, 10))
plt.imshow(figure, cmap='Greys_r')
plt.show()
```

You'll display a grid of 15 × 15 digits (255 digits total).

Transforms linearly spaced coordinates using the SciPy ppf function to produce values of the latent variable z (because the prior of the latent space is Gaussian)

Repeats z multiple times to form a complete batch

Reshapes the first digit in the batch from 28 × 28 × 1 to 28 × 28

Decodes the batch into digit images

The grid of sampled digits (see figure 8.14) shows a completely continuous distribution of the different digit classes, with one digit morphing into another as you follow a path through latent space. Specific directions in this space have a meaning: for example, there's a direction for "four-ness," "one-ness," and so on.

In the next section, we'll cover in detail the other major tool for generating artificial images: generative adversarial networks (GANs).

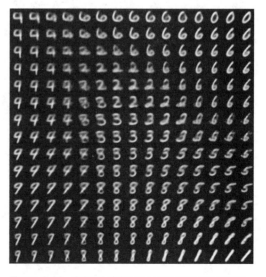

Figure 8.14　Grid of digits decoded from the latent space

8.4.4 *Wrapping up*

- Image generation with deep learning is done by learning latent spaces that capture statistical information about a dataset of images. By sampling and decoding points from the latent space, you can generate never-before-seen images. There are two major tools to do this: VAEs and GANs.
- VAEs result in highly structured, continuous latent representations. For this reason, they work well for doing all sorts of image editing in latent space: face swapping, turning a frowning face into a smiling face, and so on. They also work nicely for doing latent-space-based animations, such as animating a walk along a cross section of the latent space, showing a starting image slowly morphing into different images in a continuous way.
- GANs enable the generation of realistic single-frame images but may not induce latent spaces with solid structure and high continuity.

Most successful practical applications I have seen with images rely on VAEs, but GANs are extremely popular in the world of academic research—at least, circa 2016–2017. You'll find out how they work and how to implement one in the next section.

TIP   To play further with image generation, I suggest working with the Large-scale Celeb Faces Attributes (CelebA) dataset. It's a free-to-download image dataset containing more than 200,000 celebrity portraits. It's great for experimenting with concept vectors in particular—it definitely beats MNIST.

8.5 Introduction to generative adversarial networks

Generative adversarial networks (GANs), introduced in 2014 by Goodfellow et al.,[8] are an alternative to VAEs for learning latent spaces of images. They enable the generation of fairly realistic synthetic images by forcing the generated images to be statistically almost indistinguishable from real ones.

An intuitive way to understand GANs is to imagine a forger trying to create a fake Picasso painting. At first, the forger is pretty bad at the task. He mixes some of his fakes with authentic Picassos and shows them all to an art dealer. The art dealer makes an authenticity assessment for each painting and gives the forger feedback about what makes a Picasso look like a Picasso. The forger goes back to his studio to prepare some new fakes. As times goes on, the forger becomes increasingly competent at imitating the style of Picasso, and the art dealer becomes increasingly expert at spotting fakes. In the end, they have on their hands some excellent fake Picassos.

That's what a GAN is: a forger network and an expert network, each being trained to best the other. As such, a GAN is made of two parts:

- *Generator network*—Takes as input a random vector (a random point in the latent space), and decodes it into a synthetic image
- *Discriminator network (or adversary)*—Takes as input an image (real or synthetic), and predicts whether the image came from the training set or was created by the generator network.

The generator network is trained to be able to fool the discriminator network, and thus it evolves toward generating increasingly realistic images as training goes on: artificial images that look indistinguishable from real ones, to the extent that it's impossible for the discriminator network to tell the two apart (see figure 8.15). Meanwhile, the discriminator is constantly adapting to the gradually improving capabilities of the generator, setting a high bar of realism for the generated images. Once training is over, the generator is capable of turning any point in its input space into a believable image. Unlike VAEs, this latent space has fewer explicit guarantees of meaningful structure; in particular, it isn't continuous.

---

[8] Ian Goodfellow et al., "Generative Adversarial Networks," arXiv (2014), https://arxiv.org/abs/1406.2661.

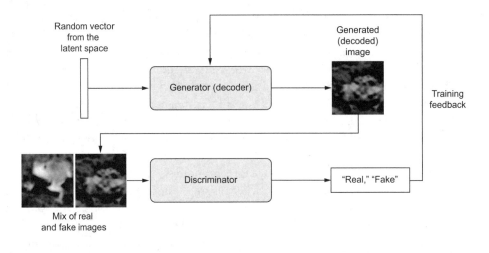

Figure 8.15   A generator transforms random latent vectors into images, and a discriminator seeks to tell real images from generated ones. The generator is trained to fool the discriminator.

Remarkably, a GAN is a system where the optimization minimum isn't fixed, unlike in any other training setup you've encountered in this book. Normally, gradient descent consists of rolling down hills in a static loss landscape. But with a GAN, every step taken down the hill changes the entire landscape a little. It's a dynamic system where the optimization process is seeking not a minimum, but an equilibrium between two forces. For this reason, GANs are notoriously difficult to train—getting a GAN to work requires lots of careful tuning of the model architecture and training parameters.

Figure 8.16   Latent space dwellers. Images generated by Mike Tyka using a multistaged GAN trained on a dataset of faces (www.miketyka.com).

8.5.1 A schematic GAN implementation

In this section, we'll explain how to implement a GAN in Keras, in its barest form—because GANs are advanced, diving deeply into the technical details would be out of scope for this book. The specific implementation is a *deep convolutional GAN* (DCGAN): a GAN where the generator and discriminator are deep convnets. In particular, it uses a `Conv2DTranspose` layer for image upsampling in the generator.

You'll train the GAN on images from CIFAR10, a dataset of 50,000 32 × 32 RGB images belonging to 10 classes (5,000 images per class). To make things easier, you'll only use images belonging to the class "frog."

Schematically, the GAN looks like this:

1. A `generator` network maps vectors of shape (`latent_dim,`) to images of shape (`32, 32, 3`).
2. A `discriminator` network maps images of shape (`32, 32, 3`) to a binary score estimating the probability that the image is real.
3. A `gan` network chains the generator and the discriminator together: `gan(x) = discriminator(generator(x))`. Thus this `gan` network maps latent space vectors to the discriminator's assessment of the realism of these latent vectors as decoded by the generator.
4. You train the discriminator using examples of real and fake images along with "real"/"fake" labels, just as you train any regular image-classification model.
5. To train the generator, you use the gradients of the generator's weights with regard to the loss of the `gan` model. This means, at every step, you move the weights of the generator in a direction that makes the discriminator more likely to classify as "real" the images decoded by the generator. In other words, you train the generator to fool the discriminator.

8.5.2 A bag of tricks

The process of training GANs and tuning GAN implementations is notoriously difficult. There are a number of known tricks you should keep in mind. Like most things in deep learning, it's more alchemy than science: these tricks are heuristics, not theory-backed guidelines. They're supported by a level of intuitive understanding of the phenomenon at hand, and they're known to work well empirically, although not necessarily in every context.

Here are a few of the tricks used in the implementation of the GAN generator and discriminator in this section. It isn't an exhaustive list of GAN-related tips; you'll find many more across the GAN literature:

- We use `tanh` as the last activation in the generator, instead of `sigmoid`, which is more commonly found in other types of models.
- We sample points from the latent space using a *normal distribution* (Gaussian distribution), not a uniform distribution.

- Stochasticity is good to induce robustness. Because GAN training results in a dynamic equilibrium, GANs are likely to get stuck in all sorts of ways. Introducing randomness during training helps prevent this. We introduce randomness in two ways: by using dropout in the discriminator and by adding random noise to the labels for the discriminator.

- Sparse gradients can hinder GAN training. In deep learning, sparsity is often a desirable property, but not in GANs. Two things can induce gradient sparsity: max pooling operations and ReLU activations. Instead of max pooling, we recommend using strided convolutions for downsampling, and we recommend using a LeakyReLU layer instead of a ReLU activation. It's similar to ReLU, but it relaxes sparsity constraints by allowing small negative activation values.

- In generated images, it's common to see checkerboard artifacts caused by unequal coverage of the pixel space in the generator (see figure 8.17). To fix this, we use a kernel size that's divisible by the stride size whenever we use a strided Conv2DTranpose or Conv2D in both the generator and the discriminator.

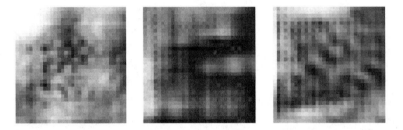

Figure 8.17 Checkerboard artifacts caused by mismatching strides and kernel sizes, resulting in unequal pixel-space coverage: one of the many gotchas of GANs

8.5.3 *The generator*

First, let's develop a generator model that turns a vector (from the latent space—during training it will be sampled at random) into a candidate image. One of the many issues that commonly arise with GANs is that the generator gets stuck with generated images that look like noise. A possible solution is to use dropout on both the discriminator and the generator.

Listing 8.29   GAN generator network

```
import keras
from keras import layers
import numpy as np

latent_dim = 32
height = 32
width = 32
channels = 3
```

```
generator_input = keras.Input(shape=(latent_dim,))

x = layers.Dense(128 * 16 * 16)(generator_input)
x = layers.LeakyReLU()(x)
x = layers.Reshape((16, 16, 128))(x)

x = layers.Conv2D(256, 5, padding='same')(x)
x = layers.LeakyReLU()(x)

x = layers.Conv2DTranspose(256, 4, strides=2, padding='same')(x)
x = layers.LeakyReLU()(x)

x = layers.Conv2D(256, 5, padding='same')(x)
x = layers.LeakyReLU()(x)
x = layers.Conv2D(256, 5, padding='same')(x)
x = layers.LeakyReLU()(x)

x = layers.Conv2D(channels, 7, activation='tanh', padding='same')(x)
generator = keras.models.Model(generator_input, x)
generator.summary()
```

Transforms the input into a 16 × 16 128-channel feature map

Upsamples to 32 × 32

Produces a 32 × 32 1-channel feature map (shape of a CIFAR10 image)

Instantiates the generator model, which maps the input of shape (latent_dim,) into an image of shape (32, 32, 3)

8.5.4 The discriminator

Next, you'll develop a `discriminator` model that takes as input a candidate image (real or synthetic) and classifies it into one of two classes: "generated image" or "real image that comes from the training set."

Listing 8.30   The GAN discriminator network

```
discriminator_input = layers.Input(shape=(height, width, channels))
x = layers.Conv2D(128, 3)(discriminator_input)
x = layers.LeakyReLU()(x)
x = layers.Conv2D(128, 4, strides=2)(x)
x = layers.LeakyReLU()(x)
x = layers.Conv2D(128, 4, strides=2)(x)
x = layers.LeakyReLU()(x)
x = layers.Conv2D(128, 4, strides=2)(x)
x = layers.LeakyReLU()(x)
x = layers.Flatten()(x)

x = layers.Dropout(0.4)(x)

x = layers.Dense(1, activation='sigmoid')(x)

discriminator = keras.models.Model(discriminator_input, x)
discriminator.summary()

discriminator_optimizer = keras.optimizers.RMSprop(
    lr=0.0008,
    clipvalue=1.0,
    decay=1e-8)

discriminator.compile(optimizer=discriminator_optimizer,
                      loss='binary_crossentropy')
```

One dropout layer: an important trick!

Classification layer

Instantiates the discriminator model, which turns a (32, 32, 3) input into a binary classifi-cation decision (fake/real)

Uses gradient clipping (by value) in the optimizer

To stabilize training, uses learning-rate decay

8.5.5   *The adversarial network*

Finally, you'll set up the GAN, which chains the generator and the discriminator. When trained, this model will move the generator in a direction that improves its ability to fool the discriminator. This model turns latent-space points into a classification decision—"fake" or "real"—and it's meant to be trained with labels that are always "these are real images." So, training gan will update the weights of generator in a way that makes discriminator more likely to predict "real" when looking at fake images. It's very important to note that you set the discriminator to be frozen during training (non-trainable): its weights won't be updated when training gan. If the discriminator weights could be updated during this process, then you'd be training the discriminator to always predict "real," which isn't what you want!

Listing 8.31   Adversarial network

```
discriminator.trainable = False

gan_input = keras.Input(shape=(latent_dim,))
gan_output = discriminator(generator(gan_input))
gan = keras.models.Model(gan_input, gan_output)

gan_optimizer = keras.optimizers.RMSprop(lr=0.0004, clipvalue=1.0, decay=1e-8)
gan.compile(optimizer=gan_optimizer, loss='binary_crossentropy')
```

Sets discriminator weights to non-trainable (this will only apply to the gan model)

8.5.6   *How to train your DCGAN*

Now you can begin training. To recapitulate, this is what the training loop looks like schematically. For each epoch, you do the following:

1   Draw random points in the latent space (random noise).
2   Generate images with generator using this random noise.
3   Mix the generated images with real ones.
4   Train discriminator using these mixed images, with corresponding targets: either "real" (for the real images) or "fake" (for the generated images).
5   Draw new random points in the latent space.
6   Train gan using these random vectors, with targets that all say "these are real images." This updates the weights of the generator (only, because the discriminator is frozen inside gan) to move them toward getting the discriminator to predict "these are real images" for generated images: this trains the generator to fool the discriminator.

Let's implement it.

Listing 8.32   Implementing GAN training

```
import os
from keras.preprocessing import image

(x_train, y_train), (_, _) = keras.datasets.cifar10.load_data()
```

Loads CIFAR10 data

```
x_train = x_train[y_train.flatten() == 6]
```
Selects frog images (class 6)

```
x_train = x_train.reshape(
    (x_train.shape[0],) +
    (height, width, channels)).astype('float32') / 255.
```
Normalizes data

```
iterations = 10000
batch_size = 20
save_dir = 'your_dir'
```
Specifies where you want
to save generated images

```
start = 0
for step in range(iterations):
    random_latent_vectors = np.random.normal(size=(batch_size,
                                                    latent_dim))
```
Samples random
points in the
latent space

Decodes
them to
fake
images
```
    generated_images = generator.predict(random_latent_vectors)
```

Combines them
with real images
```
    stop = start + batch_size
    real_images = x_train[start: stop]
    combined_images = np.concatenate([generated_images, real_images])
```

```
    labels = np.concatenate([np.ones((batch_size, 1)),
                             np.zeros((batch_size, 1))])
```
Assembles labels, discrim-
inating real from fake images

```
    labels += 0.05 * np.random.random(labels.shape)
```

Trains the
discriminator
```
    d_loss = discriminator.train_on_batch(combined_images, labels)
```
Adds random
noise to the
labels—an
important trick!

```
    random_latent_vectors = np.random.normal(size=(batch_size,
                                                    latent_dim))
```
Samples random
points in the
latent space

Assembles
labels that
say "these
are all real
images"
(it's a lie!)
```
    misleading_targets = np.zeros((batch_size, 1))
```

```
    a_loss = gan.train_on_batch(random_latent_vectors,
                                misleading_targets)
```
Trains the generator (via the
gan model, where the discriminator weights are frozen)

```
    start += batch_size
    if start > len(x_train) - batch_size:
      start = 0
```
Occasionally saves and
plots (every 100 steps)

```
    if step % 100 == 0:
        gan.save_weights('gan.h5')
```
Saves model weights

Prints metrics
```
        print('discriminator loss:', d_loss)
        print('adversarial loss:', a_loss)
```
Saves one
generated image

```
        img = image.array_to_img(generated_images[0] * 255., scale=False)
        img.save(os.path.join(save_dir,
                    'generated_frog' + str(step) + '.png'))
```

```
        img = image.array_to_img(real_images[0] * 255., scale=False)
        img.save(os.path.join(save_dir,
                    'real_frog' + str(step) + '.png'))
```
Saves one real image
for comparison

When training, you may see the adversarial loss begin to increase considerably, while the discriminative loss tends to zero—the discriminator may end up dominating the generator. If that's the case, try reducing the discriminator learning rate, and increase the dropout rate of the discriminator.

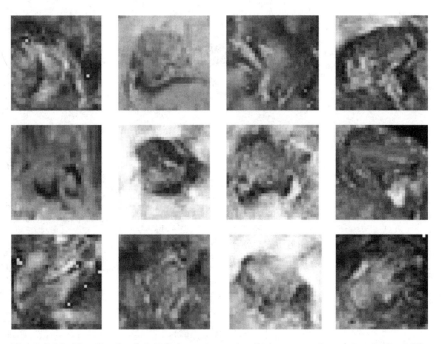

Figure 8.18   Play the discriminator: in each row, two images were dreamed up by the GAN, and one image comes from the training set. Can you tell them apart? (Answers: the real images in each column are middle, top, bottom, middle.)

8.5.7 *Wrapping up*

- A GAN consists of a generator network coupled with a discriminator network. The discriminator is trained to differenciate between the output of the generator and real images from a training dataset, and the generator is trained to fool the discriminator. Remarkably, the generator nevers sees images from the training set directly; the information it has about the data comes from the discriminator.

- GANs are difficult to train, because training a GAN is a dynamic process rather than a simple gradient descent process with a fixed loss landscape. Getting a GAN to train correctly requires using a number of heuristic tricks, as well as extensive tuning.

- GANs can potentially produce highly realistic images. But unlike VAEs, the latent space they learn doesn't have a neat continuous structure and thus may not be suited for certain practical applications, such as image editing via latent-space concept vectors.

Chapter summary

- With creative applications of deep learning, deep networks go beyond annotating existing content and start generating their own. You learned the following:
  - How to generate sequence data, one timestep at a time. This is applicable to text generation and also to note-by-note music generation or any other type of timeseries data.
  - How DeepDream works: by maximizing convnet layer activations through gradient ascent in input space.
  - How to perform style transfer, where a content image and a style image are combined to produce interesting-looking results.
  - What GANs and VAEs are, how they can be used to dream up new images, and how latent-space concept vectors can be used for image editing.

- These few techniques cover only the basics of this fast-expanding field. There's a lot more to discover out there—generative deep learning is deserving of an entire book of its own.

Conclusions 9

You've almost reached the end of this book. This last chapter will summarize and review core concepts while also expanding your horizons beyond the relatively basic notions you've learned so far. Understanding deep learning and AI is a journey, and finishing this book is merely the first step on it. I want to make sure you realize this and are properly equipped to take the next steps of this journey on your own.

We'll start with a bird's-eye view of what you should take away from this book. This should refresh your memory regarding some of the concepts you've learned. Next, we'll present an overview of some key limitations of deep learning. To use a tool appropriately, you should not only understand what it *can* do but also be aware of what it *can't* do. Finally, I'll offer some speculative thoughts about the future evolution of the fields of deep learning, machine learning, and AI. This should be especially interesting to you if you'd like to get into fundamental research. The chapter ends with a short list of resources and strategies for learning further about AI and staying up to date with new advances.

9.1 Key concepts in review

This section briefly synthesizes the key takeaways from this book. If you ever need a quick refresher to help you recall what you've learned, you can read these few pages.

9.1.1 Various approaches to AI

First of all, deep learning isn't synonymous with AI or even with machine learning. *Artificial intelligence* is an ancient, broad field that can generally be defined as "all attempts to automate cognitive processes"—in other words, the automation of thought. This can range from the very basic, such as an Excel spreadsheet, to the very advanced, like a humanoid robot that can walk and talk.

Machine learning is a specific subfield of AI that aims at automatically developing programs (called *models*) purely from exposure to training data. This process of turning data into a program is called *learning*. Although machine learning has been around for a long time, it only started to take off in the 1990s.

Deep learning is one of many branches of machine learning, where the models are long chains of geometric functions, applied one after the other. These operations are structured into modules called *layers*: deep-learning models are typically stacks of layers—or, more generally, graphs of layers. These layers are parameterized by *weights*, which are the parameters learned during training. The *knowledge* of a model is stored in its weights, and the process of learning consists of finding good values for these weights.

Even though deep learning is just one among many approaches to machine learning, it isn't on an equal footing with the others. Deep learning is a breakout success. Here's why.

9.1.2 What makes deep learning special within the field of machine learning

In the span of only a few years, deep learning has achieved tremendous breakthroughs across a wide range of tasks that have been historically perceived as extremely difficult for computers, especially in the area of machine perception: extracting useful information from images, videos, sound, and more. Given sufficient training data (in particular, training data appropriately labeled by humans), it's possible to extract from perceptual data almost anything that a human could extract. Hence, it's sometimes said that deep learning has *solved perception*, although that's true only for a fairly narrow definition of *perception*.

Due to its unprecedented technical successes, deep learning has singlehandedly brought about the third and by far the largest *AI summer*: a period of intense interest, investment, and hype in the field of AI. As this book is being written, we're in the middle of it. Whether this period will end in the near future, and what happens after it ends, are topics of debate. One thing is certain: in stark contrast with previous AI summers, deep learning has provided enormous business value to a number of large technology companies, enabling human-level speech recognition, smart assistants, human-level image classification, vastly improved machine translation, and more. The hype may (and likely will) recede, but the sustained economic and technological impact of deep learning will remain. In that sense, deep learning could be analogous to the internet: it may be overly hyped up for a few years, but in the longer term it will still be a major revolution that will transform our economy and our lives.

I'm particularly optimistic about deep learning because even if we were to make no further technological progress in the next decade, deploying existing algorithms to every applicable problem would be a game changer for most industries. Deep learning is nothing short of a revolution, and progress is currently happening at an incredibly fast rate, due to an exponential investment in resources and headcount. From where I stand, the future looks bright, although short-term expectations are somewhat overoptimistic; deploying deep learning to the full extent of its potential will take well over a decade.

9.1.3   *How to think about deep learning*

The most surprising thing about deep learning is how simple it is. Ten years ago, no one expected that we would achieve such amazing results on machine-perception problems by using simple parametric models trained with gradient descent. Now, it turns out that all you need is sufficiently large parametric models trained with gradient descent on sufficiently many examples. As Feynman once said about the universe, "It's not complicated, it's just a lot of it."[1]

In deep learning, everything is a vector: everything is a *point* in a *geometric space*. Model inputs (text, images, and so on) and targets are first *vectorized*: turned into an initial input vector space and target vector space. Each layer in a deep-learning model operates one simple geometric transformation on the data that goes through it. Together, the chain of layers in the model forms one complex geometric transformation, broken down into a series of simple ones. This complex transformation attempts to map the input space to the target space, one point at a time. This transformation is parameterized by the weights of the layers, which are iteratively updated based on how well the model is currently performing. A key characteristic of this geometric transformation is that it must be *differentiable*, which is required in order for us to be able to learn its parameters via gradient descent. Intuitively, this means the geometric morphing from inputs to outputs must be smooth and continuous—a significant constraint.

The entire process of applying this complex geometric transformation to the input data can be visualized in 3D by imagining a person trying to uncrumple a paper ball: the crumpled paper ball is the manifold of the input data that the model starts with. Each movement operated by the person on the paper ball is similar to a simple geometric transformation operated by one layer. The full uncrumpling gesture sequence is the complex transformation of the entire model. Deep-learning models are mathematical machines for uncrumpling complicated manifolds of high-dimensional data.

---

[1] Richard Feynman, interview, *The World from Another Point of View*, Yorkshire Television, 1972.

That's the magic of deep learning: turning meaning into vectors, into geometric spaces, and then incrementally learning complex geometric transformations that map one space to another. All you need are spaces of sufficiently high dimensionality in order to capture the full scope of the relationships found in the original data.

The whole thing hinges on a single core idea: *that meaning is derived from the pairwise relationship between things* (between words in a language, between pixels in an image, and so on) and that *these relationships can be captured by a distance function*. But note that whether the brain implements meaning via geometric spaces is an entirely separate question. Vector spaces are efficient to work with from a computational standpoint, but different data structures for intelligence can easily be envisioned—in particular, graphs. Neural networks initially emerged from the idea of using graphs as a way to encode meaning, which is why they're named *neural networks*; the surrounding field of research used to be called *connectionism*. Nowadays the name *neural network* exists purely for historical reasons—it's an extremely misleading name because they're neither neural nor networks. In particular, neural networks have hardly anything to do with the brain. A more appropriate name would have been *layered representations learning* or *hierarchical representations learning*, or maybe even *deep differentiable models* or *chained geometric transforms*, to emphasize the fact that continuous geometric space manipulation is at their core.

9.1.4   *Key enabling technologies*

The technological revolution that's currently unfolding didn't start with any single breakthrough invention. Rather, like any other revolution, it's the product of a vast accumulation of enabling factors—slowly at first, and then suddenly. In the case of deep learning, we can point out the following key factors:

- Incremental algorithmic innovations, first spread over two decades (starting with backpropagation) and then happening increasingly faster as more research effort was poured into deep learning after 2012.
- The availability of large amounts of perceptual data, which is a requirement in order to realize that sufficiently large models trained on sufficiently large data are all we need. This is in turn a byproduct of the rise of the consumer internet and Moore's law applied to storage media.
- The availability of fast, highly parallel computation hardware at a low price, especially the GPUs produced by NVIDIA—first gaming GPUs and then chips designed from the ground up for deep learning. Early on, NVIDIA CEO Jensen Huang took note of the deep-learning boom and decided to bet the company's future on it.
- A complex stack of software layers that makes this computational power available to humans: the CUDA language, frameworks like TensorFlow that do automatic differentiation, and Keras, which makes deep learning accessible to most people.

In the future, deep learning will not only be used by specialists—researchers, graduate students, and engineers with an academic profile—but will also be a tool in the toolbox of every developer, much like web technology today. Everyone needs to build intelligent apps: just as every business today needs a website, every product will need to intelligently make sense of user-generated data. Bringing about this future will require us to build tools that make deep learning radically easy to use and accessible to anyone with basic coding abilities. Keras is the first major step in that direction.

9.1.5   *The universal machine-learning workflow*

Having access to an extremely powerful tool for creating models that map any input space to any target space is great, but the difficult part of the machine-learning workflow is often everything that comes before designing and training such models (and, for production models, what comes after, as well). Understanding the problem domain so as to be able to determine what to attempt to predict, given what data, and how to measure success, is a prerequisite for any successful application of machine learning, and it isn't something that advanced tools like Keras and TensorFlow can help you with. As a reminder, here's a quick summary of the typical machine-learning workflow as described in chapter 4:

1 Define the problem: What data is available, and what are you trying to predict? Will you need to collect more data or hire people to manually label a dataset?

2 Identify a way to reliably measure success on your goal. For simple tasks, this may be prediction accuracy, but in many cases it will require sophisticated domain-specific metrics.

3 Prepare the validation process that you'll use to evaluate your models. In particular, you should define a training set, a validation set, and a test set. The validation- and test-set labels shouldn't leak into the training data: for instance, with temporal prediction, the validation and test data should be posterior to the training data.

4 Vectorize the data by turning it into vectors and preprocessing it in a way that makes it more easily approachable by a neural network (normalization, and so on).

5 Develop a first model that beats a trivial common-sense baseline, thus demonstrating that machine learning can work on your problem. This may not always be the case!

6 Gradually refine your model architecture by tuning hyperparameters and adding regularization. Make changes based on performance on the validation data only, not the test data or the training data. Remember that you should get your model to overfit (thus identifying a model capacity level that's greater than you need) and only then begin to add regularization or downsize your model.

7 Be aware of validation-set overfitting when turning hyperparameters: the fact that your hyperparameters may end up being overspecialized to the validation set. Avoiding this is the purpose of having a separate test set!

9.1.6 *Key network architectures*

The three families of network architectures that you should be familiar with are *densely connected networks*, *convolutional networks*, and *recurrent networks*. Each type of network is meant for a specific input modality: a network architecture (dense, convolutional, recurrent) encodes *assumptions* about the structure of the data: a *hypothesis space* within which the search for a good model will proceed. Whether a given architecture will work on a given problem depends entirely on the match between the structure of the data and the assumptions of the network architecture.

These different network types can easily be combined to achieve larger multi-modal networks, much as you combine LEGO bricks. In a way, deep-learning layers are LEGO bricks for information processing. Here's a quick overview of the mapping between input modalities and appropriate network architectures:

- *Vector data*—Densely connected network (Dense layers).
- *Image data*—2D convnets.
- *Sound data (for example, waveform)*—Either 1D convnets (preferred) or RNNs.
- *Text data*—Either 1D convnets (preferred) or RNNs.
- *Timeseries data*—Either RNNs (preferred) or 1D convnets.
- *Other types of sequence data*—Either RNNs or 1D convnets. Prefer RNNs if data ordering is strongly meaningful (for example, for timeseries, but not for text).
- *Video data*—Either 3D convnets (if you need to capture motion effects) or a combination of a frame-level 2D convnet for feature extraction followed by either an RNN or a 1D convnet to process the resulting sequences.
- *Volumetric data*—3D convnets.

Now, let's quickly review the specificities of each network architecture.

DENSELY CONNECTED NETWORKS

A densely connected network is a stack of Dense layers, meant to process vector data (batches of vectors). Such networks assume no specific structure in the input features: they're called *densely connected* because the units of a Dense layer are connected to every other unit. The layer attempts to map relationships between any two input features; this is unlike a 2D convolution layer, for instance, which only looks at *local* relationships.

Densely connected networks are most commonly used for categorical data (for example, where the input features are lists of attributes), such as the Boston Housing Price dataset used in chapter 3. They're also used as the final classification or regression stage of most networks. For instance, the convnets covered in chapter 5 typically end with one or two Dense layers, and so do the recurrent networks in chapter 6.

Remember: to perform *binary classification*, end your stack of layers with a Dense layer with a single unit and a sigmoid activation, and use binary_crossentropy as the loss. Your targets should be either 0 or 1:

```
from keras import models
from keras import layers

model = models.Sequential()
model.add(layers.Dense(32, activation='relu', input_shape=(num_input_features,)))
model.add(layers.Dense(32, activation='relu'))
model.add(layers.Dense(1, activation='sigmoid'))

model.compile(optimizer='rmsprop', loss='binary_crossentropy')
```

To perform *single-label categorical classification* (where each sample has exactly one class, no more), end your stack of layers with a Dense layer with a number of units equal to the number of classes, and a softmax activation. If your targets are one-hot encoded, use categorical_crossentropy as the loss; if they're integers, use sparse_categorical_crossentropy:

```
model = models.Sequential()
model.add(layers.Dense(32, activation='relu', input_shape=(num_input_features,)))
model.add(layers.Dense(32, activation='relu'))
model.add(layers.Dense(num_classes, activation='softmax'))

model.compile(optimizer='rmsprop', loss='categorical_crossentropy')
```

To perform *multilabel categorical classification* (where each sample can have several classes), end your stack of layers with a Dense layer with a number of units equal to the number of classes and a sigmoid activation, and use binary_crossentropy as the loss. Your targets should be k-hot encoded:

```
model = models.Sequential()
model.add(layers.Dense(32, activation='relu', input_shape=(num_input_features,)))
model.add(layers.Dense(32, activation='relu'))
model.add(layers.Dense(num_classes, activation='sigmoid'))

model.compile(optimizer='rmsprop', loss='binary_crossentropy')
```

To perform *regression* toward a vector of continuous values, end your stack of layers with a Dense layer with a number of units equal to the number of values you're trying to predict (often a single one, such as the price of a house), and no activation. Several losses can be used for regression, most commonly mean_squared_error (MSE) and mean_absolute_error (MAE):

```
model = models.Sequential()
model.add(layers.Dense(32, activation='relu', input_shape=(num_input_features,)))
model.add(layers.Dense(32, activation='relu'))
model.add(layers.Dense(num_values))

model.compile(optimizer='rmsprop', loss='mse')
```

CONVNETS

Convolution layers look at spatially local patterns by applying the same geometric transformation to different spatial locations (*patches*) in an input tensor. This results in representations that are *translation invariant*, making convolution layers highly data efficient and modular. This idea is applicable to spaces of any dimensionality: 1D (sequences), 2D (images), 3D (volumes), and so on. You can use the `Conv1D` layer to process sequences (especially text—it doesn't work as well on timeseries, which often don't follow the translation-invariance assumption), the `Conv2D` layer to process images, and the `Conv3D` layers to process volumes.

Convnets, or *convolutional networks*, consist of stacks of convolution and max-pooling layers. The pooling layers let you spatially downsample the data, which is required to keep feature maps to a reasonable size as the number of features grows, and to allow subsequent convolution layers to "see" a greater spatial extent of the inputs. Convnets are often ended with either a `Flatten` operation or a global pooling layer, turning spatial feature maps into vectors, followed by `Dense` layers to achieve classification or regression.

Note that it's highly likely that regular convolutions will soon be mostly (or completely) replaced by an equivalent but faster and representationally efficient alternative: the *depthwise separable convolution* (`SeparableConv2D` layer). This is true for 3D, 2D, and 1D inputs. When you're building a new network from scratch, using depthwise separable convolutions is definitely the way to go. The `SeparableConv2D` layer can be used as a drop-in replacement for `Conv2D`, resulting in a smaller, faster network that also performs better on its task.

Here's a typical image-classification network (categorical classification, in this case):

```
model = models.Sequential()
model.add(layers.SeparableConv2D(32, 3, activation='relu',
                                 input_shape=(height, width, channels)))
model.add(layers.SeparableConv2D(64, 3, activation='relu'))
model.add(layers.MaxPooling2D(2))

model.add(layers.SeparableConv2D(64, 3, activation='relu'))
model.add(layers.SeparableConv2D(128, 3, activation='relu'))
model.add(layers.MaxPooling2D(2))

model.add(layers.SeparableConv2D(64, 3, activation='relu'))
model.add(layers.SeparableConv2D(128, 3, activation='relu'))
model.add(layers.GlobalAveragePooling2D())

model.add(layers.Dense(32, activation='relu'))
model.add(layers.Dense(num_classes, activation='softmax'))

model.compile(optimizer='rmsprop', loss='categorical_crossentropy')
```

RNNs

Recurrent neural networks (RNNs) work by processing sequences of inputs one timestep at a time and maintaining a *state* throughout (a state is typically a vector or set of vectors:

a point in a geometric space of states). They should be used preferentially over 1D conv-nets in the case of sequences where patterns of interest aren't invariant by temporal translation (for instance, timeseries data where the recent past is more important than the distant past).

Three RNN layers are available in Keras: SimpleRNN, GRU, and LSTM. For most prac-tical purposes, you should use either GRU or LSTM. LSTM is the more powerful of the two but is also more expensive; you can think of GRU as a simpler, cheaper alternative to it.

In order to stack multiple RNN layers on top of each other, each layer prior to the last layer in the stack should return the full sequence of its outputs (each input time-step will correspond to an output timestep); if you aren't stacking any further RNN lay-ers, then it's common to return only the last output, which contains information about the entire sequence.

Following is a single RNN layer for binary classification of vector sequences:

```
model = models.Sequential()
model.add(layers.LSTM(32, input_shape=(num_timesteps, num_features)))
model.add(layers.Dense(num_classes, activation='sigmoid'))

50model.compile(optimizer='rmsprop', loss='binary_crossentropy')
```

And this is a stacked RNN layer for binary classification of vector sequences:

```
model = models.Sequential()
model.add(layers.LSTM(32, return_sequences=True,
            input_shape=(num_timesteps, num_features)))
model.add(layers.LSTM(32, return_sequences=True))
model.add(layers.LSTM(32))
model.add(layers.Dense(num_classes, activation='sigmoid'))

model.compile(optimizer='rmsprop', loss='binary_crossentropy')
```

9.1.7 *The space of possibilities*

What will you build with deep learning? Remember, building deep-learning models is like playing with LEGO bricks: layers can be plugged together to map essentially any-thing to anything, given that you have appropriate training data available and that the mapping is achievable via a continuous geometric transformation of reasonable com-plexity. The space of possibilities is infinite. This section offers a few examples to inspire you to think beyond the basic classification and regression tasks that have tra-ditionally been the bread and butter of machine learning.

I've sorted my suggested applications by input and output modalities. Note that quite a few of them stretch the limits of what is possible—although a model could be trained on all of these tasks, in some cases such a model probably wouldn't generalize far from its training data. Sections 9.2 and 9.3 will address how these limitations could be lifted in the future.

- Mapping vector data to vector data
  - *Predictive healthcare*—Mapping patient medical records to predictions of patient outcomes
  - *Behavioral targeting*—Mapping a set of website attributes with data on how long a user will spend on the website
  - *Product quality control*—Mapping a set of attributes relative to an instance of a manufactured product with the probability that the product will fail by next year
- Mapping image data to vector data
  - *Doctor assistant*—Mapping slides of medical images with a prediction about the presence of a tumor
  - *Self-driving vehicle*—Mapping car dash-cam video frames to steering wheel angle commands
  - *Board game AI*—Mapping Go and chess boards to the next player move
  - *Diet helper*—Mapping pictures of a dish to its calorie count
  - *Age prediction*—Mapping selfies to the age of the person
- Mapping timeseries data to vector data
  - *Weather prediction*—Mapping timeseries of weather data in a grid of locations of weather data the following week at a specific location
  - *Brain-computer interfaces*—Mapping timeseries of magnetoencephalogram (MEG) data to computer commands
  - *Behavioral targeting*—Mapping timeseries of user interactions on a website to the probability that a user will buy something
- Mapping text to text
  - *Smart reply*—Mapping emails to possible one-line replies
  - *Answering questions*—Mapping general-knowledge questions to answers
  - *Summarization*—Mapping a long article to a short summary of the article
- Mapping images to text
  - *Captioning*—Mapping images to short captions describing the contents of the images
- Mapping text to images
  - *Conditioned image generation*—Mapping a short text description to images matching the description
  - *Logo generation/selection*—Mapping the name and description of a company to the company's logo
- Mapping images to images
  - *Super-resolution*—Mapping downsized images to higher-resolution versions of the same images
  - *Visual depth sensing*—Mapping images of indoor environments to maps of depth predictions

- Mapping images and text to text
  - *Visual QA*—Mapping images and natural-language questions about the contents of images to natural-language answers
- Mapping video and text to text
  - *Video QA*—Mapping short videos and natural-language questions about the contents of videos to natural-language answers

Almost anything is possible—but not quite *anything*. Let's see in the next section what we *can't* do with deep learning.

9.2   The limitations of deep learning

The space of applications that can be implemented with deep learning is nearly infinite. And yet, many applications are completely out of reach for current deep-learning techniques—even given vast amounts of human-annotated data. Say, for instance, that you could assemble a dataset of hundreds of thousands—even millions—of English-language descriptions of the features of a software product, written by a product manager, as well as the corresponding source code developed by a team of engineers to meet these requirements. Even with this data, you could *not* train a deep-learning model to read a product description and generate the appropriate codebase. That's just one example among many. In general, anything that requires reasoning—like programming or applying the scientific method—long-term planning, and algorithmic data manipulation is out of reach for deep-learning models, no matter how much data you throw at them. Even learning a sorting algorithm with a deep neural network is tremendously difficult.

This is because a deep-learning model is just *a chain of simple, continuous geometric transformations* mapping one vector space into another. All it can do is map one data manifold X into another manifold Y, assuming the existence of a learnable continuous transform from X to Y. A deep-learning model can be interpreted as a kind of program; but, inversely, *most programs can't be expressed as deep-learning models*—for most tasks, either there exists no corresponding deep-neural network that solves the task or, even if one exists, it may not be *learnable*: the corresponding geometric transform may be far too complex, or there may not be appropriate data available to learn it.

Scaling up current deep-learning techniques by stacking more layers and using more training data can only superficially palliate some of these issues. It won't solve the more fundamental problems that deep-learning models are limited in what they can represent and that most of the programs you may wish to learn can't be expressed as a continuous geometric morphing of a data manifold.

9.2.1   The risk of anthropomorphizing machine-learning models

One real risk with contemporary AI is misinterpreting what deep-learning models do and overestimating their abilities. A fundamental feature of humans is our *theory of mind*: our tendency to project intentions, beliefs, and knowledge on the things around us. Drawing a smiley face on a rock suddenly makes it "happy"—in our minds. Applied to deep learning, this means that, for instance, when we're able to somewhat successfully train a model to generate captions to describe pictures, we're led to believe that the model "understands" the contents of the pictures and the captions it generates. Then we're surprised when any slight departure from the sort of images present in the training data causes the model to generate completely absurd captions (see figure 9.1).

Figure 9.1   Failure of an image-captioning system based on deep learning

The boy is holding a baseball bat.

In particular, this is highlighted by *adversarial examples*, which are samples fed to a deep-learning network that are designed to trick the model into misclassifying them. You're already aware that, for instance, it's possible to do gradient ascent in input space to generate inputs that maximize the activation of some convnet filter—this is the basis of the filter-visualization technique introduced in chapter 5, as well as the DeepDream algorithm in chapter 8. Similarly, through gradient ascent, you can slightly modify an image in order to maximize the class prediction for a given class. By taking a picture of a panda and adding to it a gibbon gradient, we can get a neural network to classify the panda as a gibbon (see figure 9.2). This evidences both the brittleness of these models and the deep difference between their input-to-output mapping and our human perception.

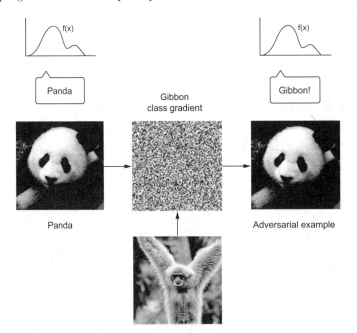

Figure 9.2   An adversarial example: imperceptible changes in an image can upend a model's classification of the image.

In short, deep-learning models don't have any understanding of their input—at least, not in a human sense. Our own understanding of images, sounds, and language is grounded in our sensorimotor experience as humans. Machine-learning models have no access to such experiences and thus can't understand their inputs in a human-relatable way. By annotating large numbers of training examples to feed into our models, we get them to learn a geometric transform that maps data to human concepts on a specific set of examples, but this mapping is a simplistic sketch of the original model in our minds—the one developed from our experience as embodied agents. It's like a dim image in a mirror (see figure 9.3).

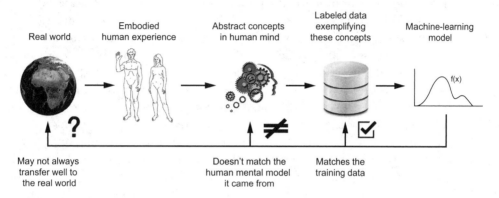

Figure 9.3 Current machine-learning models: like a dim image in a mirror

As a machine-learning practitioner, always be mindful of this, and never fall into the trap of believing that neural networks understand the task they perform—they don't, at least not in a way that would make sense to us. They were trained on a different, far narrower task than the one we wanted to teach them: that of mapping training inputs to training targets, point by point. Show them anything that deviates from their training data, and they will break in absurd ways.

9.2.2 Local generalization vs. extreme generalization

There are fundamental differences between the straightforward geometric morphing from input to output that deep-learning models do, and the way humans think and learn. It isn't only the fact that humans learn by themselves from embodied experience instead of being presented with explicit training examples. In addition to the different learning processes, there's a basic difference in the nature of the underlying representations.

Humans are capable of far more than mapping immediate stimuli to immediate responses, as a deep network, or maybe an insect, would. We maintain complex, *abstract models* of our current situation, of ourselves, and of other people, and can use these models to anticipate different possible futures and perform long-term planning. We can merge together known concepts to represent something we've never experienced before—like picturing a horse wearing jeans, for instance, or imagining what we'd do if we won the lottery. This ability to handle hypotheticals, to expand our mental model space far beyond what we can experience directly—to perform *abstraction* and *reasoning*—is arguably the defining characteristic of human cognition. I call it *extreme generalization*: an ability to adapt to novel, never-before-experienced situations using little data or even no new data at all.

This stands in sharp contrast with what deep nets do, which I call *local generalization* (see figure 9.4). The mapping from inputs to outputs performed by a deep net quickly stops making sense if new inputs differ even slightly from what the net saw at training time. Consider, for instance, the problem of learning the appropriate launch parameters to get a rocket to land on the moon. If you used a deep net for this task and trained it using supervised learning or reinforcement learning, you'd have to feed it thousands or even millions of launch trials: you'd need to expose it to a *dense sampling* of the input space, in order for it to learn a reliable mapping from input space to output space. In contrast, as humans we can use our power of abstraction to come up with physical models—rocket science—and derive an *exact* solution that will land the rocket on the moon in one or a few trials. Similarly, if you developed a deep net controlling a human body, and you wanted it to learn to safely navigate a city without getting hit by cars, the net would have to die many thousands of times in various situations until it could infer that cars are dangerous, and develop appropriate avoidance behaviors. Dropped into a new city, the net would have to relearn most of what it knows. On the other hand, humans are able to learn safe behaviors without having to die even once—again, thanks to our power of abstract modeling of hypothetical situations.

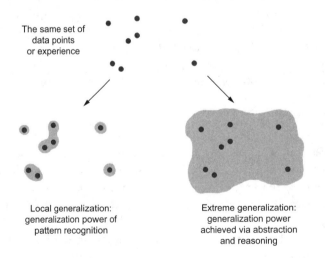

The same set of
data points
or experience

Local generalization:
generalization power of
pattern recognition

Extreme generalization:
generalization power
achieved via abstraction
and reasoning

Figure 9.4 Local generalization vs. extreme generalization

In short, despite our progress on machine perception, we're still far from human-level AI. Our models can only perform local generalization, adapting to new situations that must be similar to past data, whereas human cognition is capable of extreme generalization, quickly adapting to radically novel situations and planning for long-term future situations.

9.2.3 Wrapping up

Here's what you should remember: the only real success of deep learning so far has been the ability to map space X to space Y using a continuous geometric transform, given large amounts of human-annotated data. Doing this well is a game-changer for essentially every industry, but it's still a long way from human-level AI.

To lift some of the limitations we have discussed and create AI that can compete with human brains, we need to move away from straightforward input-to-output mappings and on to *reasoning* and *abstraction*. A likely appropriate substrate for abstract modeling of various situations and concepts is that of computer programs. We said previously that machine-learning models can be defined as *learnable programs*; currently we can only learn programs that belong to a narrow and specific subset of all possible programs. But what if we could learn *any* program, in a modular and reusable way? Let's see in the next section what the road ahead may look like.

9.3   *The future of deep learning*

This is a more speculative section aimed at opening horizons for people who want to join a research program or begin doing independent research. Given what we know of how deep nets work, their limitations, and the current state of the research landscape, can we predict where things are headed in the medium term? Following are some purely personal thoughts. Note that I don't have a crystal ball, so a lot of what I anticipate may fail to become reality. I'm sharing these predictions not because I expect them to be proven completely right in the future, but because they're interesting and actionable in the present.

At a high level, these are the main directions in which I see promise:

- *Models closer to general-purpose computer programs*, built on top of far richer primitives than the current differentiable layers. This is how we'll get to *reasoning* and *abstraction*, the lack of which is the fundamental weakness of current models.
- *New forms of learning that make the previous point possible*, allowing models to move away from differentiable transforms.
- *Models that require less involvement from human engineers*. It shouldn't be your job to tune knobs endlessly.
- *Greater, systematic reuse of previously learned features and architectures*, such as meta-learning systems using reusable and modular program subroutines.

Additionally, note that these considerations aren't specific to the sort of supervised learning that has been the bread and butter of deep learning so far—rather, they're applicable to any form of machine learning, including unsupervised, self-supervised, and reinforcement learning. It isn't fundamentally important where your labels come from or what your training loop looks like; these different branches of machine learning are different facets of the same construct. Let's dive in.

9.3.1   *Models as programs*

As noted in the previous section, a necessary transformational development that we can expect in the field of machine learning is a move away from models that perform purely *pattern recognition* and can only achieve *local generalization*, toward models capable of *abstraction* and *reasoning* that can achieve *extreme generalization*. Current AI programs that are capable of basic forms of reasoning are all hardcoded by human programmers: for instance, software that relies on search algorithms, graph manipulation, and formal logic. In DeepMind's AlphaGo, for example, most of the intelligence on display is designed and hardcoded by expert programmers (such as Monte Carlo Tree Search); learning from data happens only in specialized submodules (value networks and policy networks). But in the future, such AI systems may be fully learned, with no human involvement.

What path could make this happen? Consider a well-known type of network: RNNs. It's important to note that RNNs have slightly fewer limitations than feedforward networks. That's because RNNs are a bit more than mere geometric transformations:

they're geometric transformations *repeatedly applied inside a* for *loop*. The temporal for loop is itself hardcoded by human developers: it's a built-in assumption of the network. Naturally, RNNs are still extremely limited in what they can represent, primarily because each step they perform is a differentiable geometric transformation, and they carry information from step to step via points in a continuous geometric space (state vectors). Now imagine a neural network that's augmented in a similar way with programming primitives—but instead of a single hardcoded for loop with hardcoded geometric memory, the network includes a large set of programming primitives that the model is free to manipulate to expand its processing function, such as if branches, while statements, variable creation, disk storage for long-term memory, sorting operators, advanced data structures (such as lists, graphs, and hash tables), and many more. The space of programs that such a network could represent would be far broader than what can be represented with current deep-learning models, and some of these programs could achieve superior generalization power.

We'll move away from having, on one hand, hardcoded algorithmic intelligence (handcrafted software) and, on the other hand, learned geometric intelligence (deep learning). Instead, we'll have a blend of formal algorithmic modules that provide reasoning and abstraction capabilities, and geometric modules that provide informal intuition and pattern-recognition capabilities. The entire system will be learned with little or no human involvement.

A related subfield of AI that I think may be about to take off in a big way is *program synthesis*, in particular neural program synthesis. Program synthesis consists of automatically generating simple programs by using a search algorithm (possibly genetic search, as in genetic programming) to explore a large space of possible programs. The search stops when a program is found that matches the required specifications, often provided as a set of input-output pairs. This is highly reminiscent of machine learning: given training data provided as input-output pairs, we find a program that matches inputs to outputs and can generalize to new inputs. The difference is that instead of learning parameter values in a hardcoded program (a neural network), we generate source code via a discrete search process.

I definitely expect this subfield to see a wave of renewed interest in the next few years. In particular, I expect the emergence of a crossover subfield between deep learning and program synthesis, where instead of generating programs in a general-purpose language, we'll generate neural networks (geometric data-processing flows) augmented with a rich set of algorithmic primitives, such as for loops and many others (see figure 9.5). This should be far more tractable and useful than directly generating source code, and it will dramatically expand the scope of problems that can be solved with machine learning—the space of programs that we can generate automatically, given appropriate training data. Contemporary RNNs can be seen as a prehistoric ancestor of such hybrid algorithmic-geometric models.

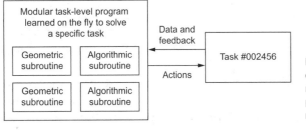

Figure 9.5   A learned program relying on both geometric primitives (pattern recognition, intuition) and algorithmic primitives (reasoning, search, memory)

9.3.2   *Beyond backpropagation and differentiable layers*

If machine-learning models become more like programs, then they will mostly no longer be differentiable—these programs will still use continuous geometric layers as subroutines, which will be differentiable, but the model as a whole won't be. As a result, using backpropagation to adjust weight values in a fixed, hardcoded network can't be the method of choice for training models in the future—at least, it can't be the entire story. We need to figure out how to train non-differentiable systems efficiently. Current approaches include genetic algorithms, evolution strategies, certain reinforcement-learning methods, and alternating direction method of multipliers (ADMM). Naturally, gradient descent isn't going anywhere; gradient information will always be useful for optimizing differentiable parametric functions. But our models will become increasingly more ambitious than mere differentiable parametric functions, and thus their automatic development (the *learning* in *machine learning*) will require more than backpropagation.

In addition, backpropagation is end to end, which is a great thing for learning good chained transformations but is computationally inefficient because it doesn't fully take advantage of the modularity of deep networks. To make something more efficient, there's one universal recipe: introduce modularity and hierarchy. So we can make backpropagation more efficient by introducing decoupled training modules with a synchronization mechanism between them, organized in a hierarchical fashion. This strategy is somewhat reflected in DeepMind's recent work on synthetic gradients. I expect more along these lines in the near future. I can imagine a future where models that are globally non-differentiable (but feature differentiable parts) are trained—grown—using an efficient search process that doesn't use gradients, whereas the differentiable parts are trained even faster by taking advantage of gradients using a more efficient version of backpropagation.

9.3.3   *Automated machine learning*

In the future, model architectures will be learned rather than be handcrafted by engineer-artisans. Learning architectures goes hand in hand with the use of richer sets of primitives and program-like machine-learning models.

Currently, most of the job of a deep-learning engineer consists of munging data with Python scripts and then tuning the architecture and hyperparameters of a deep network at length to get a working model—or even to get a state-of-the-art model, if the engineer is that ambitious. Needless to say, that isn't an optimal setup. But AI can help. Unfortunately, the data-munging part is tough to automate, because it often requires domain knowledge as well as a clear, high-level understanding of what the engineer wants to achieve. Hyperparameter tuning, however, is a simple search procedure; and in that case we know what the engineer wants to achieve: it's defined by the loss function of the network being tuned. It's already common practice to set up basic *AutoML* systems that take care of most model knob tuning. I even set up my own, years ago, to win Kaggle competitions.

At the most basic level, such a system would tune the number of layers in a stack, their order, and the number of units or filters in each layer. This is commonly done with libraries such as Hyperopt, which we discussed in chapter 7. But we can also be far more ambitious and attempt to learn an appropriate architecture from scratch, with as few constraints as possible: for instance, via reinforcement learning or genetic algorithms.

Another important AutoML direction involves learning model architecture jointly with model weights. Because training a new model from scratch every time we try a slightly different architecture is tremendously inefficient, a truly powerful AutoML system would evolve architectures at the same time the features of the model were being tuned via backpropagation on the training data. Such approaches are beginning to emerge as I write these lines.

When this starts to happen, the jobs of machine-learning engineers won't disappear—rather, engineers will move up the value-creation chain. They will begin to put much more effort into crafting complex loss functions that truly reflect business goals and understanding how their models impact the digital ecosystems in which they're deployed (for example, the users who consume the model's predictions and generate the model's training data)—problems that only the largest companies can afford to consider at present.

9.3.4 *Lifelong learning and modular subroutine reuse*

If models become more complex and are built on top of richer algorithmic primitives, then this increased complexity will require higher reuse between tasks, rather than training a new model from scratch every time we have a new task or a new dataset. Many datasets don't contain enough information for us to develop a new, complex model from scratch, and it will be necessary to use information from previously encountered datasets (much as you don't learn English from scratch every time you open a new book—that would be impossible). Training models from scratch on every new task is also inefficient due to the large overlap between the current tasks and previously encountered tasks.

A remarkable observation has been made repeatedly in recent years: training the *same* model to do several loosely connected tasks at the same time results in a model that's *better at each task*. For instance, training the same neural machine-translation model to perform both English-to-German translation and French-to-Italian translation will result in a model that's better at each language pair. Similarly, training an image-classification model jointly with an image-segmentation model, sharing the same convolutional base, results in a model that's better at both tasks. This is fairly intuitive: there's always *some* information overlap between seemingly disconnected tasks, and a joint model has access to a greater amount of information about each individual task than a model trained on that specific task only.

Currently, when it comes to model reuse across tasks, we use pretrained weights for models that perform common functions, such as visual feature extraction. You saw this in action in chapter 5. In the future, I expect a generalized version of this to be commonplace: we'll use not only previously learned features (submodel weights) but also model architectures and training procedures. As models become more like programs, we'll begin to reuse *program subroutines* like the functions and classes found in human programming languages.

Think of the process of software development today: once an engineer solves a specific problem (HTTP queries in Python, for instance), they package it as an abstract, reusable library. Engineers who face a similar problem in the future will be able to search for existing libraries, download one, and use it in their own project. In a similar way, in the future, metalearning systems will be able to assemble new programs by sifting through a global library of high-level reusable blocks. When the system finds itself developing similar program subroutines for several different tasks, it can come up with an abstract, reusable version of the subroutine and store it in the global library (see figure 9.6). Such a process will implement *abstraction*: a necessary component for achieving extreme generalization. A subroutine that's useful across different tasks and domains can be said to *abstract* some aspect of problem solving. This definition of abstraction is similar to the notion of abstraction in software engineering. These subroutines can be either geometric (deep-learning modules with pretrained representations) or algorithmic (closer to the libraries that contemporary software engineers manipulate).

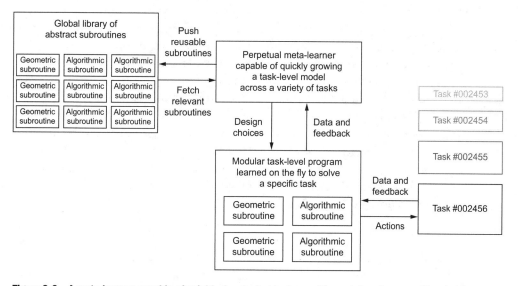

Figure 9.6 A meta-learner capable of quickly developing task-specific models using reusable primitives (both algorithmic and geometric), thus achieving extreme generalization

9.3.5 The long-term vision

In short, here's my long-term vision for machine learning:

- Models will be more like programs and will have capabilities that go far beyond the continuous geometric transformations of the input data we currently work with. These programs will arguably be much closer to the abstract mental models that humans maintain about their surroundings and themselves, and they will be capable of stronger generalization due to their rich algorithmic nature.

- In particular, models will blend *algorithmic modules* providing formal reasoning, search, and abstraction capabilities with *geometric modules* providing informal intuition and pattern-recognition capabilities. AlphaGo (a system that required a lot of manual software engineering and human-made design decisions) provides an early example of what such a blend of symbolic and geometric AI could look like.

- Such models will be *grown* automatically rather than hardcoded by human engineers, using modular parts stored in a global library of reusable subroutines—a library evolved by learning high-performing models on thousands of previous tasks and datasets. As frequent problem-solving patterns are identified by the meta-learning system, they will be turned into reusable subroutines—much like functions and classes in software engineering—and added to the global library. This will achieve *abstraction*.

- This global library and associated model-growing system will be able to achieve some form of human-like extreme generalization: given a new task or situation, the system will be able to assemble a new working model appropriate for the task using very little data, thanks to rich program-like primitives that generalize well, and extensive experience with similar tasks. In the same way, humans can quickly learn to play a complex new video game if they have experience with many previous games, because the models derived from this previous experience are abstract and program-like, rather than a basic mapping between stimuli and action.

- As such, this perpetually learning model-growing system can be interpreted as an *artificial general intelligence* (AGI). But don't expect any singularitarian robot apocalypse to ensue: that's pure fantasy, coming from a long series of profound misunderstandings of both intelligence and technology. Such a critique, however, doesn't belong in this book.

9.4 Staying up to date in a fast-moving field

As final parting words, I want to give you some pointers about how to keep learning and updating your knowledge and skills after you've turned the last page of this book. The field of modern deep learning, as we know it today, is only a few years old, despite a long, slow prehistory stretching back decades. With an exponential increase in financial resources and research headcount since 2013, the field as a whole is now moving at a frenetic pace. What you've learned in this book won't stay relevant forever, and it isn't all you'll need for the rest of your career.

Fortunately, there are plenty of free online resources that you can use to stay up to date and expand your horizons. Here are a few.

9.4.1 Practice on real-world problems using Kaggle

One effective way to acquire real-world experience is to try your hand at machine-learning competitions on Kaggle (https://kaggle.com). The only real way to learn is through practice and actual coding—that's the philosophy of this book, and Kaggle competitions are the natural continuation of this. On Kaggle, you'll find an array of constantly renewed data-science competitions, many of which involve deep learning, prepared by companies interested in obtaining novel solutions to some of their most challenging machine-learning problems. Fairly large monetary prizes are offered to top entrants.

Most competitions are won using either the XGBoost library (for shallow machine learning) or Keras (for deep learning). So you'll fit right in! By participating in a few competitions, maybe as part of a team, you'll become more familiar with the practical side of some of the advanced best practices described in this book, especially hyperparameter tuning, avoiding validation-set overfitting, and model ensembling.

9.4.2 Read about the latest developments on arXiv

Deep-learning research, in contrast with some other scientific fields, takes places completely in the open. Papers are made publicly and freely accessible as soon as they're finalized, and a lot of related software is open source. arXiv (https://arxiv.org)—pronounced "archive" (the *X* stands for the Greek *chi*)—is an open-access preprint server for physics, mathematics, and computer science research papers. It has become the de facto way to stay up to date on the bleeding edge of machine learning and deep learning. The large majority of deep-learning researchers upload any paper they write to arXiv shortly after completion. This allows them to plant a flag and claim a specific finding without waiting for a conference acceptance (which takes months), which is necessary given the fast pace of research and the intense competition in the field. It also allows the field to move extremely fast: all new findings are immediately available for all to see and to build on.

An important downside is that the sheer quantity of new papers posted every day on arXiv makes it impossible to even skim them all; and the fact that they aren't peer reviewed makes it difficult to identify those that are both important and high quality.

It's difficult, and becoming increasingly more so, to find the signal in the noise. Currently, there isn't a good solution to this problem. But some tools can help: an auxiliary website called arXiv Sanity Preserver (http://arxiv-sanity.com) serves as a recommendation engine for new papers and can help you keep track of new developments within a specific narrow vertical of deep learning. Additionally, you can use Google Scholar (https://scholar.google.com) to keep track of publications by your favorite authors.

9.4.3 *Explore the Keras ecosystem*

With about 200,000 users as of November 2017 and growing fast, Keras has a large ecosystem of tutorials, guides, and related open source projects:

- Your main reference for working with Keras is the online documentation at https://keras.io. The Keras source code can be found at https://github.com/fchollet/keras.
- You can ask for help and join deep-learning discussions on the Keras Slack channel: https://kerasteam.slack.com.
- The Keras blog, https://blog.keras.io, offers Keras tutorials and other articles related to deep learning.
- You can follow me on Twitter: @fchollet.

9.5 *Final words*

This is the end of *Deep Learning with Python*! I hope you've learned a thing or two about machine learning, deep learning, Keras, and maybe even cognition in general. Learning is a lifelong journey, especially in the field of AI, where we have far more unknowns on our hands than certitudes. So please go on learning, questioning, and researching. Never stop. Because even given the progress made so far, most of the fundamental questions in AI remain unanswered. Many haven't even been properly asked yet.

appendix A
Installing Keras and its dependencies on Ubuntu

The process of setting up a deep-learning workstation is fairly involved and consists of the following steps, which this appendix will cover in detail:

1. Install the Python scientific suite—Numpy and SciPy—and make sure you have a Basic Linear Algebra Subprogram (BLAS) library installed so your models run fast on CPU.
2. Install two extras packages that come in handy when using Keras: HDF5 (for saving large neural-network files) and Graphviz (for visualizing neural-network architectures).
3. Make sure your GPU can run deep-learning code, by installing CUDA drivers and cuDNN.
4. Install a backend for Keras: TensorFlow, CNTK, or Theano.
5. Install Keras.

It may seem like a daunting process. In fact, the only difficult part is setting up GPU support—otherwise, the entire process can be done with a few commands and takes only a couple of minutes.

We'll assume you have a fresh installation of Ubuntu, with an NVIDIA GPU available. Before you start, make sure you have `pip` installed and that your package manager is up to date:

```
$ sudo apt-get update
$ sudo apt-get upgrade
$ sudo apt-get install python-pip python-dev
```

Python 2 vs. Python 3

By default, Ubuntu uses Python 2 when it installs Python packages such as `python-pip`. If you wish to use Python 3 instead, you should use the `python3` prefix instead of `python`. For instance:

```
$ sudo apt-get install python3-pip python3-dev
```

When you're installing packages using `pip`, keep in mind that by default, it targets Python 2. To target Python 3, you should use `pip3`:

```
$ sudo pip3 install tensorflow-gpu
```

A.1 Installing the Python scientific suite

If you use a Mac, we recommend that you install the Python scientific suite via Anaconda, which you can get at www.continuum.io/downloads. Note that this won't include HDF5 and Graphviz, which you have to install manually. Following are the steps for a *manual* installation of the Python scientific suite on Ubuntu:

1 Install a BLAS library (OpenBLAS, in this case), to ensure that you can run fast tensor operations on your CPU:

```
$ sudo apt-get install build-essential cmake git unzip \
    pkg-config libopenblas-dev liblapack-dev
```

2 Install the Python scientific suite: Numpy, SciPy and Matplotlib. This is necessary in order to perform any kind of machine learning or scientific computing in Python, regardless of whether you're doing deep learning:

```
$ sudo apt-get install python-numpy python-scipy python- matplotlib
➥python-yaml
```

3 Install HDF5. This library, originally developed by NASA, stores large files of numeric data in an efficient binary format. It will allow you to save your Keras models to disk quickly and efficiently:

```
$ sudo apt-get install libhdf5-serial-dev python-h5py
```

4 Install Graphviz and pydot-ng, two packages that will let you visualize Keras models. They aren't necessary to run Keras, so you could skip this step and install these packages when you need them. Here are the commands:

```
$ sudo apt-get install graphviz
$ sudo pip install pydot-ng
```

5 Install additional packages that are used in some of our code examples:

```
$ sudo apt-get install python-opencv
```

A.2   *Setting up GPU support*

Using a GPU isn't strictly necessary, but it's strongly recommended. All the code examples found in this book can be run on a laptop CPU, but you may sometimes have to wait for several hours for a model to train, instead of mere minutes on a good GPU. If you don't have a modern NVIDIA GPU, you can skip this step and go directly to section A.3.

To use your NVIDIA GPU for deep learning, you need to install two things:

- *CUDA*—A set of drivers for your GPU that allows it to run a low-level programming language for parallel computing.
- *cuDNN*—A library of highly optimized primitives for deep learning. When using cuDNN and running on a GPU, you can typically increase the training speed of your models by 50% to 100%.

TensorFlow depends on particular versions of CUDA and the cuDNN library. At the time of writing, it uses CUDA version 8 and cuDNN version 6. Please consult the TensorFlow website for detailed instructions about which versions are currently recommended: www.tensorflow.org/install/install_linux.

Follow these steps:

1   Download CUDA. For Ubuntu (and other Linux flavors), NVIDIA provides a ready-to-use package that you can download from https://developer .nvidia.com/cuda-downloads:

```
$ wget http://developer.download.nvidia.com/compute/cuda/repos/ubuntu1604/
 x86_64/cuda-repo-ubuntu1604_9.0.176-1_amd64.deb
```

2   Install CUDA. The easiest way to do so is to use Ubuntu's apt on this package. This will allow you to easily install updates via apt as they become available:

```
$ sudo dpkg -i cuda-repo-ubuntu1604_9.0.176-1_amd64.deb
$ sudo apt-key adv --fetch-keys
 http://developer.download.nvidia.com/compute/cuda/repos/ubuntu1604/
 x86_64/7fa2af80.pub
$ sudo apt-get update
$ sudo apt-get install cuda-8-0
```

3   Install cuDNN:

   a   Register for a free NVIDIA developer account (unfortunately, this is necessary in order to gain access to the cuDNN download), and download cuDNN at https://developer.NVIDIA.com/cudnn (select the version of cuDNN compatible with TensorFlow). Like CUDA, NVIDIA provides packages for different Linux flavors—we'll use the version for Ubuntu 16.04. Note that if you're working with an EC2 install, you won't be able to download the cuDNN archive directly to your instance; instead, download it to your local machine and then upload it to your EC2 instance (via scp).

   b   Install cuDNN:

```
$ sudo dpkg -i dpkg -i libcudnn6*.deb
```

4 Install TensorFlow:

    a TensorFlow with or without GPU support can be installed from PyPI using Pip. Here's the command without GPU support:

```
$ sudo pip install tensorflow
```

    b Here's the command to install TensorFlow with GPU support:

```
$ sudo pip install tensorflow-gpu
```

A.3 Installing Theano (optional)

Because you've already installed TensorFlow, you don't have to install Theano in order to run Keras code. But it can sometimes be useful to switch back and forth from TensorFlow to Theano when building Keras models.

Theano can also be installed from PyPI:

```
$ sudo pip install theano
```

If you're using a GPU, then you should configure Theano to use your GPU. You can create a Theano configuration file with this command:

```
nano ~/.theanorc
```

Then, fill in the file with the following configuration:

```
[global]
floatX = float32
device = gpu0

[nvcc]
fastmath = True
```

A.4 Installing Keras

You can install Keras from PyPI:

```
$ sudo pip install keras
```

Alternatively, you can install Keras from GitHub. Doing so will allow you to access the keras/examples folder, which contains many example scripts for you to learn from:

```
$ git clone https://github.com/fchollet/keras
$ cd keras
$ sudo python setup.py install
```

You can now try to run a Keras script, such as this MNIST example:

```
python examples/mnist_cnn.py
```

Note that running this example to completion may take a few minutes, so feel free to force-quit it (Ctrl-C) once you've verified that it's working normally.

After you've run Keras at least once, the Keras configuration file can be found at ~/.keras/keras.json. You can edit it to select the backend that Keras runs on: tensorflow, theano, or cntk. Your configuration file should like this:

```
{
    "image_data_format": "channels_last",
    "epsilon": 1e-07,
    "floatx": "float32",
    "backend": "tensorflow"
}
```

While the Keras script examples/mnist_cnn.py is running, you can monitor GPU utilization in a different shell window:

```
$ watch -n 5 NVIDIA-smi -a --display=utilization
```

You're all set! Congratulations—you can now begin building deep-learning applications.

appendix B
Running Jupyter notebooks
on an EC2 GPU instance

This appendix provides a step-by-step guide to running deep-learning Jupyter notebooks on an AWS GPU instance and editing the notebooks from anywhere in your browser. This is the perfect setup for deep-learning research if you don't have a GPU on your local machine. The original (and up-to-date) version of this guide can be found at https://blog.keras.io.

B.1 What are Jupyter notebooks? Why run Jupyter notebooks on AWS GPUs?

A *Jupyter notebook* is a web app that allows you to write and annotate Python code interactively. It's a great way to experiment, do research, and share what you're working on.

Many deep-learning applications are very computationally intensive and can take hours or even days when running on a laptop's CPU cores. Running on a GPU can speed up training and inference by a considerable factor (often 5 to 10 times, when going from a modern CPU to a single modern GPU). But you may not have access to a GPU on your local machine. Running Jupyter notebooks on AWS gives you the same experience as running on your local machine, while allowing you to use one or several GPUs on AWS. And you only pay for what you use, which can compare favorably to investing in your own GPU(s) if you use deep learning only occasionally.

B.2   *Why would you not want to use Jupyter on AWS for deep learning?*

AWS GPU instances can quickly become expensive. The one we suggest using costs $0.90 per hour. This is fine for occasional use; but if you're going to run experiments for several hours per day every day, then you're better off building your own deep-learning machine with a TITAN X or GTX 1080 Ti.

In summary, use the Jupyter-on-EC2 setup if you don't have access to a local GPU or if you don't want to deal with installing Keras dependencies, in particular GPU drivers. If you have a access to a local GPU, we recommend running your models locally, instead. In that case, use the installation guide in appendix A.

> **NOTE**   You'll need an active AWS account. Some familiarity with AWS EC2 will help, but it isn't mandatory.

B.3   *Setting up an AWS GPU instance*

The following setup process will take 5 to 10 minutes:

1 Navigate to the EC2 control panel at https://console.aws.amazon.com/ec2/v2, and click the Launch Instance link (see figure B.1).

Figure B.1   The EC2 control panel

2 Select AWS Marketplace (see figure B.2), and search for "deep learning" in the search box. Scroll down until you find the AMI named Deep Learning AMI Ubuntu Version (see figure B.3); select it.

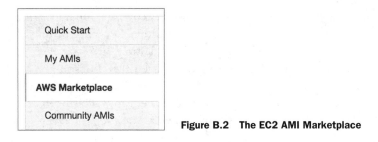

Figure B.2   The EC2 AMI Marketplace

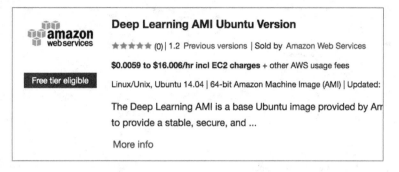

Figure B.3 The EC2 Deep Learning AMI

3 Select the p2.xlarge instance (see figure B.4). This instance type provides access to a single GPU and costs $0.90 per hour of usage (as of March 2017).

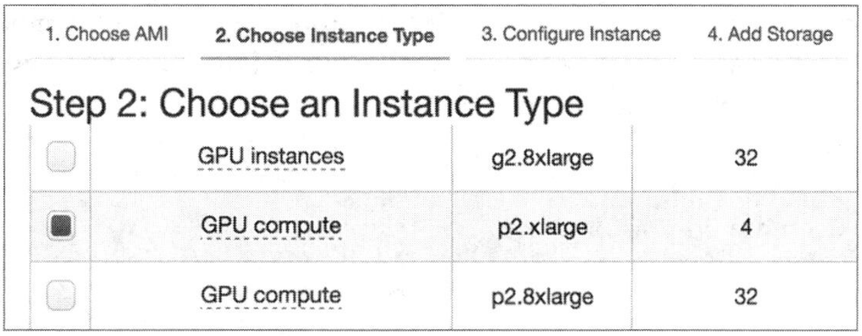

1. Choose AMI	**2. Choose Instance Type**	3. Configure Instance	4. Add Storage

Step 2: Choose an Instance Type

☐	GPU instances	g2.8xlarge	32
■	GPU compute	p2.xlarge	4
☐	GPU compute	p2.8xlarge	32

Figure B.4 The p2.xlarge instance

4 You can keep the default configuration for the steps Configure Instance, Add Storage, and Add Tags, but you'll customize the Configure Security Group step. Create a custom TCP rule to allow port 8888 (see figure B.5): this rule can be allowed either for your current public IP (such as that of your laptop) or for any IP (such as 0.0.0.0/0) if the former isn't possible. Note that if you allow port 8888 for any IP, then literally anyone will be able to listen to that port on your instance (which is where you'll run IPython notebooks). You'll add password protection to the notebooks to mitigate the risk of random strangers modifying them, but that may be pretty weak protection. If at all possible, you should consider restricting access to a specific IP. But if your IP address changes constantly, then that isn't a practical choice. If you're going to leave access open to any IP, then remember not to leave sensitive data on the instance.

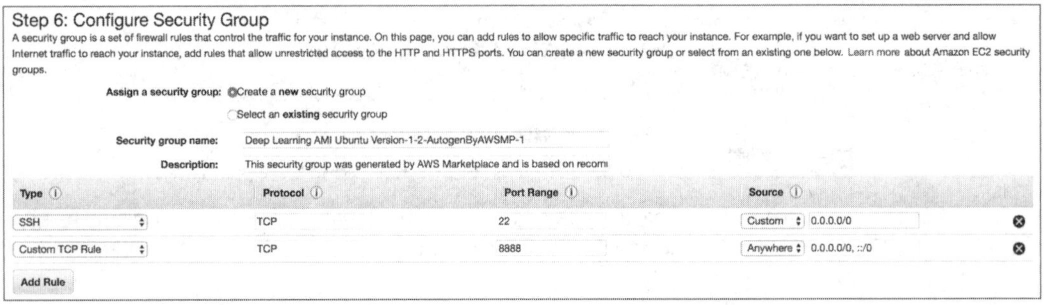

Step 6: Configure Security Group
A security group is a set of firewall rules that control the traffic for your instance. On this page, you can add rules to allow specific traffic to reach your instance. For example, if you want to set up a web server and allow Internet traffic to reach your instance, add rules that allow unrestricted access to the HTTP and HTTPS ports. You can create a new security group or select from an existing one below. Learn more about Amazon EC2 security groups.

Assign a security group: ◉ Create a **new** security group
                          ○ Select an **existing** security group

Security group name: Deep Learning AMI Ubuntu Version-1-2-AutogenByAWSMP-1

Description: This security group was generated by AWS Marketplace and is based on recom

Type ⓘ	Protocol ⓘ	Port Range ⓘ	Source ⓘ	
SSH ⇕	TCP	22	Custom ⇕ 0.0.0.0/0	✕
Custom TCP Rule ⇕	TCP	8888	Anywhere ⇕ 0.0.0.0/0, ::/0	✕

Add Rule

Figure B.5 **Configure a new security group.**

> **NOTE** At the end of the launch process, you'll be asked if you want to create new connection keys or if you want to reuse existing keys. If you've never used EC2 before, create new keys and download them.

5 To connect to your instance, select it on the EC2 control panel, click the Connect button, and follow the instructions (see figure B.6). Note that it may take a few minutes for the instance to boot up. If you can't connect at first, wait a bit and try again.

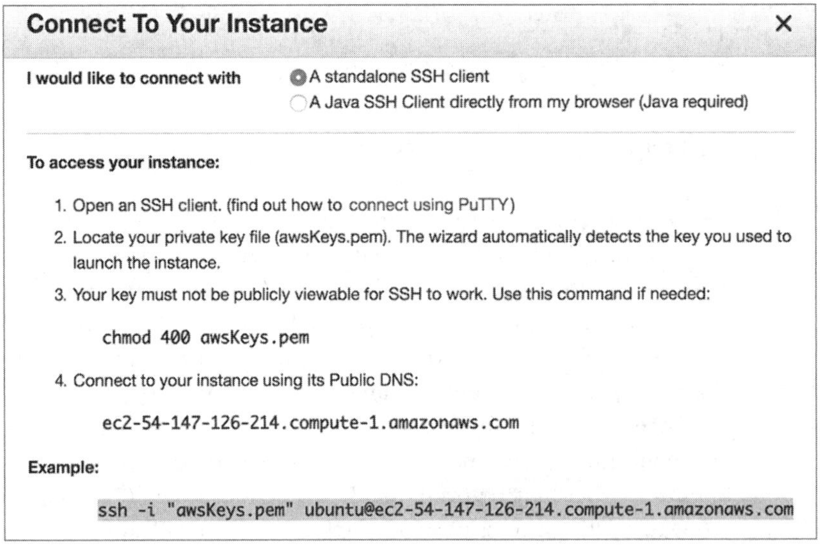

Connect To Your Instance   ✕

I would like to connect with   ◉ A standalone SSH client
                                    ○ A Java SSH Client directly from my browser (Java required)

To access your instance:

1. Open an SSH client. (find out how to connect using PuTTY)
2. Locate your private key file (awsKeys.pem). The wizard automatically detects the key you used to launch the instance.
3. Your key must not be publicly viewable for SSH to work. Use this command if needed:

        chmod 400 awsKeys.pem

4. Connect to your instance using its Public DNS:

        ec2-54-147-126-214.compute-1.amazonaws.com

Example:

    ssh -i "awsKeys.pem" ubuntu@ec2-54-147-126-214.compute-1.amazonaws.com

Figure B.6 **Connection instructions**

6 Once you're logged in to the instance via SSH, create an ssl directory at the root of the instance, and cd to it (not mandatory, but cleaner):

```
$ mkdir ssl
$ cd ssl
```

7 Create a new SSL certificate using OpenSSL, and create cert.key and cert.pem files in the current ssl directory:

```
$ openssl req -x509 -nodes -days 365 -newkey rsa:1024 -keyout "cert.key" -out
➥"cert.pem" -batch
```

2.3.1 Configuring Jupyter

Before you use Jupyter, you need to touch up its default configuration. Follow these steps:

1 Generate a new Jupyter config file (still on the remote instance):

```
$ jupyter notebook --generate-config
```

2 Optionally, you can generate a Jupyter password for your notebooks. Because your instance may be configured to be accessible from any IP (depending on the choice you made when configuring the security group), it's better to restrict access to Jupyter via a password. To generate a password, open an IPython shell (ipython command) and run the following:

```
from IPython.lib import passwd
passwd()
exit
```

3 The passwd() command will ask you to enter and verify a password. After you do, it will display a hash of your password. Copy that hash—you'll need it soon. It looks something like this:

```
sha1:b592a9cf2ec6:b99edb2fd3d0727e336185a0b0eab561aa533a43
```

Note that this is a hash of the word *password*, which isn't a password you should be using.

4 Use vi (or your favorite available text editor) to edit the Jupyter config file:

```
$ vi ~/.jupyter/jupyter_notebook_config.py
```

5 The config file is a Python file with all lines commented out. Insert the following lines of Python code at the beginning of the file:

Path to the private key you generated for the certificate

Serves the notebooks locally

Path to the certificate you generated

Gets the config object

Inline figure when using Matplotlib

```
c = get_config()
c.NotebookApp.certfile = u'/home/ubuntu/ssl/cert.pem'
c.NotebookApp.keyfile = u'/home/ubuntu/ssl/cert.key'
c.IPKernelApp.pylab = 'inline'
c.NotebookApp.ip = '*'

c.NotebookApp.open_browser = False
c.NotebookApp.password =
➥'sha1:b592a9cf2ec6:b99edb2fd3d0727e336185a0b0eab561aa533a43'
```

Don't open a browser window by default when using notebooks.

Password hash you generated earlier

> **NOTE** In case you aren't accustomed to using vi, remember that you need to press I to begin inserting content. When you're finished, press Esc, enter :wq, and press Enter to quit vi and save your changes (:wq stands for *write-quit*).

B.4 Installing Keras

You're almost ready to start using Jupyter. But first, you need to update Keras. A version of Keras is preinstalled on the AMI, but it may not necessarily be up to date. On the remote instance, run this command:

```
$ sudo pip install keras --upgrade
```

Because you'll probably use Python 3 (the notebooks provided with this book use Python 3), you should also update Keras using pip3:

```
$ sudo pip3 install keras --upgrade
```

If there's an existing Keras configuration file on the instance (there shouldn't be, but the AMI may have changed since I wrote this), you should delete it, just in case. Keras will re-create a standard configuration file when it's launched for the first time.

If the following code snippet returns an error saying that the file doesn't exist, you can ignore it:

```
$ rm -f ~/.keras/keras.json
```

B.5 Setting up local port forwarding

In a shell *on your local machine* (*not* the remote instance), start forwarding your local port 443 (the HTTPS port) to port 8888 of the remote instance:

```
$ sudo ssh -i awsKeys.pem -L local_port:local_machine:remote_port remote_machine
```

In my case, it would look like the following:

```
$ sudo ssh -i awsKeys.pem -L
➥ 443:127.0.0.1:8888 ubuntu@ec2-54-147-126-214.compute-1.amazonaws.com
```

B.6 Using Jupyter from your local browser

On the remote instance, clone the GitHub repository containing the Jupyter notebooks associated with this book:

```
$ git clone https://github.com/fchollet/deep-learning-with-python-notebooks.git
cd deep-learning-with-python-notebooks
```

Start Jupyter Notebook by running this command, still on the remote instance:

```
$ jupyter notebook
```

Then, in your local browser, navigate to the local address you're forwarding to the remote notebook process (https://127.0.0.1). Be sure you use HTTPS in the address, or you'll get an SSL error.

You should see the safety warning shown in figure B.7. This warning is due to the fact that the SSL certificate you generated isn't verified by a trusted authority (obviously—you generated your own). Click Advanced, and proceed to navigate.

⚠ Not Secure https://127.0.0.1 ☆

⚠

Your connection is not private

Attackers might be trying to steal your information from **127.0.0.1** (for example, passwords, messages, or credit cards). NET::ERR_CERT_AUTHORITY_INVALID

☐ Automatically report details of possible security incidents to Google. Privacy policy

ADVANCED   Back to safety

Figure B.7   A safety warning you can ignore

You should be prompted to enter your Jupyter password. You'll then arrive at the Jupyter dashboard (see figure B.8).

◯ Jupyter   Logout

Files   Running   Clusters

Select items to perform actions on them.   Upload   New ▾   ↻

☐ ▾ 🏠

Notebook list empty.

Figure B.8   The Jupyter dashboard

Upload   New ▾   ↻

Text File
Folder
Terminal   ing

Notebooks
Python 2
Python 3

Choose New > Notebook to get started (see figure B.9). You can use the Python version of your choice. All set!

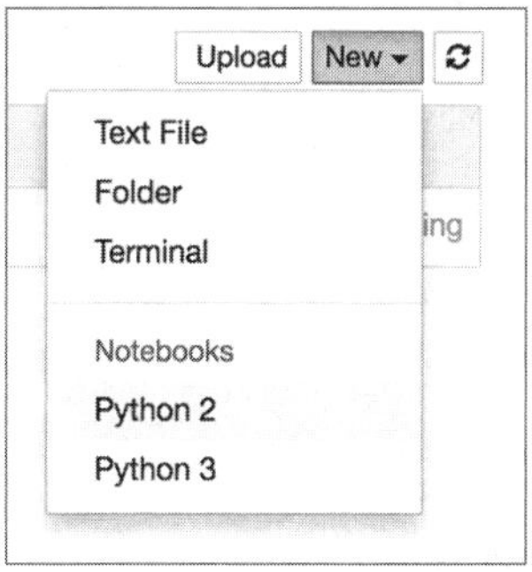

Figure B.9   Create a new notebook.

index

N

RELATED MANNING TITLES

Machine Learning with TensorFlow
by Nishant Shukla

ISBN: 9781617293870
325 pages, $44.99
December 2017

The Quick Python Book, Third Edition
by Naomi Ceder

ISBN: 9781617294037
400 pages, $39.99
December 2017

R in Action, Second Edition
Data analysis and graphics with R
by Robert I. Kabacoff

ISBN: 9781617291388
608 pages, $59.99
May 2015

Practical Data Science with R
by Nina Zumel and John Mount

ISBN: 9781617291562
416 pages, $49.99
March 2014

For ordering information go to www.manning.com